A COMPLETE GUIDE

ERIE CANAL

1ST EDITION

ERIE CANAL

Exploring New York's Great Canals

Deborah Williams

The Countryman Press
Woodstock, Vermont

To the boys . . .
Marshall J. Brown and Bart

ISBN: 978-1-58157-080-9

Cover photo by Deborah Williams
Interior photographs by the author unless otherwise specified
Maps by Mapping Specialists Ltd., Madison, WI © The Countryman Press
Book design by Bodenweber Design
Composition by PerfecType, Nashville, TN

Published by The Countryman Press, P.O. Box 748, Woodstock, VT 05091
Distributed by W. W. Norton & Company, Inc., 500 Fifth Avenue, New York, NY 10110
Printed in the United States of America

10 9 8 7 6 5 4 3 2 1

Recommended by *National Geographic Traveler* and *Travel + Leisure* magazines

A crisp and critical approach, for travelers who want to live like locals.
—*USA Today*

Great Destinations™ guidebooks are known for their comprehensive, critical coverage of regions of extraordinary cultural interest and natural beauty. Each title in this series is continuously updated with each printing to ensure accurate and timely information. All the books contain more than one hundred photographs and maps.

Current titles available:

The Adirondack Book

The Alaska Panhandle

Atlanta

Austin, San Antonio
& the Texas Hill Country

The Berkshire Book

Big Sur, Monterey Bay
& Gold Coast Wine Country

Cape Canaveral, Cocoa Beach
& Florida's Space Coast

The Charleston, Savannah
& Coastal Islands Book

The Chesapeake Bay Book

The Coast of Maine Book

Colorado's Classic Mountain Towns

Costa Rica: Great Destinations
Central America

Dominican Republic

The Finger Lakes Book

The Four Corners Region

Galveston, South Padre Island
& the Texas Gulf Coast

Guatemala: Great Destinations
Central America

The Hamptons Book

Hawaii's Big Island: Great Destinations
Hawaii

Honolulu & Oahu: Great Destinations
Hawaii

The Jersey Shore: Atlantic City to Cape May

Kauai: Great Destinations Hawaii

Lake Tahoe & Reno

Las Vegas

Los Cabos & Baja California Sur:
Great Destinations Mexico

Maui: Great Destinations Hawaii

Memphis and the Delta Blues Trail

Michigan's Upper Peninsula

Montreal & Quebec City:
Great Destinations Canada

The Nantucket Book

The Napa & Sonoma Book

North Carolina's Outer Banks
& the Crystal Coast

Nova Scotia & Prince Edward Island

Oaxaca: Great Destinations Mexico

Palm Beach, Fort Lauderdale, Miami
& the Florida Keys

Palm Springs & Desert Resorts

Philadelphia, Brandywine Valley
& Bucks County

Phoenix, Scottsdale, Sedona
& Central Arizona

Playa del Carmen, Tulum & the Riviera Maya:
Great Destinations Mexico

Salt Lake City, Park City, Provo
& Utah's High Country Resorts

San Diego & Tijuana

San Juan, Vieques & Culebra:
Great Destinations Puerto Rico

San Miguel de Allende & Guanajuato:
Great Destinations Mexico

The Santa Fe & Taos Book

The Sarasota, Sanibel Island & Naples Book

The Seattle & Vancouver Book

The Shenandoah Valley Book

Touring East Coast Wine Country

Tucson

Virginia Beach, Richmond
& Tidewater Virginia

Washington, D.C., and Northern Virginia

Yellowstone & Grand Teton National Parks
& Jackson Hole

Yosemite & the Southern Sierra Nevada

The authors in this series are professional travel writers who have lived for many years in the regions they describe. Honest and painstakingly critical, full of information only a local can provide, Great Destinations guidebooks give you all the practical knowledge you need to enjoy the best of each region.

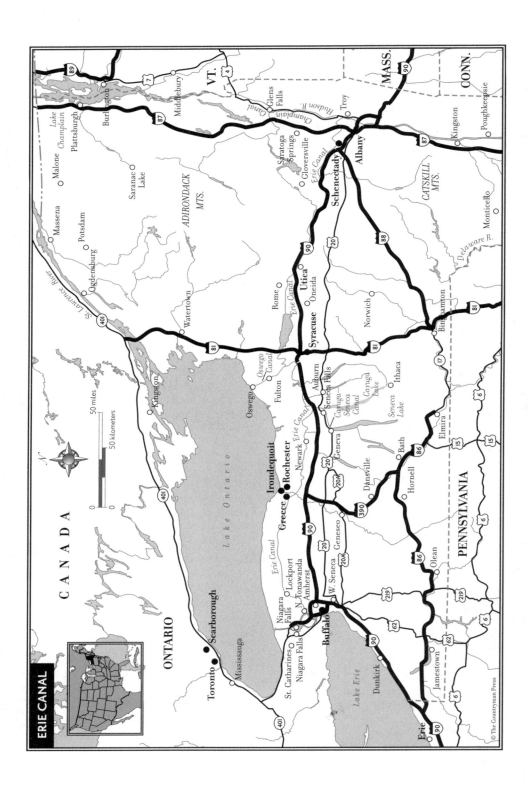

Contents

Acknowledgments

I stand in awe of the visionaries and workers who created the Erie Canal and all of the canals making up the New York State Canal System. My hat is off to the many volunteers, preservationists, and public officials who are working to preserve the remarkable history of these waterways. I and many others appreciate the pioneering efforts of Peter Wiles Sr. and his family, of Skaneateles, New York, who helped save the current canal system and led the way in introducing thousands to exploring the canals via boat tours.

Up and down the canals, many people extended a helping hand to me—too many to list here. But I would like to thank Erin Agans, of the New York State Canal Corporation, for her assistance and patience. Thanks also to Patti Donoghue and Greg Marshall, of Visit Rochester, who represent some of the most picturesque and historic towns along the Erie Canal and are always very helpful. Thanks as well to Danica Bryant, of the Syracuse Convention and Visitors Bureau, and Elizabeth Hosford, of the Albany Convention and Visitors Bureau. Tour-boat operators are some of the best ambassadors for the canals, and all were generous with their assistance.

I am grateful to Sharon Stanley, Barbara Copley, Marshall Brown, Deborah Beale, and my sister Holly Gang for their help and support. Long before I wrote this book, I listened to wonderful Erie Canal songs and sea shanties sung by my friend George Levine. These helped inspire me while writing and added to my enjoyment while traveling across the state and on the canals, and sailing off Point Abino, in the Canadian province of Ontario.

A special thanks to Countryman Press editors Lisa Sacks and Melissa Dobson.

And then there is Bart, my Labrador retriever, who is the perfect travel-writer's companion. He is always ready to take to the road and the waters, including the Erie Canal, but loves to relax in my office while I'm writing.

Introduction

A vision of New York governor DeWitt Clinton, the Erie Canal is North America's most successful and influential manmade waterway. The story of the canal is a tale of achieving the impossible with an array of improbables. The dreamers, the developers, and the diggers accomplished a truly monumental undertaking.

When completed in 1825, the 363-mile-long canal was the first all-water link between the Atlantic seaboard and the Great Lakes. The Erie Canal was a marvel, the Internet of its era, opening new vistas and changing not only the lives of those who adventured on its waters but also New York State and the entire nation. It fostered settlement in the Northeast, Midwest, and Great Plains, transformed New York City into the nation's principal seaport, and created many communities across New York State. It is impossible to overemphasize the immediate and long-lasting effects of the canal.

The 19th-century wonder has recently been rediscovered and reenergized. Today's canal—the third version—has been declared a National Heritage Corridor. When the original canal was completed, it was heralded for its speed in transporting goods and people. Today its charm lies in its ability to take boaters, bikers, walkers, and canal watchers back in time to a slower, more reflective era. With a speed limit of 10 miles per hour, there are no speeders on the canal, and for many that is one of its biggest attractions.

The New York State Canal System—which includes the Erie, Cayuga-Seneca, Oswego, and Champlain canals—connects the major upstate cities with many small towns, two Great Lakes, the longest Finger Lakes, Oneida Lake, Lake Champlain, rivers, and the waterways of the world. Beginning in the canal system, a boater can travel from Buffalo or Ithaca or Whitehall, New York, to the Caribbean, Europe, and around the world. Even today, that alone seems quite mind-boggling.

Although this is my fourth book on New York State, my travels along the canals and to the state's many communities have brought me unexpected surprises and delightful discoveries. I am continually amazed by the richness and diversity that can be found in upstate New York—many of the state's special attractions are along the canal corridor.

I learned, for example, that Winston Churchill, Britain's great World War II prime minister, had family ties to Palmyra, a canal community most famous as the birthplace of the Mormon religion. And the war was still raging in Europe when nearly a thousand refugees were transported to Oswego, a Lake Ontario port on the Oswego Canal. Their stories and others of life along the early canal are told today in museums up and down the canalway, most notably in Syracuse, site of the premier U.S. canal museum.

For many, the best way to experience the Erie Canal is to take to the water and "lock through" at the canal locks. You can charter your own canal boat for a week, take a 2- or 3-day cruise, board a small cruise ship for a 10-day excursion along the canal, or just rent a kayak or canoe for an hour or so. At the Erie Canal Village in Rome, New York, there is even a tour boat pulled by a mule named Sal. Of course, boaters are welcome to launch their own boats on the canal to cruise for a day or longer. Fortunately, tour-boat operators up and down the canal offer tours with historical narration. (If you are lucky, the tour comes with old-time canal songs.)

Numerous trails along the canal serve bikers, hikers, and walkers, who can join an organized tour or take to the trails independently and enjoy them at their own pace. Historic inns, hotels, restaurants, and attractions along the canal welcome visitors to spend time on the waterway's shores. Best of all, communities big and small have redis-covered their historic connections to the Erie Canal, and many restored cities, towns, and villages are now inviting the world to experience the attractions that they have to offer.

Celebrated in art, literature, and song, the Erie Canal is deeply grooved into the national awareness, and helped to establish an American identity both in the United States and abroad.

The Way This Book Works

This book covers the Erie Canal and the branch canals of the New York State Canal System: the Cayuga-Seneca, Oswego, and Champlain canals. The system encompasses much of upstate New York.

A history of the Erie Canal—the most remarkable canal in U.S. history—opens the book. Part II, "Transportation," focuses on the wide array of boat tours on the canals as well as the best routes into the area. Part III, "Destinations" begins with Buffalo, the western terminus of the original canal. The section then follows the canals and cities, towns and villages, eastward, with separate chapters on the Rochester area, the Cayuga-Seneca Canal (including the two largest Finger Lakes), Syracuse and the central canal region, the Oswego Canal, the Utica area, and Albany and the eastern canal region, concluding with the Champlain Canal. Each of these chapters details the area's history, lodging, restaurants, culture, recreation, and shopping, with an emphasis on key historic sites, museums, attractions, parks, and other places of interest.

Although visitor information was accurate as of publication, it is always best to call ahead. Some areas—particularly those outside the bigger cities—have seasonal hours and may be open only May to mid-October or November.

When possible, in homage to Bart, my trusted and beloved Lab, pet-friendly lodgings are noted. Again, be sure to check before you arrive. Rules can and do change.

Prices

The region is most active during the canal season, from May to November. Prices for lodging can be higher during this time. Sometimes, as in Saratoga Springs during the August racing season, rates are *much* higher. Some high-season special weekends have minimum-stay requirements.

A general price range is given. Lodging prices are per room, double occupancy, and may or may not include breakfast. Restaurant prices indicate the cost of a dinner entrée, without tax, tip, or beverages. All restaurants in New York State are nonsmoking.

Lodging Rates
Inexpensive: Up to $75
Moderate: $76–$150
Expensive: $151–$250
Very Expensive: More than $250

Dining Rates
Inexpensive: Up to $10
Moderate: $11–$25
Expensive: $26–$40
Very Expensive: More than $40

An effort was made to include a wide selection of the best in accommodations and restaurants in a variety of price ranges. Lodging and restaurants directly along the canals were included so that boaters, bikers, walkers, and water lovers can find enjoyable places to sleep and eat beside the water. Please refer to the geographically organized "Lodging by Price" and "Dining by Price" indexes at the back of this book for further information on affordability for businesses mentioned in passing or in abbreviated form in the text.

If there are places that were not included that should be considered for the next edition, we would be glad to hear about them.

Deborah Williams
www.deborahwilliams.com

CAMILLUS LANDING
← 175.47 M   ALBANY-BUFFALO   175.91 M →

Sign marking the halfway point on the original Erie Canal

1

HISTORY

October 26, 1825: The moment had arrived at last. It took just a little more than two hours for the successive canon booms to travel from Buffalo to New York City and back again. It was "a grand salute 500 miles long, announcing to the people of the state the completion of the most stupendous undertaking of their time," wrote state engineer and surveyor Roy G. Finch, in a 1925 pamphlet marking the Erie Canal's 100th anniversary. It took nearly a month for the inaugural flotilla to make the same round-trip passage. Boats and dignitaries were slowed on their incredible journey by elaborate and rousing celebrations all along the route.

October 26 was the date of the long-awaited ceremony marking the opening of the Erie Canal. An engineering marvel of its time and of all times, the canal was called by some the Eighth Wonder of the World. The 363-mile-long artificial waterway transformed not only New York State but also the young nation. It was the longest canal in the world, passing through rugged wilderness. Its construction posed seemingly impossible engineering challenges but was accomplished largely without professional engineers. Canals deal with changes in elevation by means of a succession of lift locks: The builders of the Erie Canal had to account for the fact that Lake Erie is 568 feet higher than the Hudson River at Albany. Thus the project served as the nation's first practical school of civil engineering.

American ingenuity overcame countless other problems—workers had to cut through 300 miles of primeval forest; dig through the Montezuma Swamp in slime up to their chests; construct 83 locks; erect numerous stone aqueducts, including a 1,137-foot-long stone bridge that was the longest stone-arch bridge in the world; and, in the days before dynamite, cut a 30-foot-deep channel through 3 miles of solid rock. All this was accomplished in just eight years.

The original canal was a ditch 40 feet wide at the top, 28 feet wide at the bottom, and 4 feet deep. On one side there was a 5-foot-wide berm and on the other side a 12-foot-wide towpath to accommodate mules and horses. These animals were guided by *hoggees* (Scottish for "worker"), typically boys, sometimes as young as 8, and together the teams pulled the boats along the canal's route.

Four self-made engineers—Benjamin Wright, James Geddes, Charles G. Broadhead, and Nathan S. Roberts—oversaw the project. The first three were judges who had learned land surveying to help resolve property cases; Roberts was a math teacher who had taught himself surveying.

Mile by mile, through eight years of wet, heat, and cold, canal workers felled trees and excavated, mostly by hand and animal power. They devised equipment to uproot trees and pull stumps and developed hydraulic cement that hardened under water. With hand drills and black powder, they blasted rocks.

Horse-drawn wagon ride at the Erie Canal Village in Rome offers visitors a chance to travel back in time

Disasters were commonplace. At one point malaria-carrying mosquitoes sickened nearly a thousand workers. The banks of sections of canal dug in the marshes routinely collapsed into the dredged trench overnight, requiring the building of extensive pilings to keep the banks in place.

It took resourcefulness, persistence, and sheer physical labor to make the Erie Canal the engineering and construction triumph of its time.

THE FIRST SHOVELFUL

Construction began at sunrise on July 4, 1817, just outside Rome—an appropriate name for a town that was the birthplace of a project that would turn New York into the Empire State.

Building the Canal

"And even with the spade and wheel barrow, more progress can be made in excavations than was supposed. Three Irishmen finished, including banks and towing paths, three rods of the canal, in four feet cutting each, in the space of five and a half days. This sixteen and a half days work accomplished the excavation of two hundred forty-nine and one-third cubic yards; which at twelve and a half cents per cubic yard, would produce each workmen with the very liberal wages of one dollar and eighty-eight cents per day."

—From the 1817 *Annual Report of the Canal Commissioners* regarding construction of the old Erie Canal system

The day was chosen because Independence Day had become a day of unity in the young nation—a day to put aside conflicts.

The moment was a symbol of American entrepreneurship and vision, and initiating the project at this remote spot represented a masterful political move. Canal construction proceeded simultaneously east and west from Rome to maximize 94 miles of flat terrain with relatively easily dug soil between the Mohawk and Seneca rivers. It would not be necessary to build locks or aqueducts, which would slow progress, for approximately 60 miles.

Canal commissioner Samuel Young began the proceedings with this prediction: "By this great highway, unborn millions will . . . hold a useful and profitable intercourse with all the maritime nations of the earth."

The cannons at the nearby arsenal boomed, and Judge John Richardson, the canal's first signed contractor, drove his team of oxen forward, inaugurating the construction of the Erie Canal.

DeWitt Clinton, New York's governor at the time of the canal opening, championed the canal while still mayor of New York City. He envisioned a waterway from Buffalo on the eastern shore of Lake Erie to Albany on the upper Hudson River. In those early days, the project was often sarcastically referred to as Clinton's Big Ditch.

Jesse Hawley, a miller in the town of Geneva, was one of the first to propose a canal across New York State. In 1807 Hawley was serving time in Ontario County's debtors' prison. A flour merchant, he had gone bankrupt due to the lack of an adequate transportation system to move his product to market. While in jail, he wrote a series of articles describing in great detail a prospective canal connecting Buffalo and Albany. (Hawley's ideas would prove to be remarkably accurate when the project finally came to fruition.)

Hawley won strong support from Joseph Ellicott, an agent for the Holland Land Company, in Batavia, who realized that a canal would add immense value to the land he was selling in the western part of the state. Ellicott would later become the first canal commissioner.

In 1808 Joshua Forman of Syracuse proposed that New York take the bold step of examining potential routes that would do the unthinkable: link the Hudson River and the Great Lakes by means of an artificial canal. Forman addressed the state legislature, stating for the record, "Resolved, that a joint committee be appointed to take into consideration the propriety of exploring, and causing an accurate survey to be made of the eligible and direct route for a canal, to open a communication between the tide waters of the Hudson River and Lake Erie."

Not everyone believed in the vision of Hawley, Ellicott, Forman, and Clinton. President Thomas Jefferson thought it was "little short of madness to think of [such a canal] at this day." Jefferson went on to say that he believed it was "a very fine project that might be executed a century hence."

A three-term mayor of New York City, Clinton wrote in 1816 of the proposal, which his opponents called Clinton's Folly: "As an organ of communication between the Hudson, the Mississippi, the St. Lawrence, the Great Lakes of the north and west and their tributary rivers, it will create the greatest inland trade ever witnessed." In arguing for the canal before the New York State Legislature, he said: "The canal, in reaching out to the Great Lakes, would pass through the most fertile country in the universe and would convey more riches on its waters than any other canal in the world, a free state to erect a work more stupendous, more magnificent, and more beneficial than has hitherto been achieved by the human race."

Some canal supporters favored a more direct route to Lake Ontario. However, that course would benefit Canada and further isolate western New York. The United States had recently concluded the War of 1812, which included decisive battles in Canada and along the U.S.–Canadian border. Clinton preferred the proposed route to Lake Erie so that New York State would be the main beneficiary.

In 1817 Clinton became governor of New York State, and funds for a canal from the Hudson River to the Great Lakes were quickly approved. His predictions proved right, as trade was funneled straight down the Hudson to New York City.

"The city will, in the course of time, become the granary of the world, the emporium of commerce, the seat of manufactures, the focus of great moneyed operations," the governor forecast. "And before the revolution of a century, the whole island of Manhattan, covered with inhabitants and replenished with a dense population, will constitute one vast city."

CANAL CELEBRATIONS

The canal festivities began in Buffalo with a parade led by Governor Clinton from the courthouse to the waterfront. Then Clinton and other dignitaries boarded the packet *Seneca Chief*, which was drawn by four gaily decorated gray horses. There were two elegant wooden kegs on board filled with water from Lake Erie, to be poured into the Atlantic Ocean on arrival in New York City. Other boats followed, including *Noah's Ark*, bringing a cargo of animals and birds from the west, among them two eagles, two fawns, and a bear.

The moment the *Seneca Chief* pulled away from the docks, the cannon fire began in a "cannon telegraph," an elaborately choreographed progression of gunfire. As each shot was fired, the next gun went off—all the way from Buffalo to the southern tip of New York Harbor and back again. The guns themselves had special significance. Many had been British arms captured by Commodore Oliver Hazard Perry at the battle of Lake Erie during the War of 1812.

On Friday, November 4, after an untold number of speeches, banquets, and toasts along the canal route, Clinton and his party arrived in New York City, where they were greeted by cheering crowds, calm seas, and brilliant sunshine.

As the first act of the elaborately staged ceremony marking the "Wedding of the Waters," Clinton filled several bottles with water from Lake Erie and placed them in a cedar box made by the famous woodworker Duncan Phyfe. This box was destined for France as a gift to Revolutionary War hero the Marquis de Lafayette from the people of New York State.

Then Clinton poured the Lake Erie waters into the Atlantic Ocean, declaring: "The solemnity, at this place, on the first arrival of vessels from Lake Erie, is intended to indicate and commemorate the navigable communication, which has been accomplished between our Mediterranean Seas and the Atlantic Ocean, in about eight years, to the extent of more than four hundred and twenty-five miles, by the wisdom, public spirit, and energy of the people of the state of New York; and may the God of Heavens and the Earth smile most propitiously on the work, and render it subservient to the best interests of the human race."

One of Clinton's close friends, Dr. Samuel Mitchell, then stepped up with 13 bottles of water—from the Ganges, the Indus, the Nile, the Gambia, the Thames, the Seine, the Rhine, the Danube, the Mississippi, the Columbia, the Orinoco, the Rio de la Plata, and the Amazon—and emptied them into the Atlantic.

Who Built the Canal?

The answer to this seemingly simple question is steeped in myth. After careful examination of census records and engineering and construction documents, researchers believe they know the answer. The original canal (1817–25) was built primarily by individuals of English, Welsh, and Dutch extraction living in New York, descendants of the first Europeans to settle in the state. The 1819 New York State Canal Commissioners report stated that three-fourths of the workers were "born among us." During the Erie Enlargement (1836–62) and the construction of today's barge canal (1905–18), the ethnic mix of New York changed dramatically, and immigrant labor played a much larger role, dominated by Irish and Germans. There were also Italians and immigrants from Eastern European countries such as Poland, Czechoslovakia, and Bulgaria.

Simultaneously, a giant parade set forth in Manhattan—the largest parade ever witnessed in the country up to that time. The line of participants was more than a mile and a half in length.

Back in Buffalo, the citizens eagerly awaited the homecoming of the *Seneca Chief,* and in the early morning of November 23, the boat made a triumphant return, bearing a keg of Atlantic waters. Judge Samuel Wilkeson, who had fought hardest to have Buffalo be named the terminus of the canal, stepped onto the boat and emptied the water from the Atlantic into Lake Erie amid cheers and gunfire. The Wedding of the Waters was now complete.

At one of many ceremonies marking the canal's completion, Cadwallader D. Colden, grandson of New York's surveyor general, who in 1724 advanced the idea of inland water travel, said: "The authors and the builders—the heads who planned, and the hands who

Historical marker at Buffalo harbor

executed this stupendous work, deserve perennial monuments; and they will have it. . . .
Europe already begins to admire, America can never forget to acknowledge, that they have
built the longest canal in the world in the least time, with the least experience, for the least
money, and to the greatest public benefit."

CANAL BENEFITS

The federal government had refused to pay for the project, so New Yorkers built the Erie
Canal at the then staggering cost of $7.8 million, financed through taxes and bonds. It
proved to be a very wise investment, as once in operation the canal immediately reduced
transportation costs by 90 percent, and the full debt was paid off by 1837. Most New
Yorkers had at first not considered the money spent to build the canal—$2 million over the
original estimate—a good expenditure. But this changed once the canal proved economically successful beyond even Governor Clinton's wildest dreams.

Prior to the construction of the canal, New York City was the nation's fifth-largest seaport, behind Boston, Baltimore, Philadelphia, and New Orleans. Within 14 years of the
canal's opening, New York was the busiest port in the country, moving tonnages greater
than that of Boston, Baltimore, and New Orleans combined. New York City soon climbed to
preeminence in the fields of communications, finance, law, and publishing. It also became
the cultural center of the nation.

The Erie Canal changed the course of American history, and many historians would
argue it was an important factor in affecting the outcome of the Civil War. Against the rapid
settlement of the Midwest brought on by the canal, the South lost influence over much of
the country's middle section. In the years between the opening of the canal and the out-
break of the Civil War, there was a large migration of New England residents to the
Midwest. At the same time, there was a massive emigration of northern Europeans to the
Midwest—also via the Erie Canal.

By way of the canal, packet boat passengers traveled in relative comfort from Albany to
Buffalo in five days—the same trip by crowded stagecoach took more than two weeks. The
canal opened upstate New York to the beginnings of tourism and enabled thousands of visitors to see firsthand one of the great wonders of the world: Niagara Falls.

Business of the Canal

The business of moving goods and people along the canal involved thousands of boats and their
crews. In 1845 there were 4,000 boats on the canal, operated by 25,000 men, women, and children.
A typical crew included a captain, a steersman, a cook, a deckhand, and hoggees, who drove the
teams that pulled the canal boats. Thousands more workers were employed to maintain and operate
the canal itself, including lock tenders, toll collectors, bridge operators, surveyors, repair crews, and
even bank patrollers, whose job, called the bank watch, required patrolling a 10-mile stretch of canal
looking for leaks and breaks on the bank of the canal.

Eleven years after the canal's opening, the Erie Enlargement was begun in response to the immediate overcrowding of the original canal. The enlargement expanded the canal to 70 feet wide and 7
feet deep. Most of what remains of the old Erie Canal are from the Erie Enlargement era. The majority of the canal workers on the enlargement were Irish immigrants.

Canal Terminology
- flying light—term describing boats traveling empty
- hoggee—worker who drove the draft animals along the canal's towpath
- hoodledasher—train of boats formed by tying empty boats to full boats
- mudlarked—term describing boats stuck in mud
- muleskinner—mule driver
- snubbing post—post for tying up canal boats
- towpath—path where draft animals walk when pulling canal boats
- whiffletree—bar that linked draft animals with canal boats

Although the speed of travel on the original Erie Canal was only about 4 miles per hour, the waterway was a great improvement over the primitive roads and trails of the early 19th century. The canal was so busy, there were traffic jams (and, on occasion, fistfights) at the locks as waiting boats jockeyed for position.

A typical canal boat, pulled by two draft animals, weighed nearly 50 tons, and was 77 feet long by 14 feet wide. It could also serve as a fully functioning mobile home for the many boat captains and their families who made a living on the canal. Small children could be tethered to the deck so as not to fall into the water, while older children might act as steersmen, guiding the boat along, always compensating for the sideward pull of the towrope on the vessel. Typically, the sons drove the horse or mule teams, guiding the

Sims Store Museum at Camillus Erie Canal Park

animals onto the onboard stable during shift changes and leading a fresh team out onto the towpath. They also fed and groomed the animals. Mothers and daughters, meanwhile, busied themselves with domestic chores, such as doing the wash, then hanging it out on lines that ran across the stern, and preparing meals in the family's cramped quarters.

After the canal had been operating for a decade, Jesse Hawley, the early proponent of the waterway, observed: "No single act—no public measure—except the Declaration of Independence and the formation of the U.S. Constitution had done so much to promote public prosperity and produce a new era in the history of the country as the construction of the Erie Canal."

It "proved to be America's greatest canal," Roy G. Finch wrote in his *Story of the New York State Canals.* "Its effect was soon felt, not only through the state but throughout the east and the Great Lakes region. Settlers flocked westward, forests gave way to sawmills and hamlets and these in turn grew into villages. Prosperous towns were established on the Great Lakes and a splendid chain of cities sprang up along the line of the Erie Canal."

The Erie Canal quickly became known as the Mother of Cities as it gave rise to scores of flourishing canal-side communities that forever reshaped the geography and economy of upstate New York. Businesspeople and entrepreneurs amassed enormous fortunes because of the ease and affordability of transportation on the canal. (Their fortunes are still being enjoyed today through the cultural institutions they created and homes and estates they built that have been preserved as museums.)

New York State became the most productive area in the United States and, some would argue, in the world. The canal created the science of engineering in the U.S., which in turn led to the country's predominance during the Industrial Revolution. Because of the canal, New York led the way, transforming New York State from a wilderness into the agricultural, industrial, commercial, and—in the case of New York City—financial center of the country in the 19th century.

The Erie Canal not only transformed New York City but also made the towns between Lake Erie and New York City, including Buffalo, Rochester, Syracuse, Seneca Falls, and Waterloo important centers of commerce and thought. The canal brought a flow of people as well as new ideas and inventions. Albion, a western canal town, was home to George Pullman, the inventor of the railroad sleeping car. The sleeping quarters of the canal packet boats were the inspiration for his Pullman cars. Social reform movements like abolitionism and women's suffrage, utopian communities, and various religious movements thrived in the canal corridor. The canal linked together communities that would otherwise have been isolated. The Erie Canal could be called America's first great communications network.

The Erie Canal carried more westbound immigrants than any other means, and these newcomers infused the nation with different languages, customs, practices, and religions. The canal acted as a conduit of culture, civic life, and national identity for almost a century.

Success followed success. The tremendous immediate impact of the Erie spurred the construction of more than 2,000 miles of other American canals. Some of them survive to this day, but most have been abandoned.

The canal even helped protect the Adirondack Mountains to the north. Concern that erosion caused by massive logging operations in the Adirondacks could silt up the canal was an important factor in the creation in 1885 of the Adirondack Forest Preserve. In 1892 the 6.1-million-acre Adirondack Park was established, consisting of both the preserve and private lands, making it the largest state park in the nation and protecting the public lands as "forever wild."

FROM CLINTON'S DITCH TO ROOSEVELT'S ROUTE

Theodore Roosevelt may be known as the father of conservation, but he could also be called the father of today's Erie Canal. His initiative and foresight led him to create the Committee on Canals, addressing the decline of New York's canals and facilitating their rebirth.

When Roosevelt took office as governor in 1898, the commercial supremacy of New York State was in dire peril. Competition from railroads was a major cause of the decline of the state's canals. After much investigation and deliberation, the Committee on Canals issued a plan to upgrade the canals, and in 1903 the New York State Legislature authorized construction of the New York State Barge Canal as the "improvement of the Erie, the Oswego, the Champlain, and the Cayuga and Seneca Canals."

To accommodate large barges, engineers decided to abandon much of the original man-made channel and use new techniques to "canalize" the rivers that the original canals had been constructed to avoid—the Mohawk, Oswego, Seneca, Oneida, and Clyde—and Oneida Lake. The resulting canal system was completed in 1918, and is 12 to 14 feet deep and 120 to 200 feet wide. There were 57 locks built to handle barges carrying up to 3,000 tons of cargo, with lifts of 6 to 40 feet. No towpath was required, since the boats were self-propelled instead of drawn by horse or mule. A 169-foot rise to the Mohawk Valley was handled by five locks known as the Waterford Flight, the world's largest series of high-lift locks.

With growing competition from railroads and highways, and the opening of the Saint Lawrence Seaway in 1959, commercial traffic on the New York State Barge Canal declined dramatically in the later part of the 20th century. In the early 1970s the canal, which appeared to have outlived its usefulness, was threatened with closure. Plans were even considered for filling it in. The late Peter Wiles Sr., founder of the Skaneateles-based Mid-Lakes Navigation Company, led the fight to save the waterway.

In 2001 the canal, known since 1992 as the New York State Canal System, was named the 23rd National Heritage Corridor. Administered by the U.S. National Park Service, its preservation is ensured. The National Heritage Corridor is a new kind of national park whose purpose is to help preserve and interpret the historical, natural, scenic, and recreational resources of areas of particular national significance. The designation is helping to foster revitalization of canal-side communities.

The Erie Canalway National Heritage Corridor includes 524 miles of navigable waterway making up the New York State Canal System. Along with the Erie, Cayuga-Seneca, Oswego, and Champlain canals, it includes the 234 cities, towns, and villages astride the canal system. The canalway corridor encompasses 4,834 square miles in 23 counties, and is home to 2.7 million people. Upstate New York's largest population centers—Buffalo, Rochester, Syracuse, and Albany—all grew up along the canal and are within the canalway corridor.

Today the waterway, still frequently referred to simply as the Erie Canal, is enjoying a rebirth as a recreational, historic, and economic-development resource. Commercial shipping endures on the canals. Rising fuel costs and the search for more efficient transportation has brought about a resurgence in commercial traffic. Tens of thousands of pleasure craft ply the canals' waters each year. Thousands of visitors and locals take advantage of the miles of bike and hiking paths, parks, and historic sites along the canals. Canal towns have caught the canal spirit, and the number of festivals and special events held annually has exploded in recent years. As many as four times the number of canal events took place in 2008 than were held in 2005.

The Canal's Official Ambassador

The historic tug *Urger* is the official ambassador for the New York State Canal System. It has been in service since 1901 and is listed on the State and National Registers of Historic Places. During the spring and fall, the tug travels through the canalway, offering programs for schoolchildren, and in the summer it participates in various canal festivals. It has won Best Historic Tug in New York City competitions.

Tugboat Urger *docked at Fairport*

The western section of the Erie Canal is part of the New York State Heritage Area System. This 136-mile portion of the canal, from the village of Clyde, east of Rochester, to Buffalo, flows through 5 counties, 16 villages, and the major cities of Buffalo and Rochester. The Western Erie Canal Heritage Corridor features the longest section of the canal that still follows its original path and retains its historic relationship to the communities and landscapes along its banks. Traveling along the route by land or by water, you'll find village Main Streets, lift bridges, farm fields, cobblestone and local sandstone buildings, and 20th-century locks and engineering marvels alongside historic lock ruins.

The New York State Canal System is a vital link in a vast network of navigable inland waterways, rivers, and lakes in the Northeast and is easily accessible from all points of the compass. From the south, the majestic Hudson River is the gateway to the eastern segments of the canal system for boaters entering the Erie and Champlain canals at their origins in the historic town of Waterford. From points north, Lake Champlain provides access for boaters from the Adirondack region, Vermont, and Canada. Lake Ontario is the Great Lakes gateway to the Oswego Canal, and Lake Erie is the western gateway to the Erie Canal.

CANAL SONGS, ART, AND LITERATURE

The Erie Canal instantly became famous in song and story as a result of the thousands of people who took advantage of the new inland waterway and its faster, smoother mode of travel. A source of wonder and inspiration for the artists and travelers who made their way along its waters, the canal generated an abundance and variety of art and literature.

Thousands more were employed on the canal, operating cargo boats that transported goods such as salt, flour, and textiles between Buffalo and New York City. Many of the sights and sounds of the Erie Canal were recorded by those who utilized it during its heyday.

Tourists and trekkers wrote about their experiences and impressions in both private journals and published travelogues. Artists created images of the canal in prints and paintings. And popular magazines and newspapers ran stories and illustrations featuring the canal throughout the 19th century.

The opening of the Erie Canal in 1825 enabled waves of travelers from America and Europe to visit places to the west that had been previously inaccessible. Many of these travelers chronicled a wide range of canal experiences, from the picturesque to the mundane. Jonathan Pearson wrote in his diary, August 11, 1833, "On the canal there is no Sabbath. I must say that I never witnessed so much immorality and vice, profanity and drinking in the same length of time before in my life. . . . Canal men are . . . as a whole . . . a coarse and untaught set of vagabonds whose chief delight is to carouse and fight."

The first visual representations of the canal were prints published in travel guides and magazines soon after the canal opened. Paintings quickly followed, as artists who traveled on the Erie returned to their studios to develop sketches into larger works. Some artists portrayed the canal realistically; others chose to romanticize it.

Replica wooden packet boat in Waterford

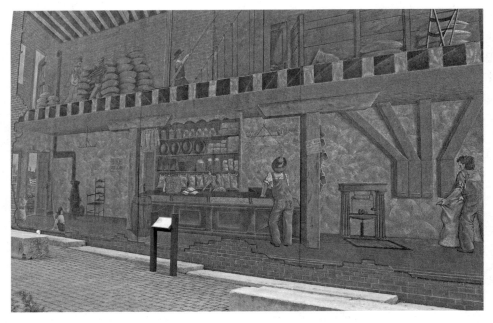

Mural outside the Erie Canal Museum in Syracuse displays a canal-side store

Popular Erie Canal scenes were also reproduced on plates, cups, and bowls; medals were cast to celebrate the opening of the canal; canal scenes were block-printed on wallpaper; a vest was produced with the words "DeWitt Clinton and the Grand Canal" covering its silk front; and a scene of a boat on a canal aqueduct over a raging river was carved into the gravestone of canal contractor Luke Hitchcock.

After journeying to the United States in 1842, Charles Dickens wrote of his experiences on the Erie Canal: "There was much in this mode of traveling which I heartily enjoyed . . . the fast, brisk walk upon the towing path, between dawn and breakfast, when every vein and artery seemed to tingle with health; the exquisite beauty of the opening day, when light came glancing off from everything; the gliding on at night so noiselessly . . . all these were pure delights."

Nathaniel Hawthorne was among the well-known American writers to document his travels on the canal, in *New England Magazine* in 1835: "I was inclined to be poetical about the Grand Canal. In my imagination, De Witt Clinton was an enchanter, who had waved his magic wand from the Hudson to Lake Erie, and united them by a watery highway, crowded with the commerce of two worlds, till then inaccessible to each other. This simple and mighty conception had conferred inestimable value on spots which Nature seemed to have thrown carelessly into the great body of the earth, without foreseeing that they could ever attain importance.

"I pictured the surprise of the sleepy Dutchmen when the new river first glittered by their doors, bringing them hard cash or foreign commodities, in exchange for their hitherto unmarketable produce. Surely, the water of this canal must be the most fertilizing of all fluids; for it causes towns—with their masses of brick and stone, their churches and theatres, their business and hubbub, their luxury and refinement, their gay dames and polished citizens—to spring up, till, in time, the wondrous stream may flow between two continuous lines of buildings, through one thronged street, from Buffalo to Albany. I embarked about thirty miles below Utica, determining to voyage along the whole extent of the canal, at least twice in the course of the summer.

"Passing on, we glide now into the unquiet heart of an inland city—of Utica, for instance—and find ourselves amid piles of brick, crowded docks and quays, rich ware-houses and a busy population. We feel the eager and hurrying spirit of the place, like a stream and eddy whirling us along with it. Through the thickest of the tumult goes the canal, flowing between lofty rows of buildings and arched bridges of hewn stone. Onward, also, go we, till the hum and bustle of struggling enterprise die away behind us, and we are threading an avenue of the ancient woods again."

In lofty prose, Hawthorne questioned the impact of the bustling commerce along the early Erie Canal. He feared that the quickening pace of life along the new canal would irreparably harm upstate communities.

He was certainly proved correct in one respect: the canal forever changed the towns and cities along its route. But ironically, Hawthorne's wish for a slower pace can now be real-ized by today's travelers on the canal, where the maximum speed is 10 mph. In the twenty-first century, canal travel provides a true escape from the fast pace of modern society.

The slow lane: Lock 24 in Baldwinsville

Touring on the Canal

In 1836 Thomas S. Woodcock made the trip from Schenectady to Buffalo and recounted his experience aboard a packet boat:

"These boats are about 70 feet long and with the exception of the kitchen and bar, is occupied as a cabin. The forward part being the ladies' cabin, is separated by a curtain, but at meal times this obstruction is removed, and the table is set the whole length of the boat. The table is supplied with everything that is necessary and of the best quality with many of the luxuries of life.

"On finding we had so many passengers, I was at loss to know how we should be accommodated with berths, as I saw no convenience for anything of the kind, but the Yankees, ever awake to contrivances, have managed to stow more in so small a space than I thought them capable of doing."

Woodcock was amazed at the restrictions posed by the waterway's bridges, noting, "The bridges on the canal are very low, particularly the old ones. Indeed they are so low as to scarcely allow the baggage to clear, and in some cases actually rubbing against it. Every Bridge makes us bend double if seated on anything, and in many cases you have to lie on your back. The man on at the helm give the word to the passengers: 'Bridge,' 'very low Bridge,' 'the lowest in the canal,' as the case may be.

"Some serious accidents have happened for want of caution. A young English woman met with her death a short time since, she having fallen asleep with her head upon a box, had her head crushed to pieces. Such things however do not often occur, and in general it affords amusement to the passengers who soon imitate the cry, and vary it with a command, such as 'All Jackson men bow down.' After such commands we find few aristocrats."

2

Transportation

The New York State Canal System is within a day's drive (400 miles) of 14 states; two Canadian provinces as well as Toronto, Canada's biggest city; New York City, the nation's largest city; and Washington, D.C., the nation's capital. Most visitors arrive by car. Others come by Amtrak, whose routes north and west follow the Erie Canal and the Champlain Canal. Airports in Buffalo, Rochester, Ithaca, Syracuse, and Albany link the region to the rest of the world. The Greyhound/Trailways system offers bus service through all the major cities. Boaters come from near and far to cruise the canals. Car rentals are available throughout the region, making it easy to drive to smaller destinations after arriving by air, train, bus, or boat.

BOATING ON THE CANAL

Whether you enjoy a quiet paddle in a canoe or kayak through locks and history, a narrated canal tour, or want to be the captain of your own canal boat, the New York State Canal System offers a wide range of options for nautical visitors. From hour-long cruises to dinner cruises to overnight cruises, there is something for everyone. During the summer the canal comes alive with festivals and fishing derbies. During the fall, cruisers can enjoy vibrant fall foliage from the water.

Mid-Lakes Navigation Company charter in Fairport

Young passengers on a Lockport tour boat

Tour-Boat Operators, Day Cruises (from west to east)

Lockport Locks & Erie Canal Cruises (716-433-6155 or 800-378-0352, www.lockport locks.com, Lockport Canal Side, 210 Market St., Lockport, NY 14094) The regularly scheduled two-hour cruises on board the *Lockview IV* and *Lockview V* take visitors through the only double set of locks on the Erie Canal and past Lockport's famous "Flight of Five." On Thursdays there are special cruises with live music. There is also a gift shop filled with canal-related items, a snack bar, and banquet facilities in a historic canal-side building.

Bon Voyage Adventures (585-345-0733 or 716-830-7555, www.roselummis.com, 5060 Ellicott Street Rd., Batavia, NY 14020) The 1953 *Rose Lummis,* a Mississippi paddle wheeler, cruises between Spencerport and Brockport. There is also a weekly luncheon cruise to the Adams Basin Inn.

Corn Hill Navigation (585-262-5661, www.samandmary.org, 12 Schoen Pl., Pittsford, NY 14534) The *Sam Patch* is an 1800s packet boat replica built by Mid-Lakes Navigation Company that docks at Pittsford's historic Schoen Place and cruises through Lock 32.

Colonial Belle (585-223-9470, www.colonialbelle.com, 400 Packett's Landing, Fairport, NY 14450) The *Colonial Belle* cruises from the heart of historic Fairport from mid-May to October. There are a variety of theme and dinner cruises. On Sunday afternoons, a singer/guitarist entertains with canal songs. The gift shop has canal-related items.

Mid-Lakes Navigation Company (315-685-8500 or 800-545-4318, www.midlakesnav .com, 11 Jordan St., Skaneateles, NY 13152) The double-decker *Emita II* cruises from Dutchman's Landing in Syracuse through Lock 24 in Baldwinsville. Enjoy lunch and dinner cruises.

Seaway Navigation & Tours (315-934-4157, www.seawaynavigationandtours.com,

Riverfront Park, 9700 Walnut St., Brewerton, NY 13029) The *Mystère* offers a variety of dinner, Sunday brunch, and theme cruises Thursday through Sunday on Oneida Lake and the Erie Canal.

Erie Canal Cruises (315-717-0350, www.eriecanalcruises.com, 800 Mohawk St., Herkimer, NY 13350) *Lil' Diamond II* is docked at Gems Along the Mohawk, a dining and shopping complex just off the New York State Thruway (I-90) in Herkimer. This Mohawk Valley cruise takes visitors through Lock 18 from mid-May to mid-October.

Erie-Champlain Canal Boat Company (518-432-6094, www.eccboating.com, 1 Tugboat Alley, Waterford, NY 12188) Although mostly a charter-boat outfit, the company offers small groups and families cruises out of historic Waterford on board one of the narrow wooden packet boats made by Mid-Lakes Navigation Company.

Champlain Canal Tour Boats (518-695-5609 or 518-695-5496, www.champlaincanal tours.com, Canal House, End of Towpath, Schuylerville, NY 12871) The *M/V Sadie* and *M/V Caldwell Belle* offer a variety of excursions, including locking through Lock C5 on the Champlain Canal from mid-May to October. There are also overnight excursions to Whitehall.

Multiday Cruises

American Canadian Caribbean Line (800-556-7450, www.accl-smallships.com, P.O. Box 368, Warren, RI 02885) Small cruise ships like the *Grande Mariner,* with accommodations for 84 to 100 passengers, offer 10-, 11-, and 12-night cruises on the Erie and Oswego canals, among other itineraries, and fall foliage cruises on the canals and the Saint Lawrence River.

Mid-Lakes Navigation Company (315-685-8500 or 800-545-4318, www.midlakesnav .com, 11 Jordan St., Skaneateles, NY 13152) The double-decker *Emita II* offers two- and three-day one-way cruises from Lockport, Macedon, Syracuse, and Albany. All meals are served on board, and passengers stay overnight in nearby hotels—some right on the canal. Transportation is provided back to the home port.

Sam Patch *near Pittsford*

Grande Mariner *cruising in Waterford*

Self-Skippered Charter Boats

Erie Canal Cruise Lines (800-962-1771, www.canalcruises.com, P.O. Box 285, Cape Vincent, NY 13618) This line offers full-week or half-week cruises on board boats that resemble traditional English canal boats. They sleep six and include TV, air-conditioning, and a microwave oven. Two bicycles are also included. Cruises begin in either Fairport or Seneca Falls and can travel on the Erie, Cayuga-Seneca, and Oswego canals.

Erie-Champlain Canal Boat Company (518-432-6094, www.eccboating.com, 1 Tugboat Alley, Waterford, NY 12188) Cruise for a week on the Erie or Champlain canals on board fully equipped narrow wooden 41-foot boats built to resemble old-time canal packet boats. The boats, which sleep six, were built by Mid-Lakes Navigation Company.

Mid-Lakes Navigation Company (315-685-8500 or 800-545-4318, www.midlakesnav .com, 11 Jordan St., Skaneateles, NY 13152) Take the helm for a weeklong cruise on a 34-, 41-, or 42-foot Lockmaster narrow wooden boat. Cruises depart from Macedon near Rochester, and you can cruise on the Erie, Cayuga-Seneca, and Oswego canals. The boats sleep four to six. Two bikes are included.

Canoes and Kayaks (from west to east)

These companies offer canoe and kayak rentals for those who want to navigate the canals at their own pace.

Canaltown Paddlesports (585-355-7855, www.canaltownpaddlesports.com, Union St., Spencerport, NY 14559)

Genesee Waterways Center (585-328-3960, www.geneseewaterways.org, 2797 Clover St., Pittsford, NY 14534, or 149 Elmwood Ave., Rochester, NY 14611)

Erie Canal Boat Company (585-748-
BOAT, www.eriecanalboatcompany
.com, 7 Liftbridge Lane West,
Fairport, NY 14450)

Mid Lakes Erie Macedon Landing
(315-986-3011 or 800-808-4511,
www.macedonlanding.com, 1865
Canandaigua Rd., Macedon, NY
14502)

Cayuga General Store (315-568-9306,
2679 Lower Lake Rd., Seneca Falls,
NY 13148)

Big Bay Marina (315-676-2223,
www.bigbayboats.com, Camic Rd.,
Central Square, NY 13036)

The Boat House (518-393-5711,
www.boathousecanoeskayaks.com,
2855 Aqueduct Rd., Schenectady, NY
12309)

Lock 12 Marina (518-499-2049,
www.visitwhitehall.com, 82 N.
Williams St., Whitehall, NY 12887)

Kayaking in Fairport along the canal

Emita II moored in Brockport

Locking Through along the Canal

When approaching the lock, boaters must stop at a safe distance and follow specified signals. Boaters must give three distinct blasts on the horn, whistle, or other signaling device.

Lock operators will reply with lights in the following manner:

Green: Lock is ready, craft may advance

Red: Craft must wait

No light: Craft must wait or tie up to approach wall

Six flashes of red or green: Remain stopped and await further instructions.

On entering the lock chamber, vessels must proceed under control at a safe, reduced speed. All boats must be equipped with adequate mooring lines and fenders. Lock operators are not required to handle or furnish lines.

Once in the lock chamber, all vessels should take their stations against the chamber walls. Boaters are required to secure their vessels to the provided mooring posts, lines, cables, or ladders.

As soon as the water in the lock chamber reaches the proper level, the gates will be opened. After the gates are fully opened, boaters should cast off all lines and proceed at a reduced speed to exit the chamber in station order.

Lockview IV *entering the lock at Lockport*

BIKING AND HIKING

The New York State Canalway Trail is a multiuse recreational trail that continues to expand. The Erie Canal trail, the longest section of the trail, is more than 260 miles long. When complete, it will be the longest continuous trail in the United States, at 348 miles. And when the Canalway Trail system is finished, including along the three smaller canals, the entire length of the trail will be 524 miles. The Canalway Trail is a popular hiking and biking trail. Each July, Parks and Trails NY sponsors an annual eight-day, 400-mile bicycle tour from Buffalo to Albany. (For more information about the Canalway Trail, call 518-434-1583, or visit www.ptny.org.)

GETTING HERE

By Car

I-90 (New York State Thruway) is a limited-access toll road that connects Buffalo, Rochester, Syracuse, Utica, and Albany and parallels the Erie Canal.

US 20 parallels much of I-90 and was used extensively before the high-speed route was built. US 20 connects towns along the Cayuga-Seneca Canal and many other towns, including Skaneateles, Auburn, and Geneva.

NY 48 parallels the Oswego Canal on the west side and **NY 481** parallels the Oswego Canal on the east side.

NY 4 parallels the Champlain Canal from Waterford to Whitehall on Lake Champlain.

I-86 crosses the southern portion of New York along the Pennsylvania border from just

Biking along the Canalway Trail in Pittsford

north of New York City to Jamestown in the southwestern corner of the state. This divided highway offers a pleasant alternative to I-90—depending on your final destination.

I-81 is the major north-south route in the center of the state from the Pennsylvania border to the Canadian border. This divided highway crosses through Syracuse and has a 65-mph speed limit for most of its length.

I-87 is the major north-south route in the eastern region of the state. It travels north from New York City to Albany, Saratoga Springs, on to the Adirondacks, and up to Quebec.

By Air
Buffalo Niagara International Airport (716-630-6000, www.buffaloairport.com, 4200 Genesee St., Cheektowaga, NY 14225) The airport is served by nine major carriers.
Greater Rochester International Airport (585-464-6000, www.monroecounty.gov/airport, 1200 Brooks Ave., Rochester, NY 14624) The airport is served by nine major carriers.
Ithaca Tompkins Regional Airport (607-257-0456, www.flyithaca.com, 72 Brown Rd., Ithaca, NY 14850) The airport is served by three major carriers.
Syracuse Hancock International Airport (315-454-4330, www.syrairport.org, 1000 Colonel Eileen Collins Blvd., 13212) The airport is served by seven major carriers and several commuter airlines.
Albany International Airport (518-242-2200, www.albanyairport.com, 737 Albany-Shaker Rd., Albany, NY 12211) The airport is served by seven major carriers.

By Bus
Adirondack Trailways (800-858-8555, www.trailwaysny.com)
Greyhound (800-231-2222, www.greyhound.com)

By Train
Amtrak (800-USA-RAIL, www.amtrak.com) Amtrak's route parallels the Erie Canal, with stations in Buffalo, Niagara Falls, Rochester, Syracuse, Rome, Utica, Amsterdam, Schenectady, and Albany-Rensselaer. This is the Empire Service, and after Albany-Rensselaer, it continues south to New York City. The *Adirondack* travels daily from New York City with stops in Albany-Rensselaer, Schenectady, Saratoga Springs, Fort Edward, and Whitehall on Lake Champlain, paralleling part of the Champlain Canal. It then continues north to Montreal, Canada.

3

Buffalo and the Western Canal Region

Niagara Falls, The Tonawandas, Lockport, Medina

Buffalo

The opening of the Erie Canal was a transforming moment for Buffalo. As a small village at the confluence of Lake Erie and the mouth of the Niagara River, Buffalo had been burned to the ground by the British on December 30, 1813, in retaliation for Americans burning Toronto during the War of 1812. Just north of Buffalo was the more substantial community of Black Rock. When discussions began regarding the route of the proposed Erie Canal, the intrigue and lobbying among community leaders grew intense; all knew that the decision would be an epic one.

General Peter Porter led the contingent advocating for Black Rock as the terminus of the Erie Canal. Samuel Wilkeson—who claimed to "have never seen a harbor"—directed a massive Buffalo harbor-building project, leading Governor DeWitt Clinton to side with

Buffalo's art deco City Hall viewed from the Erie Basin Marina

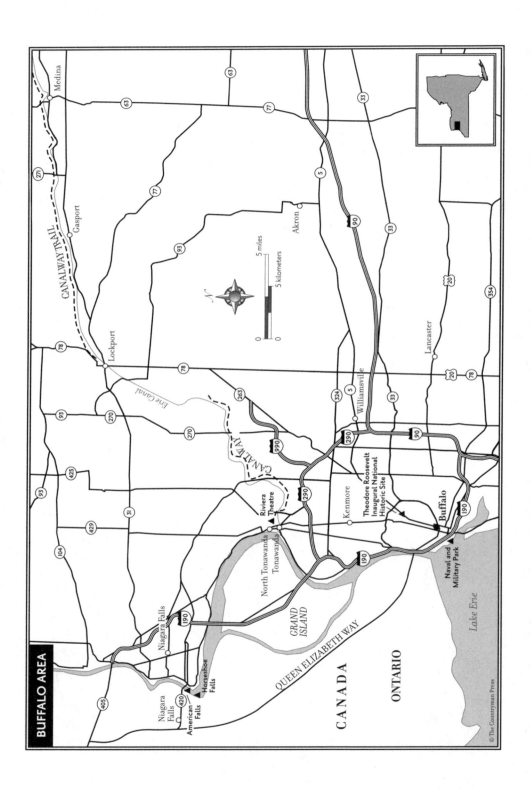

those promoting Buffalo as the canal's terminus. The Buffalo forces, of course, won, and Buffalo went on to grow so fast that it swallowed up Black Rock in 1852.

As the canal's terminus, Buffalo became one of the country's great 19th-century cities. And of all the cities along the original canal, Buffalo was the most important—growing in size and influence to become the state's second-largest city. It also became the greatest inland port in the nation, leading to it being called the Queen City of the Lakes. Great Lakes shipping and Erie Canal transport met on the Buffalo waterfront for the transfer of goods. It was here in 1842 that Joseph Dent invented the mechanized grain elevator and revolutionized the handling of wheat. By 1849 Buffalo had become the world's busiest grain-transfer port, surpassing London, Odessa, and Rotterdam. (Grain elevators still line the Buffalo River.)

The city was an outpost of the East and a gateway to the West. It profited from its privileged position as a transportation hub—when the influence of the canal declined in the later years of the 19th century, the city became a major national railroad center.

It also became one of the country's most technically advanced cities by harnessing the electricity produced in nearby Niagara Falls. The 1901 Pan-American Exposition was designed to showcase the city's industrial development and the power of electrical illumination.

President William McKinley was shot by an assassin while visiting the exposition and died in Buffalo eight days later. Vice President Theodore Roosevelt took the presidential oath of office in an elegant Delaware Avenue mansion, now the Theodore Roosevelt Inaugural National Historic Site. (The McKinley Monument in front of Buffalo's magnificent art deco City Hall honors the assassinated president.)

During the 19th century, Buffalo sent two hometown citizens to the White House: Millard Fillmore, the 13th president, and Grover Cleveland, the 22nd and 24th president. Fillmore had served in the U.S. Congress and as state comptroller, and Cleveland had been both mayor of Buffalo and governor of New York. (Cleveland remains the only president to marry while in office, and the only one to leave office and return four years later.) Fillmore

Historical marker at Buffalo harbor

retired to Buffalo, and his work following the presidency led to the creation of a number of city institutions, including the University at Buffalo and the Buffalo and Erie County Historical Society.

Another notable Buffalo resident was Mark Twain, who spent several years in Buffalo as the editor and part-owner of the *Buffalo Express* newspaper. The original *Adventures of Huckleberry Finn* manuscript is in the Mark Twain Room at the downtown Buffalo and Erie County Public Library. And famed writer F. Scott Fitzgerald spent some of his youth in the city's historic Allentown neighborhood.

Strong ethnic neighborhoods and identities have long defined the city—a rich mixture of Polish, Irish, Italian, German, and, more recently, Puerto Rican immigrants and their descendants. Buffalo has the biggest Saint Patrick's Day Parade west of New York City's Fifth Avenue and the biggest Pulaski Day Parade, a celebration of Polish heritage, east of Chicago. The city also has a strong African American history due to its proximity to Canada: It was a last stop on the Underground Railroad before escaping slaves reached freedom across the Niagara River. The Niagara Movement, the forerunner to the National Association for the Advancement of Colored People (NAACP), was founded in the city in 1905.

Buffalo is a city of both taverns and churches. But the taverns are sedate places now compared to the 19th century, when the two-block-long Canal Street on the waterfront had 93 saloons and 15 dance halls. For absolute depravity, toughness, and violence, the city had no equal and was considered one of the world's most notorious waterfront neighborhoods.

Buffalo and its elegant avenues were laid out by Joseph Ellicott, a brother of Andrew Ellicott, Pierre L'Enfant's chief surveyor in the planning of Washington, D.C. Frederick Law Olmsted, America's greatest landscape architect, designed the city's beautiful parks and parkways. The city has received worldwide recognition for its architectural treasures— structures built in the late 19th and early 20th centuries when the city was one of the wealthiest in the nation. Significant works by H. H. Richardson, Louis Sullivan, Stanford White, Eliel and Eero Saarinen, Richard Upjohn, and Frank Lloyd Wright grace the city. Wright immodestly called the 1905 Darwin D. Martin House Complex, currently nearing the end of a $50 million restoration, "a well-nigh perfect composition." It is the largest Prairie-style house complex in existence, with six buildings totaling nearly 32,000 square feet. And the Guaranty Building in downtown Buffalo, designed by Sullivan, is considered the finest example of early skyscraper design. It has been painstakingly restored and is now home to the city's oldest and largest law firm, Hodgson Russ, which dates from 1817. Attorneys who have practiced with Hodgson Russ and its predecessor firms include two presidents—the country's sole law firm with this distinction.

"In my line of work, it doesn't get any better than this," said Richard Moe, president of the National Trust for Historic Preservation, in 2007. "To come up here and in one day see the best of Upjohn, Sullivan, Richardson, Wright, Saarinen and Olmsted—nowhere else, nowhere else in the United States, with the possible exception of Chicago, do you see the rich array of 19th and 20th century architecture that you have here in Buffalo."

Gilded Age opulence can be found along Delaware Avenue. The street is lined with elegant 19th-century mansions, once home to the city's rich and powerful and now used as offices by corporations, law firms, nonprofit organizations, and medical groups.

"When I think of Buffalo, I see Lake Erie gleaming with sailboats, tree-lined boulevards of astonishing grandeur, and miles of homes, offices and civic centers designed by the greatest architects America has known," wrote Lauren Belfer, author of the 1999 best-

Power of Buffalo

"In an age of cultural tourism, an age in which people are eager to find ways to explore places that are different from other places, places that do not look like the banal Anywhere is Nowhere is Everywhere of the American Interstate, Buffalo has a kind of power, the power of the authentic place. It's an extraordinary and, in many ways, beautiful city."

—Paul Goldberger, architectural critic for the *New Yorker*

seller *City of Light,* a historical novel that celebrates Buffalo and the Niagara Frontier in the early 20th century.

Aside from its famous architecture, Buffalo is also known for—and fiercely proud of—its professional sports teams: the National Football League's Buffalo Bills and the National Hockey League's Buffalo Sabers. Furthermore, some of the Northeast's top-ranked ski centers can be found in the hills south of the city, courtesy of the bountiful snow created by winter winds whipping off Lake Erie—the famous "lake effect" snowfalls. (Buffalo is sometimes referred to as Blizzard City, a somewhat unfair designation given that Syracuse regularly wins the annual snow derby among upstate cities.)

The city suffered a significant decline and loss of population following the opening in 1959 of the Saint Lawrence Seaway, which bypassed the Port of Buffalo, and the closing of the area's massive steel mills as well as many other manufacturing plants. Today, giant wind turbines take advantage of the usually steady winds across Lake Erie to generate electricity on former steel-mill property. The futuristic-looking turbines have become tourist attractions in their own right.

Although sometimes dismissed as a declining industrial center, Buffalo is now a city that is transforming itself into a technologically and medically advanced center at the same time that it is undergoing a cultural renaissance as it seeks to recapture its former glory.

Original canal-era building foundations (foreground) were unearthed during restoration of the Commercial Slip

Buffalo's entire waterfront is currently undergoing a $400-million redevelopment with the goal of reclaiming some of the commerce and bustle of the 19th-century canal era. In 2007 the American Planning Association named the city's historic and vibrant Elmwood Village one of the country's top 10 neighborhoods. It is also a city that takes its nickname—the City of Good Neighbors—seriously.

A section of the old Erie Canal at the terminus of the canal has recently been excavated and rewatered. Known as the Commercial Slip, it once linked the canal to the Buffalo River, Lake Erie, and America's heartland. The area around the slip dates back to the beginning of the canal and was a notoriously rough neighborhood. Today the area is experiencing a dramatic resurgence. The Erie Canal Harbor has undergone a $53-million makeover. Other highlights of the once-again-bustling wharf include unearthed foundations of original canal-era buildings, a replica "bowstring" pedestrian bridge that spans the reopened slip, and a re-creation of the wooden Central Wharf. More than 500 feet of public docks line one side of the slip and the riverfront along the historic wharf. It was formally opened on July 2, 2008, when a number of dignitaries poured water from the Hudson River into the Commercial Slip. It immediately became a waterfront gathering place and has hosted concerts, lectures, and children's events.

In a note of synchronicity, this is the same point where the Wedding of the Waters was completed—marking the formal opening of the canal in 1825.

LODGING

Buffalo has a wide variety of lodging, ranging from downtown high-rises to a world-class Delaware Avenue boutique hotel to numerous bed & breakfasts. The city is a good base from which to tour Niagara Falls and the other towns and cities of the western canal region. A large concentration of national chain hotels can be found near the Buffalo Niagara International Airport and in Amherst, near the University at Buffalo North Campus. Many of the airport-area establishments offer park-and-stay rates, since the airport attracts a number of out-of-area travelers who come to take advantage of the airport's reputation for competitive airline fares. Lodging rates tend to be in the moderate range. All are for double occupancy.

Lodging Rates
Inexpensive: Up to $75
Moderate: $76–$150
Expensive: $151–$250
Very Expensive: More than $250

ADAM'S MARK BUFFALO NIAGARA
716-845-5100 or 800-444-ADAM
www.adamsmark.com/buffalo
120 Church St., Buffalo, NY 14202
Price: Moderate—Expensive
Credit Cards: Yes
Handicapped Access: Yes
Special Features: Indoor pool; some rooms with great views of Lake Erie

This waterfront hotel has 486 rooms and bills itself, because of its expansive meeting facilities, as "Buffalo's Other Convention Center." The large indoor pool and health club make it a popular choice for families. There is an airport shuttle service and two in-house restaurants. It is within an easy walk of the Erie Basin Marina and the historic canal area.

BEAU FLEUVE BED & BREAKFAST
Innkeepers: Ramona and Rik Whitaker
716-882-6116 or 800-278-0245
www.beaufleuve.com
242 Linwood Ave., Buffalo, NY 14209

Price: Moderate
Credit Cards: Yes
Handicapped Access: No
Special Features: Complimentary gourmet breakfast

Beau Fleuve means "beautiful river," the name believed to have been given to the area by early French explorer-traders. The name *Buffalo* is thought to originate from a mispronunciation of *Beau Fleuve* by non-French-speakers. This 1882 grand residence is in the Linwood Historic Preservation District and is close to downtown and Allentown. Five guest rooms celebrate the ethnic groups that settled in the area: French, Irish, German, Italian, and Polish. The French Room is decorated in shades of blue and has a private bath and a fireplace; the German Room has a four-poster bed and private bath; the Irish room is the largest of the guest rooms and features an antique brass bed and a sofa plus a private bath; the Italian and Polish Rooms share a bath. Descend a wide oak staircase, passing vibrant stained-glass windows to the dining room for an elegant breakfast that includes fresh-from-the-oven muffins, scones, and nut breads; fresh fruits, and entrées such as veggie frittata, Spanish tortilla, eggs Benedict, raspberry-almond Belgian waffles, and banana-blueberry pancakes. Guests also enjoy complimentary snacks and beverages. Michael Chapdelaine, who won first place in a classical-guitar competition held in Buffalo, was so inspired by his stay that he composed a song titled "Beau Fleuve." You can listen to it on the B&B's Web site. Beau Fleuve is not appropriate for children under ten.

BEST WESTERN INN ON THE AVENUE

716-886-8333 or 888-868-3033
www.innontheavenue.com
510 Delaware Ave., Buffalo, NY 14202
Price: Moderate
Credit Cards: Yes
Handicapped Access: Yes
Special Features: Dog friendly; complimentary continental breakfast

Located on Delaware Avenue a short distance from the theater district and the Chippewa Street entertainment district, this inn offers 61 recently renovated rooms, including eight king business rooms and five king whirlpool suites.

BUFFALO NIAGARA MARRIOTT

716-689-6900
www.marriott.com
1340 Millersport Hwy., Amherst, NY 14221
Price: Moderate
Credit Cards: Yes
Handicapped Access: Yes
Special Features: Indoor/outdoor pool

The 356 rooms and suites in this well-located hotel—it's adjacent to the University at Buffalo and 20 minutes from Niagara Falls—have been recently renovated. The hotel offers a daily breakfast buffet (not included in room rate). The popular Houlihan's Restaurant & Bar, which attracts locals as well as hotel guests, is open for lunch and dinner and is known for its creative food and drinks, including signature martinis and mini desserts. There is an indoor/outdoor pool, fitness center, and free airport shuttle. The hotel is a popular location for meetings, with 14,000 square feet of meeting space.

COMFORT SUITES DOWNTOWN BUFFALO

716-854-5500 or 800-4CHOICE
www.choicehotels.com
601 Main St., Buffalo, NY 14203
Price: Moderate
Credit Cards: Yes
Handicapped Access: Yes
Special Features: Free high-speed wireless Internet

Located in the heart of downtown, this was the former Radisson Hotel, and the all-suite 146-room hotel offers lots of square footage for a modest price. French doors divide the living room from the bedroom, and each room has a king-sized bed as well as a sofa bed, refrigerator, and microwave, making it a good choice for families.

DOUBLETREE CLUB HOTEL
716-845-0112 or 877-633-4667
www.doubletreebuffalo.com
125 High St., Buffalo, NY 14203
Price: Moderate
Credit Cards: Yes
Handicapped Access: Yes
Special Features: All rooms have refrigerators, microwaves, and free high-speed Internet

Situated in the High Street Medical Corridor—where Buffalo General Hospital and Roswell Park Cancer Institute are located—the hotel caters to hospital visitors and a corporate crowd that tend to be longer-term residents. But leisure travelers are welcome to enjoy the 100 spacious rooms, some with kitchenettes. There are also comfy public spaces, including a library where you can read or play board games. An Au Bon Pain café is located in the hotel.

HAMPTON INN & SUITES BUFFALO
716-855-2223 or 800-HAMPTON
www.hamptoninnbuffalo.com
220 Delaware Ave., Buffalo, NY 14202
Price: Moderate–Expensive
Credit Cards: Yes
Handicapped Access: Yes
Special Features: Free high-speed Internet, complimentary breakfast buffet

This is a Hampton Inn like none other and surely rates as one of the nicest of this chain anywhere. The ancient-Greek-style statue overlooking the indoor pool might be your first indication that this is a special place. The 137 rooms and suites are the shining stars of this hotel, constructed inside an existing vintage downtown building. They are enormous and come loaded with amenities such as Jacuzzis, fireplaces, and large flat-screen TVs. Some rooms have kitchenettes, and all rooms have coffeemakers. Everyone can enjoy the Hampton Inn breakfast, which is more like a full-blown breakfast buffet here. It is right in the heart of the entertainment district, and for chocolate lovers the Chocolate Bar is here (see listing under "Restaurants")—which, for some, might be the pinnacle of their journey.

HAMPTON INN WILLIAMSVILLE
716-632-0900 or 866-466-9853
www.hamptoninn.com
5455 Main St., Williamsville, NY 14221
Price: Moderate
Credit Cards: Yes
Handicapped Access: Yes
Special Features: Indoor pool; complimentary airport shuttle and high-speed Internet

Located in the heart of the village of Williamsville, this Hampton Inn has been awarded the Hampton Lighthouse Award, given to hotels that offer exemplary service. The 80 rooms are large and have custom-designed Thomasville furniture that includes a large desk for your laptop—and high-speed Internet access. The suites have whirlpools, fireplaces, and full kitchens. There is a complimentary airport shuttle and buffet breakfast as well as fitness room and indoor pool. Many village restaurants are within walking distance.

HOLIDAY INN BUFFALO DOWNTOWN
716-886-2121 or 800-HOLIDAY
www.hibuffalodowntown.com
620 Delaware Ave., Buffalo, NY 14202
Price: Moderate
Credit Cards: Yes

Handicapped Access: Yes
Special Features: Outdoor pool; complimentary airport shuttle

Located in the historic Allentown district, this hotel is across the street from the Wilcox Mansion—otherwise known as the Theodore Roosevelt Inaugural National Historic Site. The 168 rooms—all nonsmoking—have two double beds or a king. There is a fitness center and a swimming pool, and the complimentary airport shuttle is available 24 hours. The Grille 620 dining room offers a good in-house choice for breakfast or dinner. The menu is chosen with care and features such favorites as Tuscan chicken, seafood scampi, strip steak, and rack of lamb. Desserts come from Butterwood, the force behind the Chocolate Bar, and are always a delectable treat.

HOMEWOOD SUITES BY HILTON BUFFALO-AIRPORT
716-685-0700 or 800-CALLHOME
www.homewoodsuitesbuffalo.com
760 Dick Rd., Cheektowaga, NY 14225
Price: Moderate—Expensive
Credit Cards: Yes
Handicapped Access: Yes
Special Features: Complimentary breakfast buffet; all rooms with full kitchens

This is a most comfortable 77-room hotel for business travelers, families, and extended-stay guests. Every room has a fully equipped kitchen, and some suites have fireplaces and a Jacuzzi. Pets are welcome for a fee. A Manager's Reception is held Monday through Thursday, with a complimentary light meal and beverages. The hotel has an indoor pool and health club as well as an on-site convenience store. It is just a mile from the airport, and there is a complimentary shuttle.

HOSTELLING INTERNATIONAL– BUFFALO NIAGARA
716-852-5222

www.hostelbuffalo.com
667 Main St., Buffalo, NY 14203
Price: Inexpensive
Credit Cards: Yes
Handicapped Access: Yes
Special Features: Free tea and coffee and Wi-Fi

Located in a historic building in the center of the downtown theater district, this hostel has male, female, and coed dorms as well as two private rooms—48 beds total. The hostel has a communal kitchen, comfortable public rooms, and a friendly staff. Registered guests have 24-hour access.

HYATT REGENCY BUFFALO
716-856-1234 or 800-233-1234
www.buffalo.hyatt.com
Two Fountain Plaza, Buffalo, NY 14202
Price: Moderate—Expensive
Credit Cards: Yes
Handicapped Access: Yes
Special Features: Covered walkway to Convention Center

The 15-story circa-1923 Genesee Building, designed by noted Buffalo architects E. B. Green and William Wicks, was transformed into a 394-room, French Renaissance—style luxury hotel. The spectacular glass-topped lobby was added to the building during the construction, with the marble doorway of the old building serving as the entrance to the atrium. There are no cookie-cutter rooms here, since they were transformed from various-shaped offices. The rooms are all comfortable and spacious and have recently undergone a major renovation. Request one of the top-floor rooms facing Lake Erie, and you will have the added bonus of a fantastic view. This unique hotel occupies a prime Main Street location, and since it is connected to the Convention Center, it attracts a business-focused clientele, but its location also makes it a great option for leisure travelers. There is casual dining at Harriet's, featuring Buffalo's only "ice rail" bar, and fine dining and live entertainment at the award-winning E. B. Green's Steakhouse (see listing under "Restaurants"). The 21,000 square feet of meeting space makes it a popular choice for meetings, banquets, and wedding receptions.

LORD AMHERST MOTOR HOTEL
716-839-2200 or 800-544-2200
www.lordamherst.com
5000 Main St., Amherst, NY 14226
Price: Inexpensive–Moderate
Credit Cards: Yes
Handicapped Access: Yes
Special Features: Pet friendly; free high-speed Internet

Conveniently located next to I-290 not far from the University at Buffalo North Campus, Niagara Falls, and the Erie Canal, this hotel offers 100 large, comfortable rooms decorated in early-American decor. There are suites, corporate apartments, and efficiencies suitable for extended stays. Refrigerators and microwaves are available for an additional charge. There is an exercise room and an outdoor pool. A continental breakfast is included.

THE MANSION
General Manager: Gino Principe
716-886-3300
www.mansionondelaware.com
414 Delaware Ave., Buffalo, NY 14202
Price: Expensive–Very Expensive
Credit Cards: Yes
Handicapped Access: Yes
Special Features: Complimentary continental breakfast, afternoon tea and wine, and 24-hour butler service

Built as a private residence in 1869, the Mansion was transformed into one of the city's luxurious hotels in time for the 1901 Pan American Exposition. It was called the House of Light in recognition of its 175 windows (all replaced during the $3-million-plus renovation). Over the years the second Empire-style building became an apartment house popular with writers and artists and the home of the once-legendary Victor Hugo Wine Cellar. After several decades of abandonment and disrepair, the building was

The Mansion Inn on elegant Delaware Avenue

returned to its former glory and reopened in 2001 as a 28-room luxury boutique hotel—completely nonsmoking—with high ceilings, fireplaces, elegant wood everywhere, and luxurious beds. It has already been awarded Four Diamonds by AAA and is the choice for celebrities from Hillary Clinton to Faith Hill and Tim McGraw. Guests enjoy complimentary continental breakfast, afternoon tea and wine, downtown car service, and 24-hour butler service. In its current incarnation it has already become celebrated for a level of service and style that matches the luxury of a bygone era. Located between Allentown and the downtown theater district, the Mansion is the choice for visitors who are looking for a special, memorable experience.

MILLENNIUM AIRPORT HOTEL BUFFALO

716-681-2400 or 866-866-8066
www.millenniumhotels.com
2040 Walden Ave., Cheektowaga, NY 14225
Price: Moderate
Credit Cards: Yes
Handicapped Access: Yes
Special Features: Pet friendly; complimentary airport shuttle

This 300-room hotel was recently completely renovated—the most popular rooms overlook the lush, plant-filled indoor courtyard and indoor pool. It is located next to the Walden Galleria, the region's premier shopping mall with more than 200 stores, shops, restaurants, and 16 movie theaters. Special rates are offered for Canadian travelers. Enjoy fine dining in Walden's Restaurant and casual eating and drinking in the Twigs Sports Bar. It is also a good choice for meetings.

SLEEP INN AND SUITES BUFFALO AIRPORT

716-626-4000 or 800-559-PARK
www.sleepinnairport.com

100 Holtz Dr., Cheektowaga, NY 14225
Price: Moderate
Credit Cards: Yes
Handicapped Access: Yes
Special Features: Complimentary breakfast and evening cookie reception

This 88-room hotel, a three-time Gold Award property, is a popular choice for travelers flying out of the Buffalo Niagara Airport, with attractive park-and-fly packages as well as shopping packages. In-room refrigerators and microwaves are available, and guests can also choose to stay in one of 24 suites, including 6 Jacuzzi suites. The needs of guests are always foremost, starting with the buffet breakfast that begins at 4:30 am for travelers with early-morning flights. Conveniently located next to the airport, the hotel offers a courtesy shuttle 24 hours a day to transport guests anywhere within a 5-mile radius.

RESTAURANTS

The Buffalo region has a rich culinary tradition based on its diverse ethnic roots. Of course, everyone knows about buffalo wings, and then there is the famous "beef on weck" (thinly sliced roast beef on a fresh kimmelweck roll—a salty hard roll—with a dash of horseradish sauce). Buffalo is also famous for its Friday-night fish fries served in bars and restaurants, a legacy of Catholic meatless Fridays. Buffalo even made it into the *Guinness Book of Records* for the most fish fries served at once.

All restaurants are by New York State law nonsmoking. Prices are estimated per person for dinner entrée without tax, tip, or beverage.

Dining Rates
Inexpensive: Up to $10
Moderate: $11–$25
Expensive: $26–$40
Very Expensive: More than $40

Buffalo Wings and the Chicken Wing Festival

Buffalo wings take their name from the city in which the famous menu item, now served in restaurants around the globe, was created. It was one day in 1964 when Teressa Bellissimo—one-half of the eponymous team at **Frank and Teressa's Anchor Bar**—had a brainstorm. She was feeding a crowd of her son's friends and decided that instead of putting some plump chicken wings into a pot of soup, she would put them in the deep fryer. Teressa served them with a special sauce (which now comes in mild, medium, or hot), celery, and blue-cheese dressing. The rest is history. Wings are now shipped around the country. Celebrities and wing lovers make a pilgrimage to the Anchor Bar (716-886-8920; www.anchorbar.com; 1047 Main Street, Buffalo) whenever they are in town, often taking home some of the famous hot sauce as well. The walls are lined with photos of the many celebrities who have visited.

Buffalo wings inspired another creation: the **National Chicken Wing Festival.** Since 2002 the festival (www.buffalowing.com) has been held on Labor Day weekend at the downtown baseball park, and attendees have consumed nearly 200 tons of wings. The idea for the festival came from a movie called *Osmosis Jones*, which starred Bill Murray as a compulsive eater with a goal of attending the Super Bowl of junk food, the National Buffalo Wing Festival. Ironically, the festival didn't exist at the time—so Buffalo promoter Drew Cerza created it at the suggestion of *Buffalo News* columnist Donn Esmonde. The festival revolves around consuming tons of wings of every possible flavor, and the climax is a chicken-wing-eating contest sanctioned by the International Federation of Competitive Eating. Since the festival's beginning, several million wings have been consumed, and one wedding was even held with the event as its backdrop. The festival has been featured on both the Travel Channel and the Food Network.

The National Chicken Wing Festival serves up world-famous Buffalo wings

CHEF'S RESTAURANT
716-856-9187
www.ilovechefs.com
291 Seneca St., Buffalo, NY 14204
Open: Mon.–Sat.
Cuisine: Southern Italian
Serving: L, D
Price: Inexpensive–Moderate
Credit Cards: Yes
Handicapped Access: Yes
Special Features: Chef's sauce available for take-out

Opened in 1923 close to the terminus of the original Erie Canal, Chef's is a classic Buffalo institution. The Billittier family has operated it since 1954. The late Lou Billittier was known for both personally overseeing all dishes and his humanitarian work in the community. His children, Mary Beth and Louis John, are carrying on the tradition of hospitality and fine food. Served on red-and-white-checked table-cloths under grape chandeliers, meals here are what your Sicilian grandmother would make for Sunday dinner. People from all walks of life—neighborhood residents, truckers passing through, baseball and hockey fans—gather and are warmly welcomed at this 325-seat restaurant.

Homegrown Casual Food

Carl Anderson and his wife, Greta, began **Anderson's Frozen Custard** in New York City in 1946, selling custard cones and lemon ice, but soon moved back to the Buffalo area, opening their first location in Kenmore (716-875-5952, www.andersonscustard.com, 2235 Sheridan Dr., Kenmore, NY 14223). Anderson's became famous for its homemade ice cream, frozen custard, and fruit ices (lemon ice is the most popular and is served with fresh strawberries in-season) as well as beef on weck and other sandwiches and salads. This family-run operation has a mail-order business for homesick Buffaloians and other fans. Aside from the original location, other Buffalo-area locations are: 2635 Delaware Ave., Buffalo, NY 14216 (716-873-5330); 6075 Main St., Williamsville, NY 14221 (716-632-1416); 3724 Union Rd., Cheektowaga, NY 14225 (716-681-5464); 4855 Transit Rd., Lancaster, NY 14224 (716-656-7220); 6277 Robinson Rd., Lockport, NY 14094 (716-438-5615); and 2369 Niagara Falls Blvd., Amherst, NY 14228 (716-691-8970).

In 1913 Greek immigrant Theodore Spiro Liaros came to America and began operating a horse-drawn hot-dog cart near the construction site for Buffalo's new Peace Bridge over the Niagara River to Canada. When the bridge was completed in 1927, Liaros purchased a tool shed for $100 from the construction foreman's sister, who had been operating a sandwich shop for the workers, and thus the first stationary Ted's was born. Still family run, **Ted's Hot Dogs** (716-691-3731, www.tedsonline.com) has become a local legend and evokes fierce loyalty from its customers near and far. (It has even been celebrated on the Food Network.) Not every hot-dog stand motivates people to fly in from halfway across the country to taste the delectable charcoal-grilled dogs (best with Ted's own hot sauce, which is available to take home), plus hamburgers, fries, and fried onions, and salads and grilled chicken for the health conscious. Read about loyal Ted's fans on the company Web site. Eight locations in Buffalo suburbs plus one in Tempe, Arizona: 2351 Niagara Falls Blvd., Amherst, NY 14228 (716-691-7883); 1 Galleria Dr. (Walden Galleria), Cheektowaga, NY 14225 (716-683-7713); 4878 Transit Rd., Lancaster, NY 14043 (716-668-7533); 6230 Shimer Rd., Lockport, NY 14094 (716-439-4386); 333 Meadow Dr., N. Tonawanda, NY 14120 (716-693-1960); 3193 Orchard Park Rd., Orchard Park, NY 14127 (716-675-4662); 2312 Sheridan Dr., Tonawanda, NY 14150 (716-834-6287); and 7018 Transit Rd., Williamsville, NY 14221 (716-633-1700).

Politicians, community leaders, and visiting celebrities eventually find their way to Chef's, their photos showcased on the walls. Daily specials include stuffed shells, tripe, chicken livers, manicotti, eggplant Parmesan, and a local favorite of baked yellow pike. There is even fresh dandelion salad (in season). Favorite dishes include spaghetti Parmesan and ravioli. Bibs are provided, and your server will happily tie it for you. Take-out is available.

COLE'S

716-886-1449
meetmeatcoles.com
1104 Elmwood Ave., Buffalo, NY 14222
Open: Daily
Cuisine: American
Serving: L, D
Price: Moderate
Credit Cards: Yes
Handicapped Access: Yes
Special Features: Sunday brunch

This popular restaurant has been a neighborhood fixture since 1934. Winner of Best Burger in Buffalo and *Buffalo Beat* Best Casual Dining awards, it is located along the Elmwood strip close to Buffalo State College and nearby art galleries. The menu includes everything from grilled swordfish and chicken Dijon to lamb chops to more casual choices including chicken wings and, of course, those award-winning burgers.

D'ARCY MCGEE'S IRISH PUB

716-853-3600
darcymcgeesonline.com
257 Franklin St., Buffalo, NY 14202
Open: Daily
Cuisine: American-Irish
Serving: L, D
Price: Moderate
Credit Cards: Yes
Handicapped Access: Yes

Special Features: Live music on the patio bandstand

This is a fun party bar and restaurant with live entertainment in downtown Buffalo. The comfortable Irish ambiance means that no one remains a stranger. On the roof overlooking the Buffalo skyline is the famous Skybar, open for warm-weather entertainment. A wide and varied menu includes such Irish favorites as shepherd's pie, fish and chips, corned beef and cabbage, beef and Guinness stew, and braised lamb shanks, as well as down-home favorites such as roast turkey, meat loaf, roast beef, and smokehouse BBQ. Their Bailey's Irish Cheesecake, made with loads of Bailey's Irish Cream liqueur, is a popular dessert choice.

DUG'S DIVE

716-821-9600
1111 Fuhrman Blvd., Buffalo, NY 14203
Open: Daily May 1–Oct. 15
Cuisine: American
Serving: L, D
Price: Inexpensive–Moderate
Credit Cards: Yes
Handicapped Access: Yes
Special Features: Outdoor patio overlooking Buffalo Small Boat Harbor

Not far from the old Canal District, Dug's is a great place to get a taste of summer and good, classic American food with a grand view of the waterfront. The name honors the original Dug's Dive, a saloon that was situated on Commercial Street along the Erie Canal towpath. The slang term referring to a joint as a "dive" has its roots in this Buffalo bar. William Douglas, a former slave turned business owner, operated the below-street-level establishment, which was referred to as a dive because the entranceway to the basement was configured in such a way that thirsty patrons had to virtually dive down the steps to get in.

The current Dug's Dive requires no diving to enter the attractive blue dining room with large windows designed to take advantage of the view. The menu suits the location, with steamed clams, battered-fish sandwiches, steamed mussels, fresh haddock, and the usual burgers and hot dogs. After your meal pick up some ice cream cones at the attached ice cream shack, and sit by the water to watch the boats.

E. B. GREEN'S STEAKHOUSE

716-855-4870
www.ebgreens.com
2 Fountain Plaza, Buffalo, NY 14202 (inside Hyatt Regency Hotel)
Open: Daily
Cuisine: American
Serving: D
Price: Expensive to Very Expensive
Credit Cards: Yes
Handicapped Access: Yes
Reservations: Recommended
Special Features: Live entertainment

This is one of America's top-rated steakhouses, and for the past five years it has been named one of the top ten steakhouses in America. The designation is justified, and although there are seafood, chicken, and duck selections on the menu, what attracts most diners is the steak. The steaks (and other dishes) arrive perfectly prepared. Size ranges from 8 to 24 ounces. Desserts—for those who still have room—are special and include such traditional items as apple pie, cheesecake, and molten chocolate cake. This is a place designed to impress.

FAT BOB'S SMOKEHOUSE

716-887-2971
www.fatbobs.com
41 Virginia Pl., Buffalo, NY 14202
Open: Daily
Cuisine: BBQ
Serving: L, D
Price: Moderate
Credit Cards: Yes
Handicapped Access: Yes
Special Features: Take-out available

Located in the Allentown neighborhood on Virginia Place (not Virginia Street) off Allen Street, Fat Bob's specializes in authentic BBQ and ice-cold beer. Nearly everything is created from scratch, right down to the blue cheese that comes with the jumbo chicken wings. The award-winning BBQ features authentic smoked meats straight from the custom-built Texas smoker. Sides include collard greens, macaroni and cheese, and sweet-potato fries. There is an ever-changing menu of microbrews from New York and around the U.S. Draft beers include Blue Moon Belgian White, Magic Hat Circus Boy, Bass Ale, and Molson Canadian. Some of the drinks specials include Woodchuck Draft Cider, Mike's Hard Lemonade, Saranac Black & Tan, and Corona. This is a casual, fun place for anyone who loves meat and beer.

HARRY'S HARBOUR PLACE GRILLE

716-874-5400
www.harrysharbour.com
2192 Niagara St., Buffalo, NY 14202
Open: Daily
Cuisine: American
Serving: L Mon.–Sat., D Daily
Price: Expensive
Credit Cards: Yes
Handicapped Access: Yes
Special Features: Expansive outdoor patio

The view of the Niagara River, Strawberry Island, and Canada is wonderful from Harry's, which is designed to take best advantage of it all with expansive windows and an outdoor patio. Winner of a number of awards for excellence, Harry's opened in 1997 and rapidly attracted a legion of fans. Of course it's a hot spot in the spring and summer, but it's a good choice year-round. There's an extensive wine list, and the lunch and dinner menus change seasonally. Seafood occupies a choice spot on the menu, with such items as king salmon, Pacific halibut, scallops, mussels, and yellow-fin tuna. The seafood chowder is very popular. A large banquet room is available for meetings and weddings. A fun touch is the complimentary homemade cotton candy offered at meal's end.

PEARL STREET GRILL & BREWERY

716-856-2337
www.pearlstreetgrill.com
76 Pearl St., Buffalo, NY 14202
Open: Daily
Cuisine: American
Serving: L, D (open at 4 pm on Sun.)
Price: Moderate
Credit Cards: Yes
Handicapped Access: Yes
Special features: Outside patios, some with terrific views of the lake; free wireless Internet

This place has it all—and it is vast. It is also easy to find. Look for the 30-foot-high, 2-ton steel and epoxy "Lake Effect Man" mounted near the top of the four-story building. The figure is based on artwork for Lake Effect Pale Ale, a popular brand at the microbrewery. Housed in an 1841 structure, this establishment is just steps from the old Erie Canal in the heart of what has been called "the most evil square mile in America." As the menu tells us, the area was rife with crime and "the unannointed and the downtrodden." This is where the action was in the bad old days. The surroundings feature sturdy brick walls, heavy beams, and old-time fans that work on an intricate pulley system. It's a lesson in history. Pregame buffets are served on what are called "event nights" that include Buffalo Sabres and Buffalo Bisons games. Beer turns up in many places, including the Gouda soup, the brew-house chili, the beer-braised pot roast, beer-based kielbasa (rated as the Taste of Buffalo's best meat dish), and even the ice cream (made with oatmeal stout), though you really can't taste it. A full-grain brew house is featured right in the main dining room. Some of the flagship offerings include Lake Effect, Lighthouse, Street Brawler, Wild Ox Wheat, and Trainwreck. Enjoy live entertainment on weekends, and flat-screen TVs for sports fans. Upstairs there are games galore, including billiards, air hockey, and darts.

POLISH VILLA

716-683-9460
2954 Union Rd., Cheektowaga, NY 14225
Open: Daily
Cuisine: Polish
Serving: B, L, D
Price: Inexpensive
Credit Cards: Yes
Handicapped Access: Yes
Special Features: Preorder food to be on your table when you arrive

Walking into this comfortable eatery, you are greeted with "Dzien Dobry!" (Polish for "good morning"). Since 1979, Ed and Irene Kutas Sr. have welcomed diners who come for the pierogi, the potato pancakes, the Polish Platter (kielbasa, pierogi, and golabki), and the czarnina (duck soup). Breakfast is a most important meal here, and the choices are all good—a Polish omelet (kielbasa with peppers and onions), French toast, an egg wrap, or the best offering of all for many: the nalesniki, or Polish crepes. They come filled with your choice of cinnamon apples, blueberries, lemons, cherries, raspberries, strawberries, peaches and cream, sour cream, or farmer's cheese. You will never leave hungry, and you will leave as a friend. The service is always speedy.

QUAKER BONNET EATERY

716-885-7208
www.quakerbonnet.com
175 Allen St., Buffalo, NY 14201
Open: Mon.–Sat.
Cuisine: American
Serving: L Daily, D Wed.
Price: Inexpensive
Credit Cards: Yes
Handicapped Access: Yes
Special Features: Signature creations available for take-out

A Buffalo institution since the early 1930s, this eatery has always carried some of the city's finest confections. Early creations were based on recipes handed down from the owner's Quaker grandmother, and the shop was named after the family's 120-year-old Quaker bonnet. Liz Kolken, the third-generation and current owner, has kept many of the original recipes, including the sinfully rich hot-fudge sauce, cinnamon ice cream, and cakes. She added some of her own creations, such as her now-famous Buffalo Chips (fresh coconut covered in decadent dark chocolate). Eat outside on the patio during the warm weather. Menu items include sandwiches on homemade bread, salads, soups, hot entrées, and those famous desserts.

RUE FRANKLIN

716-852-4416
www.ruefranklin.com
341 Franklin St., Buffalo, NY 14202
Open: Tues.–Sat.
Cuisine: French
Serving: D
Price: Moderate to Expensive
Credit Cards: Yes
Handicapped Access: Yes
Reservations: Recommended
Special Features: Outdoor dining area

For decades Rue Franklin has been considered the best restaurant in Buffalo. Boasting the look and feel of an intimate Parisian café, it is located in a converted row house with a courtyard dining area, fountain, and garden. Sophisticated and intimate, this is an establishment with a menu that changes with the seasons. Owners Joe and Deedee Lippes take care of the smallest details and consistently offer a wonderful dining experience. On Tuesdays, Wednesdays, and Thursdays they offer a prix fixe menu with appetizer, entrée, and dessert. Entrées include Atlantic salmon, roast veal loin, Moroccan lamb stew, and Australian lamb rib rack.

SALVATORE'S ITALIAN GARDENS RESTAURANT

716-683-7990 or 800-999-8082
www.salvatores.net
6491 Transit Rd., Depew, NY 14043
Open: Daily
Cuisine: American/Italian
Serving: D
Price: Expensive
Credit Cards: Yes
Handicapped Access: Yes
Special Features: Classic car collection, including a Pierce-Arrow, a Packard, and a 1919 Ford convertible

This establishment just a mile from the airport would be right at home on the Las Vegas strip. The decor is over the top, with chandeliers everywhere (even in the ladies' room). It has consistently won accolades, including the Millennium International Award of Excellence as one of America's top 100 restaurants of the 20th century. For more than 40 years the family-run restaurant has been a fixture in the Buffalo area for special occasions, weddings, and banquets. Menu items run the gamut from the classic such as lobster tail and prime rib to more exotic items such as salmon Wellington.

SHANGHAI RED'S

716-852-7337
www.shanghairedsrestaurant.com

2 Templeton Ter., Buffalo, NY 14202
Open: Daily
Cuisine: American/Continental
Serving: L Mon.–Fri., D daily, Sun. brunch
Price: Moderate–Expensive
Credit Cards: Yes
Handicapped Access: Yes
Reservations: Required
Special Features: Outdoor patio overlooking
Erie Basin Marina

Location is everything here because
Shanghai Red's occupies the number one
piece of restaurant real estate in downtown
Buffalo. It would be hard to find a restaurant with a better view: the Erie Basin
Marina, Buffalo Lighthouse, Niagara River,
Lake Erie, and, if your timing is right, sunsets over Canada. Blazing fire pits on the
deck on the marina side of the restaurant
allow for dining and drinking outside in
cooler weather. Seafood is a big item, naturally enough, but there is something for
everyone, from pasta and steak to burgers
and sandwiches.

THE CHOCOLATE BAR

716-332-0484
www.buffalochocolatebar.com
114 Chippewa St., Buffalo, NY 14201 (inside
Hampton Inn)
Open: Daily
Cuisine: American
Serving: L, D, desserts, drinks
Price: Moderate
Credit Cards: Yes
Handicapped Access: Yes
Special features: Patio dining

This is the newest creation of Carolyn and
Bill Panzica, whose Butterwood Desserts
supplies its wondrous confections to some
of the country's top restaurants, hotels, and
sporting events. The Chocolate Bar has
something for just about anyone at any time
of the day and night—including sandwiches,
salads, and soups. Dinner specials feature
Jamaican jerk chicken and a variety of cre-

ative pasta dishes. But most everyone
comes here for—what else?—chocolate, in
just about every form imaginable. There are
chocolate martinis and chocolate bar
shooters filled with your favorite spirits.
There is drinking chocolate so intense it
just may make your toes curl. (The chocolate served here is not for the timid, or
those raised on Hershey's milk chocolate.)
The desserts are what it is all about—try the
chocolate fondue, Belgian chocolate pyra-
mid, chocolate raspberry crepes, Kahlúa
Heath Bar pie, and turtle cheesecake. For
the chocolate averse (?!), desserts include
sweet-potato bourbon pecan torte and
bananas Foster. At night, the Chocolate Bar
transforms into one of the city's hippest
bars, with over 20 different martinis.
Remember its motto: "Everything is better
with chocolate."

THE EAGLE HOUSE

716-632-7470
www.eaglehouseonline.com
5578 Main St., Williamsville, NY 14221
Open: Daily
Price: Moderate
Credit Cards: Yes
Serving: L, D
Handicapped Access: Yes
Special Features: Outdoor dining

Opened in 1827, the Eagle House is one of
the oldest restaurants and taverns in the
state and boasts the longest continuously
held liquor license in both Erie County and
New York State. The establishment's first
owner, Oziel Smith, used his quarry to provide the 2-foot-thick limestone foundation
that the Eagle House sits on today. Now
owned by the Hanny family, with five generations of experience in the restaurant
business, the Eagle House is a warm and
comfortable award-winning restaurant
along Main Street in the bustling village of
Williamsville, just outside the city of
Buffalo. Lunch menus include such tradi-

tional dishes as Welsh rarebit, buffalo wings, crab cakes, and Yankee pot roast, a house specialty. Dinner dishes include longtime favorites such as chicken potpie, beef Wellington, liver and sautéed onions, and beer-battered fish fries.

THE STILLWATER

716-884-9283
www.thestillwater.com
481 Delaware Ave., Buffalo, NY 14202
Open: Daily
Cuisine: American
Serving: L, D, Sun. brunch
Price: Expensive
Credit Cards: Yes
Handicapped Access: No
Special Features: Live entertainment
Thurs.–Sat.

This is one of the most beautiful dining spots in Buffalo. Step into a European-style cobblestone courtyard with a star-lit ceiling in one of the city's historic Delaware Avenue brick row houses, and choose from four dining rooms, each with a fireplace. Or dine in the courtyard itself, and pretend you are dining out in Rome or Paris. You could also imagine that you are dining in an elegant 19th-century Buffalo dwelling. There's a main bar and a wine bar. It's the perfect choice for a special occasion, and the elegant menu reflects the surroundings, offering char-grilled lamb, lobster tail, veal, and filet mignon, all with imaginative touches. The desserts are extra special, too, featuring such creations as passion fruit crème brûlée, molten chocolate cake, and crisp banana spring roll.

TOWNE RESTAURANT

716-884-5128
www.thetowne.net
186 Allen St., Buffalo, NY 14201
Open: Daily
Cuisine: Greek
Serving: B, L, D
Price: Inexpensive
Credit Cards: Yes
Handicapped Access: Yes
Special Features: Open 23 hours a day

Located in the heart of the historic Allentown district at the corner of Allen and Elmwood, this restaurant has a culinary tradition of serving good, ample portions of all the Greek favorites for more than 30 years. It is famous for its chicken souvlaki and rice pudding. Its family-oriented atmosphere makes it easy for patrons to imagine that they are at a real Greek taverna. It's not unusual to find a few Buffalo police officers enjoying a meal here—breakfast selections are available around the clock, and it's a popular spot for late-night meals.

W. J. MORRISSEY'S IRISH PUB

716-852-0930
www.wjmorrissey.com
30 Mississippi St., Buffalo, NY 14203
Open: Daily
Cuisine: Irish pub fare
Serving: L, D
Price: Inexpensive to moderate
Credit Cards: Yes
Handicapped Access: Yes
Special Features: All-day Irish breakfast

A special place in the city's historic Cobblestone District—the neighborhood surrounding the original Erie Canal—the immense wooden bar and all the interior furnishings of this pub were built in Ireland and shipped to Buffalo. Bartenders were also imported from the Old Sod. You can shoot the blarney with owner Dennis Brinkworth and enjoy such Irish dishes as shepherd's pie, Guinness stew, traditional corned beef, bangers and mash, and an all-day Irish breakfast as well as burgers, sandwiches, and soup. Guinness is always on tap, of course, and there's plentiful food during the daily happy hour.

CULTURE

For the past several years Buffalo has been named by *American Style,* a national arts and lifestyle magazine, as the number one arts destination among the country's midsized cities. In addition to its cultural attractions, the city has a rich architectural heritage. The National Trust for Historic Preservation chose Buffalo as the host city for its annual conference in 2011.

Museums and Historic Sites

AMHERST MUSEUM

716-689-1440
www.amherstmuseum.org
3755 Tonawanda Creek Rd., Amherst, NY 14228
Open: Tues.–Sun Apr.–mid-Oct.; Tues.–Fri. Oct.–Apr.
Admission: Adults $5, children $1.50

Polka, Pussy Willows, and Polish Pride

Buffalo claims to be the home of the world's largest **Dyngus Day** celebration. Dyngus Day is the day after Easter and heralds spring and the end of the restrictive Lenten season. Although it was celebrated in Buffalo's traditional Polish neighborhoods as far back as the 1870s, modern Dyngus Day had its start with the Chopin Singing Society in 1961. Dyngus Day parties are now held in more than 30 different venues throughout the area.

A popular polka anthem proclaims "Everybody's Polish on Dyngus Day!" Girls and women chase boys and men with pussy willow switches, and the males respond by squirting water pistols at them. The mascot of the celebration is the *Edward M. Cotter,* the country's oldest working fireboat and a National Historic Landmark that has been named the world's largest Dyngus Day squirt gun. (For more information, visit www.dyngusdaybuffalo.com.)

Fireboat Edward M. Cotter

Twilight Tours on the Lake

In the fall of 1958, just months before his death, the 91-year-old master architect Frank Lloyd Wright paid a surprise visit to **Graycliff,** the summer home of his most generous benefactor, Darwin Martin. The Wright-designed home, 20 miles south of Buffalo on the Lake Erie shore, had been purchased by a religious order, the Piarist Fathers, after the deaths of Martin and his wife. Wright was horrified at the adaptations that had been made to the structure in its use as a school.

"Who made these changes? This is not my work," he sputtered.

Today he would surely be pleased to see his creation returned to its original design. Sometimes called Wright on the Lake, it is also known as the Isabelle R. Martin House and Estate, because it was Isabelle, Darwin's wife, who had the most influence over the design of the house: Her failing eyesight led her to direct Wright to create a structure full of sunlight.

On select Friday evenings during the summer, visitors are invited on special wine-and-cheese "twilight tours," to enjoy the house and grounds and experience what Wright called "repose," or tranquillity. There are regular tours during the day. (For more information, call 716-947-9217, or visit graycliff.bfn.org or wrightnowinbuffalo.com.)

Experience 19th-century life on the Niagara Frontier. Tour historic homes, gardens, churches, a one-room schoolhouse, and a working blacksmith shop. Learn about local history through exhibits on agriculture, costumes, antique radios, and a pioneer kitchen. Learn about the Erie Canal through hands-on activities and a replica canal packet boat as well as a working model of a canal lock. The museum is accessible to boaters traveling on the canal.

BUFFALO AND ERIE COUNTY HISTORICAL SOCIETY

716-873-9644
www.bechs.org
25 Nottingham Ct., Buffalo, NY 14216
Open: Tues.–Sun.
Admission: Adult $6, students and seniors $4, children $2.50

The classic Doric-style building faced with Vermont marble is the historical society museum's largest artifact and was designed by well-known Buffalo architect George Cary. It is the only permanent building erected for the Pan-American Exposition, Buffalo's international fair that attracted 8 million people in 1901. Pan-American Exposition Walking Tours are offered regularly and guide visitors through the former expo grounds, now one of the city's most popular residential neighborhoods. The historical society's **Resource Center,** a short distance away at 459 Forest Avenue, has been transformed into a Pan-Am Exposition hall, with exhibits and displays that explore the exposition's funny and serious sides. Bflo. Made! is one of the museum's most popular permanent exhibits. Cheerios, Keri lotion, the pacemaker, the *Saturday Night Fever* disco floor, Mentholatum, Milk-Bone dog biscuits, and the kazoo are among the 700-plus inventions and products that have been made in Buffalo. The Native American Gallery tells the story of the area's earliest residents. A National Historic Landmark, the museum overlooks Delaware Park's Hoyt Lake. During the summer, the monthly Friday-evening Party on the Portico offers one of the best values in the city, with live music, food, drinks, lake views, and museum tours—all for $10.

BUFFALO AND ERIE COUNTY NAVAL & MILITARY PARK

716-847-1773
www.buffalonavalpark.org
1 Naval Park Cove, Buffalo, NY 14202
Open: Daily Apr.–Oct.; Nov., Sat. and Sun. and the Fri. after Thanksgiving. Closed Dec.–Mar.
Admission: Adults $8, children and seniors $5

This waterfront site next to the reconstructed Erie Canal Harbor is the largest inland naval park in the country. Visitors can climb aboard the USS *Little Rock,* the only guided-missile cruiser on display in the U.S., and the USS *The Sullivans,* the World War II National Historic Landmark destroyer named for five brothers who lost their lives in the Battle of the Solomon Islands when their ship sank. The submarine USS *Croaker,* another World War II—era ship, offers a glimpse into the very tight spaces of these undersea vessels. The new $1-million museum building houses a number of planes and military artifacts, including the famous P-39 Airacobra (made in Buffalo at Bell Aircraft), with its cannon that fired through the propeller shaft, capable of pulverizing trains, tanks, and ships. The museum building is modeled after the 19th-century Coit-McCutcheon building, originally in the canal harbor area. The museum offers overnight encampments onboard the ships, for scouts and other groups.

BUFFALO MUSEUM OF SCIENCE

716-896-5200
www.buffalomuseumofscience.org
1020 Humboldt Pkwy., Buffalo, NY 14211
Open: Wed.–Sun.
Admission: Adults $7, seniors $6, children and students $5

Historic battleships are on display at the Buffalo & Erie County Naval & Military Park

With more than a dozen exhibit halls, a number of interactive exhibits, and some six hundred thousand specimens in its collection—ranging from anthropology to zoology, plus several traveling exhibits—there's always something new at the museum. The Buffalo Museum of Science also has the distinction of being the first museum in the U.S. to have a school on its grounds (Drew Science Magnet).

BUFFALO TRANSPORTATION PIERCE-ARROW MUSEUM
716-853-0084
www.pierce-arrow.com
263 Michigan Ave., Buffalo, NY 14203
Open: Thurs.–Sat. (call ahead)
Admission: Adults $7, seniors $6, children $3

Learn about Buffalo's transportation history with a special focus on the Buffalo-made Pierce-Arrow automobile. (The Pierce factory was a few blocks away in the old Canal District, and became Pierce-Arrow in 1909.) Displays related to the transportation history of Buffalo include photos, paintings, china, signs, factory items, and other memorabilia. The museum is hopping on the Frank Lloyd Wright bandwagon with the construction of a Wright-designed filling station as part of a museum-expansion project. Wright designed the station in 1927 to be built on Michigan Avenue in Buffalo, and it is being constructed exactly as the architect planned—except that it will be under glass and not dispensing gas. The museum is an outgrowth of founder James T. Sandoro's love of the Pierce-Arrow, the Thomas Flyer (also made in Buffalo), and other classic cars. Some 20 autos are on display at any given time, and when the expansion is finished in 2010, there will be room for 50 cars.

DARWIN D. MARTIN HOUSE COMPLEX
716-856-3858 or 877-377-3858
www.darwinmartinhouse.org or www.wrightnowinbuffalo.com
125 Jewett Pkwy., Buffalo, NY 14216
Open: Daily Apr.–Nov., closed Tues.; Daily Dec. and Jan.–Mar., closed Tues. and Thurs. Call or check online for tour hours.
Admission: Basic tour (1 hour) adults $15, seniors $13, students $10; in-depth tour (2 hours) adults $30, seniors $28, students $25. Reservations strongly recommended for the docent-led tours

This is the largest Frank Lloyd Wright Prairie-style house complex in existence, with six buildings set in the Parkside East Historic District. Wright called it his opus, and kept a drawing of his creation pinned above his drafting table for 50 years. It was built for Darwin Martin, one of the country's wealthiest business executives; Wright assured Martin that, if he hitched his star to Wright, the world would never forget him. Wright's prophecy proved correct. Martin brought Wright to Buffalo and gave him a 2-acre corner lot, huge amounts of money, and acceptance of Wright's fanciful details. The pair developed a close friendship, and Martin became a father figure and patron to the architect. The Martin House is considered the best-documented building in American architectural history, with hundreds of letters (housed at the University at Buffalo) exchanged between Wright and Martin. Martin lost everything in the Great Depression, and the house was abandoned to weather and vandals for 16 years. Currently nearing the end of a multiyear, $50-million restoration, the complex is a National Historic Landmark and has won national awards for its preservation. The complex consists of the main Martin House, the Barton House (built for Wright's sister), the Gardener's Cottage, the rebuilt 100-foot-long Pergola (a covered walkway), the glass-roofed Conservatory, and the two-story Carriage House and Stable, as well as the Toshiko Mori–designed Visitor Pavilion, which opened in spring 2009. Wright also designed **Graycliff**, the Martin's lakeshore summer home, 20 miles to the south; the **William R. Heath House** (76 Soldiers Place), and the **Davidson House** (57 Tillinghast Place), also in Buffalo.

FOREST LAWN CEMETERY

716-885-1600
www.forest-lawn.com
1411 Delaware Ave., Buffalo, NY 14209
Open: Daily
Admission: Free

Founded in 1850, Forest Lawn is a beautiful 269-acre cemetery in the heart of the city and tells the story of Buffalo's history through the many statues and mausoleum architecture. On the New York State and National Registers of Historic Places, the cemetery is the final resting place of President Millard Fillmore and the great Seneca chief Red Jacket, as well as many area leaders. There are memorial designs by some of the country's greatest architects, including Stanford White, Richard Upjohn, and Frank Lloyd Wright. Wright's Blue Sky Mausoleum, originally designed for Darwin Martin, was built in 2004. Guided tours are held in the summer.

FRANK LLOYD WRIGHT'S ROWING BOATHOUSE

716-362-3140
www.wrightboathouse.org
194 Porter Ave., Buffalo, NY 14201

Martin House

Open: Daily
Admission: Adults $8

This 5,000-square-foot boathouse for the West Side Rowing Club, the nation's largest rowing club, is a boathouse with a difference. Frank Lloyd Wright designed the building for the University of Wisconsin, but the university decided not to build it. A Buffalo group constructed the boathouse, which was completed in 2007. One of the biggest supporters of the $5.5-million project was television producer and writer Tom Fontana, who grew up in Buffalo in a rowing family. Its official name is the Charles and Marie Fontana Boathouse, after Fontana's parents, who coached for decades. Fontana persuaded Hollywood friends including Mary Tyler Moore, Blythe Danner, and Grant Tinker to join television producer Diane English and the late newsman Tim Russert—both Buffalo natives—in contributing to the cause. Except for its location on the Niagara River with the Peace Bridge to Canada as a backdrop, the boathouse was built exactly as originally envisioned by Wright.

LOWER LAKES MARINE HISTORICAL SOCIETY
716-849-0914
66 Erie St., Buffalo, NY 14202
Open: Tues., Thurs., and Sat.
Admission: Donation

Located in an 1896 building that once housed the Howard H. Baker Company ship chandlery, this museum focuses on the maritime history of Buffalo and the Great Lakes. Housed here is an extensive collection of Erie Canal photos, along with models of many vessels that cruised the Great Lakes, the Buffalo River, and the Erie Canal.

THEODORE ROOSEVELT INAUGURAL NATIONAL HISTORIC SITE
716-884-0095
www.nps.gov/thri
641 Delaware Ave., Buffalo, NY 14201
Open: Daily
Admission: Adults $6, seniors $4, children $2

Now a museum, this National Historic Site, also known as the Wilcox Mansion, was the home of Ansley Wilcox, a close friend of Theodore Roosevelt's. Following the assassination of President William McKinley, Roosevelt rushed to Buffalo from the Adirondacks, where he had been vacationing, and was sworn in as president in this white-pillared mansion on September 14, 1901. The museum reopened in late spring 2009 after a $2-million-plus restoration. The carriage house has been rebuilt, and new interactive exhibits tell the story of the history made here. In the library, visitors can now hear an audio transmission of Roosevelt taking the oath, complete with the ambient sounds of reporters milling around and a photographer dropping his camera. Remarking about the tragic way he became president, Roosevelt said: "It is a dreadful thing to come into the Presidency in this way; but it would be far worse to be morbid about it. Here is the task, and I have got to do it to the best of my ability." Many special events are held here, including a Teddy Bear Picnic and the annual Victorian Christmas celebration.

The Theodore Roosevelt Inaugural National Historic Site

Art Galleries

ALBRIGHT-KNOX ART GALLERY

716-882-8700
www.albrightknox.org
1285 Elmwood Ave., Buffalo, NY 14222
Open: Wed.–Sun.
Admission: Adults $12, seniors and students $8, children free

Housed in a 1905 Greek Revival building, with 18 dramatic marble columns, overlooking Hoyt Lake in Delaware Park, Albright-Knox was designed by noted Buffalo architect E. B. Green, who also designed the Toledo Museum of Art. An added wing was designed by Buffalo native Gordon Bunshaft and dedicated in 1962. The Albright-Knox enjoys a world-wide reputation as an outstanding center of modern art. It is especially rich in postwar American and European works, acquired mostly though the generosity of its patron, the late Seymour H. Knox Jr. Thomas Hoving, art historian and former director of the New York's Metropolitan Museum of Art, said that "the Albright-Knox Art Gallery should be on everyone's list to see, for it's an overwhelming art experience. Small, intimate, and seductive, the museum has one of the most thumping modern and contemporary collections in the world." Plan on lunch, or dinner on Thursdays and Fridays, or Sunday brunch, at **Muse,** the excellent café overlooking the outdoor sculpture court. Free Friday-night Gusto at the Gallery is a popular family-friendly program that combines activities, games, music, and art. There are also popular Sunday jazz concerts in the summer.

BURCHFIELD-PENNEY ART CENTER

716-878-6011
www.burchfield-penney.org
1300 Elmwood Ave., Buffalo, NY 14222
Open: Tues.–Sun.
Admission: Adults $7, seniors and children $4

The museum opened its first free-standing home in November 2008. The striking futuristic $33-million art center on the grounds of Buffalo State College in the heart of the city's museum district is dedicated to renowned Buffalo artist and watercolorist Charles E. Burchfield. The works of other distinguished western New York artists are also highlighted in the galleries. Considered a top-ranking regional art museum, Burchfield-Penney works closely with the Art Department at Buffalo State College and provides a number of programs for students.

Other Attractions

BUFFALO ZOO
716-837-3900
www.buffalozoo.org
300 Parkside Ave., Buffalo, NY 14214
Open: Daily Mar.–Dec.; Wed.–Sun. Jan.–Feb.
Admission: Adults $9.50, seniors and students $7, children $6

The third-oldest zoo in the U.S., the Buffalo Zoo was established in 1875. It is undergoing a massive $75-million redevelopment, with major new exhibits and visitor facilities. The organizing theme of the new zoo is water, which was chosen because of water's historic importance to Buffalo, including the Great Lakes and the Erie Canal. The first exhibits that visitors see are those of the sea lion and river otter. The idea is to display animals in their natural habitats, and the more than 1,000 animals include polar bears, lowland gorillas, giraffes, and elephants, as well as numerous birds in an aviary. Rainforest Falls is the newest exhibit, with a replica of the world's tallest waterfall, Venezuela's Angel Falls. The Children's Zoo is always popular, and kids can interact with barnyard animals. The zoo has one of the country's finest collections of porcelain animal sculptures, created by artist and naturalist Edward Boehm.

BUFFALO AND ERIE COUNTY BOTANICAL GARDENS
716-827-1584
www.buffalogardens.com
2655 South Park Ave., Buffalo NY 14214
Open: Daily
Admission: Adults $6, seniors and students $5, children $3.

The Buffalo and Erie County Botanical Gardens are set within the Frederick Law Olmsted–designed South Park and housed in an 1899 all-glass tri-domed conservatory. The plants inside are arranged in classic Victorian style, with similar flora from throughout the world grouped together. Special gardens include the Rainforest Garden, Desert Garden, Tropical Flower Garden, Orchid Garden, Begonia Garden, and Herb Garden. Outside are all-American annuals flower gardens, a children's learning garden, a shrub garden, and even a bog garden. Special events include concerts by various groups including the Buffalo Philharmonic Orchestra. It's a popular spot for wedding photos.

Performing Arts
Alleyway Theatre (716-852-2600, www.alleyway.com, 1 Curtain Up Alley, Buffalo, NY 14202) The Alleyway Company performs in an intimate space in the heart of the theater district and specializes in innovative new plays and musicals.

Asbury Hall (716-852-8020, www.righteousbabe.com, 341 Delaware Ave., Buffalo, NY 14202) The former Asbury Delaware Methodist Church, whose exterior is made of Medina sandstone, has been renovated as a concert hall by Buffalo native and singer/singwriter Ani DiFranco. It is also the headquarters of her Righteous Babe Records as well as the gallery and screening room of Hallways Contemporary Arts Center.

Buffalo Philharmonic Orchestra (716-885-5000, www.bpo.org, Kleinhans Music Hall, 370 Pennsylvania St., Buffalo, NY 14201) The orchestra performs in the acoustically perfect 1940s music hall designed by the father-son team of Eliel and Eero Saarinen. A National Historic Site, Kleinhans Music Hall has an international reputation as one of the finest musical venues in the U.S. The orchestra was formed in 1935 and has played under the batons of some of the leading stars of the podium. The BPO has toured widely in the U.S., Canada, and Europe. Today, award-winning music director JoAnn Falletta has rekindled its distinguished history, and the orchestra performs more than 100 concerts yearly.

Center for the Arts (716-645-2787, www.ubcfa.org, 103 Center for the Arts, University at Buffalo, Buffalo, NY 14260) The largest arts organization in the region, the Center for the Arts operates four theaters and two art galleries and presents a wide range of professional performing arts.

Colored Musicians Club (716-885-9383, www.coloredmusiciansclub.org, 145 Broadway, Buffalo, NY 14203) This place has attracted such jazz greats as Count Basie, Dizzy Gillespie, and Duke Ellington, and continues to offer live jazz in an intimate setting.

Irish Classical Theatre Company at the Andrews Theatre (716-853-4282, www.irish classicaltheatre.com, 625 Main St., Buffalo, NY 14203) Founded in 1990, this theater has only three rows of seats in the round, so you are never more than 20 feet from the stage.

Kavinoky Theatre at D'Youville College (716-829-7668, www.kavinokytheatre.com, 320 Porter Ave., Buffalo, NY14207) Starting up in 1980, this award-winning professional theater company has been staging plays in a small Edwardian gem of a theater.

Shakespeare in Delaware Park (716-856-4533, www.shakespeareindelawarepark.org, Shakespeare Park, Delaware Park, Buffalo, NY 14222) A Buffalo tradition since 1976, it's the country's second most successful outdoor Shakespeare festival in terms of audience (number one is New York City). The company has two free productions each summer in the Olmsted-designed Delaware Park.

Shea's Performing Arts Center (716-847-1410, www.sheas.org, 646 Main St., Buffalo, NY 14202) A National Historic Site built in 1926 in the style of a European opera house, Shea's continues to entertain with touring Broadway productions, concerts, opera, dance, historic tours, a classic film series, and family shows.

Theatre of Youth (716-884-4400, www.theatreofyouth.org, Allendale Theatre, 203 Allen St., Buffalo, NY 14203) TOY is the resident company of the historic Allendale Theatre, built in 1913—the area's only professional theater dedicated to the entertainment of young people.

Tours

Gray Line Niagara Falls (800-695-1603, www.grayline-niagarafalls.com, 3466 Niagara Falls Blvd., N. Tonawanda, NY 14120) The Best of Buffalo Tour highlights the city's history and architecture.

Landmark Society of the Niagara Frontier (716-852-3300, www.landmark-niagara.org, 617 Main St., Buffalo, NY 14203) The Landmark Society offers a broad range of tours, including Main Street buildings and Buffalo churches.

Motherland Connextions (716-282-1028, www.motherlandconnextions.com, 176 Bridge St., Niagara Falls, NY 14305) "Conductors" dressed in period clothing take groups to stops along the Underground Railroad in western New York and southern Ontario. Tours start in Buffalo.

Preservation Coalition of Erie County (716-362-0266, www.preservationcoalition.org, 14 Allen St., Buffalo, NY 14203) Tours include houses and neighborhood walks that take in the "grand mansions" on Delaware Avenue.

RECREATION

Boating and Cruises

Buffalo Harbor Cruises (716-856-6696 or 800-244-8684, www.buffaloharborcruises .com, 79 Marine Dr., Buffalo, NY 14202) Cruise the *Miss Buffalo II* on the Niagara River and through the Black Rock Lock and Canal. The Buffalo River cruises allow passengers to see the terminus of the Erie Canal as well as World War II warships and the Buffalo waterfront, including the signature grain mills.

Moondance (716-854-7245, www.moondancecat.co, 2 Templeton Ter., Buffalo, NY 14202) Sail on a 56-foot catamaran along the Buffalo waterfront.

Seven Seas Sailing Center (716-824-1505, www.sevenseassailing.com, 284 Fuhrmann Blvd. [at RCR Yachts Skyway Marina], Buffalo, NY 14203) Sailboat rentals and lessons, plus excursions.

Fishing

The Buffalo area has some of the best smallmouth bass, muskie, king salmon, steelhead, walleye, and lake trout fishing in the world. Lake Erie has been called the smallmouth bass capital of the world, and Buffalo Harbor is one of the best-kept secrets in the world of muskie fishing. Lake Erie is also an excellent walleye fishery, and trophy fish are routinely taken here. Buffalo has hosted a number of Bassmasters Elite Tournaments, and professional fishermen have caught top numbers of fish in Lake Erie waters near Buffalo. For a complete list of local charter captains, launch sites, and marinas, visit www.erie.gov/hotspot.

Marinas

Erie Basin Marina (716-851-6503, www.eriebasinmarina, 329 Erie St., Buffalo, NY 14202) This is one of Buffalo's gems, with award-winning gardens, a small sand beach (no swimming), boat launch, 278-slip marina with full facilities, picnic tables, and an observation tower that offers great views of downtown Buffalo, the Niagara River, Lake Erie, and Canada. Here, too, is the **Hatch**, a popular casual eatery, and an ice cream stand.

Spectator Sports

Buffalo Bandits Lacrosse (716-855-4100 or 888-467-2273, www.bandits.com, HSBC Arena, 1 Seymour H Knox III Plaza, Buffalo.) The Bandits play January to April and are four-time world champions.

Buffalo Bills Football (716-648-1800 or 877-228-4257, www.buffalobills.com, Ralph Wilson Stadium, 1 Bills Dr., Orchard Park, NY 14127) The National Football League Bills play here August through December. Though the stadium is one of the largest in the NFL, the games are usually sold out.

Buffalo Bisons Baseball (716-846-2000 or 888-223-6000, www.bisons.com, Dunn Tire Park, 275 Washington St., Buffalo, NY 14203) The ballpark, close to the waterfront, has received national recognition for its design. The International League champion AAA Bisons offer family-friendly games and events with parties, fireworks, and concerts. Dine before or after the game at **Pettibone's Grill** (716-846-2100, www.pettibones .com), overlooking the field.

Buffalo Sabres Hockey (716-855-4100 or 888-467-2273, www.sabres.com, HSBC Arena, 1 Seymour H. Knox III Plaza, Buffalo, NY 14203) The National Hockey League Sabres are very popular on both sides of the U.S.–Canada border and attract a very loyal following.

Canisius College Golden Griffins Division I Basketball and Hockey (716-888-2970, www.canisius.edu/athletics, 2001 Main St., Buffalo, NY 14208) Canisius College has a long tradition of competitive basketball and games draw high-energy crowds during the summer.

Lancaster Raceway Park (716-759-6818, www.lancasterracing.com, 57 Gunnville Rd., Lancaster, NY 14086) Stock car and drag racing during the summer.

University at Buffalo Buffalo Bulls Division I Basketball and Football (716-645-6666, www.buffalobulls.com, UB Stadium and Alumni Arena, Amherst, NY 14226) The champion Buffalo Bulls football team has renewed enthusiasm for the game among students, alumni, and the Buffalo community.

SHOPPING

The area's major shopping destinations include the Walden Galleria, Eastern Hills, and Boulevard Malls, as well as many shops and boutiques along Elmwood and Hertel avenues and antiques shops in Clarence, a suburb north of Buffalo.

Malls

Boulevard Mall (716-834-8600, www.boulevard-mall.com, 730 Alberta Dr., Amherst, NY 14226) This mall offers more than 120 shops and restaurants, including the popular Bonefish Grill restaurant.

Eastern Hills Mall (716-631-5812, www.shopeasternhills.com, 4545 Transit Rd., Williamsville, NY 14221) Eastern Hills, which describes itself as "the friendliest place to shop in Western New York," is home to Sears, JC Penney, Macy's, Bon-Ton, and more than 85 specialty stores, including Orvis and Brooks Brothers. Along with a food court, you can dine at the Brick Oven Bistro or Dave & Buster's.

Walden Galleria (716-681-7600, www.waldengalleria.com, 1 Walden Galleria, Buffalo, NY 14225) The area's premier shopping destination has just undergone an expansion and now has 16 Regal Cinema movie theaters as well as more than 200 shops and restaurants, the latter including the Cheesecake Factory, Johnny Rockets, and the Melting Pot. Shops include Apple Computer, Brookstone, Build-A-Bear, Pottery Barn, Williams-Sonoma, Ann Taylor, Abercrombie & Fitch, J. Crew, and the Disney Store.

A Short Drive South

The centerpiece of the historic village of **East Aurora,** 20 miles south of Buffalo, is the more-than-century-old **Roycroft Campus,** on South Grove Street, founded by Elbert Hubbard as a community of artisans and devotees of the arts and crafts movement. Its survival as the crown jewel of this village, filled with 19th-century Victorian homes, is a tribute to residents who fought to preserve their heritage. Hubbard's philosophy was "better art, better work, and a better and more reasonable way of living."

Before becoming a philosopher, writer, and movement leader, Hubbard—known as the sage of East Aurora—was a successful soap company executive who had a genius for promotion. It was his talent for marketing that attracted some of the country's most talented artisans. At the Roycroft Movement's height, more than 500 Roycrofters were working on the campus as printers, coppersmiths, furniture makers, silversmiths, potters, artists, and innkeepers. Today, artists and craftspeople have returned to the campus. Roycroft offers a variety of artisan classes and demonstrations, and guided tours are available June through September. (For more information call 716-655-0261, or visit www.roycroftcampus.corporation.com.)

Original and reproduction Roycroft furnishings adorn the 1905 **Roycroft Inn**'s public rooms, including the dining rooms and 28 suites that still bear the names of notable personalities, including Ralph Waldo Emerson, Thomas Edison, Henry David Thoreau, and Susan B. Anthony, who journeyed to East Aurora for inspiration from Roycroft's founder. Located on Roycroft Campus, the inn was transformed by an award-winning $8 million restoration in 1995. (For more information call 716-652-5552, or visit www.roycroftinn.com.)

Just a few blocks away is **Vidler's 5 & 10** (716-652-0481 or 877-VIDLERS; on the Web at www.vidlers5and10.com). Look for the distinctive red-and-white-striped awning at 676-694 Main Street. The store occupies four connected, vintage 1890 buildings on two levels with 15,000 square feet of retail space. Inside, you'll find uneven wooden floors, an original popcorn maker that dis-

Roycroft Inn, East Aurora

Cooking demonstration at the Millard and Abigail Fillmore House Museum

penses popcorn for a dime, and a dizzying array of merchandise.

Across the street is the **Aurora Theatre** (716-652-1660; www.theaurora theatre.com), a grand movie palace that opened during silent film days in 1925 and today features first-run movies. **Tony Rome's Globe Hotel** (716-652-4221), also across the street, has been welcoming diners since 1824. Local lore has it that area residents driving livestock to Buffalo for sale would stop at the Globe for refreshment while the animals freely roamed Main Street.

It's easy to imagine a young Millard Fillmore walking across Main Street from his home to meet with the town leaders at the Globe. Fillmore, the country's 13th president, built the Greek Revival cottage for his bride, Abigail, and lived there for four years before moving his family to Buffalo.

The home has been restored and moved to Shearer Avenue from its original location. The **Millard and Abigail Fillmore House Museum** includes some original furnishings, such as Fillmore's desk and the volumes of law books in his tiny office. Fillmore made the rough wooden table in the kitchen. Climb the steep and narrow staircase to the second floor, where a quilt made by Abigail Fillmore is displayed on their bed. This quilt traveled to the White House and back to East Aurora. Next door is a child's playroom where Fillmore's son, Millard Powers Fillmore, is believed to have been born. (Seasonal hours; for more information call 716-652-8875 or 716-652-4985; or visit www.buffaloah .com/a/EastAur/shearer/mus/tc.html.)

East Aurora is known as Toy Town USA because it is the birthplace of Fisher-Price Toys. A museum founded in 1987 to preserve the area's rich toy heritage, **Toy Town Museum** is both a toy museum and children's activity center. The museum showcases early Fisher-Price toys from the 1930s including classic wooden pull toys that marked the company's debut into the toy industry as well as many other exhibits including a 12-room antique doll house, toy trains, and interactive exhibits. (For more information call 716-687-5151, or visit toytownusa.com.)

The village also boasts one of New York State's newest parks—the 633-acre **Knox Farm State Park,** named in honor of Seymour Knox, a local banker, nationally known art patron (Buffalo's Albright-Knox Art Gallery is also named for him), and philanthropist, who lived on the property amid the village's rolling acres and kept his polo ponies in the barns. The park is comprised of a variety of habitats, including 400 acres of pastures and hayfields and 100 acres of woodlands, ponds, and several wetland areas. Visitors can cross-country ski, bike, hike, or ride their horses (permit required) on the park's paths. (Phone 716-655-7200, or visit http://nysparks.state.ny.us/parks/info.asp?parkID=89.)

NIAGARA FALLS

The first "tourist" to witness the wonders of mighty Niagara Falls was Father Louis Hennepin, who served as a missionary under French explorer Robert LaSalle. In his eye-witness account, Father Hennepin revealed to the world for the first time the "incredible Cataract or Waterfall, which has no equal." Ever since that cold December day in 1678, the Falls have been one of North America's greatest tourist attractions.

In a book widely read across Europe, Hennepin wrote: "Betwixt the Lake Ontario and Erie, there is a vast and prodigious Cadence of Water . . . the Universe does not afford its Parallel. . . . The Waters which fall from this horrible Precipice do foam and boyl [sic] after the most hideous manner imaginable, making an outrageous Noise, more terrible than that of Thunder."

In 1801 Theodosia Burr, daughter of future U.S. vice president Aaron Burr, and her groom, Joseph Alston, chose the Falls to "conclude their nuptials," followed three years later by Jerome Bonaparte (Napoleon's youngest brother) and his Baltimore-born bride, Elizabeth Patterson. From this trickle of romance was born the tradition that would later become a flood: honeymooning by the cascading waters.

It was the Erie Canal that heralded the beginning of mass tourism to Niagara Falls. In the 50 years between 1820 and 1870, the tourism trade increased tenfold as the Falls became more and more accessible.

In 1985 the world celebrated a century of unrestricted viewing of Niagara Falls. It is hard to believe this natural wonder wasn't always open to all, but before 1885, the lands around the Falls had become one of the most vulgar tourist traps anywhere, with visitors having to pay for the privilege of seeing the mighty cataract. The land belonged to private owners who charged visitors a fee to view the site through peepholes in their fences. Americans—many of whom had never visited the Falls but who knew what they looked like from Frederic Church's well-known painting—found it unsettling to look through a hole to view such magnificence.

By the mid-1800s Niagara Falls had become a victim of one of the ugliest assaults on a wonder of nature, with the growth of factories, shacks, and mills around the cataract. The insult of having to pay to view the Falls helped generate a most ingenious lobbying and public relations campaign, which had one goal: Free Niagara. Spurred by this rallying cry, the Free Niagara Movement—led by a group of Americans that included landscape architect Frederick Law Olmsted—fought to return the area around the Falls to its natural state and to the world.

The campaign resulted in the establishment—on July 15, 1885—of the nation's first state park, embracing 435 acres of land along the American Falls. The Canadians followed suit on their side of the cataract, and Niagara Falls' protection was assured.

More than 20 million visitors a year come to look upon these relentless waters. They line the promenade opposite, gape from the deck of a boat below, peer from the caves behind, gaze from towers, and ogle from a helicopter above—drinking in the vista from every conceivable angle. At night the falls are illuminated with huge colored spotlights.

Niagara Falls is an awesome spectacle: a sprawling 182-foot-high cataract of thundering water, surrounded by towering clouds of mist and spray. There may be taller cataracts in Africa, South America, and even elsewhere in New York State, but the sheer size—more than half a mile wide—and tremendous volume of Niagara are unsurpassed.

Located in the Niagara River, the Falls separate the United States and Canada. The American and Bridal Veil Falls are in the U.S. and the Horseshoe Falls are on the Canadian side. Bridges make border crossings easy. Niagara Falls drives one of the world's largest hydroelectric developments. The water that flows over the Falls drains four Great Lakes—Superior, Michigan, Huron, and Erie—into the fifth, Ontario, at a rate of 700,000 gallons a second during the summer. The waterfall fluctuates with the season, less in the winter when more water is used to produce electricity.

Writers have long struggled to capture in words the immensity of the Falls. Charles Dickens gushed, "I seemed to be lifted from the earth and to be looking into Heaven." Mark Twain simply wrote: "Niagara Falls is one of the finest structures in the known world." Thomas Moore enthused: "It is impossible by pen or pencil to convey even a faint idea of their magnificence. . . . We must have new combinations of language to describe the falls of Niagara."

Any of the many vantage points can confirm Twain's view of the Falls, but perhaps the most vivid experience involves the *Maid of the Mist* boat ride. These boats have been operating more or less continuously since 1846. President Theodore Roosevelt called the ride "the only way fully to realize the Grandeur of the Great Falls of Niagara." The four *Maid of the Mist* boats can be boarded from both the U.S. and Canada sides.

In recent years there has been tremendous growth and development in Niagara Falls, Ontario, spurred on by two major casino complexes. On the American side, the Senecas have also built a casino and first-class hotel (see "Casinos," below), but changes have been occurring at a much slower pace.

ATTRACTIONS

Aquarium of Niagara (716-285-3575, www.aquariumofniagara.org,
   701 Whirlpool St., Niagara Falls, NY 14301) The most popular sea creatures at this aquarium include penguins, sea lions, seals, and sharks. The two-floor sea lion tank allows for viewing from above as well as below the water. There are a number of special programs, including a close encounter with a seal or sea lion, feeding a seal, and being a trainer for a day.

Cave of the Winds (716-278-1730,
   www.niagarafallsstatepark.com/Activities_CaveOfTheWinds.aspx,
   First St. and Buffalo Ave., Niagara Falls, NY 14303.) This Niagara Falls tour begins with an elevator ride 175 feet into the Niagara Gorge. Then, clad in a souvenir rain poncho and sandals, you'll follow a tour guide over wooden walkways to the Hurricane Deck, less than 20 feet from the torrents of Bridal Veil Falls. Tours conducted from April to October (opening day varies; call ahead).

Maid of the Mist (716-284-8897, www.maidofthemist.com,
   151 Buffalo Ave., Niagara Falls, NY 14303 [American side]). There are four boats, two on each side of the border. On the American side, board a boat at the handicap-accessible entrance to the Observation Tower in Niagara Falls State Park. The season begins in late April (depending on weather conditions) and continues through late October. This is a definite must-do for any visitor to Niagara Falls. Hooded raincoats are provided.

Casinos

Casino Niagara (905-374-3598 or 888-946-3255, wwwcasinoniagara.com, 5705 Falls Avenue, Niagara Falls, Ontario) This Canadian casino was the first in the area and offers more than 1,700 slot machines, table games, entertainment, and restaurants.

Fallsview Casino Resort (888-325-5788, www.fallsviewcasinoresort.com, 6380 Fallsview Blvd., Niagara Falls, Ontario) A 30-story, 374-room hotel is the center of the property, which also includes a large casino with 3,000 slot machines, 150 gaming tables, the Avalon Ballroom (hosting top entertainers, including Las Vegas headliners), plus a retail complex and a meeting center.

Seneca Niagara Casino & Hotel (716-299-1100 or 877-8-SENECA, www.snfgc.com, 310 Fourth St., Niagara Falls, NY 14303) Open 24 hours daily, this casino is operated by the Seneca Nation of Indians and offers a variety of restaurants, live entertainment (including top acts), and a gleaming 594-room hotel and spa. Smoking is allowed in the casino, though there is a nonsmoking section. There are more than 4,200 slot machines with progressive jackpots, including a popular Pennies from Heaven area. Table games include blackjack, craps, roulette, and poker.

THE TONAWANDAS: CITY OF TONAWANDA AND NORTH TONAWANDA

Tonawanda is a Seneca word that means "swift running water." Tonawanda Creek flows into the Niagara River and once had large stretches of rapids until it was tamed with the construction of the Erie Canal.

Tonawanda and North Tonawanda developed rapidly after the opening of the canal in 1825. Lumber shipped from the western U.S. and Canada passed through these towns, and North Tonawanda soon became known as Lumber City. Literally dozens of planking and sawmills sprang up in North Tonawanda during the 19th century, and the place became a boomtown. The waterfront was soon jammed with schooners and steamers that brought in lumber, flour, pork, grain, and livestock, much of which was transferred to railroad cars and canal boats for other destinations.

The area was the lumber capital of the world, shipping more than 1 million board feet of lumber each year. The peak year of this business was in 1890, when 719 million board feet of lumber arrived here aboard 2,023 boats. At times the waterfront took on aspects of the Barbary Coast. There was a large influx of both lake and canal sailors, and the red-light district, known as Goose Island, had a notorious reputation, and riots and fights were routine.

On a completely different note, the city is the hometown of the most famous and largest carousel company in the country, the Allan Herschell Company. Today, the Herschell Carrousel Factory Museum is the only museum in the world housed in an authentic, original carousel factory roundhouse. North Tonawanda is also the place where Rudolph Wurlitzer first developed and manufactured the Wurlitzer Organ and later the Wurlitzer Jukebox.

The Tonawandas—twin cities across from each other on the Erie Canal—are the western terminus of today's canal. The canal actually ends at the Niagara River, and boaters can travel south along the Black Rock Canal to Buffalo. The Erie Canal lift bridge here is an elaborate, counterweighted lift bridge constructed over Tonawanda Creek, which at this point serves as the Erie Canal. When the bridge was built, it was expected to permit taller lake ships into the canal, but it proved impractical, so the bridge was only lifted once in its history.

The eight-day **Canal Fest of the Tonawandas**, in mid-July, is the largest festival of its kind along the canal. Events include a golf tournament, parades, youth games, musical entertainment, midway rides, food, a car show, a boat race, and, ending the festivities, fireworks. The festival area encompasses a 2-square-mile area along both sides of the canal in the Gateway Harbor Park. Boaters are free to dock at the park. (For more information, visit www.canalfest.org.)

Attractions

Herschell Carrousel Factory Museum (716-693-1885, www.carouselmuseum.org, 180 Thompson St., N. Tonawanda, NY 14120) This museum lives up to its motto: "Once around is never enough." Admission (adults $5; seniors $4; children $2.50) includes a ride on a 1916 carousel (additional rides are 50 cents), with music provided by a Wurlitzer band organ made in North Tonawanda. A carousel ride is simple fun and evokes the spirit of an earlier time. The museum building, formerly the Allan Herschell Company factory complex, and carousel are listed on both the New York State and National Registers of Historic Places. Exhibits include 20 large hand-carved and artistically painted carousel animals. Photographs of early-20th-century carousel production adorn the walls and lend an air of authenticity to the factory, which retains its paint-

Fishing along the canal during Canal Fest of the Tonawandas

splattered walls. Watch wood carvers demonstrate how carousel horses are made. Small children can ride on a 1940s aluminum kiddie carousel. The gift shop is stocked with imaginative carousel-related items.

Riviera Theater and Performing Arts Center (716-692-2413, www.rivieratheatre.org, 67 Webster St., N. Tonawanda, NY 14120) This historic venue hosts group tours, musical events, movies, and plays, including monthly concerts on the 1926 "Mighty Wurlitzer" organ. The grand 1,150-seat restored Italian Renaissance–style theater is listed on the National Register of Historic Places. It was billed as "the showplace of the Tonawandas" when it opened in 1926. Saved several times from the wrecker's ball, the theater has undergone an extensive restoration and boasts stained-glass windows and a 15-foot-high French chandelier. It is one of just a few theaters in the country that has a silver screen and vintage projectors capable of running the nitrate film used for silent movies.

LOCKPORT

The Lockport section of the Erie Canal was the last to be completed and proved to be one of the most challenging. Lockport sits atop a massive ledge of solid rock known as the Niagara Escarpment—the same Ice Age outcropping that created Niagara Falls, 17 miles to the west. Canal boats traveling west had to be raised 70 feet to the top of the stone mountain, and those traveling east had to be lowered the same distance. It was here, said historian William L. Stone, that "nature had interposed her strongest barrier to the enterprises and strength of man."

The solution was two sets of five locks, so that two-way traffic could be maintained. The twin set of locks was known as the Flight of Five. This was the most expensive and difficult section of canal construction. It took two years to build these locks, which required blasting a deep channel into the escarpment west of Lockport. The "Deep Cut" ranged in depth from 25 to 30 feet. Special drills penetrated the surface to make a hole for gunpowder. Pieces of the blasted rock were thrown daily over Main Street, and townspeople ran for shelter when the warning cries were sounded. (According to canal lore, to increase productivity, a barrel of whiskey was placed ahead of the workers as a reward upon their reaching it.)

The primary cause of death during construction of this section of canal was snakebite. (Not to worry; the rattlers are all gone now.) When the Marquis de Lafayette visited in 1825, he declared that Niagara County possessed the greatest natural (Niagara Falls) and manmade (the canal locks) wonders known in the world. Many consider the locks at Lockport to be the jewel of the entire canal. The Flight of Five locks soon gained international acclaim and became a popular attraction for tourists of the early 19th century. They were the only locks that allowed two-way traffic on the canal.

The Flight of Five is the system's most historic structure from the original canal and remains intact after minor changes during the Erie Enlargement; it is located within the operating waterway of the current New York State Canal System. Plans are under way to make the historic locks operable for demonstration purposes.

Of course, the town was named in honor of the impressive locks. The community was centered on the locks and consisted mainly of immigrant Scottish and Irish canal workers. They remained in Lockport after the canal was completed, giving the city a heavy Celtic influence still discernible today.

Today, Lockport boasts the only set of double locks on the canal. The walls along the side of the canal here are 12 feet thick. During World War II, it was illegal to photograph or paint these locks because the mechanism was the same as that in the strategic Panama Canal. Lockport Cave tours highlight a prolific Lockport inventor, Birdsill Holly, whose many inventions include the fire hydrant, central steam heat, and the rotary pump.

LODGING

Comfort Inn (716-434-4411, www.comfortinn.com/hotel-lockport-new_york-NY098, 551 S. Transit Rd., Lockport, NY 14094) This 50-room motel is a typical Comfort Inn, well located for Lockport attractions. It has a business center and free wireless Internet in all rooms. Local calls are free and some rooms have refrigerators and microwave ovens. Pet friendly; complimentary continental breakfast.

Holiday Inn Lockport (716-434-6151, www.ichotelsgroup.com, 515 S. Transit Rd., Lockport NY 14094) The largest hotel in Lockport, with 95 rooms, the two-story Holiday Inn has business conference facilities, a restaurant, bar, indoor pool, exercise room, and a central location just a mile from the Erie Canal. It is pet friendly, and all rooms have free wireless Internet.

Lockport Inn & Suites (716-434-5595 or 877-465-4100, www.lockportinnandsuites.com, 315 S. Transit Rd., Lockport, NY 14094) Family owned and operated since 1968, this two-story hotel draws well-deserved accolades from guests who appreciate the 90 large rooms, sparkling pool, free movies, wireless Internet, and friendly staff. Some rooms have Jacuzzi tubs; all have refrigerators and microwave ovens. Considered by many travelers the best hotel in the Lockport area, it is just 2 miles from **Lockport Locks & Erie Canal Cruises.**

ATTRACTIONS

Canal Museum (716-434-3140, Richmond Ave., Lockport, NY 14094) This one-room museum by the locks is in the former powerhouse that served the double locks until the mid-1950s. Displays include photographs, tools used in canal construction, and other canal memorabilia. A word of caution: The museum is well below street level and accessible only by several flights of stairs; railings are minimal. Open daily May through October. Free admission.

Colonel William Bond House (716-439-0431, www.niagarahistory.org, 143 Ontario St., Lockport, NY 14094) Colonel Bond was a speculator who came to Lockport to purchase land where he anticipated the locks would be constructed. He built his home in 1824—it was the first brick home in Lockport. Listed on the New York State and National Registers of Historic Places, this home has 12 rooms, furnished primarily in the 1820s Empire style. The Bond house is part of the **Niagara County Historical Society** complex. Open Monday, Wednesday, and Saturday May through October; winter months by appointment.

Erie Canal Discovery Center (716-439-0431, www.niagarahistory.org/page/discovery center, 24 Church St., Lockport, NY 14094) One short block from the Lockport locks, this museum is home to the **Lockport Visitors' Center,** a state-of-the-art interpretive center that explains the Erie Canal and the role Lockport played in the canal's history. A floor-to-ceiling mural depicts the celebration surrounding Clinton's first passage

Testing out the echo effect on a Lockport canal cruise

through the famous Flight of Five locks. A film transports visitors back in time on board a re-creation of a packet boat. Enjoy a hands-on opportunity to navigate a model ship through a working series of locks. Open daily May through October. Admission: adults $6, children $4.

Lockport Cave Tours and Underground Boat Ride (716-438-0174, www.lockportcave .com, 2 Pine St., Lockport, NY 14094) A 70-minute guided tour begins with the Lockport locks, both those of the modern canal and the original Flight of Five. Learn about the city's industrial heritage during a canal walk to the cave, originally a 1,600-foot waterpower tunnel used in the 1860s. The cave features stalactites and various other geologic formations. During a 30-minute underground boat ride—the longest in the U.S.—participants experience total darkness when their guide turns off the lights. The tunnel was the creation of Lockport inventor Birdsill Holly. Open daily mid-May through mid-October. Admission: adults $9, children $6.

Lockport Locks & Erie Canal Cruises (716-433-6155 or 800-378-0352, www.lockport locks.com, 210 Market St., Lockport, NY 14094) A narrated two-hour trip down the Erie Canal allows visitors to lock through the only double set of locks on the canal and view remnants of the original Flight of Five from the early canal days; the cruise passes under the widest bridge in the U.S. (call out and hear your echo). Open daily May through October. Admission: adults $15, children $8.50. Reservations recommended.

MEDINA

Listed on the National Register of Historic Places, Medina's Main Street offers some of the finest examples of 19th-century commercial architecture on the Erie Canal. Many of the buildings are constructed of Medina sandstone; the now-famous sandstone was mined in the area and shipped via the canal around the country and the world. It was used in the construction of New York's Brooklyn Bridge and London's Buckingham Palace. For about 80 years, nearly 50 quarries were in operation mining the durable sandstone, which ranges in color from deep reddish-brown to light gray.

Medina merits two entries in *Ripley's Believe It or Not!* A couple of miles outside the village, **Culvert Road** passes under the Erie Canal, the only such road along the entire canal route. And **St. John's Episcopal Church** stands in the center of Church Street just before that street becomes East Center Street. There the street splits, passing around the historic Medina-sandstone church—creating a church in the middle of the street and another entry in Ripley's.

There is a picturesque park alongside the canal's largest turning basin. The countryside around Medina is apple country, and a giant replica of an apple greets visitors to **Lions Park,** along the canal.

Medina is also a favorite with railroad fans. The **Medina Railroad Museum** (585-798-6106; www.railroadmuseum.net; 530 West Avenue, Medina), which opened in 1997, is the largest freight-depot museum in the country. The depot itself was built in 1905 and, at 300 feet by 34 feet, is one of the largest surviving wooden freight depots in the country. The museum is the creation of Martin Phelps, a retired firefighter who lives above the museum. (His former profession is evident in the more than 500 fire helmets that line the top shelves of the museum.) The ever-growing exhibits and interactive displays show how the railroad influenced American culture, industry, and history. There are more than 4,000 historic HO-scale cars, including many famous trains such as the *Black Diamond,* the *Phoebe Snow,* the *20th Century Limited,* and the *Empire State Express.* The museum's HO-scale layout is the longest such all-on-one-floor display in the nation—an immense 14 feet by 204 feet.

Train excursions begin at the museum and travel through the scenic 34-mile **Erie Canalway National Heritage Corridor** to Lockport. There are "Santa trains" in December, winery tours in the summer and fall, fall foliage tours, and Thomas the Tank Engine rides for the little ones.

Martin Phelps, conductor and founder of Medina Railroad Museum, with two young train enthusiasts on an excursion between Medina and Lockport

Cobblestone Houses

The Erie Canal spawned a unique architecture style: cobblestone houses. Once work was completed on the canal in 1825, masons were looking for new work—and for something new. They found it in the cobblestones, a free building material that was scattered about the area and believed to be a remnant of the Ice Age.

After gathering and sorting the stones by size and hue, masons created a design and set them in their own concoction of soft lime mortar. Typically they created intricate designs for the front of the house, with plainer rows for the sides. No two cobblestone buildings were made exactly alike, although the homes were often done in Greek Revival or Federal styles.

The cobblestone building boom lasted for about four decades, ending just before the Civil War. About 900 such structures were erected in western New York during this era. Although a smattering of cobblestone buildings are in other parts of the country, 90 percent of them are within a 75-mile radius of Buffalo. NY 104, historic Ridge Road, is often referred to as "the road of the cobblestone houses," for there are more of these houses here than on any highway in America.

Cobblestones are showcased at the **Cobblestone Society Museum** (585-589-9113, www .cobblestonesocietymuseum.org, 14393 Ridge Road West [NY 98 and 104], Childs, NY 14477), about 10 miles east of Medina. The only cobblestone museum in the world, this National Historic Landmark offers guided tours of seven buildings housing artifacts from the cobblestone era, including the oldest cobblestone church in North America. The **Cobblestone School** is unique in that it is a wooden structure with only a cobblestone veneer. The interior, with its sloping floor, appears as if it might have been built in the late 19th century. The school was closed in 1952, and it became part of the museum in 1961. The museum is open Tuesday through Sunday June 23 to Labor Day, and Sunday only in September and October.

The Cobblestone Museum is just outside Medina, in Childs

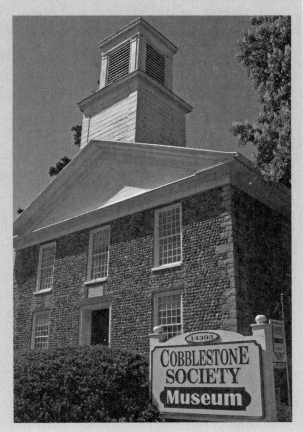

The Frederick Douglass–Susan B. Anthony Memorial Bridge spans the Genesee River in Rochester

4

Rochester Area

Pittsford, Fairport, Palmyra

ROCHESTER

Rochester has been called America's first boomtown. The third-largest city in the state, Rochester owes its existence to the Genesee River, and its growth and development to the Erie Canal.

Known as the Young Lion of the West, it catapulted from a sleepy little hamlet of fewer than 300 inhabitants in 1817 to a bustling city of over 8,000 residents a decade later. Progress was due in large part to the Erie Canal, which supplied a convenient and inexpensive route to populous markets on the East Coast. Long lines of barges loaded with flour, lumber, and other goods moved along the canal.

On May 31, 1825, the *Rochester Telegram* reported, "Our basins and wharves presented yesterday morning the appearances of a bustling commercial town—forwards and clerks, wagons and boatmen, all confusion and hurry; boats arriving and departing constantly."

Although the entire canal did not open until 1825, it reached Rochester in 1823, and shippers immediately loaded goods on it. In just the first 10 days of the opening season in 1823, Rochester shipped out 10,450 barrels of flour and 417 barrels of pork and potash on 58 boats. Forty-five incoming boats brought 4,000 gallons of beer, 2,300 gallons of whiskey, and even fresh New England oysters into Rochester.

Writer Nathaniel Hawthorne visited Rochester in the fall of 1830, traveling by the canal. Among his impressions: "The whole streets, sidewalks, and centre were crowded with pedestrians, horsemen, stagecoaches, gigs, light wagons, and heavy ox-teams, all hurrying, trotting, rattling, and rumbling, in a throng that passed continually, but never passed away."

One major problem of canal construction in the Rochester area was the deep Irondequoit Creek valley and its glacier-formed hills; by hand-carrying dirt in wheelbarrows, workers created an embankment to take the canal 70 feet above the valley floor. Now called Bushnell's Basin, it is also known as the Great Embankment and is one of the largest ever created.

Another construction problem involved crossing the roaring Genesee River in downtown Rochester; this was finally solved with the construction of an aqueduct spanning over 800 feet and supported by 11 arches. When completed, it was the largest structure of its type in the world, attracting visitors from around the globe to view its great expanse. A second, sturdier version was built in 1842 to replace the original aqueduct.

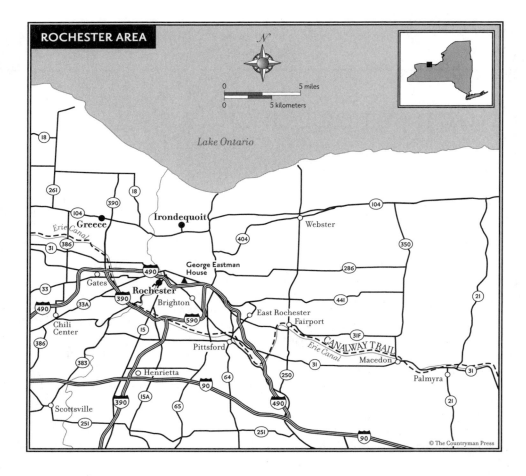

ROCHESTER AREA

Lake Ontario

© The Countryman Press

No longer serving the canal, the aqueduct is now the Broad Street Bridge, carrying hundreds of vehicles back and forth across the river each day. However, proponents are lobbying to restore the old Erie Canal, including filling the aqueduct with water as a downtown attraction.

The High Falls district is close by in the heart of downtown and features the country's highest urban waterfall: the Genesee River's 96-foot High Falls. The falls are best seen from the 858-foot-long Pont de Rennes pedestrian bridge, which spans the Genesee River Gorge.

The land of the Genesee Valley surrounding Rochester provided the richest farmland known to the country at that time. The land was particularly suited for wheat production. In a bit of synergistic luck, the Genesee Falls furnished enormous waterpower to grind the wheat into flour. Rochester is in fact named after Colonel Nathaniel Rochester, who built and developed flour mills alongside the Genesee River's High Falls. Originally called the Flour City because of these mills, the city was for a time the flour capital of the world, producing more of this product than anywhere else, flour that was world famous for its quality.

The best Rochester flour was considered to be truly superior and was highly acclaimed at the 1851 Crystal Palace Exposition in London. Britain's Queen Victoria expressed a preference for Rochester flour and said it made especially good cakes. In 1844 she ordered 6,000 barrels of the flour for the royal kitchens; it was sent to London via the Erie Canal.

Rochester later became known as the Flower City for its many flower nurseries. Ellwanger and Barry Nursery was the largest in the world in the 19th century. Traveling along the Erie Canal in the summer of 1833 on his first visit to the United States, George Ellwanger, a German immigrant, wrote: "In passing through Rochester a stop was made to unload some freight, which gave me an opportunity to inspect the then infant city on the Genesee whose appearance impressed me." Home to the world's biggest collection of lilacs—more than 500 different varieties—the city celebrates its flower heritage every May with the 10-day **Lilac Festival** (for more information visit www.lilacfestival.com).

Women's suffrage can also trace its roots to Rochester. Susan B. Anthony, a founder of the women's rights movement, arrived in Rochester in 1845 on the Erie Canal. Her home— the site of her famous arrest for voting—is now a museum. In her parlor she met and planned with reformers Elizabeth Cady Stanton and Frederick Douglass, an escaped slave and publisher of the *North Star* newspaper and a leading abolitionist. Both Anthony and Douglass are buried in Rochester's celebrated Mount Hope Cemetery, the country's first municipal Victorian cemetery. The striking, award-winning Frederick Douglass—Susan B. Anthony Memorial Bridge over the Genesee River honors the pair.

From bloomers to the fountain pen to the very first gold tooth, Rochester has had its share of firsts. Marshmallows were first commercially produced in Rochester, and it was here in 1904 that the first prepared mustard was manufactured by the R. T. French Company.

Surely, though, it is George Eastman, creator of Eastman Kodak, who brought the most fame to the city. In 1888 he launched the famous Kodak box camera, which he shipped around the country via the Erie Canal. Eastman is the father of popular photography and motion-picture film. He has also been called the father of Rochester. He gave away more than $100 million in his lifetime (more than $2 billion in today's dollars), making possible

Horse-drawn carriage transports visitors to the Lilac Festival through Rochester's Highland Park

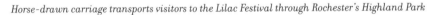

the University of Rochester's Eastman School of Music, the Eastman Theatre, the United Way, the Rochester Philharmonic Orchestra, and Strong Hospital.

The George Eastman House International Museum of Photography and Film is the oldest and one of the world's largest collections of photography and film, housed in modern archives adjacent to the National Historic Landmark Colonial Revival mansion and gardens. Eastman's home offers tantalizing details about this shy former bank clerk, who was a business genius, inventor, and great philanthropist.

The city has another important legacy related to Eastman Kodak: the Strong National Museum of Play. Margaret Woodbury Strong, Rochester's favorite collector, loved to play and loved to collect. During her lifetime, she collected more than 300,000 objects—the majority relating to play: toys, dolls, games, and books. When she died in 1969, Strong—who was the largest single Kodak shareholder—left an estate valued at $77 million. Her will directed that as much of her estate as needed be used to establish a museum to house the treasure and trivia that had preoccupied her life.

From the launch of the nationally renowned museum in 1982, Margaret Strong's collections have been its focus. Over the years the play objects have gained in emphasis, and the museum has added many interactive exhibits relating to play. After a recent major makeover, the museum nearly doubled in size, and it now also houses the National Toy Hall of Fame. The Strong is the first and only major museum in the world devoted to the study and interpretation of play; it has the most comprehensive collection of dolls, toys, and objects related to play in the world. And *Family Fun* rated the Strong National Museum of Play second in the Northeast in its "Top Picks" of regional museums for its Family-Friendly Travel Awards.

Another tourist destination is one that perhaps wouldn't automatically spring to mind: the Wegmans supermarket chain. In 1916 John Wegman opened the Rochester Fruit and Vegetable Company. Today, the innovative multistate supermarket chain is known as **Wegmans Food Markets.** Wegmans is regularly named one of the 100 best companies to work for by *Fortune* magazine (it ranked first in 2005). Now one of the country's premier

The Strong National Museum of Play is one of the city's many family-friendly attractions

supermarket chains, Wegmans stores have become tourist attractions in their own right.

Rochester has also become known as the world's image center, because it is the birthplace of high-tech giants like Xerox and Bausch & Lomb. It is also home to the University of Rochester and the Rochester Institute of Technology.

Rochester has embraced its role as a major canal city. It hosted the World Canals Conference in 2000 and will play host to the conference again in 2010, bringing together canal supporters, businesses, and officials from throughout North America and Europe.

Above all, Rochester is an extremely family-friendly city—so much so that *Child* magazine named it one of America's Top 10 Best Cities for Families.

LODGING

The Rochester area has both a special bed & breakfast and a hotel right on the Erie Canal as well as several historic B&Bs in downtown neighborhoods. There are also major chain hotels downtown and a number of suburban and airport hotels and motels. Rates tend to be moderate. All quotes are for double occupancy.

Lodging Rates
Inexpensive: Up to $75
Moderate: $76–$150
Expensive: $151–$250
Very Expensive: More than $250

ADAMS BASIN INN
Innkeepers: Pat and Dave Haines
585-352-3999 or 888-352-3999
www.adamsbasininn.com
425 Washington St., Adams Basin, NY 14410
Price: Moderate
Credit Cards: Yes
Handicapped Access: No
Special Feature: Wireless Internet; robes and slippers in rooms

This inn is located 13 miles from Rochester on the Erie Canal—on a section of the waterway that's much the same as it was when the first canal was constructed in 1823. The inn offers an opportunity to truly step back to the beginning of the canal's history. Listed on the National Register of Historical Places, the original portion of the inn has served as a rail station, general store, and a tavern. Stories say that more than just a drink was available to the packet boaters. (The Greek Revival portion of the house was added in the 1850s.) Today, there are four guestrooms, each with a private bath. The Nichols Room, decorated in a French style with a king-sized bed, offers a wonderful view of the canal. Bicyclists are especially welcome, with a locked carriage house to store bikes, free transportation to local restaurants for meals, and luggage transportation. A complimentary gourmet breakfast is served in the breakfast room, the tavern, or on the open-air porch in warm weather.

COUNTRY INN & SUITES
585-486-9000 or 800-456-4000
www.countryinns.com/henriettany_south
4635 W. Henrietta, Henrietta, NY 14467
Price: Moderate
Credit Cards: Yes
Handicapped Access: Yes
Special Features: Complimentary breakfast, nonsmoking hotel

Country Inn offers a wealth of services to guests, from evening receptions on Tuesdays and Thursdays with complimentary beer, wine, and snacks to outdoor grills with free hot dogs and hamburgers on Monday and Wednesday evenings during the summer. Enjoy complimentary freshly baked cookies and coffee 24 hours a day as well as complimentary breakfast. There is a business center, free high-speed Internet, a "read it and return" lending library, meeting facilities, indoor pool, and fitness center. The 77 rooms include family suites, studio suites, business suites, whirlpool suites, and one-bedroom suites. All suites have a refrigerator and microwave.

DARTMOUTH HOUSE

Innkeepers: Ellie and Bill Klein
585-271-7872 or 800-724-6298
www.dartmouthhouse.com
215 Dartmouth St., Rochester, NY 14607
Price: Moderate–Expensive
Credit Cards: Yes
Handicapped Access: No
Special Features: Gourmet breakfast; complimentary high-speed Internet

This is a grand 1905 English Tudor well located in the heart of the Park Avenue/East Avenue area, close to the George Eastman House and other museums. In the public rooms there is a grand piano, fireplace, cozy window seats, beamed ceilings, and pocket doors that help to create an elegant atmosphere. The five-course breakfast is always a treat, including freshly made Italian ice (either raspberry, lemon, or mango). Guests rave about the warmth and hospitality of the innkeepers. Three bedrooms on the second floor each with a private bathroom, and a two-bedroom suite on the third floor with a kitchen and bathroom. Children over 10 years old are welcome.

428 MT. VERNON

585-271-0792
www.428mtvernon.com
428 Mt. Vernon Ave., Rochester, NY 14620
Price: Moderate
Credit Cards: Yes
Handicapped Access: Yes
Special Features: High-speed Internet

Built in 1917 on two wooded acres within the city limits of Rochester, this lovely bed & breakfast is just off Highland Park, home to the world-famous Lilac Festival. It is a relaxed and comfortable place with handsome Victorian-style furnishings in the seven rooms. Close to attractions and businesses, the B&B's location and grounds give it a country atmosphere in the midst of the city. The gardens attract many birds that feed from the feeders. Breakfasts are hearty and prepared to order and include eggs, pancakes, and special French toast. Children over age 12 are welcome.

GENESEE COUNTRY INN

Innkeepers: Deborah and Richard Stankevich
585-538-2500
www.geneseecountryinn.com
948 George St., Mumford, NY 14511
Price: Moderate–Expensive
Credit Cards: Yes
Handicapped Access: Limited
Special Features: Spring-fed trout fishing

Located just a mile from the Genesee Country Village & Museum (with which there's no association), this is a perfect country inn. Before opening as an inn in 1982, the building—dating back to 1833—was a working mill for 100 years. There are two-and-a-half-foot-thick stone walls and 8 acres of grounds with waterfalls, woods, and gardens. Guests enjoy private fishing on Spring Creek, site of an early trout hatchery. The inn's 10 rooms are individually decorated with antiques and period reproductions, and some rooms have fireplaces. In the afternoon tea and home-baked cookies are offered. A full country breakfast is served daily. The **Old Mill Shoppe** in the inn is a favorite with knitters, since it stocks a wide range of lovely Bartlett yarns spun on a historic spinning machine with wool from nearby sheep farmers. Fly-fishing with lessons and other packages are available.

HOLIDAY INN ROCHESTER AIRPORT

585-328-6000
www.hirochesterairport.com
911 Brooks Ave., Rochester, NY 14624
Price: Moderate
Credit Cards: Yes
Handicapped Access: Yes
Special Features: Pet friendly; fitness center and indoor pool

There are 279 large guestrooms, including suites and executive rooms, all with complimentary high-speed Internet. There is a large indoor pool with a lifeguard, fitness center, sauna, and whirlpool. This is a popular meeting site, and there is also a complimentary business center. Restaurants include the Greenhouse Café and O'Malley's Sports Bar, with a pool table, darts, and TVs tuned in to sports channels. Check out the park-and-fly hotel specials.

HYATT REGENCY ROCHESTER

585-546-1234
www.rochester.hyatt.com
125 E. Main St., Rochester, NY 14614
Price: Moderate–Expensive
Credit Cards: Yes
Handicapped Access: Yes
Special Features: Indoor pool

The hotel is centrally located in downtown Rochester, adjacent to the Rochester Riverside Convention Center. The 338 rooms and suites have been recently renovated, offering the hotel chain's signature Grand Bed, leather armchair, ergonomic desk furniture, and luxurious linens. There is also an indoor pool, fitness facility, sundeck, and business center. The newly renovated Palladio Restaurant is open for breakfast, lunch, and dinner and serves Italian American–influenced fare, while the Focus Lounge in the lobby bar offers light fare and snacks. A complimentary shuttle service runs to the Rochester airport, Amtrak station, and Greyhound station.

INN ON BROADWAY

585-232-3595 or 877-612-3595
www.innonbroadway.com
26 Broadway, Rochester, NY 14607
Price: Expensive–Very Expensive
Credit Cards: Yes
Handicapped Access: Yes
Special Features: Complimentary breakfast

In 1929 the University Club of Rochester was built as the hub of social activity for its members. Now, after an extensive restoration, the building has been transformed into a luxury boutique urban inn. Located in the heart of the East End Theatre District, the inn boasts a variety of restaurants and shops within a short stroll. The 23 rooms and suites offer such amenities as gas fireplaces, kitchenettes, and Jacuzzi tubs, and all have either queen- or king-sized featherbeds. Even bathrobes are provided. The rooms sport old travel gear, and one room even displays a century-old Harvard Club of New York register. The main ballroom features two magnificent crystal chandeliers as well as murals of the Erie Canal, Kodak, High Falls, and the University of Rochester. The inn is home to the award-winning **Tournedoes**, a New York City–style steakhouse serving some of the best steak and seafood in the city.

RADISSON HOTEL ROCHESTER AIRPORT

585-475-1910
www.radisson.com
175 Jefferson Rd., Rochester, NY 14623
Price: Moderate
Credit Cards: Yes
Handicapped Access: Yes
Special Features: Pet friendly; indoor pool

Located on the grounds of Rochester Institute of Technology, this comfortable 171-room hotel is ideal for all members of the family, including four-legged ones. All rooms provide Sleep Number beds, and complimentary wireless Internet is available throughout the hotel. Other amenities include an indoor pool and fitness center, and Baxter's Restaurant & Lounge, featuring American cuisine, is open for breakfast, lunch, and dinner. The hotel is five minutes from the Rochester Airport, with complimentary shuttle service to the airport and businesses within 5 miles.

RADISSON RIVERSIDE HOTEL

585-546-6400
www.radissonriversidehotel.com
120 East Main St., Rochester, NY 14604
Price: Moderate
Credit Cards: Yes
Handicapped Access: Yes
Special Features: Pet friendly

Nestled on the banks of the Genesee River in the heart of downtown Rochester, this 465- room hotel is connected to the Rochester Riverside Convention Center. It is the primary link to an enclosed skyway system that encompasses more than 100 retail stores, restaurants, and office buildings. It is the largest, full-service conference hotel in the city. There are seven suites, an outdoor pool, fitness facility, and business center. Complimentary airport transportation and wireless high-speed Internet are available.

RIT INN & CONFERENCE CENTER

585-359-1800
www.ritinn.com
5257 W. Henrietta Rd., Rochester, NY 14586
Price: Moderate
Credit Cards: Yes
Handicapped Access: Yes
Special Features: Pet friendly

The Rochester Institute of Technology Inn—which is staffed by RIT students majoring in hospitality and service management—offers 304 rooms, including some designed specifically for business travelers, and both indoor and outdoor pools. The inn has easy access to the New York State Thruway (I-90), and it is close to the airport, with complimentary shuttle service. **Petals Restaurant** serves bistro-style dining for breakfast, lunch, and dinner; **Jitters** offers snacks, specialty coffees, and drinks such as fruit smoothies; and the **Charades Dining Room** is open for dinner, featuring popular favorites such as steak, tenderloin of beef, duck, salmon, and chicken.

ROCHESTER PLAZA HOTEL & CONFERENCE CENTER

585-546-3450 or 866-826-2831
www.rochesterplaza.com
70 State St., Rochester, NY 14614
Price: Moderate
Credit Cards: Yes
Handicapped Access: Yes
Special Features: Pet friendly; complimentary wireless Internet

Located in the center of downtown in a prime spot on the Genesee River, this hotel is adjacent to the High Falls neighborhood, the East End Theatre District, and the St. Paul Quarter. There are 362 rooms and suites, one of which is a Sports Suite outfitted with local teams' memorabilia from the past several decades. Invite your poker-playing friends, and the Rochester Plaza will provide the poker chips, cards, munchies, and drinks. The special pet-friendly rooms come equipped with everything you and your pet might need. Other amenities include a large outdoor pool located on the fourth floor; also on the fourth floor is the Fitness Center, with an extensive array of equipment and a sauna. The **River Club Restaurant** is open for breakfast, lunch, and dinner and offers great river views. The **State Street Bar and Grill** in the hotel's lobby has one of downtown's only outdoor seating areas and serves up a casual, upscale menu.

Origins of the Garbage Plate
The original Garbage Plate was created at **Nick Tahou Hots,** a Rochester institution since 1918. Legend has it that college students once asked Tahou for a dish with "all the garbage" on it. So he concocted an original combo plate with two hamburger patties and a choice of two sides—usually some combination of home fries, macaroni salad, and beans. The contents are often laced heavily with ketchup plus Nick Tahou's signature hot sauce and mixed together before eating. Rolls or white bread are served on the side. The Garbage Plate is considered a great late-night snack, and many college students in Rochester believe consuming the dish to be a rite of passage. Nick Tahou Hots is located at 320 W. Main Street in downtown Rochester. (For more information call 585-436-0184, or visit www.garbageplate.com.)

RESTAURANTS

Rochester has a rich culinary history, and area restaurants include numerous diverse ethnic flavors. Some unique Rochester specialties include the Garbage Plate, a dish that especially appeals to the young. Many restaurants feature Finger Lakes wines. All restaurants are by New York State law non-smoking. Prices are estimated per person for dinner entrée, without tax, tip, or beverage.

Dining Rates
Inexpensive: Up to $10
Moderate: $11–$25
Expensive: $26–$40
Very Expensive: More than $40

BAMBA BISTRO
585-244-8680
www.bambabistro.com
282 Alexander St., Rochester, NY 14607
Open: Mon.–Sat.
Cuisine: Bistro
Serving: D; L Mon.–Fri.
Price: Expensive
Credit Cards: Yes
Handicapped Access: Yes

Special Features: Happy Hour specials on weeknights from 4 to 7, with first drink free
The Bamba Bistro (formerly the Rio Bamba) is located in a beautifully restored downtown building. Inside, the brick walls and soft lighting provide a warm and cozy atmosphere. The lounge incorporates a beautiful bar. Menu items include rack of lamb, pork tenderloin, and Atlantic salmon.

CRESCENT BEACH RESTAURANT
585-227-3600
www.crescentbeachinn.com
1372 Edgemere Dr., Rochester, NY 14612
Open: Daily
Cuisine: American
Serving: L, D, Sunday champagne brunch
Price: Moderate–Expensive
Credit Cards: Yes
Handicapped Access: Yes
Special Features: Lake access for boaters

The Crescent Beach Restaurant was originally opened prior to 1900. It was a popular spot on Lake Ontario, and patrons wore tuxedos and gowns while enjoying the elegant dining room. Today it is a restaurant that welcomes people wearing tuxedos and gowns, boaters in shorts, and everyone in between. It has three dining rooms, including the main dining room where 18 oversized windows offer a great view of the lake. Seafood takes a prime spot on the menu, with grilled salmon, sea scallops, crab legs, and lobster as well as traditional favorites such as prime rib, steak, and filet mignon.

Homegrown Casual Food

Two local companies have become regional (and even national) casual-cuisine success stories. Don't miss these local favorites if you're in the area.

The story of **Abbott's Frozen Custard** (www.abbottscustard.com) dates back to 1902, when Arthur Abbott perfected his recipe for frozen custard while traveling with small carnivals along the eastern seaboard. In 1926 he settled in Rochester and opened a shop at the corner of Lake and Beach avenues, across the street from Ontario Beach Park. Hundreds lined up for the frozen treat. Today that stand remains, and there are many others, in New York, Florida, and Massachusetts. Area locations include: 4791 Lake Ave., Rochester, NY 14612, 585-865-7400; 624B Pittsford-Victor Rd., Pittsford, NY 14534, 585-385-1366; 104 Midtown Plaza, Rochester, NY 14614, 585-546-3116; 1220 Fairport Rd., Fairport, NY 14450, 585-586-4469; 1340 Mount Hope Ave., Rochester, NY 14620, 585-271-5780.

The first **Tom Wahl's** (www.tomwahls.com) opened in Avon, New York, in 1955, and customers have been known to travel great distances to enjoy a juicy Wahlburger, crispy fries, and a frosted mug of handcrafted root beer. There are nine restaurants in the Rochester area, with locations at 283 E. Main St., Avon, NY 14414, 585-226-2420; Greece Ridge Mall, 440 Greece Ridge Center Dr., Rochester, NY 14626, 585-227-2950; Market Place Mall, 671 Miracle Mile Dr., Rochester, NY 14623, 585-427-0460; 2510 Rochester Rd., Canandaigua, NY 14424, 585-393-9170; 643 Pittsford-Victor Rd., Pittsford, NY 14534, 585-586-4920; East View Mall, 7979 Victor-Pittsford Rd., Victor, NY 14564, 585-425-4860; 585 W. Union St., Newark, NY 14513, 315-331-9112; 2070 Empire Blvd., Webster, NY 14580, 585-671-5930; and 1333 Fairport Rd., Fairport, NY 14450, 585-377-8420.

DINOSAUR BAR-B-QUE

585-325-7090
www.dinosaurbarbque.com
99 Court St., Rochester, NY 14604
Open: Daily
Price: Inexpensive–Moderate
Cuisine: BBQ
Serving: L, D
Credit Cards: Yes
Handicapped Access: Yes
Special Features: Live music Mon.–Sat. nights

Opened in 1998, the Dinosaur Bar-B-Que occupies what used to be the Lehigh Valley Train Station in the heart of downtown. The original Dinosaur began down the canal in Syracuse. Overlooking the Genesee River, Rochester's version has taken on its own unique personality while offering the same great Dinosaur food and passion for blues. This is a genuine honky-tonk rib joint, and it has received national acclaim. A store sells sauces, and rubs—categorized by heat index—plus T-shirts, hats, books, and glasses. All are also available online. Take-out is available.

GOLDEN PORT DIM SUM RESTAURANT

585-256-1780
www.thegoldenport.com
105 East Ave., Rochester, NY 14604
Open: Tues.–Sun.
Cuisine: Asian
Serving: L, D
Price: Moderate
Credit Cards: Yes
Handicapped Access: Yes
Special Features: Take-out and delivery available

This award-winning establishment fuses Chinese, Thai, and Vietnam cuisines. Enjoy authentic dim sum, including Japanese, Chinese, vegetarian, and dessert items. The menu is huge and includes "make your own soup" and "make your own stir fry" sections. All dishes are individually prepared to order.

LENTO RESTAURANT

585-271-3470
www.lentorestaurant.com
274 N. Goodman St., Rochester, NY 14607
Open: Tues.–Sat.
Cuisine: American
Serving: D
Price: Expensive
Credit Cards: Yes
Handicapped Access: Yes
Special Features: Menu changes daily; special tastings, including a four-course tasting of tomato dishes.

The original wood timbers, brick walls, and high ceilings of this former factory provide the backdrop for a most comfortable and serene dining experience. Chef Art Rogers, a Rochester native, is a true believer in the tenets of the "slow food" movement: local, seasonal, fresh, and organic ingredients expertly prepared and served with flare. Lento—which takes its name from the Italian and musical term for "slow"—salutes local farmers who supply the restaurant with organic foods including heirloom vegetables. (Rich and delicious tomatoes are brought in from the chef's own garden daily in-season.) The menu includes wild coho salmon, wild Alaskan halibut, grilled sirloin steak, grilled duck breast, rabbit leg, as well as a good selection of vegetarian entrées.

MAX OF EASTMAN PLACE

585-697-0491
www.maxrochester.net
25 Gibbs St., Rochester, NY 14604
Open: Mon.–Sat.
Cuisine: American/Continental
Serving: D; L Mon.–Fri.
Price: Expensive
Credit Cards: Yes
Handicapped Access: Yes
Special Features: Live music

Since opening in 2001, Max of Eastman Place has earned a well-deserved reputation as one of the area's finest dining experiences, offering a sophisticated setting overlooking the University of Rochester's Eastman Theatre. There are changing menus, but some favorites include pan-roasted Chilean sea bass, wild Gulf of Mexico shrimp, Angus New York strip steak, and roasted rack of lamb. There is an extensive wine list and full-service bar; enjoy a drink or glass of wine in the lounge before the theater or a concert. Guests are invited to stop into the kitchen and see what's cooking.

PANE VINO RISTORANTE

585-232-6090
www.panevinoristorante.com
175 N. Water St., Rochester, NY 14614
Open: Mon.–Sat.
Cuisine: Italian
Serving: D; L Mon.–Fri.
Price: Moderate–Expensive
Credit Cards: Yes
Handicapped Access: Yes
Special Features: Live music; outdoor dining

Pane vino means "bread and wine" in Italian, and this restaurant offers contemporary Italian dishes in a rustic Tuscan setting on the Genesee River. (In-season, enjoy patio dining overlooking the water.) The restaurant, which is within walking distance to all downtown hotels and the convention center, is a good choice for a romantic dinner or a celebration. Italian dishes go beyond the ordinary to such selections as lobster ravioli and penne vodka. There are also steaks, pork chops, rack of lamb, veal, and a number of seafood dishes. The chef will gladly prepare a special meal off the menu when you call ahead.

RESTAURANT 2 VINE

585-454-6020
www.2vine.com

24 Winthrop St., Rochester, NY 14607
Open: Mon.–Sat.
Cuisine: Bistro
Serving: D Mon.–Sat.; L Mon.–Fri.
Price: Expensive
Credit Cards: Yes
Handicapped Access: Yes
Special Features: Jazz combo Thurs.–Sat. nights

This award-winning upscale bistro serves some of the freshest food available. The fish and seafood are delivered daily from Boston, and the beef is certified Angus. At 2 Vine the owners believe in the cycles of nature; accordingly, the menu changes with the seasonality of fish, seafood, and produce. Fruits and vegetables come from local farms whenever possible and are organically grown. Though this is a fine-dining establishment, it is not a stuffy place. Tablecloths are topped with white butcher paper. Bread comes in a paper wrapper. Servers have tablecloths tied around their waists for aprons. The building that houses 2 Vine was originally built around the turn of the 20th century as an ambulance garage; later, it was a new-car-prep garage; and after its transformation into 2 Vine, the owners were recognized by the Rochester-based Landmark Society of Western New York for their renovation efforts. The restaurant is located behind the Little Theatre and is a good place for dinner before or after a show.

ROHRBACH BREWING COMPANY
585-594-9800
www.rohrbachs.com
3859 Buffalo Rd., Rochester, NY 14624
Open: Daily
Price: Moderate
Cuisine: American/German
Serving: L, D
Credit Cards: Yes
Handicapped Access: Yes
Special Features: Homemade soups available to take out

John Urlaub worked for Eastman Kodak, and his job took him to Rohrbach, Germany, where he spent two years sampling as many German beers as possible. Soon after returning from Germany, he founded this small family-owned and -operated microbrewery and restaurant, naming it after the town in Germany where he had lived. The menu runs the gamut from burgers, sandwiches, soups, salads, and steak to such German specialties as sauerbraten, bratwurst, and schnitzel. A good children's menu offers items such as grilled chicken breast, pasta, and pizza. (Children under 12 eat free on Sundays.) On the brewery side of the menu, Rohrbach's most popular beer is its Scotch Ale, while its McDermott's Ale is named after head brewer James McDermott. Other brands include Highland Lager, BlueBeary Ale, Old Nate's Pale Ale, and Sam Patch Porter.

ROONEY'S RESTAURANT
585-442-0444
www.rooneysrestaurant.com
90 Henrietta St., Rochester, NY 14620
Open: Mon.–Sat.
Price: Expensive
Cuisine: Continental
Serving: D
Credit Cards: Yes
Handicapped Access: Yes
Special Features: Guest chefs; daily-changing menu

This restaurant was once a saloon on the original Erie Canal when the canal ran through downtown Rochester. The handsome 1890s building has high ceilings, a welcoming dining room fireplace, and an impressive Victorian bar. Grilled and blackened dishes are popular on the menu, which changes daily. There is wood-grilled beef tenderloin, blackened Hawaiian-orange marlin, pan-seared venison, and chestnut-crusted Atlantic salmon. Ice cream is homemade, as are the sorbets.

Chocolate lovers shouldn't miss the choco-late oblivion.

SIAM RESTAURANT
585-232-7426
www.thesiamrestaurant.com
280 Exchange Blvd., Rochester, NY 14608
Open: Mon.–Sat.
Price: Moderate
Cuisine: Thai
Serving: L, D

Credit Cards: Yes
Handicapped Access: Yes
Special Features: Outdoor dining

Located in historic Corn Hill Landing, Siam offers traditional Thai dishes with special-ties such as mango tango and king of the jungle tiger shrimp. The chic three-level restaurant features views of the Genesee River. In addition to the Thai menu, there is also a Chinese menu.

A Market for All

The **Rochester Public Market** is much more than just a market. Opened in 1905, it offers more than 300 indoor and outdoor stalls. Here immigrants to the U.S. soothe their homesickness with flavors and smells reminiscent of their homelands. The vibrant, thriving marketplace is unique in that it show-cases area farmers and purveyors. You probably won't get your chickens any fresher, and the fish mar-kets carry almost every kind of fish imaginable—some are still swimming, others are on ice.

The bazaar atmosphere of the market is heightened by the mélange of skin colors and the babel of voices, languages, and accents. But this market is a friendly meeting place where cultural and racial differences are set aside in the quest for the freshest squid or the plumpest tomato.

Special events scheduled throughout the year—such as "Greatest Garage Sales Ever" and "Flower City Days"—add to the flavor. In addition to fresh foods, flowers, and plants, there are bakeries, cheese shops, restaurants, and coffee shops, as well as crafts vendors. There is even a shop selling wild game. To find out more about the Rochester Public Market, call 585-428-6907 or visit www .cityofrochester.gov/PRHS/PublicMarket. The market is located at 280 N. Union Street, Rochester, and is open year-round Tuesday and Thursday 6 am to 1 pm and Saturday from 5 am to 3 pm.

Fresh produce at the Rochester Public Market

THE TRIPHAMMER GRILL

585-262-2700
www.thetriphammergrill.com
60 Browns Race, Rochester, NY 14614
Open: Mon.–Sat.
Price: Moderate
Cuisine: American
Serving: D; L Mon.–Fri.
Credit Cards: Yes
Handicapped Access: Yes
Special Features: Outdoor dining overlooking the Genesee River Gorge

The Triphammer building was built as a forge in 1816: a large, heavy hammer—the triphammer—was raised by waterpower and dropped to forge wrought-iron tools. The building burned in 1977, and when the rubble was cleared, a long-forgotten basement room was uncovered that housed the building's massive waterwheel. Today Brown's Race Historic District pays tribute to early-19th-century entrepreneurs. The comfortable restaurant opened in 1993, serving such items as roasted lamb shank, filet mignon, grilled salmon, and meat loaf. Diners can marvel at the original 12-ton waterwheel, still ensconced in its chamber.

CULTURE

The Rochester region has a rich history of music, art, and theater. George Eastman, the area's greatest philanthropist, was a very generous benefactor of the arts, especially music. Of course, the Eastman House and its photography museum is world class and has become a mecca for photography fans from around the world.

Museums and Historic Sites

CHARLOTTE-GENESEE LIGHTHOUSE

585-621-6179
www.geneseelighthouse.org
70 Lighthouse St., Rochester, NY 14612
Open: Weekends mid-May–Oct.
Admission: Free

Visitors can climb to the top of the 1822 tower, located on a bluff, and enjoy a beautiful view of the Genesee River, Lake Ontario, and the village of Charlotte. The 40-foot Medina sandstone lighthouse is on the National Register of Historic Places and has 4-foot-thick walls and a winding wrought-iron staircase. The Charlotte-Genesee Lighthouse Historical Society maintains the property, including the 1863 Keeper's House that accommodates a small museum. Displays portray the lighthouse, the port, Ontario Beach Park, and the village of Charlotte. Native Americans used the site as a summer encampment for hundreds of years.

GANONDAGAN STATE HISTORIC SITE

585-924-5848
www.ganondagan.org
1488 State Rt. 444, Victor, NY 14564
Open: Trails open daily; visitors' center and longhouse open Tues.–Sun., May–Oct.
Admission: Adults $3, children $2 for visitors' center and longhouse; self-guided trails free

Ganondagon, a former 17th-century Seneca village, is a National Historic Landmark. Illustrated signs mark trails where visitors can learn about the Seneca. The world's only full-sized replica of a 17th-century Seneca bark longhouse is furnished as closely as possible to an original 1670 longhouse. It has replicas of European and colonial trade goods and items created and crafted by the Seneca. Also in the longhouse are dried crops, herbs and medicines that were grown, harvested, and preserved by the Seneca, who lived atop the hill at Ganondagan. Learn about the Iroquois inspiration for the U.S. Constitution and the model matriarchal society that eventually led to women's right to vote. The site hosts historic reenactments and Native American dance and music festivals. Guided trail walks are offered on weekends.

GENESEE COUNTRY VILLAGE & MUSEUM
585-538-6822
www.gcv.org
1410 Flint Hill Rd., Mumford, NY 14511
Open: Tues.–Sun., mid-May–mid.-Oct.
Admission: Adults $15, seniors and students $12, children $9

This museum extols the 19th century. Visitors can attend a baseball game played by 19th-century rules, attend a concert in an opera house, enjoy a Victorian tea, learn to weave or quilt, and meet a tinsmith, a pair of oxen, and spring lambs. Throughout the season, special events are staged to give an in-depth look at various aspects of 19th-century life. They include Civil War reenactments, concerts, a national baseball tournament, Old-Time Fiddler's Fair, antiques show and sale, Agricultural Society Fair, Moon and Meteors Overnight, fireworks, and Native American art, dance, crafts, and storytelling.

There are 68 restored historically significant buildings in the 125-acre village. The buildings were gathered from 13 Genesee Valley counties and represent various stages in the development of the frontier. Costumed interpreters are on hand to explain and demonstrate pioneer life. They also perform crafts demonstrations such as spinning, weaving, quilting, and working with pottery and tin. Two museum buildings were the early homes of Rochester's leading citizens: Nathaniel Rochester and George Eastman. Colonel Rochester, who gave the city its name, lived in the frame-and-plank house from 1810 to 1815 with his wife, Sophia, and their nine children. George Eastman, founder of Eastman Kodak, spent his early youth in a comfortable one-and-a-half-story Greek Revival dwelling in Waterville.

Not to be missed: The John L. Wehle Art Gallery, named for the museum's founder, houses one of the country's premier collections of sporting and wildlife art.

GEORGE EASTMAN HOUSE INTERNATIONAL MUSEUM OF PHOTOGRAPHY & FILM
585-271-3361
www.eastmanhouse.org
900 East Ave., Rochester, NY 14607
Open: Tues.–Sun.
Admission: Adults $10, seniors $8, students $6, children $4

Eastman, who never married, built the grand 50-room home for his mother, who lived in it for only two years before her death. The house and gardens—designated a National

The stately Eastman House on Rochester's elegant East Avenue

Historic Landmark—have been meticulously restored as they were in Eastman's day with many original furnishings. Designed for entertaining and comfort, the house was filled with gadgets, including an elevator, 21 telephones, and a garage with its own car wash. The extensive gardens have been restored as they were in Eastman's day. It was in the gardens in 1928 that Eastman and Thomas Edison introduced the world to color motion-picture film, invented at the nearby Kodak plant.

Eastman's love of flowers can also be seen inside the house in the music room and the conservatory. The conservatory was built with a pipe organ in the wall, and soon after moving into his new house, Eastman declared its acoustics inadequate. To ensure a better sound, he had his house sliced in two and widened by 10 feet—an endeavor that cost more than constructing the original mansion. A replica of the elephant Eastman shot while on one of two African safaris dominates the music room, where the inventor ate breakfast every morning.

Eastman had his first camera on the market in 1888. During the next two decades Eastman consistently reduced the price; the simplest Brownies sold for $1 so that every family could afford a camera. On the 50th anniversary of the company, Kodak gave a Brownie to every 12-year-old child in the country. Honoring that history, the Discovery Room on the second floor is a place where kids can touch antique cameras and make their own sun prints and visit hands-on stations.

The Eastman House is connected to the International Museum of Photography, which was built to house one of the world's largest collections of photographs and films, includ-

Origin of Kodak

By 1888 George Eastman had his first camera on the market—the "No. 1 Kodak." He chose the name *Kodak* because "it is short; it is not capable of mispronunciation, and it does not resemble anything in the art and cannot be associated with anything in the art except the Kodak." Eastman also liked the letter *K*.

ing 500,000 fine art and historical prints and works of 8,000 international photographers from 1839 to the present. Film programs in the Dryden Theatre showcase the museum's world-renowned motion picture collection.

MEMORIAL ART GALLERY OF THE UNIVERSITY OF ROCHESTER
585-276-8900
www.mag.rochester.edu
500 University Ave., Rochester, NY 14607
Open: Wed.–Sun.
Admission: Adults $10, seniors $6, children $4; reduced admission $6 Thurs. 5–9 pm

The gallery was founded in 1913 and given in trust to the University of Rochester. It also serves as a community art museum—one of the few university-affiliated art museums to do so. Artists in the collection include Monet, Cezanne, Matisse, Homer, Cassatt, and O'Keeffe. Highlights include the American galleries, an interactive exhibit featuring a rare pair of ancient-Egyptian sarcophagi, a suit of 16th-century German armor, and the only full-size Italian Baroque organ in North America. Cutler's Restaurant is open for lunch daily and for dinner Thursday through Saturday and features a changing seasonal menu.

MOUNT HOPE CEMETERY
585-428-7999
www.fomh.org
791 Mount Hope Ave., Rochester, NY 14620
Open: Daily
Admission: Free

Established in 1838, this was the country's first municipal cemetery. Encompassing 197 acres, Mount Hope is also a park, a sculpture gallery, a museum, and gardens. Rochester notables buried here include Frederick Douglass, abolitionist; Susan B. Anthony, women's rights advocate; and Nathaniel Rochester, city founder. Free guided walking tours are held Saturdays and Sundays May through October.

ROCHESTER MUSEUM & SCIENCE CENTER
585-271-4320
www.rmsc.org
657 East Ave., Rochester, NY 14607
Open: Daily
Admission: Adults $10 ($15 including planetarium show or film), seniors and students $9 (including planetarium), children $8

Three floors of hands-on exhibits explore science and technology, natural science, and the region's cultural heritage. Continuing exhibits include Expedition Earth, an interactive multisensory journey delving into the region's natural environment; How Things Work, a hands-on investigation of the workings of everyday devices; Adventure Zone, with a simulator ride beneath Lake Ontario and a Genesee Gorge climbing wall; a hands-on weather station; and At the Western Door, telling the story of the Seneca people in western New York. The **Strasenburgh Planetarium** offers star shows and night laser shows, with rock-music favorites choreographed to the indoor sky.

STRONG NATIONAL MUSEUM OF PLAY

585-263-2700
www.museumofplay.org
One Manhattan Square, Rochester, NY 14607
Open: Daily
Admission: Adults $10, seniors $9, children $8; butterfly garden $3 additional

The whole family can spend the day at the only museum in the world devoted to the study of play. Just inside the museum's doors is the facility's largest and most colorful artifact, an operating 1918 Allan Herschell carousel built by the Herschell Carrousel Factory in North Tonawanda, New York. Local riders feel right at home among the brightly painted upstate New York scenes depicting the Erie Canal, Lake Ontario, and nearby High Falls. The Super Kids Market, inspired by Rochester's renowned Wegmans, remains one of the museum's most popular attractions, where kids enjoy shopping, scanning groceries, and stocking the shelves in the child-sized supermarket. Then sit on the famous *Sesame Street* stoop, visit Elmo's World, and count with the Count. Follow the Yellow Brick Road into five magical worlds inspired by children's literature. Visit the National Toy Hall of Fame and a treasure trove of play-related objects, including the world's largest collection of dolls and toys. Finally, marvel at the Dancing Wings Butterfly Garden, a glass-enclosed structure with a luminescent roof shaped like outspread wings. This is upstate New York's only indoor butterfly conservatory. Take a break from all the play at the two restaurants or the food court.

SUSAN B. ANTHONY HOUSE

585-235-6124
www.susanbanthonyhouse.org

Playing in the sandbox at the Strong Museum

A landmark in women's rights history, the Susan B. Anthony House

17 Madison St., Rochester, NY 14608
Open: Tues.–Sun.
Admission: Adults $6, seniors $5, students and children $3

Susan B. Anthony lived in this modest redbrick Victorian home for the 40 most politically active years of her life. Now a National Historic Landmark, the home tells the story of the American legend who paved the way for women to the ballot box. The house is simply decorated, perhaps harking back to Anthony's Quaker roots. Much of her own furniture is displayed here, including the desk where she helped write the words that gave American women the right to vote.

In the parlor she met and planned with famous reformers Elizabeth Cady Stanton and Frederick Douglass. It was also in this room in 1872 that a U.S. Marshal arrested her for voting. Taken by streetcar to the police station, she refused to pay her fare, insisting, "I am traveling under protest at the government's expense." (She also refused to pay her $100 fine). From 1869 to 1906 Anthony appeared before every Congress to lobby for passage of a women's suffrage amendment. In 1906 she delivered her famous "Failure is impossible" speech at her 86th birthday celebration in Washington, D.C. Less than a month later, she died at home.

One interesting personal note that visitors learn from the guides: "Susan B." bathed in cold water until she was 80—after that she apparently decided to start taking hot baths.

Other Attractions

SEABREEZE AMUSEMENT PARK
585-323-1900 or 800-395-2500
www.seabreeze.com
4600 Culver Rd., Rochester NY 14622
Open: Weekends mid-May–mid-June, daily mid-June–Labor Day
Admission: Adults $23.99, children $19.99, including unlimited rides and water park; general admission $10.99; $2 single-ride tickets with general pass

Located on the shores of Lake Ontario, this old-fashioned amusement park has more than 70 rides and attractions, including the Raging Rivers water park. Rides include such classics as a hand-carved carousel, a train that goes through an old mine tunnel, flying scooters, and a Tilt-A-Whirl. There are also four roller coasters, bumper cars, and a log flume with one of the steepest drops in the country. Seabreeze began as a waterfront picnic park in 1879, located at the end of the railroad line coming out of Rochester. Mechanical rides and other attractions were added over the years. Live shows are scheduled regularly during the day, and picnics are still allowed, although alcohol is prohibited.

SENECA PARK ZOO
585-336-7200
www.senecaparkzoo.org
2222 St. Paul St., Rochester, NY 14621
Open: Daily
Admission: Apr.–Oct., adults $9, seniors $8, children $6; Nov.– Dec. and Jan.–Mar., adults $7, seniors $6, children $4

The zoo is located in Seneca Park, one of several Rochester parks designed by noted landscape architect Frederick Law Olmsted. The park opened in 1893, and the first animals were displayed a year later. Popular animal exhibits include a pair of South African elephants, polar bears, sea lions, and wolves.

Performing Arts
Downstairs Cabaret Theatre (585-325-4370, www.DownstairsCabaret.com, 20 Windsor St., Rochester, NY 14604) With more than 400 performances of 25 to 30 different productions each year, the theater offers something for everyone—including new musicals and performers direct from off Broadway, hit comedies, world premieres, touring cabaret artists, and dramas in a year-round repertory schedule.

Eastman School of Music (585-274-1100, www.rochester.edu/eastman, 26 Gibbs St., Rochester, NY 14604) Founded by George Eastman in 1921, the Eastman School of Music is part of the University of Rochester. It is rated as one of the country's top music schools. Its famous alumni include Renée Fleming, Mitch Miller, Ron Carter, Chuck Mangione, and the late William Warfield. Each year students present hundreds of concerts at the Eastman Theatre and in settings throughout the community. Many of the concerts are free.

Garth Fagan Dance (585-454-3260, www.garthfagandance.org, 50 Chestnut St., Rochester, NY 14604) Garth Fagan, founder and artistic director, has been called "a true original" in the field of modern dance. Winner of numerous awards and choreographer for *The Lion King,* Fagan has led his dance company for more than 35 years. The troupe has performed throughout the United States, Europe, South American, the Middle East and Africa.

Geva Theatre Center (585-232-4382, www.gevatheatre.org, 75 Woodbury Blvd., Rochester, NY 14607) The Geva is Rochester's leading professional theater and the most attended regional theater in New York State. The 552-seat Elaine P. Wilson Mainstage offers a wide variety of shows from musicals to American and world classics. The 180-seat Ron & Donna Fielding Nextstage is home to Geva Comedy Improv, American Voices New Play Reading Series, Hibernatus Interuptus Festival of New Plays, the Hornets' Nest Series of New Plays, and a three-play series of cutting-edge theater.

Rochester Broadway Theatre League (585-222-5000, www.rbtl.org, 885 East Main St., Rochester, NY 14605) The Broadway Theatre League, which celebrated its 50th anniversary in 2008, is the company behind the scene of many Rochester arts and entertainment events. The 1930 Auditorium Theatre is home to major touring Broadway shows, music concerts, comedy shows, and children's events.

Rochester Philharmonic Orchestra (www.rpo.org, 585-454-2100, 108 East Ave., Rochester, NY 14604) Rochester has had a long tradition of fine orchestral music and the Rochester Philharmonic Orchestra plays a variety of classical, popular, family, and education concerts. The season runs from October through May with concerts at the Eastman Theatre and throughout the community. The orchestra also performs in the summer at the Constellation Brands-Marvin Sands Performing Arts Center in Canandaigua.

The Little Theatre (585-258-0444, www.thelittle.org, 240 East Ave., Rochester, NY 14604) Opened in 1929 and listed on the National Register of Historic Places, the theater was designed to provide an intimate alternative to the large commercial movie houses of the day. Today it is an independent art house offering the best of independent and foreign films. It also hosts exhibits of local artists, music performances and is home to a vibrant café offering casual meals, wine, micro-brewed beer, and live music nightly.

RECREATION

Cruises

Corn Hill Navigation (585-262-5661, www.samandmary.org, P.O. Box 18417, Rochester, NY 14618) The historic wooden vessel *Mary Jemison* is operated by this nonprofit company. Cruises featuring a live onboard historical narrative are offered daily from May to October and depart from Corn Hill Landing in downtown Rochester. There are also specialty cruises featuring wine tasting, history programs, and holiday celebrations.

Harbor Town Belle (585-342-1810 or 800-836-8930, www.harbortownbelle.com, Charlotte Pier, Rochester, NY 14612) The *Harbor Town Belle* is an 80-foot paddle wheeler that cruises the Genesee River, Irondequoit Bay, and Lake Ontario from the Charlotte Pier next to Ontario Beach Park. Sightseeing cruises, dinner cruises, and themed cruises are offered.

Rose Lummis (716-830-7555, www.roselummis.com, 5060 Ellicott Street Road, Batavia) The *Rose Lummis* is a 55-foot-long 1953 Mississippi River tour boat with an open upper observation deck. The boat departs from Spencerport and cruises the Erie Canal to Brockport. On Thursdays the *Rose Lummis* cruises to the **Adams Basin Inn** for lunch and a tour of the inn.

Wild Hearts **Charters** (585-671-7173 or 800-979-3370, www.wildheartscharters.com, 134 Guy Grace Lane, Webster, NY 14580) Sail on Lake Ontario from the Port of Rochester aboard the 53-foot, 49-passenger catamaran *Wild Hearts*. One-hour, two-hour, sunset, private, and corporate- charter cruises are available.

Fishing

Seth Green, known as the "father of fishes," was born in Rochester in 1817 and is credited with inventing the fishing reel. Nowadays Rochester and Lake Ontario have gained international fame in fishing circles for trophy salmon, steelhead, brown trout, lake trout, and bass. Many anglers dunk a line on Ontario Beach Park's pier for an hour or two or in the Genesee River. But for serious fishing, there are more than a dozen area fishing operations offering half- or full-day charters.

Dream Catcher Charters (585-314-2407, www.rochestercharters.com) Captain Sam Zucco offers half-, full- and extended-day charters from the Port of Rochester aboard the 1998 *Dream Catcher*, a 30-foot Penn Yan that seats eight people. All fishing equipment is provided.

Rodmaster Sportfishing Charters (585-455-5901, www.rodmastercharters.com) Captain Mike Pastore offers a variety of fishing charters on Lake Ontario aboard the *Rodmaster*, a 33-foot Trojan that can accommodate six people. Fishing equipment is provided.

Parks

Genesee Valley Park (585-753-7275, www.monroecounty.gov/parks-geneseevalley.php, 1000 E. River Rd., Rochester, NY 14620) This Frederick Law Olmsted–designed park is dominated by three intersecting waterways: Red Creek, the Genesee River, and the Erie Canal. There are baseball diamonds, soccer fields, a cricket field, and two 18-hole golf courses.

Highland Park (585-753-7275, www.monroecounty.gov/parks-highland.php, 171 Reservoir Ave., Rochester, NY 14620) Designed by famed landscape architect Frederick Law Olmsted, Highland Park is home to the world-famous Lilac Festival in May. Wander among more than 1,200 lilac bushes; 700 varieties of rhododendron, azaleas, mountain laurel, and andromeda; spring bulbs, wildflowers, a rock garden, and a large number of trees. The park's pansy bed features 10,000 plants, designed into an oval floral "carpet" with a new pattern each year. Other attractions are the **Lamberton Conservatory, Warner Castle and Sunken Garden**, and **Highland Park Bowl**, an amphitheater used for summer concerts, movies, and Shakespeare in the Park.

Ontario Beach Park (585-753-7275, www.monroecounty.gov/parks-ontariobeach.php, 4,650 Lake Ave., Rochester, NY 14612) Once known as the Coney Island of the West, Ontario Beach Park is one of Monroe County's shining jewels. It boasts an expansive white-sand beach plus a boardwalk, bathhouse, pier, boat launch, beach volleyball courts, playgrounds, picnic areas, and the historic **Dentzel Menagerie Carousel**—with its 52 riding animals and two chariots—that has been a centerpiece of the park since 1905. During the summer there are regular concerts by the shore.

Spectator Sports

Rochester Americans Hockey Club (585-454-5335, www.amerks.com, Blue Cross Arena, 100 Exchange St., Rochester, NY 14614) Established in 1956, the Rochester Americans, known as the Amerks, is one of the oldest franchises in the American Hockey League. The Florida Panthers is the parent team of the Amerks.

Rochester Knighthawks Lacrosse (585-454-5335, www.knighthawks.net, Blue Cross Arena, 100 Exchange St., Rochester, NY 14614) This National Lacrosse League team has won the league championship twice. The team plays from December through April.

Rochester Red Wings Baseball (585-454-1001, www.redwingsbaseball.com, Frontier Field, 1 Morrie Silver Way, Rochester, NY 14608) Professional baseball has had a long history in Rochester, dating back to 1877. This Triple-A farm team of the Minnesota Twins has been known as the Red Wings since 1929.

Some of the beautifully carved animals on Ontario Beach Park's Dentzel Carousel

Rochester Rattlers (585-454-5335, www.rochesterrattlers.com, Cross Arena, 100 Exchange St., Rochester, NY 14614) This major-league outdoor lacrosse team plays May through August at the downtown PAETEC Park, 460 Oak Street.

Rochester Rhinos Soccer (585-454-5425, www.rhinossoccer.com, 460 Oak St., Rochester, NY 14608) This outdoor soccer team plays at PAETEC Park.

SHOPPING

There are large suburban malls as well as boutiques and specialty shops in canal towns and along Park, Monroe, and University avenues in Rochester.

Craft Antique Co-op (585-368-0670, www.craftantiqueco-op.com, 3200 Ridge Rd., West, Rochester, NY 14626) This is New York's largest, most unique craft and antiques co-op, offering something for everyone from sportsmen to doll collectors to the purveyor of antique tools. There are more than 250 shops filled with antiques, crafts, and collectibles as well as a design center of 15 decorated room settings. It is also the home of the Dickens Christmas Festival. Open year-round Thursday to Sunday.

Eastview Mall (585-223-4420, www.eastviewmall.com, 7979 Pittsford-Victor Rd. [NY 96], Victor, NY 14564) This regional shopping center (just off the New York State Thruway, Exit 45) caters to an upscale clientele with some 30 stores that are unique to the market, including Coldwater Creek, Pottery Barn, Coach, Apple, J. Crew, and Williams-Sonoma. More than 180 stores, six restaurants—among them Bonefish Grill, Champps Americana, and P. F. Chang's China Bistro—and a Regal Cinema round out the mall.

House of Guitars (585-544-3500, www.houseofguitars.com, 645 Titus Ave., Rochester, NY 14617) Known as HOG Heaven or House of Guitars, this is a complex of five warehouses packed with everything from guitars to a pair of Elvis's leather pants. Opened in 1964 by three brothers, the music emporium has hosted a list of customers that includes Metallica, Aerosmith, Mötley Crüe, Jon Bon Jovi, and Ozzy Osbourne. The self-proclaimed "World's Largest Music Store" stocks just about every kind and brand of instrument, including more than 11,000 guitars that range in price from $60 to $50,000.

The Mall at Greece Ridge (585-225-0430, www.themallatgreeceridge.com, 271 Greece Ridge Center Dr., Rochester, NY 14626) More than 150 specialty stores, 5 anchors, and 7 big-box retailers make up this mall, including The Gap, Barnes & Noble, Bed Bath & Beyond, Old Navy, H&M, Marshalls, Macy's, Target, and Circuit City. Friendly's Restaurant, TGI Friday's, and Critic's Restaurant are among the eateries, and Regal Cinemas provides movie entertainment.

The Marketplace Mall (585-475-0757, www.themarketplacemall.com, 1 Miracle Mile Dr., Rochester, NY 14623) There are 140 specialty stores, 5 anchors, and the area's largest selection of teen apparel stores. Stores include Abercrombie & Fitch, American Eagle, Banana Republic, Lands' End, New York & Co., Victoria's Secret, and Urban Behavior.

Birthplace of Jell-O

Is there a more quintessential American food than Jell-O? Its birth and development is celebrated in its hometown of LeRoy—30 miles from Rochester—at the **Jell-O Gallery.**

The Jell-O Gallery opened in 1997, the centennial of Jell-O's birth. The story of Jell—a tribute to American marketing genius—is told in posters, exhibits, and displays. Though small, the museum offers an entertaining look at the history of this American icon.

Pearle Wait, a carpenter in LeRoy, was putting up a cough remedy and laxative tea in his home. He experimented with gelatin and came up with a fruit-flavored dessert that his wife, May, named Jell-O. He tried to market his product but lacked the capital and experience. So he sold his formula to fellow townsman Orator Frank Woodward for $450 on September 9, 1899. Woodward certainly made one of history's best business deals. In 10 years the company posted sales of more than a million dollars, and 4 years later that number doubled. In 1925 the Woodward family sold their Jell-O stock for more than $60 million. The company moved to Dover, Delaware, in 1964, where Jell-O is manufactured by Kraft/General Foods.

Some fun Jello-O facts: Immigrants at Ellis Island were served bowls of Jell-O under a sign that read "Welcome to America." (This classic photograph graces a wall with the explanation that Jell-O was seen as a unifying food.) More Jell-O is sold per capita in Utah than anywhere else in the country. On February 1, 2001, Bill Cosby appeared before the Utah legislature to support a bill declaring Jell-O the official state snack. It passed.

Listen to entertainers Kate Smith, Jack Benny, and Lucille Ball as they promoted Jell-O over the radio. See Andy Griffith, Gomer Pyle (Jim Nabors), and Bill Crosby on TV pitching Jell-O. A notebook invites visitors to contribute memorable Jell-O moments. One standout note from an anonymous visitor: "Jell-O saved my life after a flare-up of ulcerative colitis." Hard to top that, but many visitors contribute favorite family recipes.

Visit the Jell-O Gallery (585-768-7433, www.jellogallery.com) at 23 East Main Street (behind the Historic LeRoy House), LeRoy, NY 14482. The museum is open daily between April 1and December 31, weekdays from January 1 to March 31. Admission: adults $4, children $1.50.

PITTSFORD

Pittsford is a bustling Erie Canal village with one of the earliest and best-preserved collections of 19th-century structures in the region. Just a few miles down the canal from Fairport, the village was designated a "National Historic Preserve America Community" in 2005.

The village was a stagecoach trading post and a center of life on New York's western frontier. Pittsford grew rapidly after the opening of the Erie Canal, incorporating as a village on July 4, 1827. Local entrepreneurs made fortunes from both canal construction and other businesses that benefited from the canal trade. Pittsford's collection of Federal-era buildings is evidence of the prosperity the community enjoyed during this period.

Boosted by the arrival of the Rochester & Auburn Railroad in 1834, Pittsford remained an important shipping center for local grains and produce until the mid-20th century. Today's waterfront is due to the survival of historic canal warehouses, mills, and silos, many of which have been renovated as boutiques and restaurants.

In the second half of the 19th century, wealthy Rochester residents began to establish country estates in and around the village. These estates were the first step in Pittsford's evolution from a farming community to a suburb. Three of these grand homes remain within the village. Pittsford Farms, the oldest of the three village estates, was established in the 1860's by Jarvis Lord, a canal contractor. The property has retained its historic appearance and remains a 200-acre working farm. The farm's dairy plant continues to bottle milk in returnable glass containers.

Since the mid-1800s, Schoen Place alongside the Erie Canal has been a center of commerce in the village. Named for Joseph Schoen, a successful produce wholesaler and coal dealer, it was the place where residents came for provisions, loading up their wagons with coal and produce. The opening of the Erie Canal bought with it an increased demand for coal. To meet the demand, Joseph Schoen and his brother, Charles, built a coal storage silo, from which they serviced residents and canal boats.

Pittsford is one of the canal communities that parallels the original Erie Canal. The

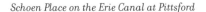

Schoen Place on the Erie Canal at Pittsford

depression in the yards of homes along South Street marks the original canal. Pick up a copy of a village walking tour in the 1819 **Little House Museum** just behind Schoen Place. It is now the home of Historic Pittsford, a historic-preservation organization. The walking tour takes about an hour.

The first stop on the tour is the **Phoenix Hotel** building just across the street. Built in 1807, it served as a hotel until the early 1900s. Daniel Webster, General Lafayette, Commodore Vanderbilt, and Governor DeWitt Clinton are all believed to have been guests. During Civil War days it was a stop on the Underground Railroad, connecting with a cavern.

Visitors can step back in time on the *Sam Patch,* a tour boat designed as an old-fashioned canal packet boat. Long and narrow to accommodate the constricted demands of the early canal, packet boats were pulled by mules or horses, carried mostly passengers, and provided food and sleeping quarters. They were the fastest way to travel, often exceeding the 4 mph speed limit, and were given priority at the locks.

Sam Patch is named for the colorful daredevil who jumped Rochester's Genesee Falls. Although Patch had twice jumped Niagara Falls and survived, he failed to surface after leaping 97 feet to the base of the Genesee Falls on Friday, November 13, 1829. His body was recovered at the mouth of the Genesee River the following spring.

The entertainer Cher traveled on the *Sam Patch* while visiting the area for a concert performance, and her photo is displayed on the boat. She also visited the nearby Pittsford **Wegmans** market dressed as, well, Cher—creating a memorable experience for the day's shoppers. This Wegmans, considered the flagship of the Rochester-based award-winning supermarket chain, features Tastings, an elegant, open-kitchen restaurant. The Food Network honored Wegmans as the Grocery Store Chain That Most Changed the Way We Shop.

Sam Patch tours depart from Pittsford's Schoen Place on the Erie Canal and are offered daily from May to October. Cruises feature a live onboard historical narrative. For more information contact Corn Hill Navigation (585-262-5661; www. samandmary.org, P.O. Box 18417, Rochester, NY 14618).

Sam Patch *cruising in Pittsford*

LODGING

Brookwood Inn Pittsford (585-248-9000, www.thebrookwoodinn.com, 800 Pittsford-Victor Rd., Pittsford, NY 14534) The 108-room Brookwood Inn, just a mile from the Erie Canal, was recently renovated and offers a number of amenities, including complimentary high-speed Internet and an indoor pool. Rooms include a sitting area with a pullout sofa. Each of the five suites is individually decorated. The Oriental Suite has Eastern decor, a living room, and kitchenette. The Manhattan Suite is perfect for honeymooners or business travelers, with a living room, dining room, refrigerator, microwave, two wide-screen TVs, and a whirlpool bathtub with a skylight. The on-site **Peter Geyer Steakhouse Restaurant & Pub** is a New York–style steakhouse, serving lighter fare in the pub. There are slate fireplaces and an extensive wine list. The inn offers free shuttle service to the Rochester Airport and local businesses.

Del Monte Lodge (585-381-9900 or 866-237-5979, www.marriott.com, 41 North Main St., Pittsford, NY 14534) This Renaissance Hotel & Spa overlooks the Erie Canal and rates as one of the top hotels on the canal. There are 97 rooms and two suites; beds sport custom duvets, pillows, and luxury linens. The award-winning **Erie Grill** serves an innovative menu with fresh local ingredients. Enjoy complimentary high-speed Internet, an indoor pool, full-service spa, and an on-site fitness center. In addition, guests have complimentary use of the nearby Midtown Athletic Club, with free fitness classes and tennis courts.

RESTAURANTS

Crystal Barn (585-381-4844, www.crystalbarn.com, 2851 Clover St., Pittsford, NY 14534) This is an authentic 1860 country barn, decorated with a pleasant blend of crystal chandeliers and Victorian motifs. The menu features a number of special dishes, including antelope medallions, sole Wellington, and mixed grill of game with antelope, quail, and wild boar chop. There are also many old favorites such as New York strip steak, filet mignon, king crab legs, and grilled Pacific ahi tuna. The wonderful array of desserts includes chocolate decadence truffle, peanut butter fudge pie, and deep-dish caramel granny apple pie. A lighter bistro menu is served all day.

Simply Crepes (585-383-8310, www.simplycrepes.com, 7 Shoen Pl., Pittsford, NY 14534) Located alongside the canal in Pittsford's historic Schoen Place, this is a perfect waterfront eatery. Here you can enjoy crepes of all types all day long: strawberry crepes, raspberry crepes, breakfast crepes with scrambled eggs, smoked salmon crepes, ham and asparagus crepes, turkey and smoked Gouda crepes, and buffalo chicken crepes, to name a few. The dessert crepes are equally wonderful, with such delicious choices as chocolate mousse, berries and crème, fudge brownie, and peaches and cream. Half portions of dessert crepes are available. Where else could you order oatmeal crème brûlée (fresh oatmeal topped with crème brûlée, bananas, and fresh berries)? Drinks include fresh fruit smoothies, blended ice drinks, and frozen hot chocolate. The wine list includes many Finger Lakes wines. Enjoy Sunday summer sails on the catamaran *Wild Hearts,* with a menu of fresh strawberry crepes.

Richardson's Canal House (585-248-5000, www.richardsonscanalhouse.com, 1474 Marsh Rd., Pittsford, NY 14534) This is a real Erie Canal jewel: the oldest original inn on the canal and listed on the National Register of Historic Places. Built in 1818, this pioneer canal hostelry was known as Bushnell's Basin Hotel; it served as a public house for more than 100 years. Prohibition forced its closing, and the building was converted to a private home, then abandoned. It even had a brief run as a nudist colony. Finally restored, it was reopened in 1979 as Richardson's Canal House. Boaters can dock next door, and diners can watch the boats cruising along the waterway. Outside dining is available. The menu changes seasonally and features such favorites as beef tenderloin, rack of lamb, salmon, Block Island swordfish, and pork tenderloin. There is also a lighter bistro menu. Desserts include crème brûlée, a perfect lemon tart, and chocolate mousse.

Tastings Restaurant (585-381-1881, www.wegmans.com/tastings, 3195 Monroe Ave., Pittsford, NY 14618) Owned and operated by the award-winning and nationally recognized Wegmans supermarket, Tastings is next door to the chain's flagship store in Pittsford. Chefs at Tastings like to boast that they have some of the freshest and widest selection of ingredients of any dining establishment anywhere, since the entire market is at their disposal. The menu changes frequently to reflect the best seasonal items. Special events are staged regularly, and diners are invited to learn more about wine or hobnob with a celebrity chef. There are also seasonal tasting menus. Dinner choices include such items as seared rare tuna, barbecued quail, and lamb loin.

FAIRPORT

Fairport, a Rochester suburb, rates as one of the crown jewels of the Erie Canal. It boasts an award-winning winery, a downtown bridge that has made it into *Ripley's Believe It or Not!* 16 times, a picturesque business district full of shops and restaurants, and the *Colonial Belle,* one of the canal's largest tour boats.

According to a popular story, the village got its name from an early traveler who stopped at Mallet's Tavern. As he was enjoying refreshments, the traveler was overheard to comment, "This is truly a fair port." When the village was incorporated in 1867, officials recalled his observation and named it Fairport. From the beginning of the canal's operation, Fairport served as a port for farmers to bring their goods for shipment. Later it became a booming industrial town.

Recreational boaters and tour boats have replaced the packet boats and barges of the past. There's modern overnight docking facilities for 30 boats right in the center of the village. The **Colonial Belle,** a tour boat under the direction of affable Captain Lee Poinan, occupies a prime spot along the canal. Offering two- and three-hour cruises on the canal, the boat passes under the famous Fairport Lift Bridge. Its claim to fame is that it is the only lift bridge in the world built on a bias. The south end is higher than the north end. No two angles in the bridge are the same, and no corners on the bridge floor are square. The boat clears the railroad bridge in Pittsford by inches. Everyone on the upper deck is ordered to sit down and duck—proving the truth of the classic canal song refrain, "Low bridge, everybody down." The *Colonial Belle* offers many theme cruises, as well as lunch and dinner cruises. The Sunday afternoon cruises feature Fred Vine playing his guitar and a selection of canal-related songs. (For more information about *Colonial Belle* tours call 585-223-9470 or visit www.colonialbelle.com.)

LODGING

Woodcliff Hotel & Spa (585-381-4000, www.woodcliffhotelspa.com, 199 Woodcliff Dr., Fairport, NY 14450) Located atop wooded hills about a mile from the Erie Canal, this 234-

Colonial Belle *under the Lift Bridge in Fairport*

room hotel has it all. There are 12 whirlpool suites, a business center, indoor and outdoor pools, a whirlpool, a nine-hole golf course, full-service spa, and a comprehensive fitness center, including professional instructors for fitness consultations and one-on-one training. Complimentary high-speed Internet is available. The Crescent Trail, directly behind the hotel, has 9 miles of trails for walking, hiking, or cross-country skiing. Also on site are the **Horizons Restaurant** and the **Horizons Lounge**, with weekend entertainment. Located 20 minutes from downtown Rochester and offering spectacular views of the city skyline, Woodcliff is a popular place for meetings and weddings.

PALMYRA
Palmyra's historic Main Street boasts four elegant churches with their distinctive spires, one on each corner. The site earned the Erie Canal village a place in *Ripley's Believe It or Not!*

A Special Winery

The award-winning Fairport **Casa Larga Vineyards** (585-223-4210, www.casalarga.com, 2287 Turk Hill Rd., Fairport, NY 14450) is Monroe County's only winery. The late Andrew Colaruotolo, a home-builder and native of Italy, started the vineyard in 1974 as a hobby, naming the winery after a vineyard his grandparents owned in Gaeta, Italy. The first wine in 1978 was an estate white wine that won a silver medal in a New York State competition. The winery has since expanded to 45 acres, and it has been winning awards ever since. Ice wines are one of the winery's specialties, rated among the world's best. The founder's wife and children are continuing the business. Tours are offered throughout the year, and there is a gift shop and expansive views from the winery, located on a hill sandwiched between Lake Ontario and Canandaigua Lake. The gift shop offers an unusual item: wine ice cream in four flavors (made with real wine). The annual **Purple Foot Grape Stomping Festival,** a very popular event, is held in September.

as the only place in the United States with a major church on each corner of a main intersection.

But it is the corner **Western Presbyterian Church** that can rightly claim a place in world history. British Prime Minister Winston Churchill's maternal grandparents, Leonard Jerome and Clarissa Hall, were married in this handsome white-columned building on April 5, 1849. Their beautiful daughter Jenny met and married Lord Randolph Churchill on a summer trip to Europe, and the couple's son Winston went on to become the famous World War II leader and British prime minister. Winston Churchill claimed Indian blood through his great-great grandmother Anna Wilcox (Clarissa's grandmother). He even had ancestors who fought the British in the American Revolution.

The village was named Palmyra after an ancient trade-route city in Syria. A thriving village when the canal came through in 1822, Palmyra soon became known as the "Queen of Erie Canal Towns." It was the setting for the Samuel Hopkins Adams novel *Canal Town,* later made into a Hollywood movie.

A waterside general store opened in 1826 to take advantage of the canal trade. In 1868 William Phelps bought the store and named it after himself. He and his family lived upstairs. After his death, his son Julius ran the store until he closed it in the 1940s. The family continued to live upstairs, and Julius's only daughter, Sibyl, lived on in the building until her death in 1976. The store and the upstairs living quarters are now a museum.

According to Bonnie Hays, executive director of Historic Palmyra, the organization that took over the former general store in 1977, "There was no electricity and no running water except what was supplied by a cistern. Sibyl was so excited when new streetlights were put in so she was able to see to read at night."

Another relic from Palmyra's past is the **Aldrich Towing-Path Change Bridge**. Volunteers were involved in rescuing and restoring the oldest iron bridge in New York State. First erected in 1858, it allowed the towpath to switch from one side of the canal to the other. The bridge now stands in **Aqueduct Park**, part of the hiking trail that runs along the canal. Nearby is Lock 29.

The community is world famous as the birthplace of the Mormon religion. Palmyra was the home of Joseph Smith Jr., founder of the Church of Jesus Christ of Latter-day Saints, and the town draws visitors from around the globe who come to see the historic places that are integral to the church.

Interactive video and audio displays as well as films at the Hill Cumorah Visitors' Center offer a good introduction to the beliefs of the church as well as to important area sites. A memorial to the Angel Moroni stands at the top of the hill. This is also the location of the famous **Hill Cumorah Pageant** (www.hillcumorah.org/pageant), where every year in July, hundreds of thousands of the faithful and curious make pilgrimages to witness the giant spectacle that constitutes the largest outdoor theatrical production in the U.S. The show sports a costumed cast of 700, a nine-level stage, and music by the Mormon Tabernacle Choir. The striking **Palmyra Temple** sits on a high ridge at the east end of the original 100 acres of the Joseph Smith Sr. farm. Only Mormons in good standing are allowed to enter the temple.

Back on Main Street is the restored Grandin Printing Shop, open to visitors. It was here in 1829 that Joseph Smith Jr. and publisher Egbert B. Grandin signed a contract to publish the Book of Mormon. The printing press was shipped along the Erie Canal from Vermont.

Historic Palmyra church played a role in Winston Churchill's family history

LODGING

Canaltown B&B (315-597-5553, www.canaltownbb.com, 119 Canandaigua St., Palmyra, NY 14522) This antiques-furnished home offers two guest rooms. Built in 1855, the home is within walking distance of Palmyra's museums and the Erie Canal. A full candlelit breakfast is included.

Liberty House B&B (315-597-0011, www.libertyhousebb.com, 131 West Main St., Palmyra, NY 14522) This home is a splendid example of Victorian Italianate architecture, featuring a cupola, gingerbread embellishment, and a wraparound porch. There are three air-conditioned rooms, including one on the first floor. The original house was built in the 1840s, and in 1879 it was transformed into the gem it is today. Children are welcome, and a full gourmet breakfast is provided. The house is within walking distance of the canal and village museums.

Palmyra Inn (315-597-8888 or 800-426-9900, www.palmyrainn.com, 955 Canandaigua Rd., Palmyra, NY 14522) This inn offers 60 rooms, all with kitchenettes. There is complimentary high-speed Internet, a continental breakfast, and a fitness center. The inn is just a five-minute walk from the historic Mormon sites the **Sacred Grove** and the Palmyra Temple. A free shuttle service transports guests to local attractions.

Thomas Galloway House B&B (315-597-6742, www.paragonfarm.com, 993 Cornwall Rd., Palmyra, NY 14522) The house was built in 1855 by masons who worked on the Erie Canal, and the home remains largely original. It is located in a bucolic setting on Paragon Farm, complete with sheep and llamas. The **Milkhouse Gift Shop** stocks spinning fibers, yarns from the farm's own flock, handcrafted items, tanned sheepskins, handmade Amish quilts, rug-hooking supplies, and locally made maple syrup. Each of the six rooms has original hardwood floors and large windows with views of the farmland, pastures, and woods. The house is furnished with antiques. A full country breakfast with the farm's own fresh eggs, homemade jams, and baked goods is included.

RESTAURANTS

Lock 29 Tavern (315-597-0286, www.lock29.com, 222 E. Main St. Palmyra, NY 14522) Named after the Palmyra canal lock just a short distance away, Lock 29 Tavern is a comfortable, fun place to eat, drink, and have a great time. There are live bands and special events regularly. Friday is karaoke night. The open kitchen lets you see your burger or wings cooking. Open daily for lunch and dinner.

Muddy Waters Café (315-502-4197, Division St. at the Marina, Palmyra, NY 14522) This café is directly on the canal and serves fresh-baked pastries, breakfast, sandwiches, and soup and salads.

ATTRACTIONS

Alling Coverlet Museum (315-597-6981, www.historicpalmyrany.com, 122 Market St., Palmyra, NY 14522) This museum houses the country's largest collection of handwoven coverlets. Named after Rochester resident and coverlet collector Mrs. Merle Alling, this museum is housed in a 1901 newspaper printing office and opened its doors on July 4, 1976, as a bicentennial project. It takes more than six years to rotate and display the entire collection of 370 coverlets. The museum also has a sizable quilt collection. Open daily; adults $2 ($5 for trail ticket to four museums), children $1 ($2 for trail ticket).

Grandin Printing Shop (315-597-5982, www.hillcumorah.org 217 E. Main St., Palmyra, NY 14522) This 1828 building was known as Thayer and Grandin's Row. It was here that Joseph Smith, the founder of the Church of Jesus Christ of Latter-day Saints, and Egbert B. Grandin, an aspiring young publisher, signed a contract to publish the Book of Mormon in 1829. The building has been restored, and visitors can see the printing presses and bindery. Open daily; free admission.

Hill Cumorah Visitors' Center and Mormon Historic Sites (315-597-5851, www.hill cumorah.org, 603 NY 21, Palmyra, NY 14522) Stop here first before visiting the Mormon historic sites. It is built at the foot of Hill Cumorah, the site of the famous summer pageant. There are free guided tours and displays with interactive audio and video telling the story of the origins of the Church of Jesus Christ of Latter-day Saints. Feature-length films are shown daily. Open daily; free admission.

Joseph Smith Farm Welcome Center (315-597-1671, www.hillcumorah.org, 843 Stafford Rd., Palmyra, NY 14522) There are daily guided tours of the re-created Smith family log home, frame home, and the Sacred Grove. It was in the Sacred Grove that Joseph Smith prayed and later showed his family and friends the gold plates from which the Book of Mormon was translated. Open daily; free admission.

Palmyra Historical Museum (315-597-6981, www.historicpalmyrany.com, 132 Market St., Palmyra, NY 14522) The building began life in 1826 as the St. James Hotel & Tavern. Remodeled in 1898, and moved to its present location in 1981, the museum features 23 themed rooms that tell the story of Palmyra. Open Tuesday through Saturday. Admission: adults $2 ($5 for trail ticket to four museums), children $1 ($2 for trail ticket).

Wm. Phelps General Store & Home Museum (315-597-6981, www.historicpalmyrany .com, 140 Market St., Palmyra, NY 14522) This store is a place where time stopped. Meet the Phelps family, who lived and worked here for 108 years. Enter through the 1826 Erie Canal doors where locals and travelers alike would come to purchase provisions. Open Tuesday through Saturday. Admission: adults $2 ($5 for trail ticket to four museums), children $1 ($2 for trail ticket).

Trinity Episcopal Church, on the Cayuga-Seneca Canal in Seneca Falls

5

Cayuga-Seneca Canal

Aurora, Ithaca, Seneca Falls, Geneva, Watkins Glen

The 12-mile-long Cayuga-Seneca Canal connects the two largest Finger Lakes with the Erie Canal—and, via the Erie, with the waterways of the world. Lush vineyards border these deep-blue lakes, and the Cayuga-Seneca Canal boasts two wine trails. The area is also the lake trout capital of the world, home of a major Ivy League university, and the birthplace of the women's rights movement.

The canal provides access to Cayuga Lake (the longest of the Finger Lakes, at 38.2 miles) and Seneca Lake (at 618 feet, the deepest of the lakes). Splendid lakeside state parks offer camping, picnicking, hiking, biking, wind surfing, sailing, waterskiing and snow skiing (cross-country and downhill), boating, fishing, hunting, bird-watching, swimming, and scuba diving.

The earliest known inhabitants of the region were Algonquin Indians. They were succeeded by the Cayugas of the Iroquois Nation. Those early Americans derived part of their livelihood from the wildlife and plants of the area's bountiful marshes.

Prior to the turn of the 20th century, the Montezuma Marsh—one of the most productive in North America—extended north from Cayuga Lake for 12 miles and was as much as 8 miles wide. Unfortunately, as with most wetlands during that era, the importance of the marsh was unrecognized. Construction of a nearby dam and changes to rivers during the building of today's canal system contributed to the loss of the marsh. By the early 1900s all but a few hundred acres had been drained.

In 1937 the Bureau of Biological Survey, which later became the U.S. Fish and Wildlife Service, purchased 7,000 acres of the former marsh. The Civilian Conservation Corps began work on a series of low dikes that would hold water and restore part of the marsh. Such restoration and preservation efforts continue today.

The Montezuma National Wildlife Refuge is located near the junction of the Erie and Cayuga-Seneca canals. It was established as a refuge and breeding ground for migratory birds and other wildlife as part of the Atlantic Flyway migration route. During the spring and fall migrations, thousands of waterfowl and shorebirds stop by. In summer Canada Geese and great blue herons nest in the refuge. After their initial release during the 1970s, bald eagles have returned to Montezuma yearly and successfully reared their young.

At the southern boundary of the refuge is the first of the Cayuga-Seneca Canal's four locks. At this point boaters can continue south on Cayuga Lake or head west on the canal, which links the north end of Cayuga Lake with the north end of Seneca Lake. The pace is

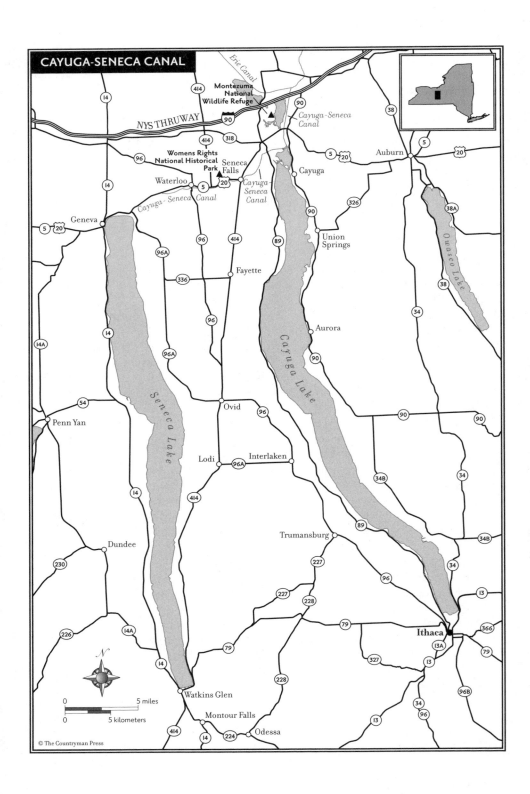

slow here, with an occasional blue heron along the water's edge. The elevation difference between Cayuga and Seneca lakes is 64 feet. Two locks with 25 feet of lift each form a double lock. The last gates open onto Van Cleef Lake in Seneca Falls.

Here we will explore the area around Cayuga Lake, the longest of the 11 Finger Lakes. Its name, translated from the Iroquois, means "boat landing."

AURORA

Dolls—the American Girl dolls, to be precise—are responsible for transforming tiny Aurora, home to Wells College, about halfway down the eastern shore of Cayuga Lake. A road sign outside the village of 750 proclaims: WHAT'S NEW IN AURORA? EVERYTHING. Old-time visitors would recognize the 19th-century brick and stone facades, but inside, just about everything is, indeed, new—or beautifully restored.

Settlers arrived in the area in the late 1790s and founded Aurora on the site of a Cayuga Indian village called Deawendote ("village of constant dawn"). The following century, in 1868, Henry Wells, pioneer of Wells Fargo & Co. and American Express, founded Wells College, overlooking Cayuga Lake. One of the country's oldest liberal arts colleges for women, Wells is a now a coed institution. The 450-student campus and most of the village are listed in the National Register of Historic Places.

Today, while retaining its bucolic charm, the village has been reborn, thanks in no small measure to the benevolence and vision of Pleasant T. Rowland, Wells College class of '62. Rowland's business acumen enabled her to finance the village's rebirth. In 1998 she sold the line of dolls and accessories she created in 1986, American Girl, to Mattel for some $700 million, and turned both her attention and resources to Aurora's renovation. She restored the historic lakefront Aurora Inn to an elegant and sumptuous establishment. Neighboring stores, pubs, and restaurants have also been renovated under her direction.

The **Aurora Inn and Restaurant** (315-364-8888, www.aurora-inn.com, 311 Main St., Aurora, NY 13026), a 10-room inn dating back to 1833, is a warm and inviting retreat that has been totally restored and renovated. Pleasant Rowland insisted on high-quality workmanship throughout, and it shows. Four rooms feature gas fireplaces; lakeside rooms

Charter canal boats tied up along the Cayuga-Seneca Canal

include a balcony with rocking chairs; two suites have skylights over a spacious whirlpool bathtub. All rooms have marble bathrooms, DVD/VCR players (movies are available for loan), and high-speed Internet access. Fires burn in the inn's public rooms during the cooler weather, while outside dining is available in warm weather. During any season, the dining room beckons, with expansive views of the lake. Rowland paid to relocate more than a dozen trees—some weighing as much as 60,000 pounds—that blocked the inn's water view. She also had 13 mature elms, each at least two stories tall, planted along Main Street. In the summer a cocktail cruise aboard the Constant Dream departs from the inn's dock.

Aurora has also benefited from the presence of **MacKenzie-Childs** (315-364-7123 or 888-665-1999, www.mackenzie-childs.com, 3260 NY 90, Aurora, NY 13026), an internationally acclaimed design firm where home furnishings are handcrafted by more than 200 artisans in a converted 19th-century dairy-farm setting. MacKenzie-Childs produces world-renowned whimsical majolica tableware and home furnishings. The 65-acre farm includes a production studio, a restored Victorian farmhouse, a duck pond, a Gothic Revival aviary, and a meadow where a herd of Scottish Highland cattle graze. The farmhouse has been totally restored and showcases MacKenzie-Childs designs in a variety of traditional interiors. Relax in the courtyard, where drinks and snacks are available during the summer. Stroll the magnificent, ever-changing gardens. The shop sells the complete line of MacKenzie-Childs products and gifts from around the world. Free studio-tour video and farmhouse tours daily; shop and grounds open daily.

ITHACA

The bumper stickers say it all: ITHACA IS GORGES.

From the lakeshore to the surrounding hillsides of Cornell University and Ithaca College, this city on the southern tip of Cayuga Lake is indeed spectacular. The educational institutions bring an international flavor and sophistication to Ithaca, which is really a small town at heart but is considered the intellectual and cultural capital of the Finger Lakes. Cornell, with more than 19,000 students enrolled in its 13 colleges and schools, has long been regarded as one of the most beautiful college campuses in the nation.

Ithaca is probably less well-known as the home of a Buddhist monastery where Courtney Love brought two handfuls of the ashes of her husband, Kurt Cobain, for a consecration ritual.

An Offbeat Look at Ithaca History

Visitors can step through time with a souvenir slide viewer called a HistoryCam, a palm-sized viewer that holds a dozen historical images of downtown Ithaca. These images are choreographed in a half-mile, self-guided walking tour that matches modern streetscapes with identical views from earlier centuries. The viewer comes with a booklet describing the historical significance of each site. Designed by the **History Center** in Tompkins County, the tour showcases images from the center's collection of more than 100,000 historical photographs. HistoryCams are available for $9.95 throughout the city in hotels, B&Bs, gift shops, visitor information centers, and at the History Center (607-273-8284; www.thehistorycenter.net; 401 E. State St., Ithaca, NY 14850. Open Tuesday, Thursday, and Saturday).

It is also a most family-friendly city. Downtown Ithaca abounds with seasonal festivals, concerts, and indoor and outdoor performances. The Commons, a pedestrian mall, is the centerpiece of downtown. The mall has an international flair, with more than 100 specialty shops, including several filled with imaginative and well-made toys from around the world.

Center Ithaca on the Commons features two levels of stores that surround a skylight-covered atrium café. The city is known for fine dining, having restaurants that offer a range of tastes to please every palate. The Sagan Planet Walk—named in memory of Cornell professor, NASA space adviser, and astronomer Carl Sagan—begins at the Commons and is a true-to-scale, walkable model of the solar system.

Between 1912 and 1920 the movie industry flourished in Ithaca, and the city's gorges were backdrops for many films. This is prime waterfall country (150 waterfalls grace the area, including some in the middle of the city), and some segments of *The Perils of Pauline* were filmed in Buttermilk Glen. Cool trails take hikers uphill and alongside Buttermilk Creek, which drops more than 500 feet in a series of cascades and rapids.

LODGING

Ithaca has the largest number of rooms in the Cayuga-Seneca Canal area, with chain hotels and motels, inns, and many historic bed & breakfasts. Cornell University has a well-known School of Hotel Administration, with its own hotel (the Statler), and some graduates have stayed to operate local inns and hotels. Special weekends (including Cornell graduations) have minimum-stay requirements, and reservations are needed far in advance. All price quotes are for double occupancy.

Lodging Rates
Inexpensive: Up to $75
Moderate: $76–$150
Expensive: $151–$250
Very Expensive: More than $250

LA TOURELLE RESORT AND SPA
607-273-2734
www.latourelle.com
1150 Danby Rd., Ithaca, NY 14850
Price: Expensive–Very Expensive
Credit Cards: Yes
Handicapped Access: Yes
Special Features: Pet friendly, spa

This is an elegant and luxurious 54-room resort and spa. There are pet-friendly rooms with private walk-out patios onto the surrounding grounds, providing easy access for a walk. For the ultimate in romantic getaways try the Tower Room. The shape is reminiscent of a palace turret. There's a queen-sized bed, mirrored ceilings, and a step-up Jacuzzi. Standard features include high-speed Internet. Many rooms have refrigerators. The **August Moon Spa** offers personalized spa treatments incorporating local ingredients, such as the Cayuga Cabernet Scrub, using crushed grape seeds from local wineries, and the Taughannock Falls and Buttermilk Falls body treatments. Massages include the Finger Lakes Grape Massage, using grape seed oil.

STATLER HOTEL AT CORNELL UNIVERSITY
607-257-2500
www.statlerhotel.cornell.edu
130 Statler Dr., Ithaca, NY 14853
Price: Expensive–Very Expensive
Credit Cards: Yes
Handicapped Access: Yes
Special Features: Use of Cornell's athletic facilities

The 153-room Statler is the teaching hotel of Cornell University's School of Hotel Administration. Located on the campus, this high-rise facility would be at home in a big city, with its marble floors, dark woods, and large modern rooms with views of the campus and countryside. Guests have access to Cornell's athletic facilities including an Olympic-sized swimming pool. There is an in-hotel fitness center and free high-speed Internet. Three restaurants are on the premises, as well as conference and banquet facilities. Guests speak glowingly of the student employees, who are rated as the best ambassadors for Cornell University.

TAUGHANNOCK FARMS INN

607-387-7711
www.t-farms.com
2030 Gorge Rd., Trumansburg, NY 14886
Price: Moderate—Very Expensive
Credit Cards: Yes
Handicapped Access: Yes
Special Features: Easy access to
Taughannock Falls State Park

The main building was built in 1873 as the summer home of John Jones, of Philadelphia, a wealthy resident and his family. Many of the lavish furnishings Jones brought with him are still in use today. When you enter the inn, take a look at the mammoth antique mirror on the right-hand wall of the entry. If you stand at just the right angle, you'll see little points of light, like stars, in the glass. That's diamond dust, a feature of mirrors made in the 19th century. The family lived on the property for 72 years. There was even a private horse-racing track for their enjoyment. In the 1930s most of the 600-acre estate was given to New York State for the creation of a state park. This Victorian mansion has five guest rooms with antique furnishings and four guest houses. In addition, there is a new ten-unit facility, Edgewood Guest House, designed to blend in with the property's historic ambiance. An award-winning restaurant is on the premises.

WILLIAM HENRY MILLER INN

607-256-4553
www.millerinn.com
303 N. Aurora St., Ithaca, NY 14850
Price: Expensive
Credit Cards: Yes
Handicapped Access: Yes
Special Features: Complimentary afternoon tea and evening dessert

Part of the East Hill Historic District, the main house was built as a private home in 1880 by Cornell University's first student of architecture, William Henry Miller. It is rich in architectural detail, with stained-glass and American chestnut windows, working fireplaces, seven spacious bedrooms, and large common areas. The carriage house, built in 1892, is directly behind the main house and has two additional bedrooms with private baths. Rooms are lovingly furnished with antiques and period reproductions. A favorite is the Library, featuring a queen cherry sleighbed, corner fireplace, bookshelves, and spacious sitting area. Gourmet breakfasts, served in the dining room or front porch, include a fruit course and a choice of two entrées, such as eggs scrambled with smoked salmon and dill, poached eggs with sun-dried tomato hollandaise, and crème brûlée French toast. Afternoon tea is served in the parlor, and evening dessert, including the inn's signature white chocolate brownies or freshly baked apple pie, is offered. Located in a residential area just off the Ithaca Commons, guests can walk to restaurants, shops, and nightlife.

RESTAURANTS

Ithaca offers more restaurants per capita than New York City, including the world-

The elegant William Henry Miller Inn

famous vegetarian Moosewood Restaurant. Its roster of diverse restaurants of various cuisines reflects the cosmopolitan tastes of area residents. Dine at the waterfront, in elegant country inns, or city bistros. All restaurants are by New York State law non-smoking. Prices are estimated per person for dinner entrée, without tax, tip, or beverage.

Dining Rates
Inexpensive: Up to $10
Moderate: $11–$25
Expensive: $26–$40
Very Expensive: More than $40

ANTLERS
607-273-9725
www.antlersrestaurant.com
1159 Dryden Rd., Ithaca, NY 14850
Open: Daily
Cuisine: American
Serving: D
Price: Moderate
Credit Cards: Yes

Handicapped Access: Yes
Special Features: Live music

Owned and operated by Toby McDonald and Bill Openshaw, a pair of Cornell grads, Antlers claims to be the oldest restaurant in Ithaca under continuous ownership. The menu includes many traditional items such as London broil, roast duckling, salmon, and pork ribs, as well as pasta, sandwiches, soups, and salads. There is live music on Sundays and Mondays. Every night there is a different special, including lobster on Thursdays and "fryless" fish fries on Fridays. Of course, there are lots of antlers on the hunter green walls.

DIJON BISTRO
607-256-0503
www.dijonbistro.com
311 Third St., Ithaca, NY 14850
Open: Daily
Cuisine: French bistro
Serving: D; L Mon.–Fri.
Price: Moderate
Credit Cards: Yes

Handicapped Access: Yes
Special Features: Extensive wine selection

This French bistro would be at home in Paris. Owner and chef Mark Papera, a graduate of Cornell University's School of Hotel Administration, spent years in New York City at various restaurants including the famed Windows on the World at the World Trade Center. He and his wife, Courtnay, opened Dijon in 2006, and soon attracted an enthusiastic local following. Lunch selections include the omelet of the day, poached salmon, mussels, open-faced sandwiches, and classic desserts including chocolate mousse, lemon tart, and crème brûlée. Dinner selections include steak, pork chops, chicken, and specials of the day such as bouillabaisse and coq au vin.

MAXIE'S SUPPER CLUB AND OYSTER BAR
607-272-4136
www.maxies.com
635 W. State St., Ithaca, NY 14850
Open: Daily
Cuisine: Cajun/seafood
Serving: D; Sun. brunch
Price: Moderate
Credit Cards: Yes
Handicapped Access: Yes
Special Features: Live music nightly

This is a lively, fun New Orleans–style restaurant that offers live music at night ranging from blues, jazz, and bluegrass, and serves some of Ithaca's best food. Every afternoon from 4 to 6 there are half-priced raw oysters and clams. This restaurant is popular with all sorts of folks and it serves up a good selection of Finger Lakes wines as well as microbrew beers. Are you craving some Cajun or southern comfort food? This place has it all, as well as a great staff who help make dining a memorable experience.

MOOSEWOOD RESTAURANT
607-273-9610
www.moosewoodrestaurant.com
215 N. Cayuga St., Ithaca, NY 14850
Open: Daily
Cuisine: Vegetarian
Serving: L, D
Price: Moderate
Credit Cards: Yes
Handicapped Access: Yes
Special Features: Outdoor dining

Moosewood has deservedly become a mecca for vegetarians through the internationally known Moosewood cookbooks, which have helped popularize its healthy menus. *Bon Appetit* magazine named Moosewood one of the 13 most influential restaurants of the 20th century. Now in its fourth decade, it is run by a collective that delivers imaginative cooking. The menu changes frequently but always features fresh, locally grown produce and whole grains. Fresh fish is also on the menu and there are popular kids' menus. Eat indoors or outdoors in-season.

TAUGHANNOCK FARMS INN
607-387-7711
www.t-farms.com
2030 Gorge Rd., Trumansburg, NY 14886
Open: Daily May–Oct.; Thurs.–Sun. Apr. and Nov.
Cuisine: American
Price: Moderate–Expensive
Credit Cards: Yes
Handicapped Access: Yes
Special Features: Lake views

This large Victorian inn across from Taughannock Falls State Park has an elegant dining room overlooking Cayuga Lake. The prix fixe menu includes appetizer, salad, entrée, and dessert—meals are traditional favorites such as New York strip, rack of lamb, prime rib, and the catch of the day. The desserts are all homemade, and there are more than a dozen selections. Time your visit to watch the sunset over the lake. Diners may overnight in the elegant inn (see "Lodging" section above).

Birthplace of the Ice Cream Sundae

One Sunday in 1892, Ithaca fountain owner Chester Platt served Rev. John M. Scott a surprising new treat: fresh vanilla ice cream topped with cherry syrup and a candied French cherry. Pronouncing the innovation delightful, Scott proposed it be named for the day it was created, and thus the "ice cream Sundae" was born. Today, other cities claim the discovery, but none offers documentation predating Ithaca's. An ad in the *Ithaca Daily Journal*, dated April 5, 1892, remains the oldest written record of America's favorite ice cream treat.

CULTURE

Ithaca can rightly claim to be the cultural center of the Finger Lakes, primarily because of Cornell University and Ithaca College. There are a range of unique museums, parks, and performing arts venues. Both educational institutions sponsor entertainment, sporting events, and other attractions open to the public.

Museums and Exhibits

Herbert F. Johnson Museum of Art (607-255-6464, www.museum.cornell.edu, Central and University Aves., Ithaca, NY 14853) The view alone makes a visit to this I. M. Pei–designed museum, on the campus of Cornell University, a must-see. It is built on the site where Ezra Cornell is said to have stood when he announced his intention to found a university. Sweeping views of Cayuga Lake, the campus, and Ithaca are offered from expansive windows on the third floor. The museum houses an impressive collection that spans forty centuries and five continents, with particular strengths in Asian and contemporary art. A new $17-million wing is currently under construction to provide more exhibit space. The museum's **Two Naked Guys Café,** named for the sculpture *Conflict* by William Zorach, which stands in the lobby, is open weekdays. Open Tuesday through Sunday; free admission.

Museum of the Earth (607-273-6623, www.museumoftheearth.org, 1259 Trumansburg Rd. [Rt. 96], Ithaca, NY 14850) Unique specimens include massive skeletons of the Hyde Park Mastodon and Right Whale #2030. Experience what life was like in three ancient worlds of New York State. Bring home a fossil. Touch and feel history by working with fossils at the Discovery stations. Witness passages of time through audiovisual presentations. Dinosaur fans will be able to immerse themselves in the dinosaurs that walked and lived in New York. The exhibit A Journey Through Time comprises the bulk of the museum and takes the visitor from the dawn of life on earth to present day. Open daily in summer; rest of year closed Tuesday and Wednesday. Adults $8, children $3.

Sagan Planet Walk (607-272-0600, www.sciencenter.org/saganpw, 601 First St., Ithaca, NY 14850) The "walk" is a scale model of the solar system extending along a three-quarter-mile route from the center of the Commons to the Sciencenter, a hands-on museum. The walk starts with a representation of the Sun and was created in memory of Ithaca resident and Cornell professor Carl Sagan, who was a founding member of the museum. Download a free audio tour from the Web site or buy a $2 "Passport to the Solar System" with facts about each planet. Passports are available at the Sciencenter, many downtown stores, and at the **Ithaca/Tompkins County Convention and Visitors Bureau** (607-272-1313, www.visitithaca.com, 904 E. Shore Dr., Ithaca, NY 14850).

Right Whale skeleton at Museum of the Earth

Sciencenter (607-272-0600, www.sciencenter.org, 601 First St., Ithaca, NY 14850)
Visitors can walk into a giant camera, splash around a water flume, and pet a snake at this hands-on museum and outdoor playground, with more than two hundred interactive exhibits and a science store. Families can experiment with finger painting and optical illusions in the Discovery Space. Children under four can explore the Curiosity Corner. Kids of all ages can learn about the world around them by tinkering with all kinds of deceptively simple gadgets. But be careful—what appears to be a seesaw may be a device that teaches a physics lesson. Watergates is a unique flume exhibit where visitors can control how fast and where water flows and how to channel its strength. Counting On You lets you measure your strength, height, and pulse and compare them to other visitors. There is also Galaxy Golf, an outdoor miniature golf course that challenges players with a different principle of science or math at each hole. Open daily July and August, closed Monday rest of year except holidays. Adults $7, seniors $6, children 3–17 $5.

Performing Arts
Hangar Theatre (607-273-4497, www.hangartheatre.org, Rt. 89, Ithaca, NY 14850) The Hangar Theatre, which opened in 1975 in a renovated municipal airport hangar, is one of the area's most well-regarded theaters. It produces five shows every summer, including full-scale musicals, classics, comedies, dramas, and regional premieres. Special children's programs and more avant-garde productions are held in a smaller theater on-site.

Ithaca College Theatre (607-274-3920, www.ithaca.edu/theatre, 201 Dillingham Center, Ithaca College, Ithaca, NY 14850) The Ithaca College Department of Theatre Arts, housed in the Dillingham Center for Performing Arts, is one of the nation's most respected training programs. Each season the center presents a diverse collection of professional productions. The musical shows and operas are done in conjunction with the School of Music.

The Sciencenter offers numerous opportunities for hands-on discovery

Kitchen Theatre Company (607-273-4497, www.kitchentheatre.org, 116 N. Cayuga St., Ithaca, NY 14850) Located in the historic Clinton House, a renovated 175-year-old hotel, this is downtown Ithaca's year-round professional theater. Critically acclaimed, the nationally renowned organization offers four performance series, Mainstage Season, Kitchen Counter Culture, Kitchen Sink, and Family Fare Theatre for all ages. A mix of contemporary, regional, and world premiere plays and musicals are presented in an intimate 73-seat venue.

Schwartz Center for the Performing Arts (607-254-ARTS, www.arts.cornell.edu/theatrearts, 430 College Ave., Ithaca, NY 14850) The Schwartz Center is home to Cornell University's Department of Theatre, Film, and Dance. Events include plays by Shakespeare, Oscar Wilde, and other dramatic masters, dance productions, and film.

State Theatre of Ithaca (607-273-6633, www.statetheatreofithaca.com, 107–113 W. State St., Ithaca, NY 14850) This historic theater is being restored to its original 1928 glory. It presents works by nationally known and outstanding regional performers. The Shanghai Circus, humorist David Sedaris, and cellist Yo-Yo Ma have appeared in recent years.

Other Attractions

Cayuga Nature Center (607-273-6260, www.cayuganaturecenter.org, 1420 Taughannock Blvd., Ithaca, NY 14850) There are 5 miles of trails, a lodge filled with exhibits, and live animals in both indoor and outdoor exhibits. Kids love the six-story tree house that sits at the edge of a gorge overlooking Denison Falls. It comes complete with rope ladders and many stairs. Open daily, main lodge open Tuesday through Sunday. Adults $3, seniors $2, children $1.

Cornell Plantations (607-255-3020, www.plantations.cornell.edu, 1 Plantation Rd., Ithaca, NY 148450) From early spring to late fall, blooms can be found at the nearly 4,000-acre Cornell Plantations, a unit of Cornell University that includes the Arboretum, Botanical Garden, and Natural Area. Cornell was among the nation's first land-grant institutions, so it is not surprising that faculty and students still display a green thumb. Come in May and June to see some 300 rhododendrons in full bloom. One of the unique specialty gardens is the Walter C. Muenscher Poisonous Plants Garden. The Robinson York State Herb Garden has been designed to serve as a living reference for herb study and research. There are 9 miles of trails. Open daily; free admission.

Farms and Farm Markets

Ithaca Farmers' Market (607-273-7109, www.ithacamarket.com, Third St., off Rt. 13, Ithaca, NY 14850) This market is a cooperative with more than 150 vendors who live within 30 miles of Ithaca. Farm vendors grow and offer high-quality fruits, vegetables, meats, eggs, poultry, and dairy products. Food vendors bring a wide variety of baked goods, jellies, honey, and sauces as well as meals to eat at the market. Many artists and craftspeople sell their locally made items. Musicians liven up the scene. Tuesday markets are at Dewitt Park; Thursday, Saturday, and Sunday markets are at Steamboat Landing on the shore of Cayuga Lake.

Lively Run Goat Dairy (607-532-4647, www.livelyrun.com, 8978 County Rd. 142, Interlaken, NY 14847) Lively Run is home to many goats including Alpine, Nubian, Saanen, and South African Boer breeds as well as crossbreeds. All the goats have names and are considered members of the Messmer family. The family invites the public to come for a visit and "let your kids pet our kids." The goat milk cheeses contain no preservatives, food colors, or artificial additives of any kind. Cheeses include fresh and aged cheeses such as Lively Run Chèvre, Cayuga Blue, and Lively Run Feta. Open for tours and farm purchases Monday through Friday, June 15 through October 30. Tours: adults $6, children 5–16 $3. The cheese and gift store is open daily except Thursday and Sunday.

RECREATION

Fishing
With more than 120 species of fish in the area, Cayuga Lake was named one of the top ten bass-fishing lakes by *Sports Afield* magazine. For charters you will need a valid New York State fishing license, a cooler to transport your catch home, snacks, and beverages.

Finger Lakes Angling Zone Guide Service (607-387-3098, www.fingerlakesanglingzone .com) Half- and full-day charters with Captain John Gaulke, a New York State–licensed guide who teaches Introduction to Freshwater Angling and Introduction to Fly Fishing at Cornell University.

Parks
Allan H. Treman State Park (607-273-3440, www.nysparks.state.ny.us, 105 Enfield Falls Rd., Ithaca, NY 14850) This marine park is one of the largest inland marinas in New York State. It boasts 370 seasonal, 30 transient, and 30 dry boat slips. The park has picnic areas and playing fields. It is within Robert H. Treman State Park.

Buttermilk Falls State Park (607-273-5761, www.nysparks.state.ny.us, c/o Robert H. Treman State Park, 105 Enfield Falls Rd., Ithaca, NY 14850) This park takes its name from the foaming cascade formed by Buttermilk Creek as it flows down the steep valley side toward Cayuga Lake. The upper park has a small lake, hiking trails through woodlands and along the gorge and rim, picnic areas, and playing fields. The lower park has a campground, pool, and playing fields. Beyond is Larch Meadows, a moist, shady glen and wetland area through which a nature trail winds.

Robert H. Treman State Park (607-273-3440, www.nysparks.state.ny.us, 105 Enfield Falls Rd., Ithaca, NY 14850) This is an area of wild beauty with the rugged gorge Enfield Glen as its scenic highlight. Winding trails follow the gorge past 12 waterfalls, including the 115-foot Lucifer Falls, to a spot where visitors can see a mile and a half down the wooded gorge as it winds its way to the lower park. There are tent and RV sites as well as cabins. Enjoy 9 miles of hiking trails or swim in a stream-fed pool beneath a waterfall. Bow hunting for deer is permitted in-season.

Stewart Park (607-273-8364, www.ci.ithaca.ny.us, corner Rt. 13 and 34, Ithaca, NY 14850) This city park hugs the shoreline of Cayuga Lake and offers playing fields, a playground, picnic area, concession stand, tennis courts, a restored carousel, a spray pool, a duck pond, a municipal golf course, and a bird sanctuary.

Taughannock Falls State Park (607-387-6739, www.nysparks.state.ny.us, 2221 Taughannock Rd., Trumansburg, NY 14886) The park's namesake waterfall is one of the outstanding natural attractions of the Northeast. Taughannock Falls plunges 215 feet past rocky cliffs that tower nearly 400 feet above the gorge. Gorge and rim trails offer spectacular views from above the falls and from below at the end of the gorge trail. Campsites and cabins overlook Cayuga Lake, with a marina, boat launch, and beach nearby. A multiuse trail for hiking and cross-country skiing winds past sledding slopes and natural sledding ponds. The park also offers organized activities including tours throughout the Taughannock Gorge and summer concerts along the lakefront. Bow hunting for deer is permitted in-season.

SENECA FALLS

Water played an important role in the development of Seneca Falls. The rapids originally found in the Seneca River attracted businesses that used waterpower to develop mills, distilleries, tanneries, and factories of all types.

By 1818 locks had been constructed, creating the first version of the Cayuga-Seneca Canal, which allowed boat traffic to avoid the rapids. Ten years later, the Cayuga-Seneca was linked to the Erie Canal. The cultural diversity of Seneca Falls is a result of the arrival

Seneca Falls statue depicts Amelia Jenks Bloomer introducing Susan B. Anthony to Elizabeth Cady Stanton in 1851

Downtown Seneca Falls along the canal

of immigrant workers who originally came to build the canal and the railroad, staying to make Seneca Falls their home. The manufacture of pumps has been a large part of Seneca Falls' history since the early 1800s.

By the mid-1800s Seneca Falls was also building a reputation as a center for social and religious reform. Abolition of slavery, temperance, and women's rights were issues supported by many local residents. As the canals helped spread ideas and ferment, Seneca Falls and other canal towns became centers of commerce and thought. Seneca Falls resident Amelia Jenks Bloomer drew international attention to the women's rights movement by advocating for and wearing the undergarment that bears her name.

As a 32-year-old mother of three, Elizabeth Cady Stanton told friends she felt like a "caged lioness," trapped and isolated in her home. "Radical reform must start in our homes, in our nurseries, in ourselves," she wrote. When she shared her frustration with a group of women Quaker abolitionists, they not only agreed with her but took immediate action. On July 11, 1848, they placed a notice in the *Seneca County Courier* newspaper announcing "a convention to discuss the social, civil and religious condition and rights of women."

On July 19, 1848, they convened the first Women's Rights Convention calling for women's suffrage. "The right is ours," Stanton told the gathering. "Have it we must. Use it we will." The convention is viewed as the starting point of the women's rights movement in

A Revolutionary Document

It was in the modest Seneca Falls home where the Stanton family lived that Elizabeth Cady Stanton wrote the first draft of the Declaration of Sentiments—"We hold these truths to be self-evident; that all men and women are created equal . . ." It was modeled after the Declaration of Independence and presented and passed by the first Women's Rights Convention in Seneca Falls. It included a women's bill of rights and listed demands for social equality, including women's suffrage.

the United States. It may be difficult to understand how radical the idea of women's rights was back in 1848. But at the time, women could not vote nor even own property.

The remnants of Wesleyan Chapel, where the convention was held, Stanton's house, and other properties constitute the Women's Rights National Historical Park. Stanton saved her press clippings, and reproductions are on display in the visitors' center. On August 19, 1848, the *Mechanics Advocate* newspaper editorialized on the radicalism of the women's platform and warned that its goals, if achieved, "would set the world by the ears."

The Women's Rights Park was dedicated in 1993. An idea park, it aims to educate and bring history alive. Its strength is in its storytelling.

In 1915 New York State widened the old Cayuga-Seneca Canal and replaced the smaller locks with the larger two-lock combination that exists today, in the process flooding what was once known as the Flats. This flooding erased from existence over 116 industrial buildings and over 60 homes. Van Cleef Lake was created during this project as a reservoir for the locks, and the falls were eliminated from Seneca Falls.

Seneca Falls received national attention as the likely inspiration for the fictional town of Bedford Falls in Frank Capra's classic holiday movie *It's a Wonderful Life*. The connection is celebrated with a special weekend in December.

WATERLOO

Much of the planning for the Women's Rights Convention took place just 3 miles from Seneca Falls, in Waterloo, at the Hunt and McClintock houses.

This lovely little village is famous as the birthplace of Memorial Day. On May 5, 1866, Waterloo conducted the nation's first formal, continuing remembrance of veterans who had died in the Civil War. In 1966 the federal government formally recognized Waterloo as the birthplace of Memorial Day. In September 2008 the village dedicated the marble, limestone, and gold **American Civil War Memorial** next to Lock 4 on the canal. At the **Memorial Day Museum** (315-539-9611, www.waterloony.com/mdaymus.html, 35 E. Main St., Waterloo, NY 13165), visitors are taken room by room through the origins of the national holiday; those responsible for its founding in Waterloo in 1866; and the changing face of Memorial Day into the 21st century. The newest exhibit, "One Family, One Scrapbook: A WWI Story of Courage and Sacrifice," focuses on the experiences and death of a local soldier in the rescue of the "Lost Battalion" in France's Argonne Forest. Open Tuesday through Saturday, May 15 to November 15; additional times by appointment.

Waterloo is also the site of the **Peter Whitmer Log Home** (315-539-2552, www.hill cumorah.org, 1451 Aunkst Rd., Waterloo, NY 13165), where on April 6, 1830, Joseph Smith and five others formally organized the Church of Jesus Christ of Latter-day Saints (Mormons). The first and second church conferences were also held here. The log home was reconstructed in 1980 and is furnished with household artifacts of the period. Open daily; free admission.

LODGING

Most of the accommodations in the Seneca Falls area are bed & breakfasts in historic homes, although chain hotels also serve the region.

Barrister's Bed and Breakfast (315-568-0145 or 800-914-0145, www.sleepbarristers .com, 56 Cayuga St., Seneca Falls, NY 13148) Built in 1888 by attorney T. J. Yawger, the

Colonial Revival home was designed with fine details such as quarter-sawn oak paneling, carved oak mantels, stained-glass windows, and expansive porches. It is in the
heart of the historic district. There are five comfortable rooms, all with private baths.
At the end of the day there is tea, cider, and homemade desserts served in the dining
room, where breakfast is also served. Delicious choices include fruit pizza, almond-
crusted French toast, and ham and cheese egg roulade.

Holiday Inn Waterloo (315-539-5011, www.hiwaterloo.com, 2468 Rt. 414, Waterloo, NY
13165) Many of the facility's 148 rooms have a view of the heated outdoor swimming
pool, courtyard, and tennis court; some are handicapped-accessible. Pets are welcome
at this hotel, which also offers business services, free high-speed wireless Internet, and
a fitness center. The on-site Heritage Café restaurant serves breakfast, lunch, and dinner.

Hubbell House on VanCleef Lake (315-568-9690, www.hubbellhousebb.com, 42 Cayuga
St., Seneca Falls, NY 13148) This beautiful 1855 restored Gothic cottage on Van Cleef
Lake and the Cayuga-Seneca Canal has four rooms with bathrooms, a private dock for
boaters, a screened porch overlooking the lake, and paddleboats available for guests'
use. The house and rooms are decorated with antiques in the Victorian style. Breakfast
is served by candlelight in the formal dining room or on the porch, weather permitting.
The menu includes homemade breads and muffins, fresh fruit, special hot entrées, and
juice. There is free wireless high-speed Internet.

John Morris Manor Bed & Breakfast (315-568-9057, www.johnmorrismanor.com, 2138
Rt. 89, Seneca Falls, NY 13148) This beautifully restored 1838 Greek Revival farmhouse
sits atop a secluded hill on nearly six acres. It is 3 miles from the center of Seneca Falls.
There are five rooms, three with private baths and two with a shared bath—all are different. Two rooms are available for pets and "their well-behaved owners." In summer
guests can enjoy the in-ground swimming pool. A full, hearty breakfast is served.

RESTAURANTS

Most restaurants in the area are casual, and several are right on the canal or lake.

Abigail's Restaurant (315-539-9300, www.abigailsrestaurant.com, 1978 Rt. 5 and 20,
Waterloo, NY 13165) Dine on the deck alongside the canal or inside in the expansive
dining room. This popular family-run restaurant offers good food at reasonable prices.
The deli lunch buffet is a good choice for $6.99. Dinner entrées include a full range of
beef, seafood, chicken, pasta, veal, and Italian dishes. Chef Marshall Grady's Blue Bayou
chicken wings took top honors in the Great Chicken Wing Hunt, which became the sub-
ject of a TV documentary.

Henry B's (315-568-1600, www.henrybs.com, 84 Fall St., Seneca Falls, NY 13148) This
sophisticated Italian dining room offers family-style service. According to the chefs at
Henry B's, the menu is all about interactive dining. Instead of trying only one or two
items, you can taste a variety of dishes, getting everyone involved.

The Deerhead Inn (315-568-2950; www.deerheadlakeside.com, 2554 Lower Lake Rd.,
Seneca Falls, NY 13148.) Come by boat from Memorial Day to Labor Day. This fun place
right on Cayuga Lake takes full advantage of its location. The history of the inn dates
back to 1929, and the Gustafson family has been welcoming guests to Deerhead for
more than 25 years. The specialty of the house is prime rib, served daily. Seafood,

Italian dishes, and lighter items including sandwiches and burgers are also on the menu. The lunch buffet is popular with locals and visitors. Save room for dessert, including rich chocolate lava cake and lemon custard pie.

CULTURE

Museums and Historic Sites

Elizabeth Cady Stanton House (315-568-2991, www.nps.gov/wori, 32 Washington St., Seneca Falls, NY 13148) There is little furniture in the Stanton House, but tour guides deliver plenty of fascinating material about Stanton's intellectual development and her life here with her seven children and her lawyer husband. The brood shared two bedrooms. Her boys helped with housework and her girls played freely. The Stantons were staunch abolitionists. Their honeymoon had taken them to the World Anti-Slavery Convention in London in 1840. It was in this house that she wrote the speeches that fellow suffragette Susan B. Anthony delivered. "I forged the thunderbolts and Susan fired them," explained Stanton. The house is open by appointment.

National Women's Hall of Fame (315-568-2936, www.greatwomen.org, 76 Fall St., Seneca Falls, NY 13148) Operated by a private organization and housed in an old bank building, the site honors several hundred American women of achievement, from Abigail Adams and Edith Wharton to Ruth Bader Ginsberg and Billie Jean King. Learn how the women inducted into the National Women's Hall of Fame contributed to such diverse fields as the arts, education, business, government, humanities, philanthropy, and science. Open daily May through September; Wednesday to Sunday October through April. Closed January. Admission: adults $3, students and seniors $1.50.

Women's Rights National Historical Park (315-568-2991, www.nps.gov/wori, 136 Fall St., Seneca Falls, NY 13148) The park consists of the visitors' center, the next-door remains of the Wesleyan Methodist Chapel where the Women's Rights Convention took place, and Stanton's house. A 25-minute film, *Dreams of Equality,* offers a good overview of the women's rights movement. Park rangers conduct walking tours of Seneca Falls, telling stories of village life in 1848. Open daily; adults $3.

Seneca Falls Heritage Area (315-568-2703; Visitors' Center, 115 Fall St., Seneca Falls, NY 13148) The area, an urban cultural park, encompasses 365 acres. The visitors' center explores the village's reform movement and industrial and transportation histories. Learn about the history of Seneca Falls through a 17-minute video. There is a life-size statue of Elizabeth Cady Stanton and exhibits that tell the story of the historic Women's Rights Convention. Open daily; free admission.

Seneca Falls Historical Society (315-568-8412, www.welcome.to/sfhs, 55 Cayuga St., Seneca Falls, NY 13148) Many of the furnishings in this three-story, 23-room Queen Anne mansion are from the Becker family, who lived here for more than 50 years. It grew from a one-room early-1800s house to its present style in the 1880s. Mannequins dressed in period clothing are scattered throughout the house. There are French carpets, stained-glass windows, and carved oak woodwork and furniture that portray what life was like for a wealthy Victorian family. Open daily in the summer, weekdays rest of year; adults $5.

Seneca Museum of Waterways and Industry (315-568-1510, www.senecamuseum.com, 89 Fall St., Seneca Falls, NY 13148) A 35-foot mural depicts the Cayuga-Seneca Canal along with original drawings, engineers' plans, and photographs. Exhibits show how a pump works, how the Erie Canal was built, and how a canal lock works. An exhibit shows the development of Seneca Falls using push-button lights that pinpoint the location of important sites. Open Tuesday through Sunday in July and August; Tuesday through Saturday rest of year. Admission: $2 per person, $5 per family.

Trinity Episcopal Church (315-568-5145, 27 Fall St., Seneca Falls, NY 13148) One of the most beautiful and most photographed structures on the entire canal system, Trinity Episcopal is located on the Van Cleef Lake shore. Built in 1885 in the Anglo-Gothic style, it is famous for its rising tower and stained-glass windows, some of which were made by the renowned Tiffany Studios.

Other Attractions

Cayuga Lake State Park (315-568-5163, www.nysparks.state.ny.us, 2678 Lower Lake Rd., Seneca Falls, NY 13148) This park on the shores of Cayuga Lake was named one of the top 100 campgrounds in the nation in 2007. It has a boat launch, playground, and playing field as well as a beach. There are cabins and tent/trailer sites. A special feature is the vacation rental house with an enclosed porch and a view of the lake. It has three bedrooms, a fully equipped kitchen, one and a half baths, a wood stove, and a sleeper sofa in the living room.

Frank J. Ludovico Sculpture Trail (Visitors' and Arts Center at 61 Ovid St., Rt. 414, Seneca Falls, NY 13148) This one-and-three-quarter-mile trail extends along the south side of the Cayuga-Seneca Canal from Seneca Falls west to Sucker Brook. The trail is home to numerous sculptures inspired by the women's rights movement and created primarily by women sculptors.

Montezuma National Wildlife Refuge (315-568-5987, www.fws.gov/r5mnwr, 3395 Rt. 5 & 20 East, Seneca Falls, NY 13148) In 1806 Dr. Peter Clark named his hilltop home after the palace of the Aztec emperor Montezuma. Eventually, the surrounding marsh and refuge acquired the name as well. This 7,000-acre refuge includes a visitors' center, a viewing platform that offers good views of nesting eagles and ospreys and a three-and-a-half-mile wildlife drive. Every spring and fall the refuge attracts thousands of migratory birds. Open daily; free admission. Visitors' center and wildlife drive closed December 1 through April 1.

Seneca River Crossing Canals Historic District

The Seneca River Crossing Canals Historic District, listed on the State and National Registers of Historic Places, illustrates one hundred years of canal engineering in New

Outlet Shopping

Waterloo Premium Outlets (315-539-1100, www.premiumoutlets.com, 655 Rt. 318, Waterloo, NY 13165.) Visible from the New York Thruway (I-90) between Exits 41 and 42, this is the largest shopping complex in the Finger Lakes area, with more than 100 shops and a food court. Outlet stores include Bose, Harry & David, Coach, OshKosh B'Gosh, Tommy Hilfiger, Puma, Jones New York, Guess, and Ann Taylor Factory Store. There is weekend entertainment and various sales on top of the outlet pricing. Open daily.

York State. The 70-acre district on the Seneca River contains intact portions of the original 1817–25 Erie Canal, the Cayuga-Seneca Canal, the 1835–62 enlarged Erie Canal, and the 1905–18 New York State Barge Canal (today's canal) as well as the archaeological remains of a lock tender's house and a commercial drydock.

The **Richmond Aqueduct** (www.co.cayuga.ny.us/parks/trails), built in 1849–57 and partially dismantled in 1917, is the centerpiece of this district. Named for canal engineer Van R. Richmond, the aqueduct, as originally built, was almost 900 feet in length and 86 feet in width. Its towpath was carried above a Roman-inspired limestone structure comprised of 31 massive arches. Eight arches and their related piers and abutments remain today.

River crossings, flood plains, and swamps stood as major challenges in engineering the original Erie Canal. In crossing the Seneca River, locks lowered the original canal to river level and canal boats were led across the river itself with the aid of a wooden towpath. This arrangement proved less than satisfactory due to periodic flooding, silting, unstable canal walls, and periodic damage from river ice. Separating the canal from the river with the use of an aqueduct ultimately corrected these deficiencies but proved to be a major investment of time and money. Construction of the aqueduct began in 1849 as part of a long-term program of enlargements and improvements to the Erie Canal designed to increase the canal's capacity.

The aqueduct project involved the placement of almost 5,000 pilings, thousands of tons of limestone blocks, and large quantities of hydraulic cement. The aqueduct was completed and opened for use in 1857. It was celebrated as one of the engineering marvels of the canal at the time. The aqueduct and its approaches followed a different alignment from the original canal, portions of which remain intact at the site.

Today's canal uses the Seneca River for a portion of its length. This necessitated the removal of much of the aqueduct structure and the dredging of the river. Fortunately, portions of the aqueduct were spared, leaving evidence of this remarkable 19th-century engineering feat. Lock 11 of the Cayuga and Seneca Canal was abandoned and remains well preserved today.

Richmond Aqueduct near Montezuma

> **A Magnificent Aqueduct**
>
> "Near the heart of the swamp we came upon the grandest remains of the old canal, a romantic ruin waiting for its Wordsworth, a capital piece of nineteenth-century engineering: the eight remaining stone arches of the Richmond Aqueduct; fifteen feet above our deck, the packet boats once floated their passengers and kippage across, drawn by the aerial clop of mules."
> —William Least Heat-Moon, *River-Horse: Across America by Boat* (2001)

To visit the aqueduct, drive east on Route 31 from Montezuma, cross the Seneca River, and turn right on High Street until you reach Chapman. Follow Chapman a short distance until you see a parking lot on your right. On the edge of this parking lot is a trail head that leads west to impressive remains of the Richmond Aqueduct less than a mile away.

GENEVA

In Geneva, on the northern tip of Seneca Lake, visitors can sleep in the ballroom of a lakeside 19th-century home transformed into a hotel that is reminiscent of a German castle, or stay in an inn that was modeled after a 16th-century Italian villa. Wines can be sampled in award-winning wineries that hug the lakeshore.

Seneca Lake is named after the Seneca Indians, one of the Six Nations of the Iroquois. At more than 600 feet, it is the deepest of the Finger Lakes—the U.S. Navy continues to test sonar equipment here. Known as the Lake Trout Capital of the World, it is famous for its annual Memorial Day weekend trout derby.

Geneva is a town where education dominates. Ivy-covered Hobart (for men) and William Smith Colleges (for women) add a cosmopolitan atmosphere and contribute to the rich and elegant feeling with their stately homes and buildings overlooking the lake.

The most well-known pioneering student in the city was surely Elizabeth Blackwell, who is remembered today with a historic marker and statue on the Hobart campus. She became the first woman medical school graduate in the United States when she graduated first in her class from Geneva College on January 23, 1849. Geneva College was later renamed Hobart College in honor of its founder, Episcopal bishop John Henry Hobart. The medical school later became part of Syracuse University.

William Smith also built the Smith Opera House, an elegant theater that has been lovingly restored. Opened in 1894, it is one of the oldest theaters in the country and hosts a wide variety of movies, concerts, performers, and other entertainment.

This is orchard country, and home of the New York State Agricultural Experiment Station, which is responsible for creating one of the country's finest apples—the Empire. **Red Jacket Orchards** on Routes 5 and 20 were originally planted in 1917 and have been owned and operated by three generations of the Nicholson family. With 500 acres of fruit production and more than 280,000 fruit trees, the orchards produce more than 14 varieties of apples as well as strawberries, cherries, prunes, plums, peaches, and apricots.

Early in the 19th century Geneva was considered the commercial center of central New York. Steamboats between Geneva and Watkins Glen carried up to 2,000 passengers daily to railroad connections at either end. The Cayuga-Seneca Canal connects the city with the Erie Canal.

Red Jacket Orchard Store in Geneva

When electricity arrived in 1883, Geneva's industrialization began in earnest with an explosion of factories and foundries clustered on the waterfront. The city's most dramatic growth occurred during the 1940s, when Sampson Naval Base (now Sampson State Park) trained more than 400,000 recruits for World War II. During the Korean War, the base became Sampson Air Force Base.

The Seneca Lake Whale Watch Festival is celebrated here in August. You won't spot any whales in Seneca Lake, but the creators of the festival guarantee a whale of a good time, with food, music, arts, crafts, and entertainment.

Lodging

Geneva has two of upstate New York's most spectacular lakefront hotels—Geneva-on-the-Lake and Belhurst Castle. There are also a number of good bed & breakfasts and two newer chain hotels along the lake and downtown.

Belhurst (315-781-0201, www.belhurst.com, 4069 Rt. 14S, Geneva, NY 14456) The Belhurst Castle could be a private estate on the shore of Lake Geneva in Switzerland instead of Geneva Lake in the Finger Lakes. Guests are transported back into a luxurious gilded age—the original owner had 22 servants. Carrie Harron Collins had the house built from 1885 to 1889. Noted architect Albert W. Fuller and 50 workmen labored six days a week for four years to create her fantasy. After her death, it was operated as a speakeasy and casino. The castle sports carved oak, cherry, and mahogany and more stained glass than many churches. On the third floor, the Victorian ballroom, with 18-foot ceilings, has been converted into the Tower Suite, with a Finnish sauna and a lookout in the turret. On the second floor a spigot in the hallway spouts complimentary wine from Belhurst's winery (see entry under "Seneca Lake Wine Trail" later in chapter). Each room is very different, so it is a good idea to take a look at the photos on the Web site before booking. Today, Belhurst operates as three distinct hotels: the 11-room castle and three cottages, the connecting newer 20-room **Vinifera Inn**, with in-room

Jacuzzis, fireplaces, and elevators, and the 11-room **White Springs Manor** (plus one house) down the road in the midst of a vineyard. There is a gift shop, winery tasting room, large Garden Room popular for weddings and meetings, and fine dining at **Edgar's** and more casual fare at **Stonecutters.**

Geneva-on-the-Lake Resort (315-789-7190 or 800-3-GENEVA, www.genevaonthelake .com, 1001 Lockland Rd., Rt. 14S, Geneva, NY 14456) Geneva-on-the-Lake is a 1911 Italianate villa built by malt tycoon Bryon Nester. It was modeled after the Villa Lancellotti, a 16th-century villa in Frascati, near Rome. It has been a Capuchin monastery, an apartment complex, and, since 1981, a small elegant resort with 29 luxury suites. It was beautifully restored by the Schickel family, and photos of the family with visiting celebrities, including actor Paul Newman, line the walls in the office. Although William Schickel still serves as general manager, the resort is now owned by the Audi family, owner of L. & J. G. Stickley, the well-known Syracuse-area furniture maker, and Stickley furniture is used throughout. One suite, the Classic, has two bedrooms, two working fireplaces, a canopy bed, a balcony, and a kitchen. The Library Suite features floor-to-ceiling bookcases stocked with family books, a working fireplace with a carved stone mantel, and tall windows opening out to the formal gardens, 70-foot swimming pool, and the lake. The resort's pontoon boat is available to take guests on a sunset cruise. There are also boat moorings so guests may come by boat to stay overnight and dine in the elegant **Lancellotti Dining Room,** with its marble columns, wall tapestries, and live music. During warm weather, there is outdoor dining.

Belhurst Castle in Geneva is one of the area's premier accommodations

The resort is listed on the National Register of Historic Places and has received the coveted AAA Four Diamond Award for 25 years.

Hampton Inn Geneva (315-781-2035 or 800-426-7866, www.hamptoninn.com, 43 Lake St., Geneva, NY 14456) Located across the street from Seneca Lake State Park, this newer 55-room hotel offers good value and is popular with business travelers. There is complimentary high-speed Internet, a hot breakfast, and a swimming pool.

Ramada Geneva Lakefront (315-789-0400 or 800-990-0907, www.genevaramada.com, 41 Lakeshore Blvd., Geneva, NY 14456) Located in a prime spot on the north shore of Seneca Lake and next to Seneca Lake State Park, this newer hotel boasts great views and is within walking distance of downtown. Docks permit visitors and guests to arrive by boat. There are 148 comfortable and attractively furnished rooms and a very small indoor pool. The **Pier House** is a popular on-site restaurant, and there is an expansive outdoor patio.

RESTAURANTS

In addition to the eateries listed here, the city's historic inns (Belhurst and Geneva-on-the-Lake) and the largest hotel, the Ramada, have popular restaurants.

Cobblestone Restaurant (315-789-8498, www.cobblestone-restaurant.com, 3610 Pre Emption Rd., Geneva, NY 14456) This elegant dining room is in a restored 1825 farmhouse that was originally built as a tavern and stagecoach stop in 1790. It serves northern Italian cuisine, seafood delivered daily from Boston, wood-grilled steaks, and chops and pastas. The wine list includes a number of Finger Lakes wines.

Crow's Nest Restaurant (315-781-0600, www.thecrowsnestrestaurant.com, 415 Boody's Hill Rd., Geneva, NY 14456) Crow's Nest is located at the mouth of Seneca Lake on the canal, close to Seneca Lake State Park. It takes full advantage of its waterside location with a glass-enclosed dining room, the longest outside bar in the region, and plenty of docks. The menu includes a good choice of grilled items, seafood, burgers, salads, and sandwiches. The restaurant is open daily for lunch and dinner; closed January 1 to March 15.

Halsey's Restaurant (315-789-4070, www.halseysgeneva.com, 106 Seneca St., Geneva, NY 14456) This is a handsome restaurant featuring lots of dark wood and original brick. The menu features daily specials as well as choices such as a grilled Jamaican pork chop, grilled mahimahi, cioppino (seafood stew), and grilled chicken and prosciutto linguini. There is an extensive wine list including many Finger Lakes wines. Open Tuesday through Saturday for dinner.

Nonna's Trattoria (315-789-1638, www.nonnastrattoria.com, 1 Railroad Pl., Geneva, NY 14456) *Nonna* means "grandmother" in Italian and *trattoria* means "small family restaurant," and Marylou and Joe Cosentino invite everyone to *manga bene* (eat and enjoy). This handsome red brick building offers outdoor seating across the street from the lake and close to downtown attractions. The menu includes such Italian classics as pasta pollo, chicken cacciatore, manicotti, lasagna, and eggplant parmigiana, as well as seafood, beef, chicken, and veal dishes. The kid's menu goes beyond the standard chicken fingers and burgers and includes lasagna, ravioli, and broiled haddock. Open daily for dinner and weekdays for lunch.

ATTRACTIONS

Air Force Museum at Sampson (315-585-9555, www.sampsonvets.com, 6096 Rt. 96A, Romulus, NY 14541) This museum was created by the thousands of members of the Sampson World War II Navy Veterans organization, to whom it is dedicated. It features veterans' artifacts, photos, guns, and other memorabilia. Open Wednesday through Sunday May 30 to Labor Day, and on weekends from Labor Day to Columbus Day. Free admission after park gate fee ($7 per car in summer).

Finger Lakes Scenic Railway (315-781-1234. www.fingerlakesscenicrailways.com) Headquartered in Geneva, the scenic railway offers excursions along the lake and a variety of theme trips.

Prouty-Chew House & Museum (315-789-5151, www.genevahistoricalsociety.com, 543 S. Main St., Geneva, NY 14456) Early in the 19th century Geneva was considered the commercial center of central New York. Steamboats between Geneva and Watkins Glen carried up to 2,000 passengers daily to railroad connections at either end. This history is shown in displays and exhibits at the 1829 Prouty-Chew Federal-style house, which houses the Geneva Historical Society Museum. It contains four period rooms as well as changing exhibits. The museum offers information for a self-guided walking tour of Geneva's historical district along South Main Street and a driving tour of noteworthy homes. Open Tuesday through Saturday (Sunday in July and August). Free admission.

Rose Hill Mansion (315-789-3848, www.genevahistoricalsociety.com, Rt. 96A, Geneva, NY 14456) Robert Selden Rose was a Virginia plantation owner who moved to Geneva in 1802. In 1809 Rose erected a simple frame house, Rose Hill Farm, now used as the reception center and gift shop for the Rose Hill Mansion, a Greek Revival mansion and National Historic Landmark. Built in 1839 by Gen. William Kerley Strong, it passed into the hands of Robert Swan in 1850. Rose Hill is furnished in the Empire style popular during the Greek Revival period. Many furnishings were possessions of the Swan

Prouty-Chew House and Geneva Historical Society Museum

Rose Hill Mansion, Geneva

family, including a first edition of Noah Webster's 1828 dictionary and an original Singer sewing machine. Open daily May 1 to October 31; adults $7, seniors and children $5.

Sampson State Park (315-585-6392, www.nysparks.state.ny.us, 6096 Rt. 96A, Romulus, NY 14541) Sampson was once a naval training station and then an Air Force base before becoming a state park. Military roads and buildings have been replaced with grasses, wildflowers, and shrubs and trees on flat, rolling woodlands surrounding ravines. The focal point of the park is the 123-berth marina for seasonal and transient boaters. There are 245 electric campsites and 64 nonelectric sites, picnic areas, playground and playing fields that include tennis, basketball, and volleyball courts, a swimming beach, a recreation building, and organized activities including tours, hikes, and wildlife watches. Open daily; $7 per car in summer.

Seneca Lake State Park (315-789-2331, www.nysparks.state.ny.us, 1 Lakefront Dr., Geneva, NY 14456) This park hugs Seneca Lake in the heart of Geneva offering a beach and a prime spot for swimming. Children will be especially delighted with the Sprayground and playground facilities. The Sprayground is the first of its kind built in the New York Parks system with more than 100 water jets that spontaneously spray water. There are two marinas with a total of 132 electric slips and 84 nonelectric slips. Transient slips are available at both marinas. Open daily; $7 per car in summer.

Smith Opera House (315-781-LIVE or 866-355-LIVE, www.thesmith.org, 82 Seneca St., Geneva, NY 14456) Built in 1894 by local philanthropist William Smith (of William Smith College fame), this handsome Richardson Romanesque structure is listed on the National Register of Historic Places and is among the country's oldest operating theaters. In the early 1930s the interior was renovated with a combination of art deco and baroque motifs as well as Victorian and Moresque influences. In recent years it has undergone a $2-million restoration and is the center of the region's cultural life, hosting a variety of concerts, movies, and live stage performances.

WATKINS GLEN

Watkins Glen, a once sleepy village now undergoing a moderate growth spurt, is on the southern end of Seneca Lake. It is named after a New York City physician, Dr. Samuel

Watkins, who owned 25,000 acres of land in the area. He arrived in 1828 and built an imposing three-story Federal-style home that is still standing. Watkins brought the bricks with which he built the home from his Harlem farm via the Erie and Cayuga-Seneca canals. His large carriage house has also been well preserved.

The boardwalk and fishing pier in Watkins Glen provide some of the most beautiful views of any vantage point in the Finger Lakes. It is the perfect place to get out on the water, and there are several charter boat operators serving the area.

The big attraction here is a spectacular gorge that traces its origins back 10,000 years to the end of the Ice Age. The chasm forms the heart of **Watkins Glen State Park**. The best way to experience the beauty of the glen is to hike the gorge trail, which is more than one and a half miles long and has more than eight hundred stone steps. The glen drops about 700 feet in two miles and is highlighted by rock formations and 18 waterfalls.

In places you will walk behind some of the waterfalls and at some points you will actually be standing on the floor of an ancient sea. Cliffs rise 200 feet above the stream; a 165-foot-high bridge spans the glen, which is lit at night.

Watkins Glen is also known as the home of American road racing. Road races are no longer held on the village streets but on the hills above the village at **Watkins Glen International**. Every August the track at "the Glen" hosts a NASCAR race. Every September the U.S. Vintage Grand Prix celebrates the first race here in 1948 with a reenactment of the famous race through the village.

The marina has been revitalized and new hotels and condominiums have been built. Seneca Harbor Park has a 300-foot fishing pier, a marina, and lake cruise boats. Near the park on North Franklin Street is the last remaining salt derrick in the state.

Finger Lakes National Forest, the only national forest in New York State, just northeast of Watkins Glen, is between Seneca and Cayuga lakes.

On a hillside above Watkins Glen is the home of the 175-acre **Farm Sanctuary**, offering respite for abused and abandoned farm animals. Gene Baur, cofounder and president of the animal refuge, is the author of *Farm Sanctuary: Changing Hearts and Minds about Animals and Food.*

LODGING

Inns and bed & breakfasts predominate in the area, along with a new full-service hotel.

Benjamin Hunt Inn (607-535-6659, www.benhunt.com, 305 Sixth St., Watkins Glen, NY 14891) The 1871 inn is in the heart of the village nestled on a quiet street convenient to the lake. Each of the three rooms has a private bath, refrigerator, and air-conditioning, and is filled with period antiques. A full breakfast is included and it is served in front of a cozy fireplace.

Farm Sanctuary B&B (607-583-2225, www.farmsanctuary.org, 3100 Aikens Rd., Watkins Glen, NY 14891) This unique B&B, a totally vegan establishment on the grounds of the Farm Sanctuary, offers three cabins in the midst of the 175-acre animal sanctuary. Visitors' companion animals are also welcome. A continental breakfast is served. Guests are welcome to pitch in with farm chores or enjoy the companionship of the farm animals. Bathrooms and showers for cabin guests are located in the visitors' center. Open May to October.

The Pearl of Seneca Lake (607-243-5227 or 866-50-PEARL, www.thepearlofseneca lake.com, 4827 Red Cedar Lane, Dundee, NY 14837) Peter and Mary Muller opened this lakefront B&B in 2005. There are four rooms, including one on the first floor that is handicapped accessible. Rooms are filled with furniture made by local Mennonite craftsmen. Guests have access to a canoe and a rowboat, and there is an 80-foot-long dock with a bench at the end for lake viewing. There is full wireless Internet access. A full breakfast is included and there is a hiking trail with lake views. In-room massages can be arranged. Two-night minimum stay during summer weekends.

Watkins Glen Harbor Hotel (607-535-6116, www.watkinsglenharborhotel.com, 16 Franklin St., Watkins Glen, NY 14891) The first full-service hotel in Watkins Glen, this 104-room waterfront hotel opened in July 2008. It has an indoor pool, fitness center, conference facilities, and a ballroom. There are wonderful views throughout and an outdoor patio. Many rooms have lake views. The Coldwater Bar features Finger Lakes wines, and the BluePointe Grill is open daily for breakfast, lunch, and dinner.

RESTAURANTS

Included here are establishments in town. Many nearby wineries have restaurants or cafés onsite. See listings under "Wine Trails" later in chapter.

Savard's Family Restaurant (607-535-4538, 601 N. Franklin St., Watkins Glen, NY 14891) A longtime village favorite, Savard's lives up to its name as a family restaurant with popular American dishes and a kid's menu. There's steak, burgers, pasta dishes, and meatloaf. Open daily for breakfast, lunch, and dinner (except Monday and Tuesday, when the restaurant closes midafternoon).

Seneca Harbor Station (607-535-6101, www.senecaharborstation.com, 1 N. Franklin St., Watkins Glen, NY 14891) This restaurant occupies a prime spot on the southern tip of Seneca Lake. The dining room is part of the original 1876 train station. The 16-foot ceilings, custom mahogany bar, and original hardwood floors give Seneca Harbor a distinctive flavor. Outside, there is a covered deck overlooking the marina. The lunch menu includes a wide array of burgers, salads, and sandwiches, as well as special desserts including a chocolate truffle sundae and raspberry bongo. Dinner includes prime rib, steaks, seafood, pasta, and smoked ribs. Children's menus are available. Open daily for lunch and dinner, April 10 through New Year's Eve.

The Wildflower Café and Roosterfish Brewing (607-535-9797, www.roosterfishbrewing .com, 223–301 N. Franklin St., Watkins Glen, NY 14891) Three blocks from the lake along the main drag, this establishment features a wide-ranging menu with an emphasis on fresh ingredients. There are burgers galore, steak, seafood, chicken and turkey, pizza, and salads and soups, and a changing choice of desserts. Roosterfish Brewing serves eight microbrews including Old Cascade Amber Ale, Dogtooth Pale Ale, and Cocoa Porter. All are brewed using organic malts, American hops, and Seneca Lake water. The wines served in the Wildflower Café are all local Finger Lakes wines. There is live music on weekends. Open daily for lunch and dinner.

ATTRACTIONS

Farm Sanctuary (607-583-2225, www.farmsanctuary.org, 3100 Aikens Rd., Watkins Glen, NY 14891) Founded in 1986, this sanctuary, the United States' largest farm-animal-rescue facility, is home to about 750 animals, including cows, pigs, sheep, chickens, turkeys, and goats. There are also some 30 cats that happened by and found a home. Some animals were rescued from abusive farms and others were displaced during natural disasters or abandoned. The tour begins with a short video and then heads to a cow pasture where visitors meet Sunny, a formerly abused and malnourished cow rescued from a New York dairy farm in 2005. There's Juniper, a goat who lost part of its leg due to frostbite, as well as pigs and sheep. All have sad stories but now live a life of comfort and serve to educate the public. Guided one-hour tours Wednesday to Sunday on the hour from 11 am to 3 pm in July and August, and on weekends in May, June, September, and October. Adults $3, children under 12 $1.

Finger Lakes National Forest (607-546-4470, www.fs.fed.us/r9/forests/greenmountain/ htm/fingerlakes/f_home.htm, 5218 State Rt. 414, Hector, NY 14841) The only national forest in New York, the 16,000-acre preserve is nestled between Seneca and Cayuga Lakes. It has over 30 miles of interconnecting trails that traverse gorges, ravines, pastures, and woodlands. There's hiking, cross-country skiing, snowmobiling, horse trails, primitive camping, fishing, hunting, berry picking, and bird-watching.

Sugar Hill State Forest (607-776-2165, www.dec.ny.gov/lands/37446.html) Located about 7 miles west of Watkins Glen, this forest covers approximately 9,000 acres. During the Depression, the Civilian Conservation Corps planted thousands of pine and spruce trees. The main trailhead for the 40-mile-long Six Nations Recreation Trail System is near the north end of the Sugar Hill State Forest, off Tower Hill Road. Here there is parking, restrooms, a fire tower, picnic area, and pavilion, 16 horse stalls, recreation building, archery targets, and camping area. National and international archery tournaments are held here and there is a wheelchair course designed for tournament competition. Horseback riding and snowmobiling are allowed.

Watkins Glen International (607-535-2486, www.theglen.com, 2790 County Rt. 16, Watkins Glen, NY 14891) On the hills overlooking the village, the Glen, as the racetrack is familiarly known, is the site of major racing weekends each year, including NASCAR events. The track and the village really heat up in early August, when the NASCAR Nextel Cup series is held. The race, constituting the area's largest sporting weekend, draws many thousands of spectators and fills every hotel, inn, and campground for miles around. The Vintage Grand Prix, held in September, is another popular event.

Watkins Glen State Park (607-535-4511, www.nysparks.state.ny.us, Rt. 14, Watkins Glen, NY 14891) Opened in 1863, this is the most famous of the Finger Lakes state parks, with a reputation for leaving visitors spellbound. Within 2 miles, the glen's stream descends 400 feet past 200-foot cliffs, generating 19 waterfalls along its course. The gorge path winds over and under waterfalls and through the spray of Cavern Cascade. Rim trails overlook the gorge. Hikers should wear appropriate hiking shoes since the trails are often wet. Shuttle buses ($3) return walkers to the entrance; it's also possible to walk back along a relatively flat Indian trail that parallels the gorge. Visitors can enjoy the Olympic-sized pool, scheduled summer tours through the gorge, tent and trailer campsites, picnic facilities, and top fishing in nearby Seneca Lake or Catherine Creek, which is renowned for its annual spring run of rainbow trout.

Cruises

Captain Bill's Seneca Lake Cruises (607-535-4541, www.senecaharborstation.com, 1½ N. Franklin St., Watkins Glen, NY 14891) The *Stroller IV*, a 1934 vintage motor vessel, offers hour-long sightseeing cruises from May 15 to mid-October. (adults $12.50,

children $6). The larger *Seneca Legacy* offers lunch, dinner, Sunday brunch, and enter-
tainment cruises.

Malabar VII (607-535-LAKE, www.schoonerexcursions.com, Fishing Pier, Seneca
Harbor Park, Watkins Glen, NY 14891) Get swept away on this vintage schooner yacht,
originally built in 1926 and victorious in the 1926 Bermuda Race. The *Malabar VII* is the
epitome of the fine wooden racing and cruising schooners designed by John Alden. Try
your hand at the helm, trim the sails, or simply sit back and take in the beauty of the
vineyards, waterfalls, and cliffs of the southern waters of Seneca Lake. Cruises May
through October (weather permitting); offered are two-hour cruises (adults $30–$40,
children $15–$20), and a two-and-a-half-hour sunset cruise ($40).

Wine Trails

The state's two biggest wine trails are part of the Cayuga-Seneca Canal system. Some
wineries are accessible by boat, making it possible to cruise from the waterways of the
world to a Seneca or Cayuga lake winery.

The explosive growth in the numbers and quality of the vineyards and wineries is credited with the development of many related businesses including restaurants, inns, bed &
breakfasts, and specialty winery tour companies. Some wineries themselves offer restaurants and overnight accommodations. Today, the wineries are regarded as the biggest success story in New York State agriculture and the impetus for the growth of a
multimillion-dollar tourism industry. Tasting rooms are friendly and inviting and the
wines have won state, national, and international awards. The growth of the wineries took
off after the passage of the Farm Winery Act in 1976.

Hammondsport, on neighboring Keuka Lake, is known as the birthplace of Finger Lakes
wineries. It was 1829 when the Reverend William Bostwick transplanted Isabella and
Catawba grapevines from the Hudson Valley to his rectory garden at St. James Episcopal
Church, with the aim of making sacramental wine for his parishioners. The grapes flourished, and news of Bostwick's success spread rapidly among nearby farmers.

These farmers soon discovered that the origins of the Finger Lakes led to ideal conditions for growing grapes. Iroquois legend has it that the Finger Lakes region was formed
when the Great Spirit placed his hand in blessing on this favored land. The geologists'
explanation is more prosaic: The lakes were created when Ice Age glaciers retreated about
a million years ago. The intense pressure of those ice masses created the long, narrow
lakes lying side by side, the deep gorges with rushing falls, and the wide, fertile valleys that
extend south for miles. These features are found nowhere else in the world.

The moving ice masses deposited a shallow layer of topsoil on sloping shale beds above
the lakes, providing the drainage crucial for grape growing. Grapevines don't like having
"wet feet." The glaciers also furnished the vineyards with protection from the region's
sometimes fickle climate. The deep lakes retain their summer warmth in the fall and their
winter cold in the spring, moderating the temperature along their shores.

CAYUGA LAKE WINE TRAIL

The Cayuga Lake Wine Trail is the first organized and longest-running Wine Trail in New
York. The vision began in 1983 when four small wineries along the lake had a dream of
working together to bring more visitors to their doors to taste the fruits of their labors.
This wine trail became a model for other wine trails in the state and around the country.

The trail sponsors a variety of special events throughout the year. Favorites include the Annual Mardi Gras on the first Saturday in February; the Wine & Herb Festival on the last weekend in April and the first weekend in May; the Greyhound Wine Tour, with special treats for greyhound owners and their dogs, including an ice cream social, during the last weekend in July; a month-long celebration in September called the Wine Festival and Harvest Hoopla; and the annual Holiday Shopping Spree in late November and early December.

The wines produced along the trail have won nearly 5,000 national and international medals and four Governor's Cups, known as the Oscars of New York wines. Today, there are 15 wineries, a cidery, a meadery, and four distilleries along the trail. Most wineries are also pet friendly. (For more information call 800-684-5217, or visit www.cayugawinetrail.com.)

The following wineries begin at the north end of the lake and follow south along the west side and then north along the east side of the lake. All offer tastings and wine or hard-cider sales.

Montezuma Winery (315-568-8190, www.montezumawinery.com, 2981 Auburn Rd., [Corner Rtes. 5/20 and 89], Seneca Falls, NY 13148) On the north end of Cayuga Lake, Montezuma Winery offers over 25 award-winning wines ranging from dry to sweet. In addition to traditional grape wines, the winery specializes in meads (honey wines) and a wide range of fruit wines including their "almost world-famous Cranberry Bog." They also produce distilled spirits and premium vodkas made from honey. There's an extensive gift shop perfect for buying souvenirs or gifts for wine lovers.

Swedish Hill Vineyard (315-549-8326 or 888-549-WINE; www.swedishhill.com, 4565 State Route 414, Romulus, NY 14541) The first of the wineries on the west side of the lake, this vineyard produces the lake's largest selection of wines, ranging from dry to sweet, classic to unique, including champagne, port, and brandy. Set on 35 acres, the winery has a rustic red barn with a deck overlooking a pond. Picnic facilities are available. Be sure to say hello to Doobie, the owners' pet miniature donkey. Try owners Dick and Cindy Peterson's famed Doobie Blues wine. The Petersons host many annual events including the Scandinavian Festival and a Champagne and Dessert Wine Festival.

Cobblestone Farm Winery & Vineyard (315-549-8797, www.cobblestonefarmwinery .com, 5102 State Route 89, Romulus, NY 14541) Enjoy wine tasting with a view of the vineyard, cherry orchard, and Cayuga Lake. Sample jellies, preserves, mustards, salsas, butters, and BBQ sauces. Linger in the old-fashioned rocking chairs on the front porch with a glass of wine, or picnic on the grounds. July visitors can pick sweet and sour cherries in the orchard.

Knapp Winery and Vineyard Restaurant (607-869-9271 or 800-869-9271, www.knapp wine.com, 2770 County Rd., Romulus, NY 14551) This winery offers more than 25 wines and five cordials and brandies. Enjoy lunch in the seasonal vineyard restaurant, dining either indoors or on the patio, with lovely views of the grounds and vineyards. Boat access available.

Goose Watch Winery (315-549-2599, www.goosewatch.com, 5480 State Route 89, Romulus, NY 14541) This winery offers a great lake view and a selection of premium wines in an elegant tasting room. Wines include Pinot Grigio, Traminette, Viognier, Merlot, and White Port. Sample some seasonal farm-raised chestnuts. Picnic area and boat docking are available.

Buttonwood Grove Winery (607-869-9760, www.buttonwoodgrove.com, 5986 State Route 89, Romulus, NY 14541) This winery produces classic European wines in a spectacular lakeside setting with a waterfall, ponds, ducks, and even goats. There's an extensive gift shop and picnic area, and three rustic but comfortable cabins with kitchenettes, appropriately named Cabernet, Chardonnay, and Merlot, available for rent. Boat access is available.

Cayuga Ridge Estate Winery (607-869-5158 or 800-598-9463, www.cayugaridgewinery .com, 6800 State Route 89, Ovid, NY 14521) Owners Susie and Tom Challen feature a wide array of wines, including Cayuga White, Cranberry Essence, and Cranberry Frost. Tastings are offered in a gigantic rustic barn decorated with gothic church lights. The gift shop offers the usual wine-related products, as well as antiques and artwork. There's a cheese shop and picnic area. The winery sponsors the Vigneron Vine Leasing Program, where individuals can "rent a grapevine" and learn to grow, tend, and harvest vines with the option of selling them to the vineyard and paying to have them made into wine.

Thirsty Owl Wine Company (607-869-5805 or 866-869-5805, www.thirstyowl.com, 6799 Elm Beach Rd., Ovid, NY 14521) This 150-acre winery debuted in 2003 and produces Dry Riesling, Vidal Blanc, Riesling, Blushing Moon, Red Moon, Pinor Noir, Merlot, and Chardonnay. There's a seasonal bistro for casual lunch and dinner. The nearly half a mile of frontage on the lake offers great lake views.

Hosmer Winery (607-869-3393 or 888-HOS-WINE, www.hosmerwinery.com, 6999 State Route 89, Ovid, NY 14521) Producing award-winning wines since 1985, the 50-acre Hosmer Winery has won the Governor's Cup for their Rieslings. The Rieslings and Cabernet Franc have set the benchmark for these varieties in the state and across the country. Try the luscious Raspberry Rhapsody made from fresh raspberries and grape wine. There's a gift shop, picnic area, and snacks for sale.

Sheldrake Point Vineyard & Simply Red Lakeside Bistro (607-532-9401 or 866-743-5372, www.sheldrakepoint.com, 7448 County Rd. 153, Ovid, NY 14521) Enjoy estate wines such as Ice Wine while dining in the bistro surrounded by lavender and rose gardens, overlooking the vineyards and lakeshore. The restored 1830s farmhouse is available for private events and business retreats. This is a boat-accessible winery. Lunch, dinner, and Sunday brunch are served in the bistro.

Lucas Vineyards (607-532-4825 or 800-682-WINE, www.lucasvineyrds.com, 3862 County Rd. 150, Interlaken NY 14847) Founded in 1980, this is Cayuga Lake's oldest winery. Ruth Lucas's sense of humor is displayed in the colorful bottles, unique labels, and nautical-inspired "Tug Boat" and "Nautie" wines. The tasting room offers lovely views of the lake below. One of the area's largest gift shops is stocked with hundreds of wine, grape, nautical, and butterfly items. Picnic facilities are available.

Bellwether Hard Cider (607-387-9464 or 888-862-4337, www.cidery.com, 9070 State Route 89, Trumansburg, NY 14886) This is the trail's only hard-cider producer and offers a distinctively different winery experience. Tours and tastings introduce visitors to a new "old" beverage that once reigned as America's most popular drink. Hard cider (made from apples) is enjoying a revival. The gift shop is filled with apple- and cider-related items.

Americana Vineyards & Crystal Lake Café (607-387-6801 or 888-600-8067, www .americanavineyards.com, 4367 East Covert Rd., Interlaken, NY 14847) Americana offers a wide selection of wines and homemade fudge for chocolate lovers. Browse through a selection of gourmet foods and gifts in the restored 1800s timber-framed barn. The Crystal Café serves gourmet sandwiches, local coffees, soups, and desserts.

Six Mile Creek Vineyard (607-272-WINE or 800-260-0612, www.SixMileCreek.com, 1551 Slaterville Rd., Ithaca, NY 14850) Ithaca's own winery features memorable wines that can be enjoyed in the tasting room overlooking a panoramic valley with the vineyard, pond, and gardens. A new line of distilled specialties, including vodka, limoncella, and grappa is offered for tastings and purchase.

King Ferry Winery (315-364-5100 or 800-439-5271, www.treleavenwines.com, 658 Lake Rd., King Ferry, NY 13081) One of two wineries of the east side of Cayuga Lake, King Ferry specializes in Rieslings and barrel-fermented Chardonnays. Peter and Tacie Saltonstall produce award-winning wines in this small farm winery, where the grapes are hand tended. Wines are bottled under the Treleaven label (named for the family who owned the lands before the Saltonstall family). Picnic tables are available.

Long Point Winery (315-364-6990, www.longpointwinery.com, 1485 Lake Rd., Aurora, NY 13026) The other east side winery, this winery produces award-winning wines. Winemaker Gary Barletta focuses his attention on the dry red wines such as Merlot and Syrah. There is boat access and a gift shop.

SENECA LAKE WINE TRAIL

Created in 1986, the Seneca Lake Trail boasts nearly 40 wineries growing hardy native grapes and premium hybrids as well as more delicate varieties such as Riesling, Chardonnay, Cabernet Franc, and Pinot Noir. There is a wine for just about every taste on this trail, which is one of the largest in the Northeast. The wineries are particularly well known for their Rieslings.

A number of wineries are accessible by boat and many are pet friendly. The trail sponsors a range of special events during the year. Highlights include the annual Chocolate & Wine Weekend the second weekend in February; Cruisin' the Tropics Weekend, the last weekend in March; Spring Wine & Cheese Weekend, the last weekend in April; the Golden Nose Awards: A Finger Lakes Wine Experience, at the end of May; and the Annual Deck the Halls, late in November and early December. (For more information call 607-535-8080 or 877-536-2717, or visit www.senecalakewine.com.)

The following are a sampling of Seneca Lake wineries beginning at the northern end of the lake in Geneva, following the lake along the west side to Watkins Glen, and then continuing north along the east side of the lake.

Belhurst Winery (315-781-0201, www.belhurst.com, 4069 State Route 14 South, Geneva, NY 14456) Visitors to the Belhurst Winery tasting room, adjacent to the stunning Belhurst Castle overlooking the lake, can enjoy dining in the castle at Edgar's or in the Vinifera Inn at Stonecutters. The Belhurst tasting room in the gift shop offers an array of award-winning Belhurst wines including Carrie, named after Carrie Collins, who built the Belhurst in 1899, Neptune, Golden Pheasant, Pinot Grigio, Cayuga, Riesling, Chardonnary, Syrah, Pinot Noir, Cabernet Franc, and Merlot.

White Springs Winery (315-781-9463, www.whitespringswinery.com, 4200 State Route 14 South, Geneva, NY 14456) The land has a rich history dating back to the 1700s. White Spring Farm is named for the beautiful clear springs on the property and was home to world-famous sheep and Guernsey cattle before it became one of the foremost fruit farms in the Northeast. It became a vineyard and winery in 2003 and today produces Riesling, Chardonnay, Merlot, Pinot Gris, Pinot Noir, Cabernet Franc, Gewurztraminer, and Sauvignon Blanc wines.

Fox Run Vineyards (315-536-4616 or 800-636-9786, www.foxrunvineyards.com, 670
State Route 14, Penn Yan, NY 14527) A winner of the Governor's Cup for Best New York
State Wine, as well as national and international awards, Fox Run offers a lovely barn
with a deck overlooking the lake. There is a gift shop and cafe with gourmet sandwiches,
salads, and soups. The 55 acres produce a wide range of fine wines. Owner Scott Osborn
is a strong advocate of the place of wine in a healthy lifestyle. The Dry Riesling and
Chardonnay have been hailed by national wine magazines as "best buys."

Red Tail Ridge Winery (315-536-4580, www.redtailridgewinery.com, 846 State Road 14,
Penn Yan, NY 14527) One of the newest area wineries, the tasting room opened in
August 2007 on a ridge overlooking the lake in the middle of the vineyard. The winery is
named after the two nesting pair of hawks who live in the woods next to the vineyard.
The small winery produces Chadonnary, Riesling, and Lemberger wines. Owners Mike
Schnelle and Nancy Irelan create fine handcrafted wines in small lots.

Seneca Shore Wine Cellars (315-536-0882 or 800-LUV-VINO, www.senecawine.com,
State Route 14 and Davy Rd., Penn Yan, NY 14527) Seneca Shore bills itself as the
Medieval Winery of the Finger Lakes. The vineyards were first planted in 1979 and the
winery started in 1997 with a medieval castle–themed tasting room. Enjoy wines on a
deck overlooking the lake. Picnic tables are available.

Prejean Winery (315-536-7524 or 800-548-2216, www.prejeanwinery.com, 2634 State
Route 14, Penn Yan, NY 14527) Award-winning Prejean Winery grows eight grape vari-
eties that originated in Europe: Merlot, Cabernet Sauvignon, Cabernet Franc, Riesling,
Gewurztraminer, Chardonnay, Pinor Noir, and Pinot Gris. Elizabeth and the late James
Prejean started the winery in 1985. Today, Elizabeth runs it with her son Tom.

Torrey Ridge Winery (315-536-1210, www.torreyridgewinery.com, 2770 State Route 14,
Penn Yan, NY 14527) Mennonite farms surround this winery on the west side of the lake
midway between Geneva and Watkins Glen and next to its sister winery, Earle Estates.
Enjoy one of the best panoramic views in the area from the second-floor tasting-room
balcony. The owners have a sense of humor and produce award-winning wines including the fun Red Neck Red and Red Neck White. The gift shop has a large collection of
wine-related gift items as well as hand-painted glassware, pottery, gourmet sauces,
shirts, and hats.

Earle Estates Winery (315-536-6755, www.meadery.com, 2770 State Route 14, Penn Yan,
NY 14527) Since 1993, the family-owned Earle Estates Winery has offered a refreshingly
different taste in wines with the production of more than 20 diverse honey wines
(mead), fruit wines, and grape wines. The winery has been consistently recognized at
national and international wine competitions and has received gold, silver, and bronze
medals as well as several fruit and mead championships and best of class awards. In-
season, visitors can also view the honeybee-observation hive, taste fresh honey, and
learn about the culture of bees and mead making.

Miles Wine Cellars (607-243-7742, www.mileswinecellars.com, 168 Randall Crossing
Road, Himrod, NY 14842) One of the newest wines produced at Miles is Ghost, a blend
of Chardonnay and Cayuga wines, that is a tribute to some of the inhabitants of the
handsome Greek Revival mansion overlooking the lake. Clairvoyants who have visited
just to taste the wine have told owner Doug Miles that spirits live in the house. It wasn't
news to him, since he has had his share of supernatural encounters. The winery has
won a number of awards for its more traditional Pinot Noir, Riesling, Cayuga White,
and Cabernet Franc.

Villa Bellangelo (607-243-8602, www.bellangelo.com, 150 Poplar Point Rd., Dundee, NY 14,837) Established in 2004, this award-winning Italian-style winery, whose name means "beautiful angel," is one of the region's newer wineries. The entire Litterio family is involved in the winery, and young daughters Francesca, Bella Bianca, and Sophia all have wines named in their honor.

Glenora Wine Cellars (607-243-5513 or 800-243-5513, www.glenora.com, 5435 State Route 14, Dundee, NY 14,837) The oldest winery on Seneca Lake, Glenora produces 45,000 cases of wine a year and has won 75 medals at international wine competitions in one year alone. In addition to Riesling, Niagara, Chardonnary, Port, Merlot, Glenora, and Cabernet Sauvignon, the winery features fruit wines including Blueberry Breeze, Cranberry Chablis, Peach Passion, and Raspberry Rose. The Inn at Glenora Wine Cellars has 30 inviting guest rooms featuring Stickley furniture. There's also a restaurant with magnificent views of the lake.

Fulkerson Winery (607-243-7883, www.fulkersonwinery.com, 5576 State Route 14, Dundee, NY 14,837) Sayre Fulkerson, 6th generation on the family farm, with his wife, Nancy, opened the award-winning winery in 1989. In 2005 they opened a new and expanded tasting room, expanded juice plant, and gift shop. In addition to the more common Riesling, Pinot Noir, Merlot, and Cabernet Sauvignon, Cabernet Franc, the winery produces Ice Wine, Dornfelder, Lemberger, and Caleb wines.

Arcadian Estate Winery (607-535-2068 or 800-298-1346, www.arcadianwine.com, 4184 State Route 14, Rock Stream, NY 14,878) The main building is a 170-year-old barn that is home to the winery, tasting room, gift shop and gallery featuring an artist of the month. This is a fun winery that features such wines as Watkins Way Cool Blush, Watkins White, and Watkins Red. There are also a number of fruit wines including Afternoon Delight Cranberry, Shine on Me Pear, Cool Hand Peach, Cherry Fantasy Cherry, and Midnight Train Blueberry.

Lakewood Vineyards (607-535-9252, www.lakewoodvineyards.com, 4024 State Route 14, Watkins Glen, NY 14,891) Three generations of the Stamp family produce award-winning wines on their sprawling 70-acre vineyards. In 1988 after nearly 37 years of growing and selling grapes, the Stamp family founded Lakewood. Winemaker Chris Stamp has the job description "Winemaker/Owner/Operator/Prisoner" on his business card. Everyone is welcome to enjoy the sunflowers, picnic facilities, and the playground. In addition to the Chardonnay, Riesling, white Catawba, Delaware, and Niagara, the winery also produces the highly prized Ice Wine.

Castel Grisch Winery (607-535-9614, www.castelgrisch.com, 3380 County Route 28, Watkins Glen, NY 14,891) Castel Grisch promotes itself as "a little touch of Europe in the Finger Lakes." The winery was founded by a Swiss family and developed at this location on the lake because of its similarities to their native Switzerland. Today the Malina family carries on the founders' European traditions with the restaurant, winery, tasting room, gift shop, and vineyards.

Atwater Estate Vineyards (607-546-VINE or 800-331-7323, www.atwatervineyards.com, 5055 State Route 414, Hector, NY 14,841) Located 7 miles north of Watkins Glen on the eastern shore of the lake, this is a small award-winning boutique winery. Owner Ted Marks features Riesling, Pinor Noir, Cabernet Sauvignon, Syrah, and Lemberger. Special events include the memorable and delicious summer Vine Dining evenings with five courses of locally grown food and paired wines served in the vineyard.

Chateau LaFayette Reneau (607-546-2062 or 800-469-9463, www.clrwine.com, 5081 State Route 414, Hector, NY 14841) This is one of the state's most photographed wineries. It has been designated the International Winery of the Year and won a host of other awards. There are 140 acres of vineyards, ponds, woodlands, and a renovated barn for tastings. Featured wines include Cabernet Sauvignon, Pinot Noir, Merlot, Cuvée Rouge, Roaring Red, Chardonnay, Johannesburg Riesling, Northern White, and Emperor's Blush.

Red Newt Cellars (607-546-4100, www.rednewt.com, 3675 Tichenor Rd., Hector, NY 14841) Red Newt is set on the east side of the lake, and owners David and Debra Whiting are committed to the best in wine and food. The Bistro restaurant highlights locally grown food and produce. Featured wines include Sauvignon Blanc, Pinot Gris, Riesling, Gewurztraminer, Salamander White, Red Newt White, Cabernet Franc, Cabernet Sauvignon, Merlot and Syrah.

Hazlitt 1852 Vineyards (607-546-WINE or 888-750-0494, www.hazlitt1852.com, 5712 State Route 414, Hector, NY 14841) Enjoy fresh popcorn and a cozy barn decorated with antiques and artifacts while sampling wines around the famous horseshoe-shaped bar. The Hazlitt family has a long history of growing grapes and fruit in this area, dating back to 1852 when David Hazlitt and his wife Clarissa purchased 153 acres. Their fruit trees and orchards provided produce that they shipped by wagon, train, and the Erie Canal. The late Jerry Hazlitt and his wife, Elaine, founded this winery in 1984, and today Elaine and sixth-generation Hazlitts, Doug and Leigh, operate the winery that has gained national and international attention. One of the fun wines is named Red Cat.

Wine tasting at the Ventosa Vineyards, Geneva

Wagner Vineyards (607-582-6450 or 866-924-6378, www.wagnervineyards.com, 9322 State Route 414, Lodi, NY 14860) Wagner Vineyards was founded in 1979 by Bill Wagner, a lifelong resident of the area and grape grower for over 40 years. This is one of the largest operations in the Finger Lakes. Tastings are conducted in the distinctive, eight-sided building designed by Wagner. All grapes are grown in the 250-acre vineyard. There's also a German-style brewery and, during the summer, Pub Nights on the Brewdeck every Friday with live entertainment, beer, and food. Lunch and Sunday brunch served daily in-season at the popular Ginny Lee Café overlooking the lake and vineyards.

Lamoreaux Landing Wine Cellars (607-582-6011, www.lamoreauxwine.com 9224 State Route 414, Lodi, NY 14860) Lamoreaux Landing is named after a 19th-century steamboat landing on Seneca Lake; the pilings from the landing can still be seen below the vineyards. Owner Mark Wagner has produced award-winning wines since its opening in 1992. His great-grandfather began the family grape business. The soaring architect-designed Greek Revival wine-tasting building offers great lake views and is one of the more beautiful tasting rooms in the region.

Ventosa Vineyards (315-719-0000, www.ventosavineyards.com, 3440 State Route 96A, Geneva, NY 14456) One of the newest of the Finger Lakes wineries, Ventosa is across the road from Rose Hill in Geneva. Ventosa, whose name means "windy" in Italian, offers an elegant Tuscan setting overlooking the lake. The 350-seat banquet room is popular for weddings and meetings. A café serves lunch daily. Eat inside or outside on the expansive terrace. Wines include Chardonnay, Riesling, Merlot, Vino Rosso, and Saggio.

Clinton Square in downtown Syracuse is a popular gathering spot Wainright Photography

6

Syracuse and the Central Canal Region

Auburn, Skaneateles, Baldwinsville, Oneida Lake, Sylvan Beach

Syracuse

Syracuse, the state's fourth-largest city, enjoys a prime location in the middle of New York State and was a halfway point on the original Erie Canal. The first people who were known to live in the area were the "people of the Longhouse," or Haudensaunee. Today, these Native Americans are known as the Onondaga Nation.

They were attracted by the brine springs on Onondaga Lake. Chief Hiawatha chose the Onondaga Nation settlement as the capital of the Iroquois Confederacy. Today, the Onondaga are still the keepers of the council fire and their reservation lands are south of the city, in Nedrow.

In 1656 French missionaries built Fort Sainte Marie de Gannentaha on the shores of Onondaga Lake. They abandoned the settlement two years later because of hostility from the Native Americans. The fort has been re-created and today costumed interpreters portray life in the 17th-century fort.

European settlement increased after the Revolutionary War when tracts of land were given to war veterans. Towns and villages in the area reflect the era's craze for classical Greece and Rome with towns named Manlius, Marcellus, Camillus, Tully, Ovid, Homer, and Pompey.

The salty swampland waters around Onondaga Creek proved to be much more valuable than the surrounding forest lands. Before refrigerators, salt was very important as a way to cure meat so it would not spoil. Everyone needed salt. When water from the area's salt springs was boiled away, salt was left. Salt production peaked at 9 million bushels in 1862, and the local industry slowly declined and ended in 1926.

A special tariff on Syracuse salt helped New York State raise $3.5 million to pay for construction of the Erie Canal. When the canal opened, the cost of transporting salt dropped from $100 a ton by land to $12 a ton by water. The local salt industry boomed and so did Syracuse.

In the early 19th century the growing community wanted a post office and an official name. John Wilkinson, the man who was to become the village's first postmaster, suggested the name "Syracuse." He had read about a city in Sicily called Siracusa that sounded

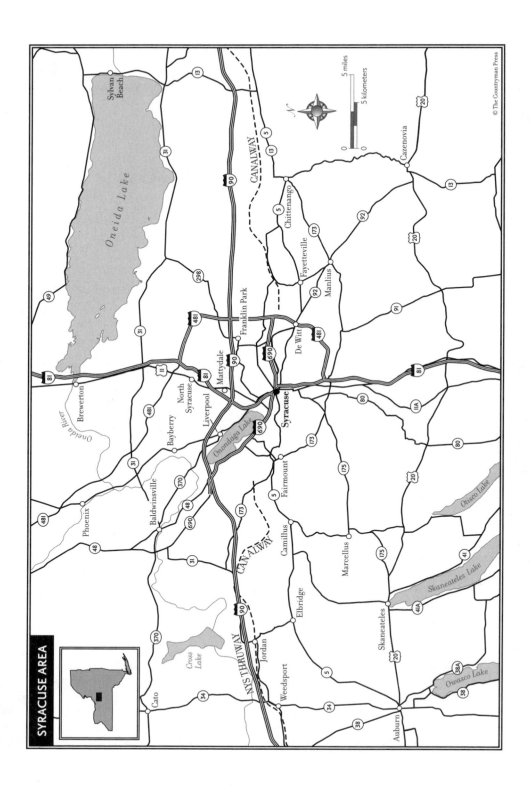

SYRACUSE AREA

© The Countryman Press

a lot like the settlement. So Syracuse became a village, just in time for the opening of the Erie Canal.

Syracuse's low, swampy land was ideal for canal construction. The Erie Canal opened in Syracuse in 1819 and quickly established the village's dominance over nearby settlements. It has been said that Syracuse, nicknamed the Salt City, is the city that salt built. But in reality, the city was built because of the Erie Canal, which continued to run through the heart of downtown until the mid-1920s.

Clinton Square in the center of downtown was known as America's Main Street during the heyday of the canal. From the earliest years of the canal's history, Clinton Square had been a meeting point. The square's wide-water design allowed canal boats to unload cargo without impeding traffic flow.

The skyline created in Clinton Square dates from the 19th-century canal days and includes some of the finest architecture in central New York. Many tolls collected on the 19th-century canals were deposited in the elegant banks that anchor the square. Today, where the canal boats once discharged their passengers and goods, people can ice skate in winter or enjoy concerts and festivals through the spring and summer season. Canal waters once flowed along the route of today's Erie Boulevard.

Warehouses called double-enders sprang up all along the canal. The rear of these buildings was located directly alongside the canal, with the front on the street side; an ornate storefront facade was designed to attract customers. The merchants who operated out of these buildings saved money in transportation costs by unloading directly from the canal boats into their buildings and then selling their merchandise out the front.

Today's Erie Canal Museum is housed in a signature Syracuse canal structure, the 1850 Weighlock Building, which was used to weigh boats and cargo to assess tolls. On the National Register of Historic Places, it is the only remaining canal weighlock in the United States and houses what is considered the country's premier canal museum. Out of seven weighlocks on the canal it was the busiest, in part because it sat at the juncture of two canals—the Erie and the Oswego—that met in downtown Syracuse. After tolls were abolished in the 1880s, the building continued to serve as canal administration offices. Much of today's canal was designed in the building's second-floor offices. When the building was threatened with demolition, volunteers rallied to save it and transform it into a place that today extols the fascinating history of the canals.

The origins of the city's ceramics trade date to the pottery of the native Onondaga people. Syracuse China was founded in 1871 as the Onondaga Pottery Company. Until it closed its Syracuse operations in 2009, it was one of the world's leading suppliers of commercial

America's Longest-Running State Fair
The Great New York State Fair, held in Syracuse, dates back to 1841. The city was picked because of its central location and the ease of transportation it offered, beginning with the Erie and Oswego canals and later railroads and major highways. The fair is a 12-day showcase of New York State's agriculture, education, entertainment, industry, and technology. It is held in late August, ending on Labor Day. Nearly 1 million people visit each year to take in the midway, farm animals, shows, food, and big-name entertainment, such as the Jonas Brothers and Kenny Chesney. Fireworks open and close the fair. For more information, call 315-487-7711 or visit www.nysfair.org.

china for the foodservice industry. The traffic light, the dental chair, the serrated knife, and the Brannock Device for converting foot measurements to shoe size were also invented in Syracuse.

The city is home to Syracuse University, with its signature Carrier Dome, the country's largest domed stadium on a college campus and the largest of its kind in the Northeast. The stadium hosts the Syracuse University Orange sports teams as well as a wide range of concerts including headline groups like the Rolling Stones. The Haudensaunee people invented lacrosse, and both Syracuse University and LeMoyne College hold men's national lacrosse championship titles.

Syracuse Medical College, which became part of Syracuse University, was the first medical college in the United States to adopt coeducation as a policy in 1849. The first woman to argue a case before the U.S. Supreme Court was Syracuse University graduate Belva Lockwood, in 1879.

Syracuse had a national role in the arts and crafts movement, which flourished in the early 20th century. The movement stressed the use of quality materials, craftsmanship, and simplicity of design. Gustav Stickley was a major spokesman for the style. He began making his characteristic oak furniture in 1900. His brothers established the L. and J. G. Stickley Company, which also produced distinctive furniture. During the same period, Adelaide Robineau, a master art potter, and Henry Keck, a stained-glass craftsman, earned national recognition while living and working in Syracuse. The city continues to enjoy a

Syracuse's Inner Harbor connects to the Erie Canal Wainright Photography

Armory Square offers ample opportunities for outside dining in summer Wainright Photography

lively arts community, with potters, cabinetmakers, and other artisans carrying on the arts and crafts tradition.

Many citizens were strong abolitionists. They risked arrest by spiriting fugitives to freedom on the Underground Railroad. Neither below the earth nor a railway, the Underground Railroad was a series of safe houses and trusted "conductors" who helped fugitive slaves escape to freedom in Canada. The Syracuse Vigilance Committee was comprised of citizens who vowed to "pledge their lives, their fortunes and their sacred honor that no person would be taken from Syracuse and returned to slavery." The Jerry Rescue Monument in Clinton Square commemorates the rescue of fugitive slave William "Jerry" Henry. Citizens stormed his jail cell, helping him escape to freedom along the Underground Railroad.

Just two blocks south of bustling Clinton Square is the historic Armory Square neighborhood. Listed on the National Register of Historic Places, Armory Square contains the most significant collection of commercial and industrial architecture in the city. Over the years, the district has escaped the modernization and demolition that has occurred in many other downtown districts. Today, it is home to top museums, a hotel, and more than 50 dining, shopping, music, and specialty establishments—all in 19th- and early-20th-century buildings.

Golden Snowball Award

Though Buffalo is probably better known for abundant snowfalls, Syracuse has been the winner in the snow derby in recent years. The Golden Snowball Award goes annually to the snowiest big city in upstate New York. Since 2003, the big winner has been Syracuse. The glittering award, a gold-flecked crystal ball, is now on display in the Syracuse mayor's office.

Currently, the Syracuse Inner Harbor is undergoing a major redevelopment that will make it one of the grandest stopovers along the canal. Previously home to a barge canal terminal, the harbor project is within walking distance of the Carousel Center, central New York's largest shopping mall, which is also in the midst of a major expansion designed to transform it into one of the nation's largest shopping malls and entertainment complexes, known as Destiny USA. Currently, the Inner Harbor hosts festivals and concerts.

Weighing a Canal Boat

Canal boats weighed in Syracuse were enclosed inside a weighlock chamber, where water drained through a sluice gate at the bottom into a culvert leading to Onondaga Creek. As the water level dropped, so did the boat, until it came to rest on a wooden cradle at the bottom of the weigh chamber. The cradle was suspended by a series of iron rods and levers. These rods distributed the weight of the boat to a single rod attached to the beam scale. The weight of the empty boat, recorded and filed as part of an annual state registration, was subtracted from the full weight. A toll was assessed on the remaining cargo weight based, in part, on the type of goods on board. This entire process took just 15 minutes.

An "Irish" Traffic Light

After the canal was completed and later enlarged, many Irish canal workers from County Tipperary settled in Syracuse on a hill overlooking the canal that became known as Tipperary Hill. When the city first started to install traffic signal lights in the 1920s, workers put one at the corner of Tompkins Street and Milton Avenue. Reportedly, some youths were incensed that British "red" was above Irish "green" and broke the light. The city replaced the light but it was broken again. After a few rounds of this, the city decided that if there was going to be a light at the intersection, it would have to be an inverted one with green on top. It remains a unique green-on-top light to this day.

Sculpture showcasing Tipperary Hill's famous streetlight Wainright Photography

LODGING

Syracuse has several centrally located downtown hotels and a number of suburban hotels and motels as well as historic bed & breakfasts. Nearby, there are good choices for overnight accommodations in Skaneateles and Baldwinsville on Lock 24. Rates as listed are for double occupancy.

Lodging Rates

Inexpensive: Up to $75
Moderate: $76–$150
Expensive: $151–$250
Very Expensive: More than $250

BED & BREAKFAST WELLINGTON

Innkeepers: Wendy Wilber and Ray Borg
315-474-3641 or 800-724-5006
www.bbwellington.com
707 Danforth St., Syracuse, NY 13208
Price: Moderate
Credit Cards: Yes
Handicapped Access: No
Special Features: Complimentary high-speed Internet

This lovely 1914 brick and stucco Tudor-style home is listed on the National and State Registers of Historic Places. Prolific architect Ward Wellington Ward designed the home. There are five guest rooms decorated with Stickley mission furniture. The Gang Suite is named after the family for whom the house was built. The suite has a bedroom with a queen-sized bed, a private bath, dining area, living room with fireplace, an efficiency kitchen, and a library. The Lakeview Room is named for its view of Onondaga Lake and has a high queen-sized sleighbed. A complimentary continental breakfast is served on weekdays and a full gourmet breakfast is served on weekends. There are a variety of ethnic restaurants within walking distance. Children are welcome.

CRAFTSMAN INN

315-637-8000, 800-797-4464
www.craftsmaninn.com
7300 E. Genesee St., Fayetteville, NY 13066
Price: Moderate–Expensive
Credit Cards: Yes
Handicapped Access: Yes
Special Features: Complimentary high-speed Internet

The Craftsman Inn opened in 1995 and is dedicated to the ideals of the arts and crafts community as represented by the Stickley furniture company, founded in the Syracuse suburb of Fayetteville nearly 100 years ago. The building, furniture, and other decor are designed in the arts and crafts style. There are 70 rooms and 21 lodge suites. The rooms are decorated with Stickley furniture. The theme continues in the **Limestone Grill**, where breakfast, lunch, and dinner are served. A lighter lounge menu is available in the evening. Dinner selections include Angus steaks, grilled Atlantic salmon, rack of lamb, and veal Oscar.

DOUBLETREE HOTEL SYRACUSE

315-432-0200
www.doubletree1.hilton.com
6301 Rt. 298, East Syracuse, NY 13057
Price: Moderate–Expensive
Credit Cards: Yes
Handicapped Access: Yes
Special Features: Indoor and outdoor pools

Situated in a corporate park just off the New York State Thruway (I-90), the 250-room Doubletree offers comfortable accommodations in a serene setting just minutes away from downtown Syracuse. In addition to the swimming pools, there is a fully equipped health club with sauna, exercise room, and whirlpool. A complimentary airport shuttle and business center are available. There are 14 meeting rooms including the Grand Ballroom and the Harbour Ballroom. Of course, the Doubletree Hotel Syracuse carries on the great Doubletree tradition with warm chocolate-chip cookies upon check-in. The **Regatta Bar & Grille** serves American cuisine for breakfast, lunch, and dinner. A children's menu is also offered.

EMBASSY SUITES HOTEL

315-446-3200 or 800-362-2779
www.syracuse.embassysuites.com
6646 Old Collamer Rd., E. Syracuse, NY 13057
Price: Expensive
Credit Cards: Yes
Handicapped Access: Yes
Special features: Complimentary cooked-to-order breakfast, manager's reception

This is a good choice for business travelers and families. All rooms are suites with two TVs, a bedroom, and living room with sofa bed, refrigerator, and microwave. There is an indoor pool and fitness center. The cooked-to-order buffet breakfast includes omelets and pancakes, and the two-hour nightly manager's reception offers complimentary drinks and snacks. The **Stillwater Restaurant** is open for lunch and dinner and the hotel is conveniently located close to area attractions and restaurants. Airport transportation is provided.

GENESEE GRANDE HOTEL

315-476-4212 or 800-365-4663
www.geneseegrande.com
1060 E. Genesee St., Syracuse, NY 13210
Price: Moderate–Expensive
Credit Cards: Yes
Handicapped Access: Yes
Special Features: Complimentary airport shuttle

Located in the heart of Syracuse's historic University Hill neighborhood, the 159-room hotel is just four blocks from Syracuse University and the Carrier Dome. One of Syracuse's newest hotels, it is also one of the most upscale places to stay in the area. The fitness center is equipped with high-end equipment and plasma TVs, and

for joggers there are virtual tours and maps of suggested running routes. The elegant **1060 Restaurant**, which has an extensive wine list, with wines available by the glass, has been selected as a *Wine Spectator* Restaurant Award winner.

JEFFERSON CLINTON HOTEL

315-425-0500
www.jeffersonclintonhotel.com
416 S. Clinton St., Syracuse, NY 13202
Price: Expensive
Credit Cards: Yes
Handicapped Access: Yes
Special Features: Complimentary breakfast with made-to-order omelets

A member of the National Trust Historic Hotels of America, the Jefferson Clinton opened in 1927 and catered to the clientele of the D. L. & W. Railroad; the railway station was then adjacent to the hotel. It was also popular with vaudeville performers playing at the nearby Landmark Theater. Today the totally renovated hotel prides itself on its eco-friendly policies. There are 60 suites, all with full kitchen, complimentary high-speed Internet, and DVD players. Guests have access to an exercise room and meeting facilities. The hotel is in the heart of historic Armory Square, and there are more than 50 restaurants within a six-block radius. The complimentary breakfast includes organic foods from local farms.

HOLIDAY INN–CARRIER CIRCLE

315-437-2761 or 800-465-4329
www.holidayinn.com/syr-i90
6555 Old Collamer Rd. South, E. Syracuse, NY 13057
Price: Moderate
Credit Cards: Yes
Handicapped Access: Yes
Special features: Pet friendly, complimentary high-speed Internet

Located just off Exit 35 of the New York State Thruway (I-90), this 203-room hotel is a good choice for the entire family, even four-legged ones. Kids eat for free and there are game and fitness rooms and laundry facilities. Guests can enjoy the wonderful large heated pool and whirlpool. There is a complimentary continental breakfast on weekdays and a business center. The hotel is just 4 miles from downtown Syracuse. The Stockyard Grill serves breakfast, lunch, and dinner.

RENAISSANCE SYRACUSE DOWN-TOWN
315-479-7000 or 877-843-6279
www.marriott.com
701 E. Genesee St., Syracuse, NY 13210
Price: Moderate–Expensive
Credit Cards: Yes
Handicapped Access: Yes
Special Features: Pet friendly; complimentary covered parking

Convenient to popular downtown attractions including the Carrier Dome, this 279-room, 20-story hotel faces Syracuse University. There are three suites and a Club Level with access to the lounge and complimentary breakfast and evening appetizers. This is a smoke-free hotel. There is a fitness center and guest privileges at the nearby YMCA. The largest of the 16 meeting rooms, Horizons, on the 20th floor, has expansive views of the city. **Redfield's Restaurant** is a Manhattan-style bistro open for breakfast, lunch, and dinner.

SHERATON SYRACUSE UNIVERSITY HOTEL & CONFERENCE CENTER
315-475-3000 or 800-395-2105
www.sheratonsyracuse.com
801 University Ave., Syracuse, NY 13210
Price: Expensive
Credit Cards: Yes
Handicapped Access: Yes
Special Features: Free high-speed Internet, dog friendly

Well located on the campus of Syracuse University, this 236-room hotel is also a popular meeting site, with ten conference rooms and two elegant ballrooms. Rooms are large and comfortable. There are family packages that feature free kids meals for the 12-and-under set. Free shuttle service is available to the airport and train station. The indoor pool and fitness facility are popular with guests. This is a totally smoke-free environment. The on-site **Seasons Bar & Grille** offers a number of TVs for sports enthusiasts, as well as pool tables and dartboards. The menu features pizza, burgers, sandwiches, and salads. **Rachel's** is the alternate fine-dining restaurant, serving up such entrées as lamb chops, orange chicken, and grilled Atlantic salmon.

THE MAPLEWOOD INN
315-451-1511
www.themaplewoodinn.com
400 7th North St., Liverpool, NY 13088
Price: Moderate
Credit Cards: Yes
Handicapped Access: Yes
Special Features: Elan Therapeutic Massage spa on premises

This 137-room luxury boutique hotel has large, well-appointed rooms with a complimentary breakfast bar, free local calls, high-speed Internet, an indoor pool, fitness facilities, and meeting space that is popular for weddings. The inn features pillow-top mattresses and luxury linens. **Elan Therapeutic Massage** offers a wide range of massages from prenatal to ginger and lemongrass to sea salt to hot stone to Swedish. Facials are also offered.

RESTAURANTS
Syracuse has a rich culinary history, and area restaurants include many diverse ethnic flavors. Many restaurants feature Finger

SYRACUSE AND THE CENTRAL CANAL REGION **161**

Lakes wines. All restaurants are by New York State law nonsmoking. Prices are estimated per person for dinner entrée without tax, tip, or beverage.

Dining Rates
Inexpensive: Up to $10
Moderate: $11–$25
Expensive: $26–$40
Very Expensive: More than $40

ALE 'N' ANGUS PUB

315-426-9672
www.alenanguspub.com
238 Harrison St., Syracuse, NY 13202
Open: Daily (closed Sat. and Sun. in July and Aug.)
Price: Moderate
Credit Cards: Yes
Cuisine: American
Serving: L, D
Handicapped Access: Yes
Special Features: Across the street from Onondaga County War Memorial

This comfortable pub is popular with both downtown workers and event-goers. Although it serves generous portions of creative dishes, the traditional Angus burger is one of the most popular choices. Decorated with neon beer signs, the spacious dining room adjoins a friendly barroom. The menu offers everything from Buffalo chicken wings to pesto fettucine to Icelandic haddock. Of course, steak is always a favorite in a place that goes by

"Angus." The signature dessert is a "mud-ball" (ice cream rolled in crushed Oreo cookies and topped with chocolate sauce and whipped cream).

ARAD EVANS INN

315-637-2020
www.aradevansinn.com
7206 Genesee St., Fayetteville, NY 13066
Open: Mon.–Sat.
Price: Expensive
Credit Cards: Yes
Cuisine: American
Serving: D
Handicapped Access: Yes
Special Features: Casual bistro in addition to dining room

Housed in an 1840s Federal-style house, the inn offers dinner in the formal dining rooms or the more casual bistro area, which features smaller entrées and items such as Kobe burgers. The dining room menu includes Kobe sirloin steak, grilled swordfish, smoked duck breast, and New Zealand lamb rack. The dessert menu features some special treats for chocolate lovers—flourless chocolate torte, chocolate pudding cake, chocolate tower, and double chocolate torte.

COLEMAN'S AUTHENTIC IRISH PUB

315-476-1933
www.colemansirishpub.com
100 South Lowell Ave., Syracuse, NY 13204
Open: Daily

Pizza for Chocolate Lovers

The Food Network has made a pilgrimage to the **Chocolate Pizza Company** (www.chocolatepizza .com, 315-673-4098, 60 E. Main St., Marcellus, NY 13108), ten minutes from Skaneateles in Marcellus. Chocolate fans come to this colorfully decorated shop for the famous chocolate pizza (milk or dark chocolate mixed with English toffee, walnuts, pecans, almonds, and white chocolate on top) served in a pizza box. There are many variations on this theme, as well as wings (rippled potato chips with peanut butter dipped in chocolate), cookies, specialty chocolates, and freshly made gelato. Items can also be ordered online. Open daily.

Price: Moderate
Credit Cards: Yes
Cuisine: American/Irish
Serving: L, D
Handicapped Access: Yes
Special Features: Live music Thurs.–Sun.

Coleman's has been a Syracuse institution since it was established as a workingman's saloon in 1933 on historic Tipperary Hill. Since then, the restaurant has tripled in size while maintaining the small-pub atmosphere. It is decorated with an Irish theme that even includes a special leprechaun's door. Signature dishes include Guinness beef stew, roast Irish chicken, corned beef and cabbage, and sea scallops. In March the beer flows green. The shop sells Coleman's logo items including a Coleman's glass with the green-on-top traffic light in honor of the unique Tipperary Hill light.

COLORADO MINE CO. STEAKHOUSE

315-451-6956
www.coloradomine.com
1333 Buckley Rd., N. Syracuse, NY 13212
Open: Daily
Price: Moderate
Credit Cards: Yes
Cuisine: American
Serving: L, D
Handicapped Access: Yes
Special Features: Take-out available

This popular western-themed steakhouse offers traditional western-cut strip steaks, filets mignons, and Delmonico and porterhouse steaks, plus rack of lamb. The whole-rack, hickory-smoked and slow-cooked baby back ribs are a favorite. Other menu items include chicken, seafood, and pasta dishes. There is a children's menu.

DANZER'S GERMAN & AMERICAN RESTAURANT

315-422-0089
www.danzers.com

153 Ainsley Dr., Syracuse, NY 13210
Open: Daily
Price: Moderate
Credit Cards: Yes
Cuisine: German/American
Serving: L, D
Handicapped Access: Yes
Special Features: Popular spot for private parties and banquets

Opened in 1946, Danzer's resembles a Bavarian chalet and is a comfortable, family-oriented restaurant. In addition to the popular burgers, huge deli sandwiches, and an array of American dishes, German dishes are a specialty. They include hearty portions of bratwurst, knackwurst, schnitzel, and sauerbraten.

DINOSAUR BAR-B-QUE

315-476-4937
www.dinosaurbarbque.com
246 W. Willow St., Syracuse, NY 13202
Open: Daily
Price: Moderate
Credit Cards: Yes
Cuisine: BBQ
Serving: L, D
Handicapped Access: Yes
Special Features: Live music

This original Dinosaur opened in 1988 and has spawned offshoots in Rochester and New York City. It advertises itself as a "genuine honky tonk rib joint," and that it is. The Dinosaur has received well-deserved national acclaim and awards for its food and blues music. It offers hearty dishes of great-tasting pork, beef, and chicken, all smoky and delicious. The Dino menu boasts of "slathering" sauce and it is rated by heat index. Take out is available, and there is a **Dino Store** with sauces, rubs, clothing, and other merchandise. Located in the historic Armory Square district.

L'ADOUR RESTAURANT FRANCAIS

315-475-7653

www.ladour.com
110 Montgomery St., Syracuse, NY 13202
Open: Daily
Price: Moderate–Expensive
Credit Cards: Yes
Cuisine: French
Serving: B, L, D
Handicapped Access: Yes
Special Features: Tasting menus and wine pairing menus

Named after a river in co-owner and chef Yann Guigne's childhood village in France, it is a vision of Guigne and Alexia Falcone, who honed their culinary skills in Prague. In 2001 the couple opened this restaurant in the newly renovated Courier Building across from City Hall, in the heart of Alexia's hometown. This is truly a perfect French restaurant down to the imported and classically trained French wait staff. Of course, there is an extensive wine list featuring French wines. Menu choices include such items as roasted red deer, roasted sea scallops, and roasted rabbit tournedos. Chocolate lovers should save room for the all-chocolate plate.

LEMON GRASS

315-475-1111
www.lemongrasscny.com
238 W. Jefferson St., Syracuse, NY 13202
Open: Daily
Price: Moderate
Credit Cards: Yes
Cuisine: Thai
Serving: D; L, Mon.–Sat.
Handicapped Access: Yes
Special Features: Special prix fixe menus on holidays, including Thai New Year on Apr. 13

Located in the heart of Armory Square, this is the best Thai restaurant in central New York. Well known for its large menu, some of the longtime favorites include Long Island duck, sweet tamarind sauce with large shrimp or yellow fin tuna, and Himalayan mango cashew nuts with shrimp or chicken.

The wine list is internationally renowned, and *Wine Spectator* honored Lemon Grass with the Award of Excellence for eight consecutive years. Signature desserts include homemade ice cream in flavors including burnt sugar, ginger, mango, and espresso, and homemade fruit sorbets.

PASCALE WINE BAR & RESTAURANT

315-471-3040
www.pascalerestaurant.com
204 W. Fayette St., Syracuse, NY 13202
Open: Daily
Price: Moderate
Credit Cards: Yes
Cuisine: American
Serving: D
Handicapped Access: Yes
Special Features: Live jazz on Sat.

Pascale has been voted Syracuse's most romantic restaurant many times over because of its fine food, friendly service, eclectic art on the stucco walls, and candlelight. In the Armory Square district, it is a good choice for a pretheater dinner. The menu changes seasonally and features such choices as the game sampler featuring antelope medallions, roasted squab, rabbit sausage with wild huckleberry sauce, and Alaskan halibut. The award-winning wine list is extensive. A lighter bistro menu is also available.

PASTABILITIES

315-474-1153
www.pastabilities.com
311 South Franklin St., Syracuse, NY 13202
Open: Daily
Price: Moderate
Credit Cards: Yes
Cuisine: Italian
Serving: D; L Mon.–Fri.
Handicapped Access: Yes
Special Features: Outdoor dining and live music

A downtown mainstay since 1982, Pastabilities has evolved from a one-room lunch spot into a three-dining-room establishment with a full-service bar and seasonal outdoor dining. It moved to its current location in 1985, becoming the restaurant centerpiece in the redevelopment of Armory Square. Everything is made from scratch, and as the demand for its bread grew, Pastabilities opened **Pasta's Daily Bread** directly across the street at 308 South Franklin. The menu includes a variety of homemade pasta dishes, chicken Parmesan, and Jamaican jerk mahimahi.

STELLA'S DINER

315-425-0353
home.twcny.rr.com/stellas

110 Wolf St., Syracuse, NY 13208
Open: Daily
Price: Inexpensive
Credit Cards: Yes
Cuisine: American
Serving: B, L, D (except Mon. and Tues.)
Handicapped Access: Yes
Special Features: Take-out available

Close to the Carousel Center, this is a classic old-fashioned diner, distinguished by its profusion of Betty Boop memorabilia. The menu is extensive; diner-favorite dishes include liver and onions, grilled ham steak, and roast turkey dinner. There is also a children's menu.

CULTURE

Syracuse has a full cultural heritage and boasts many performing arts venues of a caliber usually found only in much larger cities. It is also a region that values its history, and volunteers have worked hard to save many architectural and historic treasures.

Museums and Historic Sites

ERIE CANAL MUSEUM

315-471-0593
www.eriecanalmuseum.org
318 Erie Blvd. East, Syracuse, NY 13202
Open: Daily
Admission: Free

Housed in the museum's largest artifact—an 1850 weighlock building, the only such building remaining in the country—this is the nation's top canal museum. It is also home to the Syracuse Heritage Area Visitor Center. Currently in the midst of a major renovation project, the site has become a combination science and history museum. Displays include historic artifacts, models, dioramas, and photographs that tell the story of the canal's construction and of life along and on the canal. A highlight is the *Frank B. Thomson,* a replica 65-foot-long passenger and cargo line boat that museum goers are invited to board. Visitors learn about aquatic elevators, or locks, sources for canal waters, and types of Erie Canal boats. Start your tour with a 12-minute film on the history of Syracuse and the canal. Visit a weighmaster's office that features a desk from the mid-1800s used in the Rochester weighlock office. The Penny Postcard Arcade showcases 19th- and early-20th-century postcards showing scenes of Syracuse and the Erie Canal complete with personal messages written on the backs.

When children arrive they are given a clipboard, a pencil, and a *Towpath Detective* booklet. As they make their way through the museum and onto the boat, they follow the signs to answer questions in the booklet. It's a fun way for kids to learn while they explore. At the end of the visit, a staff member will tally the score. Depending on the number of correct answers, children will be named Captain, Steersman, Hoggee, or Mule.

MATILDA JOSLYN GAGE HOUSE

315-637-9511
www.matildajoslyngage.org
210 E. Genesee St., Fayetteville, NY 13066
Open: By appointment
Admission: Free

Matilda Joslyn Gage was an ardent women's rights supporter. Along with Susan B. Anthony and Elizabeth Cady Stanton, she was a founding member of the National Woman Suffrage Association. Her home was also a station on the Undergound Railroad. She spoke out against what she called the brutal and unfair treatment of Native Americans and was adopted into the Wolf Clan of the Mohawk Nation. Her lifelong motto appears on her gravestone in Fayetteville: "There is a word sweeter than Mother, Home or Heaven; that word is Liberty." In 1882 L. Frank Baum, author of *The Wonderful Wizard of Oz*, married Gage's youngest daughter Maud in the home's parlor. The house is a popular stop for Oz fans while visiting nearby Chittenango, birthplace of Baum.

MILTON J. RUBENSTEIN MUSEUM OF SCIENCE & TECHNOLOGY

315-425-9068
www.most.org
500 So. Franklin St., Syracuse, NY
Open: Wed.–Sun.
Admission: Adults $5, seniors $4, children $4

Located in the heart of the historic Armory Square district and known by the acronym MOST, this museum is located in a former armory. Fun and educational for the whole fam-

The MOST

ily, it includes the **Bristol Imax Omnitheater,** where visitors can rock with the Rolling Stones or swim with dolphins on the 6-story-high screen. This hands-on museum recently opened two new major exhibits. They are the Science Playhouse and the Earth Science Discovery Cave. They mark the beginning of a phased-in revitalization of the MOST. The Playhouse is a giant climbing maze that combines basic scientific principles based on levers, pulleys, and bridges with special effects and fun for all. It offers nine levels over five floors. The Earth Science Adventure Cave is a realistic cave experience that invites visitors to explore various facets of geology by crawling or walking through the large cave, which features dripping water and cool, damp air. The exhibit features many hands-on activities centering on geology, including stalactites, rock formations, mineral deposits, and water. There are also hands-on exhibits, planetarium shows, and lively science demonstrations.

OCTAGON HOUSE OF CAMILLUS

315-488-7800
www.townofcamillus.com
5420 W. Genesee St., Camillus, NY 13031
Open: Sun.
Admission: Free

This landmark structure was built in 1856 by Isaiah Wilcox out of cobblestones, rubble, and concrete, with a stucco finish. Each of its eight sides is 17 feet long and 22 inches thick at the base. There are eight square rooms, eight triangular rooms, and ten closets. The deep closet was rumored to have been part of the Underground Railroad.

ONONDAGA HISTORICAL ASSOCIATION MUSEUM

315-428-1864
www.cnyhistory.org
321 Montgomery St., Syracuse, NY 13202
Open: Wed.–Sun.
Admission: Free (suggested $3 donation)

This museum houses one of the nation's largest regional collections of historical treasures. Exhibits include Onondaga County: the Heart of New York, exploring the area's people, commerce, architecture, and transportation systems; The Franklin and the Rise of the Automobile Age, showcasing the grand Syracuse-based Franklin Automobile Company, from its beginning in 1902 until its demise in 1934; Freedom Bound: Syracuse and the Underground Railroad; and Our Sporting Life: The Heroes, the Highlights, the History. There are also exhibits on the history of brewing in Syracuse and Syracuse China.

SAINTE MARIE AMONG THE IROQUOIS

315-453-6768
http://onondagacountyparks.com/sainte-marie
Rt. 370/Onondaga Lake Parkway, Liverpool, NY
Open: Tues.–Sun., mid-May–mid-Oct.
Admission: Adults $3, seniors $2.50, children $2

This is a re-creation of the French mission that stood on the shores of Onondaga Lake from 1656–58. Museum browsers learn about the 17th-century culture of the Iroquois, the

French, and their meeting here. At the Interpretive Center, visitors can converse with knowledgeable staff in period dress about daily life in the 1650s. Demonstrations in carpentry, blacksmithing, cooking, and other activities are offered. Although it takes only a minute to walk from the visitors' center to the "living history" mission, the transformation is quite amazing. An actor portraying a Jesuit priest describes the arduous two-month trip from Quebec as he readies the small chapel. Led by Iroquois guides, seven Jesuits, twelve soldiers, and thirty craftsmen and workers traveled in 20 canoes into the unknown wilderness. An interpreter depicting Major Zacharie Dupois, commander of the settlement, bids you *bienvenue*, or welcome, at the doorway to the cookhouse, where an apprentice cook is mixing bread.

SALT MUSEUM

315-453-6715
www.onondagacountyparks.com/olp/salt-museum
6790 Onondaga Lake Trail, Liverpool, NY 13088
Open: Mid-May–mid-Oct.
Admission: Free

Located on the shores of Onondaga Lake in Onondaga Lake Park, the museum invites visitors to learn about the history of salt production in Syracuse, the city that once supplied the entire nation with salt. Explore the site of an original boiling block, where brine (salt water) was turned into what was then one of the country's most precious commodities. See the actual kettles, wooden barrels, and other equipment that were used in the process, which came to an end in this region in the 1920s. The building was constructed from timbers taken from actual salt warehouses and has a number of exhibits and salt-related artifacts.

Other Attractions

EVERSON MUSEUM OF ART

315-474-6064
www.everson.org
401 Harrison St., Syracuse, NY 13202
Open: Tues.–Sun.
Admission: Free (suggested $5 donation)

This is the first museum designed by famed architect I. M. Pei, and it is internationally acclaimed for its uniqueness. The Everson houses roughly 11,000 pieces of art: American paintings, sculpture, drawings, graphics, and one of the largest collections of American ceramics in the nation. The innovative ArtZone is designed to acquaint art viewers with the visual arts. The gallery helps visitors, particularly children and families, interpret the collection by engaging in creative activities that teach basic art principles.

ROSAMOND GIFFORD ZOO AT BURNET PARK

315-435-8511
www.rosamondgiffordzoo.org
One Conservation Pl., Syracuse, NY 13204
Open: Daily
Admission: Adults $6.50, seniors, $4.50, students and children $4

Well known in zoo circles for its successful Asian elephant–breeding program, the Rosamond Gifford offers regular demonstrations of the elephants' skills and intelligence. The zoo participated in a cooperative breeding program with other zoos to breed and release red wolves back into the wild. Before the release, this species had become extinct in the wild. Throughout the zoo there are easy-to-understand explanations about the animals and their declining habitat.

At the barnyard-animal area visitors can watch a sheepdog herding sheep, and children can take pony rides. In the "social animal" area there are gibbons, ring-tailed lemurs, meerkats, and mandrills. We watched a mother mandrill gently caress her baby, born just a week earlier. It's possible to look through glass windows at the zoo kitchen and veterinary hospital. During our visit, a turtle was recuperating from an accident that damaged part of its shell. Meet-the-keeper events and animal demonstrations are scheduled throughout the summer.

Performing Arts

Mulroy Civic Center Theaters at Oncenter (315-435-8000, www.oncentercomplex.com, 411 Montgomery St., Syracuse, NY 13202) Three theaters are housed here, hosting concerts, stage presentations, meetings, dance recitals, workshops, and lectures.

Salt City Center for the Performing Arts (315-475-9749, www.saltcitycenter.com, 204 Lincoln Park Dr., Syracuse, NY 13203) Begun in 1968, the center is a nonprofit performing arts and teaching center presenting a year-round season of musicals, dramas, and comedies. The center also offers a full complement of classes in acting, dance, voice, and playwriting for all ages. *Jesus Christ Superstar* is performed annually during Lent and is the longest-running annual performance in the area.

Syracuse Area Landmark Theatre (315-475-7979, www.landmarktheatre.org, 362 S. Salina St., Syracuse, NY 13202) This grand 3,000-seat concert and movie palace was built in 1928 and now presents everything from Dora the Explorer to Josh Groban to David Copperfield. Listed on the National Register of Historic Places, it is the last remaining Depression-era movie palace in the area.

Syracuse Civic Theater (315-449-2134, www.syracusecivictheatre.com, Carrier Theater, 421 Montgomery St., Syracuse, NY 13202) This theater repertory group produces five shows a year at the Carrier Theater in the Mulroy Civic Center. The productions include two children's performances.

Syracuse Opera Company (315-475-5915, www.syracuseopera.com, 411 Montgomery St., Syracuse, NY 13202) Central New York's only year-round professional opera company, it offers three main-stage productions each season plus outreach and education programs.

Syracuse Stage (315-443-3275, www.syracusestage.org, 820 E. Genesee St., Syracuse, NY 13210) Besides seven main-stage plays, Syracuse Stage, central New York's only professional theater, produces a New Play Festival and a Young Playwrights Festival. It presents an entertaining mix of comedies, dramas, and musicals.

Syracuse Symphony Orchestra (315-424-8200, www.syracusesymphony.org, 411 Montgomery St., Syracuse, NY 13210) Founded in 1961, the Syracuse Symphony has received national acclaim and plays 200 full orchestra and chamber ensemble concerts per season.

RECREATION

Syracuse enjoys a wealth of recreational opportunities thanks to its lakes, parks, and other leisure facilities. Its proximity to the Adirondacks and the Tug Hill area to the north, and the Finger Lakes to the south, make the area popular for outdoor enthusiasts.

Parks

Chittenango Falls State Park (315-655-9620, www.nysparks.state.ny.us, 2300 Rathburn Rd., Cazenovia, NY 13035) A picturesque 167-foot waterfall is the main attraction of this park. Glacial sculpting over 400-million-year-old bedrock is responsible for this scenic feature. Visitors can view the falls from the top, walk the winding trail into the gorge, view the falls from a footbridge, and return to the top along the small trail on the opposite side of the gorge. Activities include fishing, hiking, and picnicking.

Clark Reservation State Park (315-492-1590, www.nysparks.state.ny.us, 6105 East Seneca Turnpike, Jamesville, NY 13078) This park is a geologic wonder of the last ice age and a botanist's paradise. Guided nature walks leave from the Nature Center building, which also offers numerous exhibits. Hikers may choose from five trails, including the cliff trail, which has a ledge overlook 175 feet above the water.

Green Lakes State Park (315-637-6111, www.nysparks.state.ny.us, 7900 Green Lakes Rd., Fayetteville, NY 13066) The park's outstanding features are its two glacial lakes surrounded by upland forest. Both Round and Greek lakes are meromictic lakes, which means that there is no fall and spring mixing of surface and bottom waters. Another special feature of the park is an 18-hole golf course designed by Robert Trent Jones, where visitors can snowshoe in winter, and there are 10 miles of trails that cross-country skiers can use. There is also a nature center, campsites, cabins, a beach, boat rentals, and a playground.

Onondaga Lake Park (315-453-6712, www.onondagacountyparks.com, 6790 Onondaga Lake Trail, Liverpool, NY 13088) Known as the Central Park of central New York, this park has it all. There is a boat launch, marina, fishing, a skate park, bike and skate

The skyline of Syracuse is visible from Onondaga Lake Park Wainright Photography

rentals, boat rental, archery targets, and **Wegmans Playground. Wegmans Good Dog Park** is a top-of-the-line off-leash dog park with a separate section for small dogs, water, benches for people, agility equipment for dogs, and shade trees for all. Near the dog park is Mud Lock, dating back to the early Erie Canal, it allowed passage to the Oswego Canal and was the site of a lively tavern. The Salt Museum is in the park. There is even free outdoor wireless Internet in the area of the **Griffin Visitor Center.**

Spectator Sports

Syracuse Crunch Hockey (315-473-4444, www.syracusecrunch.com, Onondaga County War Memorial at Oncenter Syracuse, 800 South State St., Syracuse, NY 13202) This hockey team is an affiliate of the American Hockey League's Columbus Blue Jackets.

Syracuse Salty Dogs Pro Soccer (315-635-3216, www.syracusefc.com, P & C Stadium, One Tex Simone Dr., Syracuse, NY 13208) The Salty Dogs play professional A-League Soccer all summer.

Syracuse Skychiefs (315-474-2658, www.skychiefs.com, P & C Stadium, One Tex Simone Dr., Syracuse, NY 13208) The Skychiefs are the AAA affiliate of the Toronto Blue Jays and a community-owned team.

Syracuse Sting Women's Pro Football (315-418-0905, www.syracusesting.com, P & C Stadium, One Tex Simone Dr., Syracuse, NY 13208) The Syracuse Sting is one of the premier women's pro football teams in New York and has earned the title Champions of the Eastern Division twice in three years. It is one of 125 professional women's football teams in the U.S.

Syracuse University (315-443-2121, www.suathletics.com, 888-DOMETIX, Carrier Dome Box Office, 900 Irving Ave., Syracuse, NY 13244) Syracuse University, better known as the Orange, is known nationally for its champion teams in basketball, lacrosse, and football. Women's basketball, men's and women's soccer, women's lacrosse, track and field, field hockey, women's volleyball, rowing, crew, softball, swimming, and diving have all garnered national honors.

Syracuse University Orange fan Wainright Photography

SHOPPING

City shopping revolves around the historic Armory Square area and the expanding Carousel Center. There are two major malls in the suburbs.

Armory Square (www.armorysquare .com) In the heart of downtown Syracuse, the historic Armory Square district is home to a number of galleries, shops, boutiques, and restaurants, as well as cultural institutions such as the Most and the Landmark Theater. The district also hosts a number of special events throughout the year including the celebrated Syracuse Winterfest.

A Canal-Side Park

Camillus Erie Canal Park (315-488-3409, www.eriecanalcamillus.com, 5750 Devoe Road, Camillus, NY 13031) near the village of Camillus, just north of Syracuse, is a lovely canal-side park managed and run entirely by volunteers through the Camillus Canal Society. It was the midpoint on the original Erie Canal. This 300-acre park includes a restored section of the canal (the second canal), 9 miles of trails, and two picnic areas.

Volunteers cleared the canal bed and trails and built bridges, boats, and boathouses, as well as the Sims Store Museum. Volunteers continue to maintain the park, staff the boat cruises, and are now working to restore the 1844 Nine Mile Creek Aqueduct. This impressive stone aqueduct was built to carry the Erie Canal 144 feet above the creek.

The **Sims Store Museum** serves as the park's headquarters. It is actually a reproduction of the 1856 Sims' Canal Store, which was located about 2 miles from the park. The original Sims building was both a general store and a departure point for canal travel. It was destroyed by fire in 1963; the new store was built in 1976.

The main floor features a re-creation of a 19th-century general store. On the second floor is a small museum with exhibits about the Erie Canal including early photos, local artifacts, and models of locks, aqueducts, and canal boats. Just outside Sims Store is an operating lock exhibit demonstrating how a canal boat was taken from one level to the next, and a replica lock tender's shanty.

Canal dinner cruises traveling 4 miles round-trip are available throughout the summer. Boat rides on the ***Ontario,*** a replica turn-of-the-century excursion boat, are offered during the May-to-October canal season.

The park offers 9 miles of trails and a picnic pavilion. The canal waters are popular for canoeing, fishing, and kayaking. Towpath and trail activities include hiking, bird watching, jogging, cross-country skiing, and bicycling. Dogs on leashes are welcome. Grounds open daily; museum open Saturday and Sunday, May through October.

Nine Mile Creek Aqueduct at Camillus Erie Canal Park

Carousel Center (315-466-6000, www.carouselcenter.com, 9090 Carousel Center Dr., Syracuse, NY 13290) The centerpiece and namesake of the mall is an antique carousel built in Philadelphia in 1909. The 42 horses were all hand carved and have been meticulously restored after spending years at Long Branch Park in Syracuse and Canandaigua's Roseland Park. Riding the carousel is popular for visitors of all ages. There are more than 170 stores and shops, restaurants, and a 19-screen Regal Cinemas complex. Anchor stores include H&M, Macy's, and Lord & Taylor. Other stores include Apple, Borders Books, Eastern Mountain Sports, Guitar Outlet, Coach, and Brookstone.

Great Northern Mall (315-622-4449, www.greatnorthernmall.com, 4155 Rt. 31, Clay, NY 13041) This mall offers nearly 100 stores, plus a food court and Regal Cinemas.

ShoppingTown Mall (315-446-09160, www.shoppingtownmall.com, 3649 Erie Blvd. E., DeWitt, NY 13214) There are more than 85 stores and restaurants plus Regal Cinemas. Anchor stores include Macy's, Sears, and Dick's Sporting Goods.

AUBURN

William H. Seward traveled throughout the world on extended trips, but it was to his Auburn home that the city's most famous citizen was drawn "by an irresistible spell."

Devout abolitionists, Seward and his wife, Frances, were friends of Harriet Tubman, who led hundreds of slaves to freedom on the Underground Railroad. Seward convinced Tubman to leave Canada and make her home in Auburn, where he helped her buy property down the street from his home.

Today, visitors can visit their homes, as well as the only complete example of a Tiffany-designed church interior, and a well-kept county park on the shores of Owasco Lake, a lovely and little-known Finger Lake just 30 miles southwest of Syracuse.

In 1815, when DeWitt Clinton visited, Auburn was the largest village in central and western New York. It grew into a major industrial center and used the nearby Erie Canal to transport its varied manufactured goods.

Seward's home in the city's historic district is one of the most remarkable in the state.

The William Seward House in Auburn

Seward, who lost the presidential nomination to Abraham Lincoln but went on to be secretary of state for eight years under Lincoln and President Andrew Johnson, lived in the home for nearly half a century. Seward was also a New York state senator, New York governor, and U.S. senator. It was as secretary of state that he negotiated the purchase of Alaska from Russia. At the time skeptics called it Seward's Folly, or Seward's Icebox.

What makes the Seward House so special is that it was enjoyed by four generations of the family from 1816 to 1951. It was then given to a foundation that operates the home today. The Sewards kept everything, and the house is large enough to display many of the family's possessions. Everything is original to the property—a rarity in historical houses. The front parlor features a fireplace painted by Brigham Young, then a sixteen-year-old journeyman painter and carpenter. He later became famous as a pillar of the Mormon Church. Much of the furniture in this room was originally in Seward's formal parlor in his Washington, D.C., home in the 1850s and 1860s. Lincoln sat on the gold leaf chairs during his frequent visits to Seward's home to escape the chaos of the White House during the Civil War.

The house has an impressive collection of souvenirs from Seward's extensive career and world travels. The flowers that covered Lincoln's casket are on display, as are pieces of the bloodstained sheets from Seward's bed. On the night that Lincoln was assassinated, Seward himself was attacked in his bed and almost killed. Seward amassed one of the most extensive Civil War libraries in the nation. Many of the books are autographed by their authors. His collection includes two original editions of *Uncle Tom's Cabin*.

Guides point out the hidden room where the Sewards hid slaves fleeing on the Underground Railroad led by Harriet Tubman. Born a slave herself, Tubman guided several hundred fellow slaves to freedom. In all she made 19 trips to the South—risking everything for freedom. She always had a six-shooter strapped at her side.

"There was one of two things I had a right to—liberty or death. If I could not have one, I would have the other, for no man should take me alive," Tubman is oft-quoted as saying.

In 1863 she led a group of African American Union soldiers on raids in South Carolina. There she met a soldier named Nelson Davis. They were married in Auburn in 1869, with the Sewards among the many friends in attendance. Davis and Tubman lived in a brick house on the property until his death in 1888. Tubman herself died in 1913 at age 95.

The Willard sisters lived at the Willard-Case Mansion, a beautifully preserved 1836 Greek Revival mansion. It is now the Cayuga Museum showcasing history and art of the area. The sisters commissioned Louis Comfort Tiffany and the Tiffany Glass & Decorating Company to design the interior of the Willard Memorial Chapel, an extremely rare example of a Tiffany church interior.

The chapel showcases 14 opalescent nave windows, a nine-paneled rose window, nine Moresque-style chandeliers, a large memorial mosaic bronze and gilt tablet, hand-carved oak-inlay furnishings, a ceiling with gold-leaf stencils, and extensive mosaic flooring. Musical performances are played on the chapel's historic Steere-Turner tracker-style organ.

Theodore Case, a cousin of the Willard sisters, lived in the mansion from 1916 to 1930. He created the Case Research Lab in a former greenhouse in the backyard. It was there that he developed, in 1923, the first commercially successful system of recording sound on film. Case went into partnership with William Fox and together they gave the new sound system the name Movietone, with the slogan, "It speaks for itself." Movietone made its public debut in 1927 and created a sensation with a sound film of Charles Lindbergh's transatlantic flight.

ATTRACTIONS

Cayuga Museum (315-253-8051, www.cayuganet.org/cayugamuseum, 203 Genesee St., Auburn, NY 13021) Housed in the 1836 Willard-Case Mansion, the museum offers exhibits on local figures and events including a special exhibit, A Child's World, that explores how children lived in the area in the 19th century. There is also an exhibit on the Auburn State Correctional Facility, built in 1816 and the number one area employer. Next door to the mansion is the **Case Research Lab Museum and Carriage House,** with exhibits on the origin and development of sound film. Open Tuesday through Sunday; closed January. Suggested donation $3.

Harriet Tubman Home (315-252-2081, www.harrietthouse.org, 180 South St., Auburn, NY 13021) Known as the Moses of Her People, Tubman settled in Auburn after the Civil War and operated this home for aged and indigent blacks, which is now open for tours. She died here in 1913. Open Tuesday through Saturday.

Merry-Go-Round Playhouse (315-255-1758, www.merry-go-round.com, Emerson Park, Rt. 38A, Auburn, NY 13021) Known as the Broadway of the Finger Lakes, this professional theater performs favorite Broadway musicals in this historic carousel building in Emerson Park, on the shores of Owasco Lake. Open May to October.

Steward House (315-252-1283, www.sewardhouse.org, 33 South St., Auburn, NY 13021) A registered National Historic Landmark, this house has hosted such visitors as Presidents John Quincy Adams, Martin Van Buren, Andrew Johnson, William McKinley, and Bill Clinton. There are special programs through the year such as summer garden parties and Women of the Seward House tours. Open Tuesday through Sunday July to mid-October; rest of year, closed Sunday. Closed January. Admission: adults $7, seniors $6, students $2.

Harriet Tubman Home, Auburn

Willard Memorial Chapel (315-252-0339, www.willardchapel.org, 17 Nelson St., Auburn, NY 13021) The chapel and adjoining Welch Memorial Building are the only remaining buildings that were once part of the Auburn Theological Seminary. This Tiffany-designed treasure is on the State and National Registers of Historic Places and is a popular wedding venue and concert hall. Open Tuesday through Friday, also Sunday during the summer. Suggested donation $3.

SKANEATELES

The year was 1807 and Issac Sherwood decided to build a tavern and inn at the edge of a dense cedar swamp in what is now the picturesque village of Skaneateles. Today, the Sherwood Inn is one of the oldest continuously operating inns in New York State and has led the way in the revival of this lakeside Finger Lakes community.

Elegant stairway in Seward House

The cedar swamp is gone, replaced by an attractive lakeside park, and Skaneateles Lake remains one of the loveliest in the region. Hard to spell and hard to say (pronounced skinny-ata-less), *Skaneateles* is an Iroquois word meaning "long lake."

When William Eberhardt, the current owner, bought the Sherwood Inn in 1974, it was declining rapidly. There was no tourist trade to speak of back then, and ten empty storefronts in town at the time. He credits the well-publicized summer vacations by President Clinton and his family in 1999 and 2000 for putting the pristine village on the national

---

A Shopping Mecca for Outdoor Enthusiasts

Bass Pro Shops have become major tourist destinations, drawing shoppers from near and far. The one in Auburn (315-258-2700, www.basspro.com, Fingerlakes Mall, 1579 Clark St., Auburn, NY, 13022) is the only Bass Pro Shop in New York State, and at 100,000 square feet, it is designed like an enormous Adirondack-style lodge. It offers hunting, fishing, and marine gear, men and women's clothing, and a wide range of products for hiking, backpacking, outdoor cooking, and much more. Be sure to check out the wall murals, each one depicting a region of New York State. There is a 22,000-gallon native fish aquarium, and the fish-feeding sessions at noon on Tuesdays, Thursdays, and Saturdays are very popular. Visitors can test their shooting skills at the laser shooting arcade. Dogs are welcome in the store and will likely be greeted with a biscuit treat. The shop hosts a variety of special events and seminars by outdoor experts. Open daily.

and international map. The Clintons stayed in a home of a friend in one of the massive lakeside homes that dot the 16-mile-long lake.

The lake is considered the bluest of the Finger Lakes. According to Indian legend, the sky spirits used to lean out of their home to admire themselves in the lake's reflection when the heavens were nearer to the earth than they are now. The lake spirits fell in love with the sky spirits and absorbed the color of their robes, thus giving the lake its beautiful deep blue color.

After traveling around the world and returning to his home in nearby Auburn, the American statesman William H. Seward proclaimed Skaneateles Lake "the most beautiful body of water in the world." The water is considered some of the state's cleanest, and quenches the thirst of Syracuse-area residents 20 miles to the northeast.

The village of 2,600 is the only one in the region whose Main Street backs right up to the curved shore of the lake. For such a small village, it is surprisingly well endowed with independent shops and boutiques, galleries, restaurants, and attractions.

The town hosts festivals throughout the summer, including free band concerts at the gazebo in Clift Park on Skaneateles Lake on Friday and Saturday evenings; the **Finger Lakes Antique and Classic Boat Show** (315-685-0552, www.skaneateles.com) the last week of July; and the widely attended **Skaneateles Festival** (315-685-7418, www.skan.fest .org), which features chamber music as many as five nights a week at several venues throughout August and early September. The park is also the site of the local high school graduation; to cap off the ceremonies, the new graduates, by time-honored tradition, jump into the lake.

One of the more unique summer experiences is the mail boat ride around the lake. For nearly 150 years the mail has been delivered by boat to the cottages—many are inaccessible by regular roads. The mail boy or girl puts the mail in mailboxes on docks, or residents row out to the *Barbara S. Wiles* to pick it up. Guests are invited to cruise along.

Sailing on Skaneateles Lake

Judge Ben Wiles *and* Barbara S. Wiles *(foreground) docked in Skaneateles*

There are also regular cruises on the *Barbara S. Wiles* as well as the double-decker *Judge Ben Wiles*. Mid-Lakes Navigation Company, founded by the late Peter Wiles, who named the boats after his parents, operates both boats. The captains are full of lake lore. At the southern end of the lake is Glen Haven, the onetime home of W. C. Thomas, a doctor who in 1841 founded a health spa where patients came to take the waters. Thomas was a walking advertisement for his treatments; he lived to the age of 107.

LODGING

Skaneateles has historic inns, a number of bed & breakfasts, family-style motels, and a most elegant and critically acclaimed spa resort.

Hobbit Hollow Inn (315-685-3405, www.hobbithollow.com, 3061 W. Lake Rd., Skaneateles, NY 13152) This early-20th-century Colonial Revival farmhouse offers lake views as well as views of the meadows, vineyards, and the farm's barn and stables. Each of the five elegant rooms has a private bath and is furnished with period furniture. There is a complimentary full country breakfast served in the cheery yellow dining room. Wine and cheese or tea and cookies are offered each afternoon. The property is managed by the Sherwood Inn.

Mirbeau Inn & Spa (315-685-5006, www.mirbeau.com, 851 W. Genesee St., Skaneateles, NY 13152) This 34-room spa resort has drawn raves and accolades since its opening in 2000. The Four Diamond AAA boutique country inn boasts a world-class spa and a nationally acclaimed dining room, Giverny (see entry under "Restaurants," below). There are six buildings clustered around beautifully landscaped ponds and impressionist gardens. The architecture and decor are reminiscent of an Old World French country estate. All guest rooms feature a fireplace and oversized bathrooms. All the first-floor rooms have patios. There is a DVD player with complimentary DVD library. A variety of spa packages are available.

Sherwood Inn (315-685-3405 or 800-374-3796, www.thesherwoodinn.com, 26 W. Genesee St., Skaneateles, NY 13152) Since 1807, this comfortable inn has been the hub of village life. It is directly across the street from Clift Park on the lake. Sensitively restored with original hardwood floors and four-poster and canopy beds in many of the 24 rooms, a number of the rooms have fireplaces and lake views and all are spacious and distinctively decorated. The Sun Room Suite, ideal for families, has a queen-sized bed overlooking the lake and an adjoining sunroom with a queen sleeper sofa, fireplace, and whirlpool bath. The romantic Red Room also overlooks the lake, with a queen bed, fireplace, and two-person whirlpool bath. The elegant restaurant has a beautiful porch with unequaled lake views. There is also a clubby tavern with wooden booths and green leather chairs. Breakfast is included.

Restaurants

Doug's Fish Fry (315-685-3288, www.dougsfishfry.com, 8 Jordan St., Skaneateles, NY 13152) Since 1982, Doug's has been serving "decent portions at fair prices." Seafood is delivered by truck on crushed ice five days a week. The compact menu offers seafood, including steamed clams, oysters, and lobster, chicken, soup, and beer, wine, and ice cream. To assure the freshest ingredients, clams are only available on Tuesdays, oysters on Saturdays and Sundays. There are no waiters and no tipping. Eat in or outside on picnic tables or take your meal down to the park by the lake.

Giverny (315-685-5006, www.mirbeau.com, 851 W. Genesee St., Skaneateles, NY 13152) Mirbeau Inn & Spa's award-winning restaurant takes its inspiration from Claude Monet's French Country home, with beamed ceilings and Provençal-style table settings. Chef Edward Moro prepares and presents extraordinary dishes that could be paintings themselves. This is the place for a special occasion. Though expensive, it will be a memorable experience. There are four- or five-course tasting menus carefully chosen by the chef to reflect a palette of tastes. There is also lunch and a lighter bistro menu.

Sherwood Inn

Shops and restaurants line W. Genesee Street, which runs along the lake in Skaneateles

Rosalie's Cucina (315-685-2200, www.rosaliescucina.com, 841 W. Genesee St. Skaneateles, NY 13152) This friendly Tuscan restaurant has earned a well-deserved reputation among its loyal customers, who appreciate the hearty and delicious food and outstanding service. President Bill Clinton and his family have dined here. There is a bakery in the back with hand-rolled pastries, specialty breads, and wonderful desserts.

The Krebs (315-685-5714, www.thekrebs.com, 53 W. Genesee St., Skaneateles, NY 13152) Since 1899, the Krebs has been serving summer guests from May to the last Saturday in October. It is one of the area's most famous dining rooms. A visit to the Krebs is a step back into another era. There are no menus in the main dining room, which features the traditional multicourse prix fixe dinner including lobster Newburg, prime rib, chicken, fresh seasonal vegetables, and a platter of homemade brownies and angel food cake for dessert. Dinners and Sunday brunch are served family style. The tavern offers a lighter menu.

ATTRACTIONS

Mid-Lakes Navigation Company (315-685-8500 or 800-545-4318, www.midlakesnav .com, 11 Jordan St., Skaneateles, NY 13152) Founded in 1968, the company offers sightseeing, mail boat, and champagne dinner cruises aboard the *Judge Ben Wiles* and *Barbara S. Wiles,* two wooden tour boats named after the owners' grandparents. Cruises are offered from May 19 to September 30. The company also offers a variety of Erie Canal cruises.

Skaneateles Historical Society (315-685-1360, www.skaneateleshistoricalsociety.org, 28 Hannun St., Skaneateles, NY 13152) Housed in a former creamery that opened in 1899, this small museum is filled with archives and historical exhibits. There is a special exhibit on the Lightning class sailboat produced by Skaneateles Boats. The company produced Lightning #1 in 1938. Village walking tours are offered during the summer.

SHOPPING

Skaneateles is a big draw for shoppers, and its picturesque shopping district along the lake, lined with specialty shops, is a popular destination for visitors.

Creekside Books & Coffee (315-685-0379, www.creeksidecoffeehouse.com, 35 Fennell St., Skaneateles, NY 13152) This wonderful two-story bookstore and coffeehouse offers a wide selection of nonfiction, fiction, local interest, travel, and children's books. There are also home decor items, toys, gifts, and book-related items. The coffee is roasted on the premises and there are teas, smoothies, and other beverages as well as breakfast foods, desserts, and comfort foods.

Frog Alley Toys (315-685-0359, 22 Jordan St., Skaneateles, NY 13152) This shop offers quality wooden ride-on toys, books, puppets, science kits, building blocks, and stuffed animals. T. C. Timber/Haba hardwood trains are sold here.

Imagine (315-685-6263, www.imagineskaneateles.com, 8 E. Genesee St., Skaneateles, NY 13152) Browse the collection of fine and handcrafted jewelry, timepieces, American blown glass, kaleidoscopes, jewelry boxes, woodwork, and other gift items.

Skaneateles Artisans (315-685-8580, www.skaneatelesartisans.com, 11 Fennell St., Skaneateles, NY 13152) This artist-owned and -operated gallery is devoted to showcasing and selling a unique blend of high quality art in a wide variety of mediums.

The Country Ewe (315-685-9580, www.countryewe.com, 18 E. Genesee St., Skaneateles, NY 13152) This shop offers classic women's apparel and specializes in hand-knit sweaters from around the world.

BALDWINSVILLE

In 1828 John McHarrie Jr. and Stephen Baldwin built a three-story gristmill on the Seneca River north of Syracuse. The construction took thousands of man-hours and two years to complete. Today, visitors can spend the night in luxurious rooms created in this same 1828 mill building alongside the Erie Canal. Original massive timbers and beams enhance the rooms, hallways, and public rooms in what has become the **Red Mill Inn** (315-635-4871 or 800-841-0411, www.theredmillinn.com, 4 Syracuse St., Baldwinsville, NY 13027), a name that evokes its humble origins.

Throughout its history, the mill was known as both the Farmers Mill and the Red Mill. The timber-framed mill building was the first gristmill to be built in the area and it is the area's last mill building still in existence today. The Baldwin and McHarrie families also began many other businesses in the area and were instrumental in the founding of the community that is now the village of Baldwinsville.

The mill operated as a flour and grain mill until 2002. In 2006 it was transformed into the 32-room Red Mill Inn on the river and Lock 24, one of the Erie Canal's busiest locks. It is one of the canal's most historic and comfortable inns. Some rooms have a sleeper sofa, kitchenette, spiral staircase, and loft bedroom. All are filled with Stickley furniture. The inn is pet friendly, and a complimentary continental breakfast is included.

Baldwinsville is currently undergoing a renewal of its waterfront, with new restaurants and upscale housing. Red Mill Inn guests can enjoy easy walks to canal-side restaurants. Just behind the inn is an amphitheater on Paper Mill Island—the only amphitheater on the canal. Concerts are held here throughout the summer and it is a popular destination for boaters.

Until the completion of the Erie Canal in 1825, Baldwinsville had always been part of the east-west water-transportation system. However, the original Erie Canal bypassed the village. In 1917 when the present route of the Erie Canal was completed, Baldwinsville again became part of the state's water-transportation system.

Visitors to the **Beaver Lake Nature Center** (315-638-2519, www.onondagacounty parks.com/parks/beaver, 8477 E. Mud Lake Rd., Baldwinsville, NY 13027) can spy on the wetland homes of minks, herons, and bullfrogs. Walk, hike, canoe, snowshoe, or cross-country ski through the area's 8 miles of maintained trails. Canoes and kayaks are available for rental. A wide variety of nature programs are offered at the nature center, which is open daily (admission: $2 per car).

The Erie Canal proceeds eastward from Baldwinsville on the Seneca River to the Oneida River and Oneida Lake from Three Rivers Point, the confluence of the Oneida, Oswego, and Seneca rivers. Fishing is popular in Baldwinsville, and the village has hosted national carp tournaments.

Oneida Lake

Oneida Lake, northeast of Syracuse, is the largest lake located entirely within New York State. While not included as one of the Finger Lakes, it is sometimes referred to as the other lakes' "thumb." At 22 miles long and up to 5 miles wide, it is an integral part of today's Erie Canal, entering on the east end at Sylvan Beach and exiting on the west end at Brewerton.

Prior to European exploration, Native Americans utilized Oneida Lake's fishery. Artifacts that document their occupation have been discovered at Brewerton, Shackelton Point, and other sites by the lake.

Canal-side at the Red Mill Inn

Later, the Oneidas and Onondagas, members of the powerful Iroquois Confederacy, settled in the region. The Oneidas, who called the lake Tsioqui (meaning "white water"—a reference to the impressive wave action common to the lake), constructed fishing villages near Oneida Creek's mouth and along Fish Creek, near Sylvan Beach. Their Atlantic salmon harvest yielded tons of a once-common Oneida Lake fish and was vital to their sustenance. The Onondagas also valued the lake's fishery and they netted eels, salmon, catfish, pike, and related bounty.

Oneida Lake is known nationally as a fishing mecca, especially for walleye pike. The lake is the site of the Biological Field Station at Shackelton Point, a Cornell University field station on the lake's southern shore. This facility is home to the world's foremost walleye biologists. Meanwhile, on the north side of the lake near Constantia, the state operates a hatchery, where biologists strip over 400 million walleye eggs each year.

Unlike many of the Finger Lakes to the south, Oneida is very shallow, with a maximum depth of 55 feet and an average depth of about 20 feet. The region is Syracuse's boating and fishing recreation area. The lake is used year-round. Summer activities center on fishing, lake cruises, beaches, and campgrounds, while winter activities feature ice-fishing, cross-country skiing, and snowmobiling.

The original canal bypassed Oneida Lake. However, the lake was linked to the canal by the Oneida River and through two Oneida Lake canals. Today's canal was completed in this area around 1916 and used Oneida Lake as a part of its course. The lake thus became an important cog in the state's water-transportation network.

This canal was able to accommodate ships large enough to sail on the open seas.

Hundreds of tugs and barges used the lake during the canal's peak cargo years, and

Fishing along the Erie Canal where the canal joins Oneida Lake

Brewerton and Sylvan Beach became active canal ports. The completion of Interstate 81 in the 1960s transformed the distance from Oneida Lake to Syracuse into an easy commute.

Brewerton

Today, Brewerton is a hamlet at the west end of Oneida Lake at its outlet into the Oneida River. It is located near the former Fort Brewerton, erected in 1759 to defend the passage from Albany to the port of Oswego.

In 1615 explorer Samuel de Champlain stopped along the north shore of the Oneida River and beheld the present site of Brewerton. The historic site of Fort Brewerton, a communications center during the Revolutionary War, remains a popular spot for visitors.

Settlers arrived in 1789 to engage in the fur trade. In the late 1700s two Presbyterians, Rev. John Shepard and Deacon George Ramsey, started preaching in the area near the Fort Brewerton embankment. The **Fort Brewerton Block House Museum** (315-668-8801, www.fortbrewerton.org, 9 U.S. Rt. 11, Brewerton, NY 13029) contains local relics dating back to Paleo-Indian times, as well as displays narrating the history of the area and the fort. Open Saturday June through September; free admission.

Brewerton is known today for great fishing. Auto racing is also very popular. Opened in 1948, **Brewerton Speedway** (315-668-6906, www.brewertonspeedway.com, Rt. 11 Brewerton, NY 13029) has a long history of stock car races, which today are held April through October.

Part of the Onondaga County Park system, **Oneida Shores Park** (315-676-7366, www.onondagacountyparks.com, 9400 Bartell Rd., Brewerton, NY 13029) offers a wide sand beach on the shore of Oneida Lake, campgrounds, a boat launch, kayak and paddle boat rentals, and picnic shelters.

SYLVAN BEACH

It could be a movie set: a perfect mile-long white sand beach, breathtaking sunsets, a fish-filled lake, an old-fashioned amusement park, lakeside dining establishments, a beach-front chapel that has been welcoming visitors and locals since 1882, and the bustling Erie Canal.

In fact, Sylvan Beach, on the eastern shore of Oneida Lake, *was* a movie set back in 1968. A budding young actress strolled along the beach, danced in the water, and sat in front of a campfire in the sand behind the Sylvan Beach Union Chapel. She kissed her costar in the pews of the historic church and spent time at Oudin's Court (now Sunset Cottages).

The actress was Liza Minnelli and the film, released a year later, was *The Sterile Cuckoo*. Local children took a week off from school to watch the filming. The film made Minnelli a star.

Sylvan Beach was known as the playground of central New York, and drew headline entertainers in the 1940s and '50s. Frank Sinatra, Duke Ellington, and the Dorsey Brothers all enjoyed the beachside village.

Just down the beach from Sunset Cottages is the Sylvan Beach Amusement Park, featuring 21 rides including the Galaxi, central New York's largest roller coaster. Admission is free and it's fun to walk over and enjoy a few rides. The amusement park is just steps from the canal.

Sylvan Beach became an active canal port; today's canal was built here in 1916. The village has it all—the lake and beach, a multitude of restaurants, and a casual, relaxed atmosphere where most everything is within easy walking distance.

The village is a popular fishery. During the summer, bass and perch are quite active.

Oneida has been dubbed the Walleye Lake of New York State. Spring and fall are usually the best times for walleye fishing, and it is not uncommon for anglers to catch their limit during these times. Fish Creek empties into Oneida Lake at Sylvan Beach and serves as the spawning stream for walleye. Anglers are often found trolling in their waders or fishing off the pier just before sunrise and at sunset, hoping to catch their dinner. One of the best places to catch walleye is at the canal's entry to the lake at Sylvan Beach.

Just outside Sylvan Beach is McConnellsville, home to the world-famous Harden Furniture Company, the nation's oldest family-owned and -operated furniture manufacturer. Charles Harden Sr. crafted the first Harden chairs in 1844 at his sawmill on Fish Creek in McConnellsville. Today, Greg Harden is the fifth generation of Hardens to run the company.

LODGING

Cinderella's Café & Suites (315-762-4280, www.cinderellasrestaurant.com, 1208 Main St., Sylvan Beach, NY 13157) Daily and weekly rates are available at these suites, which feature refrigerators and microwaves; some include Jacuzzi tubs. It is connected to a family-style restaurant open for breakfast, lunch, and dinner.

Sunset Cottages (315-762-4093, www.sylvanbeach.com/sunset, 801 Park Ave., Sylvan Beach, NY 13157) These one-, two-, three-, and four-bedroom, fully equipped cottages with kitchens are located directly on 3 miles of a sandy beach on Oneida Lake. The site is within walking distance of restaurants, shopping, fishing, and the Sylvan Beach Amusement Park. One-week-minimum rentals during the summer season.

RESTAURANTS

Most Sylvan Beach restaurants are seasonal and are closed November to February. During the spring and fall, many have reduced hours. Be sure to call ahead.

Canal View Café (315-762-5623, www.canalviewcafe.com, 9 Canal St., Sylvan Beach, NY 13157) The Canal View has a view of the canal as well as Oneida Lake and is decorated with old Sylvan Beach memorabilia. It is a great choice for boaters, with dockage out front along the canal. One of the featured offerings is Chicken Riggies (a dish native to the nearby Utica-Rome area). The wide-ranging menu includes seafood and Italian dishes as well as sandwiches, burgers, streak, and fried chicken. A children's menu and take-out are also available. Open for lunch and dinner.

Eddie's Restaurant (315-762-5430, www.sylvanbeach.com/Eddies, 901 Main St., Sylvan Beach, NY 13157) A Sylvan Beach institution since 1934, the third generation of the Stewart family operates this expansive restaurant, which serves everything from hot dogs, hot hams, ice cream, fish, and Italian dinners. Eddie's is famous for its home-made pies. All manner of entertainers have dined here, including Liza Minnelli, Desi Arnaz, Harry James, and Frank Sinatra. Open March to October.

Harpoon Eddie's (315-762-5238, www.sylvanbeach.com/Harpoons, 611 Park Ave., Sylvan Beach, NY 13157) Another Stewart-family-operated restaurant, this one is right on the beach, with a glass-enclosed dining room and two patios for outdoor seating—perfect for watching the sunset over Oneida Lake. There is live entertainment during the summer. The menu features seafood, burgers, chicken wings, and such specialties as Harpoon sirloin and Mediterranean chicken and pasta.

The Crazy Clam (315-761-2526, www.crazyclam.com, 129 Canal St., Sylvan Beach, NY 13157) The Clam has a prime spot alongside the canal, and seafood has prime billing on a menu that includes sandwiches, burgers, and prime rib. This is a fun place, hosting a popular happy hour weeknights during the summer.

ATTRACTIONS

Harden Furniture (315-245-1000, www.harden.com, 8550 Mill Pond Way, McConnellsville, NY 13401) Tours Wednesday 10 am; showroom open Monday to Saturday.

Sylvan Beach Amusement Park (315-762-5212, www.sylvanbeach.org, Main St., Sylvan Beach, NY 13157) This old-fashioned amusement park overlooking Oneida Lake features 21 rides including a roller coaster, games, arcades, a gift shop, and a full-service restaurant. Open April to September.

Verona Beach State Park (315-762-4463, www.nysparks.state.ny.us, Box 245, Verona Beach, NY 13162) Named in 2007 as one of the top 100 campgrounds in the nation, this park, about 2 miles outside Sylvan Beach, has it all. The shaded picnic areas and campground are adjacent to the beach, with an excellent view of Oneida Lake. The lake, Black Creek, cattail marshes, and bottomland hardwood swamps give Verona Beach one of the most diverse aquatic habitats in central New York. The winter season hosts snowmobilers, cross-country skiers, and ice-fishing fans. The eastern portion of the park is open for hunting deer, small game, and waterfowl in-season. Hunting is by permit only.

Communing with seagulls at Verona Beach State Park

Historic Canal Towns

Along the old canal south of Oneida Lake are the historic canal towns of **Chittenango and Canastota.**

Chittenango is where the yellow brick road begins. It was the birthplace of L. Frank Baum, author of *The Wonderful Wizard of Oz,* which became the 1939 MGM classic film. There's even a real yellow brick road in the center of town. Since 1978, the village has celebrated its Oz connection with an annual **Oz-Stravaganza** (www.chittenango.org). Honored guests have included actors who played Munchkins in the 1939 film, and descendants of L. Frank Baum.

The **Chittenango Landing Canal Boat Museum** (315-687-3801, www.chittenangolandingcanal boatmuseum.com, 7010 Lakeport Rd., Chittenango, NY 13057) is within the Old Erie Canal State Park on Boatyard Road in Chittenango. A three-bay dry dock in which canal boats were built and repaired in the 19th and 20th centuries has been excavated and fitted with reconstructed drop gates. There actually were two dry-dock facilities in Chittenango serving the canal at various times in its history—one on "Clinton's Ditch" about 1830–58, and the other on the enlarged Erie about a half mile south of the first, from about 1855 until the second canal closed. Chittenango has the state's only restored dry dock.

An on-site interpretive center and library at the museum provide hands-on activities and exhibits. There's also a sunken canal boat, blacksmith shop, sawmill, stable, warehouse, and woodworking shop. During the 19th and 20th centuries, 96-foot-long cargo boats were also constructed and maintained at the facility.

Canastota Canal Town Museum

The museum displays the workings of the restored dry docks and depicts the social history of the canal era. Visitors can touch the massive gate timbers, handle canal-boat construction tools, and walk the towpath leading to a 150-year-old aqueduct. The museum includes information about lifestyles of boatbuilders and their families, examples of maritime tools, small replica boats, artifacts found at the site, and a diorama about life on the Erie Canal.

Many voices from the past tell of life at the boatyard. Stories are told of the ghost of a forlorn lover who perished in the feeder; of someone killed in a boiler explosion; of a woman who ran the local boardinghouse for the rough canalers.

The museum is open daily in July and August, and weekends in May and June and September and October. Adults $4, children under 14 free.

Canastota also owes its development to the Erie Canal. The canal was adjacent to the village, and canal workers and travelers helped to create a thriving community. Canastota is one of the original canal towns, although today's canal bypasses the town.

The town and the small **Canastota Canal Museum** (315-697-3451, 122 Canal St., Canastota, NY 13032) preserve the history of the 19th-century era when Canastota flourished. The museum building housed a bakery and residence around 1860 and is one of the oldest structures on Canal Street. The museum displays canal memorabilia, a canal-boat cabin replica, and exhibits about local businesses that served canalers. It is open Tuesday through Saturday, April through November.

Because of its proximity to the center of the original canal Canastota soon became one of the leading towns in the middle of the state. Distinguished glass art and wagon manufacturers were based in Canastota, and today Canastota Cut Glass and Sherwood sleds are valued in the antiques world. The "mucklands" around the town produced highly prized onions and potatoes. Many well-preserved Victorian homes still exist in Canastota, a testament to the town's former prosperity.

The village has been prominent in the sport of boxing, producing two world champions. The **International Boxing Hall of Fame** (315-697-7095, www.ibhof.com, 1 Hall of Fame Dr., Rt. 13, Canastota, NY 13032) celebrates the area's rich boxing history. The hall of fame opened in 1989 initially to honor local boxing champions—Carmen Basilio and his nephew, Billy Backus. The museum is now recognized as a boxing shrine. Each June, inductions into the hall are held here. Famous fighters including Muhammad Ali and Jersey Joe Walcott have attended induction weekends. Fist castings of every boxer who has attended induction ceremonies are on display alongside sports photographs. Videos of classic fight films are available for viewing.

The old Erie Canal scenic towpath adjacent to Canastota is used for walking, bicycling, horseback riding, and snowmobiling. The water still flows through Canastota to New London, where the old Erie Canal becomes a feeder for today's canal.

The Oswego Canal offers some of the best fishing in the Northeast Harrison Wilde

7

OSWEGO CANAL

Phoenix, Fulton, Oswego

Opened in 1828, just three years after the completion of the Erie Canal, the 24-mile-long Oswego Canal was known as one of the country's most successful inland waterways. The original canal had 18 locks and connected Oswego to the Erie Canal in Syracuse. It was a separate waterway from the Oswego River. The canal transported goods from the Great Lakes and the Midwest to markets all along the eastern seaboard, and also served as a path to freedom for many fugitive slaves heading north to Canada.

Parts of the old canal can still be seen from the river today. The only remaining intact lock of the old Oswego Canal is Mud Lock, in Onondaga Lake Park in Liverpool. Its name reflects the conditions under which it was built.

Today the Oswego Canal is a "canalized" river comprised of seven locks flowing north to Oswego and Lake Ontario. It is one of the few rivers in the United States that flows north. It begins today at Three Rivers, west of Syracuse, where the Erie Canal meets the Oswego River.

The river offers some terrific fishing—some of the best in the Northeast. It also offers top bird-watching.

Grande Mariner *cruise ship docked in Oswego* Kelly Jordal

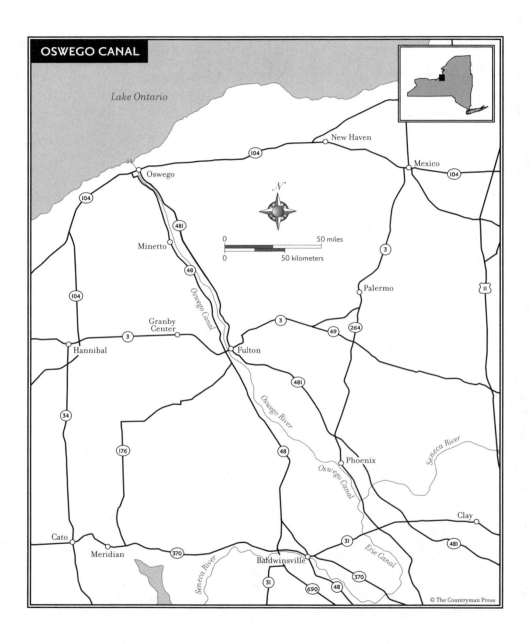

The Oswego River and the Oswego Canal transverses an area steeped in history. Boaters traveling north from the Erie Canal pass historic Stowell Island. According to legend, 50 Frenchmen set up a mission on the island intending to convert the Onondaga Indians to Christianity in 1656. Amid rumors of impending attacks, the French fled the island in 1658, supposedly leaving behind a cannon and gold. The gold has never been found, and hence the island is also known as Treasure Island.

PHOENIX

Phoenix was originally a point of portage that allowed travelers to avoid difficult rapids in the Oswego River. By the 1870s, the village was a manufacturing hub, with boatyards, paper-manufacturing companies, furniture factories, a silk mill, and a distillery. On a September evening in 1916 the fate of this small prosperous village changed forever. Fire consumed the entire manufacturing and retail district and all of downtown, including many homes. The manufacturing businesses were never restored. However, a number of historic homes and public buildings remain.

Stop at Lock 1 at the Bridge House, built in 1917 to house the controls needed to operate a drawbridge over the canal. The bridge was replaced in 1989, and the building now houses the **Bridge House Museum** (315-695-1308, www.bridgehousebrats.us, Henley Park, State and Lock Sts., Phoenix, NY 13135). The old bridge controls are exhibited in the museum, along with other historical displays and a barge boat replica. The museum is maintained and staffed by the "Bridge House Brats," who also oversee the adjacent community park. The Brats are a group of about 50 young people ages 8–21, who work every day during the canal season welcoming boaters to Phoenix. This group of entrepreneurial youths has captivated boaters in recent years with their friendly smiles and work ethic. They provide visitor information, give tours of the museum, and serve a variety of boaters' needs, taking on everything from boat cleaning to sewage pump-outs to running errands. They also operate a café out of the **Buoy House** at the Bridge House, nicknamed the Brats' Shack. Visitors peruse menus from area restaurants, and Brat "runners" pick up the food, bring it to the shack, and serve it to their customers. They also offer free lemonade and sell ice cream sundaes for $1.

Continuing north past Phoenix, keep your eyes open for remnants of the old Oswego Canal on the east shore. Parts of the stone foundation of a lock remain underwater, along with a portion of the canal. The water is very shallow here so be sure to view this relic safely from inside the channel. Pass Walter Island, which was known to canal boatmen as "Fiddler's Elbow."

Past the Hinmansville Bridge is the site of what became a well-known bottled-water company long before bottled water became the rage. In 1888 the Great Bear Spring Company was formed here. The business expanded and for decades the company bottled water from this site and sold it throughout the Northeast. Great Bear began selling to the City of Fulton in the 1960s. The spring is no longer used, although the company continues.

FULTON

The next stop on the journey north along the Oswego Canal is Fulton. The area was called Quehok by the Native Americans who used it as a portage to carry their boats around the great Oswego Falls. The community was called Oswego Falls until 1826, when the name was changed to Fulton, after Robert Fulton, inventor of the steamboat, because of the impact community leaders thought shipping would have on the area. It grew quickly because of the abundant waterpower. Eels were caught at the base of the falls, smoked, and transported to New York City for sale.

Continuing north, there's Pathfinder Island on the east side of the channel. The island was named after the title character in James Fennimore Cooper's *The Pathfinder*, one of his Leatherstocking Tales. Much of the action in *The Pathfinder* takes place during a trip down the Oswego River in 1759. The book tells of a fictitious skirmish occurring on this island between the main character in the book, Natty Bumppo, and the Iroquois Indians. Published in 1840, it was written after Cooper served as a naval officer at Fort Ontario from 1808 to 1809.

LODGING

Battle Island Inn Bed & Breakfast (315-593-3699, www.battle-island-inn.com, 2167 State Route 48 North, Fulton, NY 13069) This 1840s Italianate inn, featured in *New York Ghosts* because of its purported supernatural visitors over the years, is perched atop a hill between Fulton and Oswego and across from Battle Island State Park and its lovely golf course. Take in the view from one of the four porches or from the cupola. Enjoy fresh homemade cookies all day and relax in the handmade knitted slippers supplied with each room. Each room also has a private bath, TV, and DVD player. The Garden Room has a canopy bed and Jacuzzi, with views of the lovely gardens. The King Room, with flowered wallpaper, offers a king-sized bed as well as twin sofa bed and desk. There are two sitting rooms for relaxing and an extensive movie collection and library. A full country breakfast is included; innkeeper Diane Sokolowski recently published *Inn the Kitchen: Battle Island Inn Cookbook*, featuring her signature breakfast creations as well as favorite family recipes. She also offers gourmet-food-tasting parties. A gift shop offers handcrafted items from local artisans. The inn is home to two shy cats, Molly and Abby.

Riverside Inn (315-593-2444, www.riversideinnonline.com, 930 South First St., Fulton, NY 13069) Located on the banks of the Oswego River, this 69-room hotel was built in 1987 and recently underwent a complete renovation. Many rooms have a water view. There are two-room suites and high-speed Internet and refrigerators in all rooms. Pet friendly, the inn has an outdoor pool. The on-site **Riverview Restaurant** is open for breakfast and dinner daily, and features Friday-night beer-batter Haddock fillet and all-you-can-eat Prime Rib Saturdays. There are daily happy hours with 25-cent chicken wings.

Why Is There No Lock 4?

Those traveling the Oswego River by boat may notice that Lock 3 is followed by Lock 5. The original plans for the barge canal did include a Lock 4, but as construction progressed, engineers determined that the lock wasn't needed. At that time, all of the plans and diagrams were done by hand; it was simpler to leave out the lock than relabel the others. The situation isn't unique to the Oswego Canal—the Champlain is missing Lock 10, and the Erie has no Lock 31.

The Pathfinder

"The Oswego is formed by the junction of the Oneida and the Onondaga, both of which flow from lakes; and it pursues its way, through a gentle undulating county, a few miles, until it reaches the margin of a sort of natural terrace, down which it tumbles some ten or 15 feet, to another level, across which it glides, or glances, or pursues its course with the silent stealthy progress of deep water, until it throws its tribute into the broad receptacle of Ontario."
—*The Pathfinder*, by James Fennimore Cooper, 1840

ATTRACTIONS

Battle Island State Park Golf Course (315-593-3408, 2150 NYS Rt. 48, Fulton, NY) This 18-hole, par-72 golf course at Battle Island State Park overlooks the site where on July 3, 1750, the British officer John Bradstreet was ambushed by a party of French soldiers and their Native American allies. Bradstreet's party was traveling by boat to Schenectady after delivering badly needed supplies to the forts in Oswego. The British counterattacked from the small island and the French retreated after about an hour. The course is challenging for the budding professional and amateur player. It is used in the winter for cross-country skiing.

Pratt House Museum (315-598-4616 177 S. First St., Fulton, NY 13069) Operated by Friends of History in Fulton, this Italianate-style home dates back to 1861. The house is listed on the National Register of Historic Places and features industrial exhibits, a period kitchen, early sports equipment, military artifacts, and genealogical and historical research materials. There are also exhibits on the early days of the Erie Canal, as well as guided and self-guided tours. Open Tues.–Fri. Admission: $2 donation.

Fulton Speedway (315-668-RACE, www.fultonspeedway.com, 1603 County Rt. 57, Fulton, NY 13069) Opened in 1961, the speedway is built into a hilly area on the banks of the Oswego River. The speedway is home to DIRT 358 Modifieds, DIRT Sportsman, and DIRT Pro Stocks and Pure Stocks. Cars race on a one-third-mile clay track. Open from the end of April to September. Races are held on Saturday nights.

Willow Creek Farm Alpacas (315-592-5889, www.alpacanation.com/willowcreek.asp, 388/390 Lakeshore Rd., Fulton, NY 13069) Tour the alpaca farm and get a close-up look at these adorable creatures. The farm store is filled with items made from alpaca fleece, including yarn, socks, teddy bears, ponchos, and more.

Marinas

City of Fulton Canal Park Marina (315-592-2474, S. First St., Fulton, NY 13069) The marina's 20 slips can handle boats up to 42 feet long. Although there are no restaurants at the marina there is a good choice of eateries within a block or two. Fulton is very welcoming to visiting boats, and boaters may stay for free for an overnight or two.

OSWEGO

Oswego, on Lake Ontario, was established as a port in 1725, making it the country's first freshwater port. It gets its name from a Native American word, *Osh-we-geh*, which means "pouring-out place." The name refers to the point where the river waters pour into Lake Ontario.

View of Lake Ontario from Oswego marina Mary Ellen Barbeau

Today, the city is famous as the host to one of the canal system's largest summer festivals, known as **Harborfest** (www.oswegoharborfest.com). It is held the last weekend in July and attracts several hundred thousand people for entertainment, historical reenactments, fireworks, juried arts and crafts, and children's activities. Oswego is also an important port for scuba divers and recreational fishing enthusiasts.

Iroquois Indians lived in the area long before white settlers arrived in the mid-to-late 1600s. The first nonnative people here were missionaries who sought to Christianize Native Americans, and British and Dutch traders who came to capitalize on the area's fur trade and other rich resources.

In the 1700s the British built two forts at the mouth of the river—Fort Oswego on the west bank, which is no longer standing, and Fort Ontario on the east bank. The British maintained control of Oswego well after the American Revolution had been won. This was an attempt to make the American government reimburse British loyalists who fled to Canada after the revolution, leaving behind their property.

During the boom years of the canal, packet boats were built in boatyards along the river and larger vessels were built in the harbor for lake travel. The Oswego Canal quickly became a popular shipping alternative to the western section of the Erie Canal, especially for boats destined for Lake Ontario. In 1842 Thomas Kingsford developed a new way to make starch from corn, and six years later he opened in Oswego the largest starch factory in the world.

Fort Ontario was the site of what many have considered one of World War II's best-kept secrets. On August 5, 1944, the citizens of Oswego awoke to an extraordinary sight—train cars full of refugees from the war in Europe.

They were nearly 1,000 Holocaust survivors, primarily Jewish although about 100 were

Christian. Many had survived concentration camps and were beginning life anew at the Fort Ontario Emergency Refugee Shelter, the only shelter on U.S. soil created for Holocaust victims.

Fort Ontario has had a long history in America. The British built the first fortification in 1755. The French destroyed it in 1756. The second Fort Ontario was built in 1759. It was destroyed by American troops during the American Revolution in 1778. The British rebuilt Fort Ontario for the third time, and it wasn't until 13 years after the end of the Revolution that the British turned the fort over to the United States.

During the War of 1812 the fort was attacked and destroyed by overwhelming British land and naval forces. The threat of another war with Great Britain and a possible invasion from British-held Canada caused the United States to re-garrison the ruined post in 1838. Between 1839 and 1844 the present-day Fort Ontario was built.

Oswego has had a tradition of welcoming visitors and people in need. The citizens of the area were very active in the abolitionist movement, and the city was a prime station on the Underground Railroad. Many buildings used as way stations for escaping slaves are still standing and marked with signs. Pick up a copy of the Underground Railroad driving tour from the **Oswego County Visitors Center** (315-349-8322, www.visitoswegocounty.com, 46 E. Bridge St., Oswego, NY 13126) and drive along the route. Some fleeing slaves headed for the port where ships could carry them across the lake to Kingston, Ontario. Others crossed the nearby Saint Lawrence River. A number remained in Oswego and built their lives and families.

LODGING

Along the Oswego Canal the city of Oswego offers the most places to stay. During especially busy times such as Harborfest and Oswego State College graduation, visitors can find other lodging options in Syracuse, 25 miles to the south. Some Oswego establishments require two-night-minimum stays during these weekends. There are hotels, motels, chain hotels, and several bed & breakfasts.

Restored fort building, Fort Ontario, Oswego

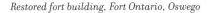

The Honorable Doctor

Dr. Mary E. Walker, who is buried in Oswego, was the first and only woman ever to be awarded the Congressional Medal of Honor—honoring her bravery during the Civil War as a surgeon for the Union Army. A noted women's activist, Walker, who died in 1919, was famous for defying the restrictive women's dress code of her day, stating, "Corsets are coffins."

Lodging Rates

Inexpensive: Up to $75 per couple
Moderate: $76–$150 per couple
Expensive: $151–$250 per couple
Very Expensive: More than $250 per couple

BEST WESTERN CAPTAIN'S QUARTER'S

315-342-4040
www.bestwesternnewyork.com/oswego-hotels
23 East First St., Oswego, NY 13126
Price: Moderate
Credit Cards: Yes
Handicapped Access: Yes

Special Features: Indoor swimming pool, free breakfast

This riverfront hotel offers great views of Oswego Harbor and Lake Ontario. Located less than a mile from Oswego State College and within walking distance of downtown attractions including Fort Ontario, this 93-room riverfront hotel offers complimentary breakfast served each morning in the **Harbor View Lounge**. There is an indoor swimming pool, hot tub, sauna, steam room, and fully equipped fitness center. There is also free wireless Internet and complimentary coffee, tea, and juice available 24 hours a day.

Oswego bustles in the summer, especially during Harborfest, in July Mary Ellen Barbeau

ECONOLODGE INN & SUITES

315-343-1600
www.econolodge.com/hotel-oswego-
new_york-NY613
70 E. First St., Oswego, NY 13126
Price: Moderate
Credit Cards: Yes
Handicapped Access: Yes
Special Features: Harbor-front rooms, free
high-speed Internet

Some of the 92 rooms in this facility overlook the Oswego harbor and have refrigerators and microwaves. The Business Suites
include a living room and separate bedroom. Efficiency Suites have a complete
kitchen. There is free coffee, tea, and juice
in the morning. The popular **GS Steamers
Bar and Grill**, on the lobby level, is rated as
Oswego's hottest cocktail lounge. Steamers
features live entertainment, weekday happy
hours, and nine TVs. It serves traditional
pub fare and is open nightly until 1 am. A
large outdoor deck opened in 2008. GS
Steamers is also host of the Labatt's
Riverfront Concert Series, which runs on
Thursday nights in the summer.

KING ARTHUR'S SUITES

315-591-4866
www.kingarthurssuites.net
7 W. Bridge St., Oswego, NY 13126
Price: Moderate–Expensive
Credit cards: Yes
Handicapped Access: Yes
Special Features: Fully equipped kitchens
and free Internet and local calls

Located in the center of downtown, this
historic building was built in the 1850s by
abolitionist Abram Buckout and was known
as a final stop on the path to freedom for
many runaway slaves. Each of the eight
rooms is individually decorated. Some have
portions of the historic stone exposed,
while others boast vaulted ceilings and spiral staircases leading up to lofts.
Nonsmoking suites are available. Small

dogs up to 10 pounds are allowed. The 8-
foot windows offer views of Oswego's canal
and river walk. The kitchens make it convenient for extended stays. The highly rated
King Arthur's Steakhouse and Brewpub (see
entry under "Restaurants," below) offers a
popular choice for overnight guests.

SERENDIPITY BED & BREAKFAST

Innkeeper: Dale Bixter
315-343-6406 or 800-267-4996
www.oswego-serendipity.com
7225 state Rt. 104, Oswego, NY 13126
Price: Moderate
Credit cards: Yes
Handicapped Access: No
Special Features: High-speed Internet in all
rooms

This 1870s Federal-style home with 2-story
white pillars has four guest rooms—two
with private baths and the other two sharing a bath. Each room is different—the
Dragon Room has red walls and Oriental
accents and the Van Gogh Room has a print
of Van Gogh's Sunflowers, yellow walls, and
oak furniture. The gourmet breakfast
includes such treats as lemon-filled French
toast, cranberry scones, and fresh berries
from the garden. Located on six acres, with
natural woodlands and scenic trails. Easily
accessible cross-country skiing, hiking,
and biking trails maintained by Oswego
State College are situated in back of the
property.

RESTAURANTS

Most Oswego Canal dining establishments
are in Oswego. Some cater to the college
crowd from Oswego State College. Italian
restaurants are a favorite in the area. All
restaurants are by New York State law nonsmoking. Prices are estimated per person
for dinner entrée without tax, tip, or beverage.

Dining Rates
Inexpensive: Up to $10
Moderate: $11–$25
Expensive: $26–$40
Very Expensive: More than $40

BRIDIE MANOR

315-342-1830
www.bridiemanor.com
1830 Bridie Manor, Oswego, NY 13126
Open: Daily
Price: Moderate
Credit cards: Yes
Cuisine: Italian, American
Serving: L, D
Handicap Access: Yes
Special features: Waterfront location

Built in 1833, the site is Oswego's only surviving flour mill. Bridie Manor was originally known as Ontario Mills. It is an
integral part of the city's industrial history
and produced over 1 million barrels of
finely ground wheat annually. Now owned
by the Lombardo family, it overlooks the
water and offers an extensive lunch and
dinner menu and a well-designed kids'
menu. Appetizers include fried calamari,
clams casino royal, and Maryland crab
cakes. There are an array of pasta dishes
including pasta primavera, Italian potato
dumplings, and fettuccine carbonara, as
well as a good selection of steaks, chops,
veal, chicken, and seafood.

CANALE'S RESTAURANT

315-343-3540
www.canalesrstaurant.com
156 W. Utica St., Oswego, NY 13126
Open: Daily
Price: Moderate
Credit cards: Yes
Cuisine: Italian
Serving: L, D
Handicap Access: Yes
Special features: Canale's house dressing

and tomato and marinara sauce available to
take home

This establishment was started in 1954 by
brothers Mike and Dom Canale using their
mother Anna's recipes. She and her husband, Nick, were Italian immigrants. Mike is
famous for saying "Mangia, Beve, a Salute"
which means, "Eat, drink and be healthy."
Canale's is still using Anna's recipes. Menus
include steak and chops, veal, seafood, and
chicken dishes, as well as Italian specialties
such as baked manicotti, baked ziti, and
baked eggplant parmigiana. Diners are
invited to create their own pasta dishes. This
is a great family place with a wide array of
items on the kids' menu including cavatelli,
gnocchi, shrimp, pizza, and even a kids'
salad. In a hurry? Meals can be ordered
online and picked up for take out.

FAJITA GRILL

315-326-0224
www.fajitagrill.com
244 Route 104 West, Oswego, NY 13126
Open: Daily
Price: Inexpensive
Credit cards: Yes
Cuisine: Mexican
Serving: L, D
Handicap Access: Yes
Special features: Wi-Fi and take-out avail-
able

All food at this restaurant is prepared from
scratch. Using an assembly-line style, diners become part of the process. Choose
what you want and monitor the preparation
from start to finish. There are burritos, rice
bowls, tacos, quesadillas, nachos, salads,
fajitas, soups, and a kids' menu.

KING ARTHUR'S STEAK HOUSE & BREW
PUB

315-343-1300
www.kingarthurssteakhouse.com
7 W. Bridge St., Oswego, NY 13126

Open: Daily
Price: Moderate
Credit Cards: Yes
Cuisine: American
Serving: D weekdays; L, D weekends
Handicap Access: Yes
Special features: Reservations recom-
mended, Brewpub happy hour, weekdays
4–7 pm

King Arthur's is located in the historic
Buckout-Jones building, which played a
prominent part in the city's history. The
brick building was constructed in the 1850s
by abolitionist Abram Buckout and soon
became known as a point on the path to
freedom for many runaway slaves. From
here some would find ships to carry them
across the lake to Canada. Later, Charles
Smith and Tudor E. Grant, former slaves,
operated a barbershop in the basement.
Today, it is considered the best steakhouse
in the city and was voted best place to take
an out-of-town visitor, with an extensive
menu including steaks, chops, roasts, veal,
chicken, and seafood, as well as traditional
pub items such as steak and shepherd's pie.
The Brewpub features such home brews as
Downtown Nut Brown, Camelot Cream Ale,
Okoberfest Ale, Bridge Street Wheat, and
Oatmeal Stout.

PORT CITY CAFÉ & BAKERY

315-343-2412
www.portcitycafe.com
209 W. First St., Oswego, NY 13126
Open: Daily
Price: Inexpensive
Credit Cards: Yes
Cuisine: American
Serving: B, L, D weekdays; B, L weekends
Handicap Access: Yes
Special features: Box lunches and bakery
items to go, delivery available.

This is a bakery and restaurant offering
sandwiches and soups including lobster

bisque daily. There are deli sandwiches,
wraps, paninis, subs, quesadillas, and salads and pasta salads. Breakfast sandwiches
include the Athens, West Coaster, the Mexi
Melt, Denver, and Southern Style. Bakery
choices include cookies, muffins, and low-
fat, low-sugar muffins, brownies, and
turnovers. Gelato is made fresh daily. Port
City Café is a great place to pick up a picnic
to enjoy along the canal or lake or on a fishing expedition.

THE PRESS BOX

315-343-0308
29 East First St., Oswego, NY 13126
Open: Daily
Price: Inexpensive
Credit cards: Yes
Cuisine: American
Serving: L, D, weekdays; B, L, D weekends
Handicap Access: Yes
Special features: More than a dozen TV
screens

A casual restaurant popular with sports
fans, who come to catch their favorite
teams on the numerous TVs. It serves a
wide variety of burgers billed as "creative,"
and traditional American pub fare.

RUDY'S LAKESIDE

315-343-2671
www.rudyshot.com
78 County Rt. 89, Oswego, NY 13126
Open: Daily Mar.–Sept.
Price: Inexpensive
Credit Cards: No
Cuisine: American
Serving: L, D
Handicap Access: Yes
Special features: Take-out available,
including the famous Rudy's Texas Hot
Sauce

Since 1946, the opening of Rudy's has heralded spring in Oswego even if there is still
ice on Lake Ontario. People come from

Oswego State College just a quarter mile away, as well as from afar, to enjoy an Oswego tradition. They come for the fish and chips, the fish plates, the Coney hot dogs (spicy white hot dogs made by the Syracuse-based Hofmann Sausage Company) and Rudy's Texas Hot Sauce, burgers, fish sandwiches, and ice cream. They also come for the beautiful lakefront location and to enjoy the sunset over the lake while dining. This is one of Oswego's most popular warm-weather establishments.

VONA'S RESTAURANT

315-343-8710
www.vonasofoswego.com
West 10th and Utica Sts., Oswego, NY 13126
Open: Daily

Price: Moderate
Credit cards: Yes
Cuisine: Italian
Serving: D; L, Mon–Fri
Handicap Access: Yes
Special features: Open for banquets, take-out available

An Oswego tradition since 1946, when Tom and Mary Vona started a small family restaurant using Mary's recipes that very soon became well loved and very popular. Today, her recipes remain the same, as does the tradition of welcoming diners by three generations of the Vona family. Vona's is a warm, family, friendly establishment that offers steaks, seafood, chicken sandwiches, and a wide array of traditional Italian dishes including ziti, manicotti, and lasagna.

CULTURE

Although the communities along the Oswego Canal are small, the area's rich cultural heritage has fostered preservation of important historic homes and sites. The presence of Oswego State College also enriches the region's visual and performing arts. Oswego even supports an opera organization that mounts regular productions.

Museums and Historic Sites

FORT ONTARIO STATE HISTORIC SITE

315-343-4711
www.fortontario.com
Foot of E. Seventh St., Oswego, NY 13126
Open: Tues.–Sun. and Mon. holidays mid-May–Oct.
Admission: Adults $4, students and seniors $3, children free.

The fort is currently being restored to its 1868–72 appearance. This period is the common age of the fort's surviving buildings. Room furnishings re-create the lives of officers, enlisted men, and civilians at Fort Ontario during the period between May 1868 and April 1869 when the fort was garrisoned by Company F, 42nd Infantry Regiment, Veteran Reserve Corps. The Veteran Reserve Corps was composed of wounded or disabled Civil War veterans. The Officers' Quarters and Enlisted Men's Barracks have been restored and furnished with period furniture and displays. Outside the walls of the fort is the post cemetery, containing the graves of generations of soldiers and civilians who served or lived at Fort Ontario from the time of the French and Indian War, and up until World War II.

Special events include Civil War, Revolutionary, and French and Indian War encampments, drills, a kite festival, and October candlelit evening ghost walks.

H. LEE WHITE MARINE MUSEUM

315-343-0480
www.hleewhitemarinemuseum.com
W. First St. Pier, Oswego, NY 13126
Open: Daily mid-May–Dec. 23, Mon.–Sat., Jan. 2–mid-May
Admission: Adults $4.50, children $2.50

The main museum building is filled with nautical artifacts from the 18th to the 20th centuries and is open year-round. The museum's boats are open to visitors from mid-May through October. The centerpiece of the boat collection is the LT-5 Tugboat, which saw military service in the Atlantic and Pacific theaters during World War II, when it was used in the D-Day attack to bring in supplies for the soldiers, and actually shot down a German airplane. From 1946 to 1989 it was a harbor tug in Buffalo, and it is now a National Historic Landmark. It is the only LT-5 remaining in the U.S. Derrick Barge No. 8, which was built in 1925 for dredging and repairing the New York State Canal System. It is the last remain-

Inside Officers' Quarters at Fort Ontario, Oswego

French and Indian War reenactment at Fort Ontario John Rozell/NYS Parks, Recreation, and Historic Preservation

ing steamboat on the New York State Canal. The third vessel is the *Eleanor D,* a 40-ton fishing vessel built in 1948. Owned by three generations of the Cahill family of Oswego, it was the last commercial fishing vessel on the lake and survived 25-foot seas.

JOHN D. MURRAY FIREFIGHTERS MUSEUM
315-343-0999
East Side Fire Station, E. Cayuga St., Oswego, NY 13126
Open: Tues., Thurs., Sat. July–Aug., rest of year by appointment.
Admission: Free

This museum is fun for firefighter buffs. There are vintage fire trucks and equipment, photos, and historic displays.

OSWEGO PUBLIC LIBRARY
315-341-5867
www.oswegopubliclibrary.org
120 E. Second St., Oswego, NY 13126
Open: Daily
Admission: Free

Founded in 1853, the library is listed on the National Registry of Historic Places and is one of the state's oldest buildings to have continuously housed a library. The building sports battlements, a tower, turrets, and arcaded windows and reflects the romantic era of the pre–Civil War period. Gerrit Smith, a wealthy abolitionist, gave $25,000 for the building and another $5,000 for books. The money was given with the stipulation that the library be open to both men and women regardless of color. Recently the facility underwent an extensive expansion and renovation.

RICHARDSON-BATES HOUSE MUSEUM/OSWEGO COUNTY HISTORICAL SOCIETY

315-343-1342
135 E. Third St., Oswego, NY 13126
Open: Tues.–Sun.
Admission: Adults $4, seniors and students $2

One of the most elegant houses in the city, construction was completed in 1867 for local attorney Maxwell Richardson. This National Register house offers a look at Victorian America's fascination with history, art, education, and travel. The luxurious interiors are 95 percent original to the house and portray the family's wealth. There are also exhibits about Oswego County history.

SAFE HAVEN MUSEUM AND EDUCATION CENTER

315-342-3003
www.oswegohaven.org
2 E. 7th St., Oswego, NY 13126
Open: Tues.–Sun. Memorial Day–Labor Day weekends, Wed.–Sun. rest of year
Admission: Adults $4, seniors $2, children $1

This little-known museum is filled with photographs, artifacts, and quotes that tell the story of Safe Haven on the grounds of Fort Ontario. The Wall of Remembrance lists the names, ages, and countries of all 982 World War II refugees who were given a new life in Oswego. The most powerful exhibit is a video with interviews of survivors who began new lives at Safe Haven. The shelter was closed in February 1946 after the war's end. Despite a widespread campaign to keep the residents in the U.S., Congress voted to send the refugees home. Most had no homes to which they could return. President Truman signed an executive order giving them priority permission to remain, and after traveling to Canada to receive visas (thereby complying with U.S. immigration law), they returned to the U.S. and to freedom.

WEST PIERHEAD LIGHTHOUSE

315-342-7245
Oswego Harbor, Lake St., Oswego, NY 13126
Not open to the public
Built in 1934 and automated in 1978, this lighthouse is one of the city's most recognizable landmarks. It offers a good photo opportunity.

Performing and Visual Arts

Arts & Culture for Oswego County (315-342-1109, www.artshappening.org) A 24-hour cultural-events hotline.

Safe Haven Museum, Oswego

Art Association of Oswego (315-343-5675, www.oswegoarts.com, Civic Arts Center at Fort Ontario, Oswego, NY 13126) The Art Association mounts between eight to ten exhibitions annually. It also offers classes in a wide variety of media for children and adults as well as a Children's Summer Art Institute in July and August. Another popular program is "Art for Me!" which brings art experiences to nursing homes and community centers for those who cannot come to the Arts Center.

Oswego Opera Theatre Company (315-342-1039; www.oswegoopera.com, Waterman Theater, Oswego State College, Oswego, NY 13126) Founded in 1976, Oswego Opera stages two productions annually at the Waterman Theater, Oswego State College. It has collaborated with the Syracuse Opera and the Bronx Opera Company. Popular and critically acclaimed productions have included *Carmen, Carousel,* and *The Barber of Seville*.

Oswego Players (315-342-0639, Francis Marion Brown Theatre in Fort Ontario Park, Oswego, NY 13126) Founded in 1938 by Francis Marion Brown, this is one of the oldest continuous running theatre companies in the country. Each year the group offers approximately eight shows from dinner theatre format to traditional drama, comedy, and musicals.

Holocaust Survivors

The remarkable stories of World War II Holocaust survivors and the tale of Oswego's role in their survival is told in the Safe Haven Museum and Education Center in the former shelter administration building on the grounds of Fort Ontario.

Survivors recount their experiences in a video presented at the museum. "I remember my feet were measured for shoes," Walter Greenberg says simply. "When I got to the camp I had no shoes. I stood on brown paper, they traced the outline of my feet and gave me shoes."

Chiam Fuchs recalls his first impressions of the U.S.: "Here we are free. Here we will be able to work and regain our health and peace of mind. I cannot tell you how much we owe the United States for giving us this home."

There were 982 refugees from 18 countries. Ruth Gruber, a young Jewish woman, was sent by Interior Secretary Harold Ickes to escort the refugees on their way from Naples, Italy, to the United States, aboard the troop-transport ship *Henry Gibbons*, and chronicle their stories.

While at the shelter, refugees went to school in the community, participated in scout organizations, learned English and job skills, and operated a newspaper and theater group. A couple got married, and children were born. Eleanor Roosevelt, President Roosevelt's wife, visited the shelter and championed the cause of the refugees.

Safe Haven displays trace a remarkable journey

Tyler Art Gallery (315-312-2113, Oswego State College, 7060 State Rt. 104, Oswego, NY 13126) The college art gallery presents several free exhibitions each year including paintings, prints, sculptures, photographs, ceramics, and metalwork.

RECREATION

It would be hard to find an area with a wider array of recreation opportunities than the Oswego Canal region, from world-class fishing and hunting, scuba diving on historic wrecks in Lake Ontario, snowmobiling in an area with the highest snowfall east of the Rockies, boating on lakes, rivers, and the canal, bird-watching, hiking in thousands of acres of public forests, and golfing on uncrowded rural courses.

Auto Racing

Oswego Speedway (315-342-0646, www.oswegospeedway.com, 300 East Albany St., Oswego, NY 13126) Built in 1951, this five-eighths-of-a-mile supermodified track features supermodifieds and limited modifieds. The unique configuration of sweeping turns and wide racing surface make two- and three-abreast racing a common sight at Oswego. Spectator capacity is in excess of 15,000 people. There is a family section that is alcohol free and a dedicated handicapped entrance and viewing area. Saturday-night races from April to mid-October. Snocross racing in winter.

Fishing

Oswego, the Oswego River and Canal, and Lake Ontario have been called the fishing capital of the Northeast. Anglers seeking record-breaking salmon or trout, the popular walleye, bass, perch, and other species can expect to reel in fine catches. Few areas in the region can match the quality and diversity of the fishing here.

There are more than 30 species of fish in the canal. Some popular species include Chinook salmon, black crappie, northern pike, walleye, rock bass, smallmouth bass, and white perch. Fishing enthusiasts have reeled in ten world and state records in area waters. Some of the river's hot spots are Battle Island, Ox Creek, Three Rivers, Big Island, and Oswego.

Much of the fishing in this area is catch and release. However, for those who want to catch and eat, the New York State Department of Health has guidelines for the consumptions of certain species of fish from the Oswego River and Lake Ontario that may contain contaminant levels exceeding federal food standards. For specific guidelines refer to the Health Advisory section in New York State Fishing Regulations, a free booklet available where fishing licenses are purchased, or contact the NYS Department of Health at 800-458-1158.

Oneida Lake Fish Cultural Station (315-623-7311, www.dec.state.ny.us, NYS Rt. 49, Constantia, NY) Owned and operated by the New York State Department of Environmental Conservation, this fish hatchery rears walleye and lake sturgeon. It is the largest walleye hatchery in the United States.

Salmon River Fish Hatchery (315-298-5051, www.dec.state.ny.us, 2133 County Rd, Altmar, NY) Owned and operated by the New York State Department of Environmental Conservation, the Salmon River Hatchery is the major stocking source of several strains of salmon and trout for Lakes Ontario and Erie. More than three million salmonids are produced annually. There are displays and exhibits on salmon and trout. Egg collection takes place on weekends.

The *Flying Fish* (315-963-7310, www.catfishcreek.com, 118 Chase Dr., New Haven, NY 13121) Fish Lake Ontario aboard the *Flying Fish*, a fully equipped 26-foot Penn Yan boat. Morning and evening as well as full-day charters are available. **Catfish Creek Fishing Camp** offers lodging, docking, boat launch, tackle shop, and fishing licenses. There is also a private fish-cleaning station and freezer space to hold your catches.

The Other Woman (315-427-1470 or 800-400-6232, www.otherwomanfishcharters .com, 8887 Shellman Dr., Cicero, NY 13039) Captain Ronald J. Hill Sr. is a full-time charter captain with more than 30 years' experience on Lake Ontario in the Oswego area. A full-time mate is always on board the four boats that are all more than 30 foot. Steelhead, salmon, trout, and walleye fishing are offered. Lodging is also available.

Golf

The area's rolling and rural landscape offers an ideal setting for golf. The public courses offer challenging fairways and greens to match all levels of skill. Dr. George Franklin Grant was born in Oswego in 1846 and invented the golf tee. Grant received a patent for his invention in 1899, the blueprint for today's wooden and plastic tees. He was a descendant of Tudor E. Grant, who escaped slavery to settle in Oswego in the 1830s.

Dropping a line along the Oswego Canal

The Club at Caughdenoy Creek (315-676-4653, www.caughdenoycreek.com, 344 County Rt. 33, Caughdenoy, NY 13036) Caughdenoy Creek winds through this challenging 18-hole, par-72 course. The fairways total 6,196 yards. The restaurant offers sandwiches, burgers, and appetizers and is open year-round. The restaurant features two big-screen TVs and is popular during football season. The restaurant is snowmobile accessible. Early-bird specials are offered. Greens fees: $18; cart, $14.

Griffin's Greens (315-343-2996, 229 NYS Rt. 104A, Oswego, NY 13126) This 18-hole, par-70 course with 5,200 yards of fairways is a real country gem in a rural setting. There is a rustic clubhouse in a 100-year-old barn. Greens fees: $16; cart, $10.

Riverside Country Club (315-676-7714, 647 County Rt. 37 West, Brewerton, NY 13036) This is an 18-hole, par-58 course with 3,485 yards of fairways. There is a small clubhouse and restaurant serving burgers and hot dogs. Greens fees: $13, or $16 with a cart.

Marinas

Oswego International Marina (315-349-8322, Lake St., Oswego, NY 13126) There are 100 slips available at this marina, along with a yacht club and a bar open to the public. No fuel or pump-out available, but there is a boat launch.

Oswego Marina, Inc. (315-349-8322, 3 Basin St. [end of NYS Rt. 481 N.], Oswego, NY 13126) This is Oswego's major marina, with 50 slips able to handle boats up to 100 feet long. There are showers, laundry room, and fuel as well as electric, water, and cable hookups. There is a small store and restaurants within close walking distance. Stepping of masts is available (putting up masts for those entering Lake Ontario and taking down masts for those continuing on the Oswego Canal). There is also a boat launch.

Parks and Camping

Nestled between the western edge of the Tug Hill Plateau and the Lake Ontario shoreline, the area's unique geography makes it a perfect place for those who appreciate the outdoors. The area has more than 100 lakes and ponds and it is covered with thousands of acres of public forests and wildlife-management areas.

With the highest recorded snowfall east of the Rocky Mountains, the Tug Hull region offers vast territory for skiing, snowshoeing, and snowmobiling. There are 340 miles of state-designated snowmobile trails crossing public and private lands in Oswego County.

Curtiss-Gale Wildlife Management (800-388-8244, ext. 217, www.dec.ny.gov, County Rt. 57, Granby, NY 13069) The area consists of 45 acres on the east side of the Oswego River. Birding, cross-country skiing, and snowshoeing. It is 1 mile south of Fulton.

Deer Creek Marsh (800-388-8244, ext. 217, www.dec.ny.gov, Rainbow Shores Rd., Richland, NY 13142) There are 1,195 acres of wetland and uplands between Lake Ontario and NYS Rt. 3 in the town of Richland. There is a viewing tower, parking area, boat access, and handicapped access, as well as scenic vistas, bird watching, cross-country skiing, snowshoeing, hunting, fishing, and trapping. The marsh is accessible from Rainbow Shores Rd.

Derby Hill Bird Observatory (315-963-8291, www.derbyhill.org, 36 Grand View Ave., Mexico, NY 13114) This is a prime location for viewing migrating birds of prey and waterfowl. More than 40,000 birds are counted here annually. The observatory is internationally known for the spring hawk migration. Thousands of red-tailed hawks and

Underwater Oswego

Oswego is rapidly becoming a scuba diver's paradise. Some historians estimate that there have been more than 160 shipwrecks off the coast of Oswego in Lake Ontario. It is host to New York State's first Great Lakes diving preserve. The **New York State David W. Mills Submerged Cultural Preserve and Dive Site** (315-342-5753, www.visitoswegocountry.com) features the shipwreck of the 202-foot steam freighter *David W. Mills*, which slammed into a shoal 4 miles off Oswego on August 11, 1919. Sitting in just 12 to 25 feet of water, it attracts all levels of divers. The Oswego Maritime Foundation has published a maritime heritage educational guide to the site.

hundreds of bald eagles fly over this site each spring. The sharp-eyed may even spot a golden eagle or a ruby-throated hummingbird. In the fall, look for many species of geese, ducks, terns, and other migrating water birds. It is owned by the Onondaga Chapter of the New York State Audubon Society.

Littlejohn State Wildlife Management Area (800-388-8244, ext. 251, www.ny.gov, County Rt. 17, Boylston and Redfield) This site offers 8,020 acres of uplands and wetlands, with 18.8 miles of trails. Hiking, birding, cross-country skiing, snowshoeing, hunting, fishing, and trapping are available. Primitive camping is offered by permit only.

Salmon River Falls Unique Area (315-298-7467, Falls Rd., Orwell, NY 13426) The 110-foot waterfall provides a breathtaking view at all times of the year. The footpath to the bottom of the gorge is open May 1 to November 15. Areas of the gorge are restricted, and visitors should use extreme caution. The footpath is closed in winter except to ice climbers, who must register at sign-in areas. The site is owned by NYS Department of Environmental Conservation.

Sandy Island Beach State Park (315-387-2657, www.nysparks.com, 3387 County Rt. 15, Pulaski, NY 13142) This park has 11 acres of sandy beach on Lake Ontario and is part of the unique Eastern Lake Ontario Dune and Watershed Systems. The dunes were formed by wind and wave motion of a giant inland sea that preceded Lake Ontario. It is the only significant freshwater dune site in the northeastern United States. Walkovers and viewing platforms have been built to protect the fragile dune environment. There is excellent swimming, fishing, birding, hiking, canoeing, and kayaking.

Selkirk Shores State Park (315-298-5737, www.nysparks.com, 7101 NYS Rt. 3, Pulaski, NY 13142) This 980-acre multiple-use park overlooking Lake Ontario offers a swimming beach, camping, fishing, hiking, biking, snowshoeing, cross-country skiing, and snowmobiling. It includes a day-use picnic area, pavilions, nearby Pine Grove boat launch, and woodland trail. The campsites overlook a bluff on Lake Ontario to take advantage of the spectacular sunsets over the lake. It was named in 2005 as one of Reserve America's Top Outdoor Locations. Selkirk Shores is on the direct migration route for a wide variety of bird species.

Winona State Forest Recreation Area/Tourathon Ski Trails (www.tughillskiclub.com, 315-376-3521, Center Rd., Boylston, NY) This 9,233-acre state forest area on the western edge of Tug Hill Plateau contains 31 miles of trails through unplowed roads and state and county forests. There is skiing, snowmobiling, hiking, mountain biking, hunting, fishing, trapping, dog sledding, birding, and horseback riding. This is the site of Tug Hill Tourathon cross-country skiing events. Take County Rt. 22 from Lacona north to Center Rd. Continue five and a half miles down Center Rd. Parking areas are on north side of Center Road at the intersection of Wart Road and Bargy Road.

SHOPPING

Though the mostly rural Oswego Canal region is not a typical shopping destination, there are some surprising discoveries, including community bookstores, a jam-packed comic store, country stores full of collectibles, antiques, exotic items from Central America, and many farm markets.

Farms and Farm Markets

C's Farm Market, Inc. (315-343-1010, www.csfarmmarket.com, 7 Third Ave., Oswego, NY 13126) Apples and vegetables. C's participates in the Pride of New York Program, designed by New York State to highlight state-grown agricultural products, and the Cornell Farm to School Program, delivering farm-fresh produce to local schools. A wide range of drinks including beer is available in the Beverage Center.

Godfrey's Last Stand (315-593-7291, 1232 NYS Rt. 264, Phoenix, NY 13135) Retail and "U-pick" (pick your own) strawberries, blueberries, and garden vegetables.

Ferlito's Berry Path (315-343-7159, 1269 County Rt. 53, Oswego, NY 13126) Retail and U-pick strawberries and blueberries.

Fruit Valley Orchard (315-342-3793, 507 Bunker Hill Rd., Oswego, NY 13126) Retail and U-pick sweet and sour cherries, apples, fruit, vegetables, flowers, and gourmet fruit juices.

Ontario Orchards (315-343-6328, www.ontarioorchards.com, 7735 Route 104, Oswego, NY 13126) For over 40 years, Ontario Orchards has been bringing locally grown produce, fresh-pressed cider, and wonderful baked goods from its in-house bakery to Oswego. There are more than 26 flavors of jumbo muffins, 30 flavors of pies including no-sugar fruit pies, 36 pastries, and jumbo cookies, plus an assortment of breads. It is one of the largest, most complete family-owned and -operated farm market. Offerings include apples, cider, fruits, and vegetables as well as U-pick apples and pumpkins. Open year round.

Flying Kites

Strong, steady western prevailing winds make Oswego an excellent place to fly a kite. Fort Ontario is the setting for some of the state's best kite flying. The Kiwanis Club hosts the annual **Kites over Fort Ontario** on Armed Forces Day each year, giving away hundreds of kites for children to enjoy. At the **Fort Ontario Fall Fun Fly** learn the dynamics of building your own kite from paper, sticks, and string, and decorate it before launching it into the wild blue. (For more information call 315-342-1960 or visit www.fortontario.com.)

Books

River's End Bookstore (315-342-0077, www.riversendbookstore.com, 19 W. Bridge St., Oswego, NY 13126) This independent, family-owned community bookstore is located in the heart of Oswego's historic downtown at the corner of West First and Bridge Streets. Enjoy coffee and tea from the **Coffee Connection** while you browse. Story time for preschoolers is held every Tuesday at 10:30 am. There are many special events including weekly book readings.

Time & Again Books and Tea (315-342-7552, http://users.westelcom.com/keptwo, 18 E. Utica St., Oswego, NY 13126) The book room houses a variety of topic areas with gently used, new, and out-of-print books. There is scattered seating throughout the shop where you can enjoy your tea while you preview your purchases. Outside, there is seating on the secluded deck. This nostalgic shop features poetry readings, writing groups, and book, art, and music discussion groups.

Gifts and Collectibles

The Comic Shop (315-343-8435, www.oswegocomicshop.com, 112 E. Bridge St., Oswego, NY 13126) Arlene Spizman opened this shop in 1992 after running an antique and collectible business. Since then, it has grown into a full-service popular-culture store catering to kids of all ages. Toys, sports cards, games, Japanese DVDs, card games, posters, and sci-fi and fantasy novels are all here, as well as a huge collection of Star Wars toys, both new and old. The store has taken on the personality of its owner, and Spizman is determined that everyone leaves with a smile.

Country Cabin Country Store (315-342-3390, www.countrycabinoswego.com, 456 Meyers Rd., Oswego, NY 13126) This log cabin is filled with primitives, folk art, pewter, furniture, lights, china, and assorted gifts. Every Thursday is senior citizen day, when seniors enjoy 10 percent off all items.

Harbor Towne Gifts and Souvenirs (www.harbortownegifts.com, 43 West Bridge St., Oswego, NY 13126) This is a browsers' paradise, filled with collectibles of all kinds including the popular Webkinz. New York State jams and jellies as well as New York State wildflower coasters are featured. There is also jewelry, frames, and trading cards.

Kathmandu (315-342-6818, www.kathmanduinc.com, 167 Water St., Oswego, NY 13126) Located on a cobblestone street near the river, the shop is filled with exotic jewelry, shoes, sandals, dresses and separates, sweaters, skateboarding attire, and T-shirts. The inventory is ever changing.

Oswego Chocolate Shoppe (315-326-0114, www.oswegochocolateshoppe.com, 191 W. First St., Oswego, NY 13126) This is the place for chocolate lovers. There is even sugar-free milk or dark chocolate. All the chocolates are handmade and lovingly presented.

Ozzie's Antiques & Country Co-Op (315-598-3732, 2 County Rt. 85, Fulton, NY 13069) This co-op's 50 dealers offer an amazing array of stuff in 28 rooms, including jewelry, books, furniture, dishes, antiques, art—something for everyone who has some time to browse.

!Que Colores! (315-326-0116, 193 W. First St., Oswego, NY 13126) This shop showcases gifts from the Central American country of Guatemala. There's Fair Trade handcrafted jewelry, distinctive home decor, and colorful children's gifts. There are original oil paintings by Guatemalan artists, carved wooden masks and saint sculptures, organic, shade-grown coffee, hand-blown glassware, handwoven home furnishings, traditional Mayan outfits for American Girl dolls, books, note cards, and other items.

Remembrance Gift Basket & Balloon Shoppe (315-342-7609, www.oswegogiftbaskets .com, 191 West First St., Oswego, NY 13126) Gift baskets and balloons for any occasion. The gift basket items can be purchased separately, and include many unusual New York State—made food items.

8

Utica Area

Rome, Ilion, Herkimer, Little Falls

Utica

In 1758 Fort Schuyler was built on the site of what is today the city of Utica. It was named in honor of Colonel Peter Schuyler, an officer who had distinguished himself in the French and Indian War.

A settlement grew up around the fort, and in 1798 the village was incorporated. Residents gathered at Bagg's Tavern to select a name for the new village. Erastus Clark suggested Utica, an ancient city in northern Africa whose history was as colorful as he wished for his hometown.

Home to a premier art museum, one of the country's last remaining family-owned regional breweries, a pioneering children's museum, an elegant restored theater, a bustling canal-side park, and a historic railway offering scenic excursions to the Adirondacks, Utica is a Mohawk Valley city of history and bygone glory.

The city's colonial past was revealed to the world when it became the setting for the 1939 movie *Drums along the Mohawk*, the story of colonial life in upstate New York during the Revolutionary War.

The onetime knit-goods center of the world, Utica has lost residents and manufacturing jobs in recent decades. However, it has managed to preserve its irreplaceable treasures.

Dog days at the Erie Canal's Lock 20 in Utica

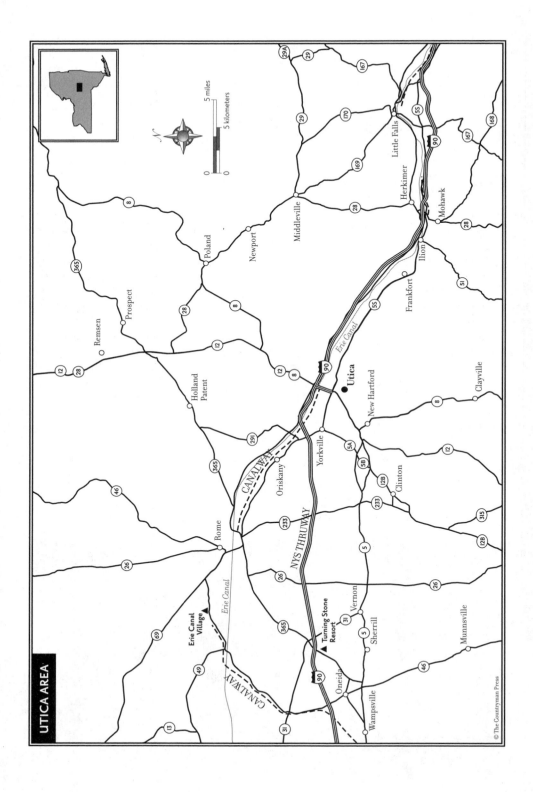

UTICA AREA

© The Countryman Press

Fountain Elms, a restored 19th-century Italianate mansion, is part of the Munson-Williams-Proctor Arts Institute, Utica

The former Erie Canal boomtown that welcomed 19th-century fortune seekers has attracted Bosnian refugees in the late 20th and early 21st centuries, helping to increase the population base.

In 1823 Albert Munson and his new bride, Elizabeth, arrived in the city, where boats were already gliding along the first section of the Erie Canal. Recognizing the potential of the waterway, Munson began marketing millstones up and down the canal. When the canal was completed two years later, permitting transportation of his merchandise on Great Lakes ships to Midwest markets, he invested in lake steamboats as well as canal packet and freight boats.

The enormous fortune he amassed would lead to the creation in the 20th century of the city's cultural centerpiece—the Munson-Williams-Proctor Arts Institute—which includes a celebrated art museum, a performing arts center, the historic house Fountain Elms, and a school of art. The institute is named for three generations of Munson's family.

Down Genesee Street is another Utica cultural institution—the Stanley Theatre. It opened September 10, 1928, and has been a premier showplace for central New York ever since.

The Children's Museum, officially the Children's Museum of History, Natural History, Science, and Technology, is one of the oldest children's museums in the country. Today it is located in the downtown Main Street neighborhood across from the historic 1914 Union Train Station in the former John C. Heiber Dry Goods Building, now a national and state historic landmark. For years, visitors came by train from Albany and Syracuse to shop here.

The only New York Central steam locomotive on public display is located at Union Station. Utica is considered a gateway to the Adirondacks to the north. Vintage excursion trains leave the city on day trips through the scenic Adirondacks to Thendara, near Old Forge.

Utica is home to the **Boilermaker Road Race,** the largest 15k race in the country. It regularly attracts more than 9,000 runners including many of the country's elite runners. The race is the main event of the National Distance Running Hall of Fame's annual Hall of Fame weekend. The Hall of Fame was established in 1998 to honor distance runners. The race ends at the Matt Brewing Company with what many in running circles consider the country's best postrace party.

The Matt Brewing Company has been a Utica institution since 1888. In 1885 F. X. Matt left his career at the famous Duke of Baden Brewery in the Black Forest region of Germany for the United States with the dream of owning his own brewery. He reorganized a faltering brewery that quickly became one of the largest and most successful of the 12 breweries operating in the city at the time. Today, the third and fourth generations of the family head up the brewery, which produces Utica Club (the first beer sold after Prohibition), Saranac beers, and a variety of soft drinks including root beer and ginger beer.

LODGING

Utica has a relatively large concentration of accommodations and is a good base from which to tour the area's other canal cities and towns. Many national chain hotels and motels are here, as is a historic hotel that recently underwent an extensive restoration.

Best Western Gateway Adirondack Inn (315-732-4121, www.bestwestern.com, 175 N. Genesee St., Utica, NY 13502) This pet-friendly inn offers free local calls, high-speed Internet, and a complimentary breakfast buffet. Just off the New York State Thruway (I-

Runners finishing the Boilermaker 15k can enjoy drinks provided by the Matt Brewing Company at the postrace party

90), it is close to Utica's attractions and within walking distance of several restaurants. Some of the 89 rooms have a refrigerator and a microwave.

Holiday Inn Utica Hotel (315-797-2131, www.ichotelsgroup.com, 1777 Burrstone Rd., New Hartford, NY 13413) Located in the Utica Business Park close to I-90, Utica attractions, and Utica College, this Holiday Inn offers 100 rooms and four suites with a full kitchen and a separate living room. There is a fitness center and an outdoor pool. Kids eat free in the hotel's **Moose River Restaurant**, which features ingredients indigenous to the Adirondacks, and American-style pub fare.

Hotel Utica (315-724-7829, www.hotelutica.com, 102 Lafayette St., Utica, NY 13502) A 1912 city landmark, the hotel almost fell to a wrecker's ball after closing, falling into disrepair and spending time as an adult residence. Before closing, it had attracted many celebrities including Judy Garland, who sang at the hotel, aviator Amelia Earhart, Kate Smith, Johnny Cash, President William Taft, and First Lady Eleanor Roosevelt. The once "Grand Lady of Lafayette Street" reopened in 2001 after a $13-million, two-year restoration that brought back the hotel's grandeur and former glory. While the public rooms and exterior of the hotel look as they did when it was first built, the guest rooms were completely updated to meet today's expectations. There are 111 units including 14 one-bedroom suites. Free high-speed Internet access is available. The elegant hotel is now a member of the prestigious National Trust Historic Hotels of America.

Radisson Hotel Utica (315-797-8010, www.radisson.com, 200 Genesee St., Utica, NY 13501) There is free high-speed Internet and free breakfast on weekdays. Centrally located, just down Genesee Street from the Stanley Center and the Munson-Williams-Proctor Arts Institute, this is the area's largest hotel, with 162 rooms. There is an indoor pool and fitness center as well as conference facilities and a business center.

RESTAURANTS

Utica's restaurants include many longtime Italian dining establishments, reflecting the city's strong Italian heritage. Tomato pie is a traditional Utica dish available in almost every area eatery. It can be served hot or cold, but most locals prefer it at room temperature.

Castronovo's Original Grimaldi's Restaurant (315-732-7011, www.grimaldisutica.com, 418 Bleecker St., Utica, NY 13501) Utica is well known for Italian restaurants and this is one of the best. Founded in 1943 by the Grimaldi family, it was acquired by the Castronovo family in 1989. There is live entertainment on weekends. Diners come for the signature entrées including veal and steak dishes. Open daily for lunch and dinner.

Delmonico's Italian Steakhouse (315-732-2300, www.delmonicositaliansteakhouse.com, 151 N. Genesee St., Utica, NY 13502) One of Utica's finest restaurants, it is famous for its 24-ounce steaks, Italian dishes, friendly service, and elegant dining room. The walls are covered with photos of celebrities who have dined here. Open daily for dinner.

Dominique's Chesterfield Restaurant (315-732-9356, www.chesterfield1713.com, 1713 Bleecker St., Utica, NY 13501) This is another well-loved Italian establishment that has been offering favorite Italian dishes for more than 60 years. Open daily for lunch and dinner.

Tom Cavallo's Restaurant (315-735-1578, www.tomcavallos.com, 40 Genesee St., New Hartford, NY 13413) Established in 1949, Tom Cavallo's has become an area landmark. Recent additions include Cavallo's Hava Cigar Bar and an open-air deck. The menu has something for everyone including pizza, pasta, burgers, wings, seafood, steak, and sandwiches. Open daily for lunch and dinner.

Thornberry's Downtown Grill & Pub (315-735-1409, www.thornberrysrestaurant.net, 1011 King St., Utica, NY 13501) This popular downtown eatery located behind the Stanley Theatre is a convenient choice for pretheater dining. The menu covers a wide range including seafood, roast beef, chicken, steak, burgers, and sandwiches. Open daily for lunch and dinner.

ATTRACTIONS

Adirondack Scenic Railroad (315-724-0700 or 800-819-2291, www.adirondackrr.com, Union Train Station, 321 Main St., Utica, NY 13511) The railway offers various tours, including a scenic excursion from Utica to Thendara. The full-day trip passes many flag stops including Holland Patent, Remsen, Forestport, Woodgate, and Otter Lake. The journey is two hours each way, with a four-and-a-half-hour layover in Thendara in the summer.

Children's Museum (315-724-6129, www.museum4kids.net, 311 Main St., Utica, NY 13511) This hands-on learning center emphasizes local history, environmental science, the arts, and space science. The National Aeronautic and Space Administration (NASA) and the Department of Energy's Office of Science have adopted the museum and contributed to the science exhibits. It is also home to the International Bicycling Hall of Fame and the International Halls of Fame for Rowing, Canoeing, and Kayaking. Open daily except Wednesday and Sunday. Adults $9, seniors $8, children $7.

Matt Brewing Company (315-732-0022 or 800-765-6288, www.saranac.com, 830 Varick

Many opportunities for play await young visitors to the Children's Museum

St., Utica, NY 13502) Open for tours daily June through August, Friday and Saturday rest of year; $5 includes two beer or root beer drinks in the elegant wood-paneled brewery bar.

Munson-Williams-Proctor Arts Institute (315-797-0000, www .mwpai.org, 310 Genesee St., Utica, NY 13502) This is a remarkable institution, especially for a small city. The museum is a landmark 1960 Philip Johnson– designed building, connected to Fountain Elms, a superbly restored 1850 Italianate mansion, by the museum education wing. The art collection features more than 25,000 American 18th-, 19th-, and 20th-century paintings, drawing, sculptures, 19th-century decorative arts, photographs, European paintings, and European and Asian works on paper. Also featured is the popular "Voyage of Life" series by Thomas Cole. Fountain Elms has been restored as a showcase for the finest in Victorian-era decorative arts. Open Tuesday through Sunday. Free admission.

Tours of the Matt Brewing Company include an icy cold one—or two

This abstract sculpture is among the Munson-Williams-Proctor's diverse holdings

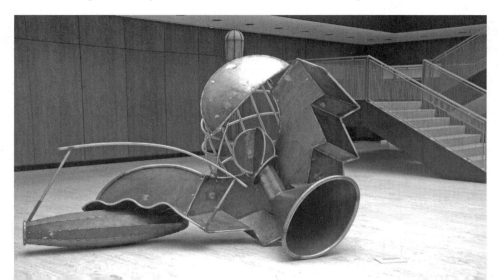

Stanley Center for the Arts (315-724-4000, www.stanleytheatre.net, 259 Genesee St., Utica, NY 13501) This elegant 1928 theater is home to the Utica Symphony Orchestra, the Leatherstocking Ballet, and the Mohawk Valley Ballet, and hosts a Great Artists series and Broadway shows.

Parks

Old Erie Canal State Park (315-687-7821, www.nysparks.state.ny.us, RD #2, Andrus Rd., Kirkville, NY 13082) Old Erie Canal State Park is accessible at various points along NY Rts. 5 and 46. This scenic 36-mile linear park is along the first enlargement of the Erie Canal, which operated between Rome and Syracuse from 1836 to 1862. Designated as a National Recreation Trail by the National Park Service, the approximately 850-acre park runs from DeWitt to Rome. Recreational opportunities include bicycling, canoeing, fishing and ice fishing, hiking, horseback riding, picnicking, and snowmobiling. The parallel towpath trail is part of the **New York State Canalway Trail**, which provides a continuous route for towpath and canal activities. The scenic trail passes through a variety of natural and cultural landscapes including open farmland, dense woods, and old canal communities. Historic points of interest include aqueducts, a change bridge, lime kiln remains, and canal-era buildings. Park facilities are wheelchair accessible. Pets are welcome but must be leashed.

Val Balias Recreation Center (315-266-0454, www.cityofutica.com/ParksAndRecreation/Recreation/Skiing.htm, Memorial Pkwy, Utica, NY 13501) This is one of only two city-owned ski centers within city limits in the Lower 48. Named after local three-time Olympian ice skater Valentine Bialas, it is located in **Roscoe Conkling Park.** There's a chairlift, towrope, night skiing, new ski chalet complete with a snack bar and double-sided fireplace. There are five trails of varying degrees of difficulty and a separate sledding hill, as well as 7 miles of groomed cross-country trails.

ROME

For thousands of years the ancient trail that connects the Mohawk River and Wood Creek served as a vital link for people traveling between the Atlantic Ocean and Lake Ontario. Travelers used this well-worn route through Oneida Indian lands to carry and trade goods. Native Americans called the area *Deo-Wain-Sta* ("the great carrying place"), referring to the portage between the Mohawk River and Wood Creek.

When Europeans arrived, they called this trail the Oneida Carrying Place, beginning a significant period in American history. It was a period when nations fought for control of not only the portage, but the Mohawk Valley, the homelands of the Six Nations Confederacy, and the rich resources of North America. Boats coming up the Mohawk River had to transfer their cargo and boats 1.7 miles overland to continue west to Lake Ontario.

Fort Stanwix was built in 1758 to guard this strategic area. The city was first laid out in 1796 by Dominick Lynch, a New York City merchant who naturally enough named the settlement Lynchville. Residents wanted to steer clear of the implications of that designation and decided upon the much more grand and classical name of Rome.

The construction of the Erie Canal began here on July 4, 1817. Two years later, with much fanfare, the first section of the canal, 15 miles between Rome and Utica, was opened. Two of the construction geniuses and self-made engineers of the canal, Benjamin Wright and John B. Jervis, lived in Rome.

The old Erie Canal as it runs through Rome at the Erie Canal Village

Brass and copper also brought fame to Rome. The largest firms in the city were brass and copper companies. Ten percent of all U.S. copper used in manufacturing was consumed in Rome. In 1944, 175 million pounds of copper wire was shipped around the world from Rome.

Fort Stanwix had disappeared under the streets of Rome until the National Park Service re-erected the fort on its original foundations, following plans retrieved from archives in England. The fort reconstruction was a federal Bicentennial project.

Known as "the fort that never surrendered," Fort Stanwix, under the command of Colonel Peter Gansevoort, successfully repelled a prolonged siege in August 1777 by British, German, Loyalist, Canadian, and American Indian troops. This success was an important step leading to the dramatic surrender of Gen. John Burgoyne at Saratoga—changing the course of the Revolutionary War in favor of the colonial rebels.

Out of the approximate 800 American Continentals and civilians inside the fort during the three-week Siege of 1777, only 21 were wounded and 4 people died. A baby girl was born on August 22, 1777, the final day of the British siege. To this day the names of the mother and child are unknown.

Entering the fort over a drawbridge, visitors are challenged by a sentry in the uniform of the 3rd New York Regiment, a colonial unit. The sentry and others in the fort portray members of the garrison force. A park ranger often impersonates Captain Aaron Aorson, a light infantry company commander. "The Oneidas trade with us regularly," he says, as if the Indians are still waiting outside the gate with pelts in hand.

At the Willett Visitors Center, visitors receive an orientation from the ranger on duty. The museum displays military arms, clothing, hardware, Indian artifacts, furniture, and furnishings from the French and Indian War and American Revolutionary War periods. Three short trails encircle the fort. One of the trails follows a portion of the Oneida Carrying Place. The other two trails include interpretive markers relaying the history of the siege.

Visitors can view the officers' quarters, dark rooms with a brick hearth and a four-poster bed. The officers ate off fine china and many pieces were preserved and are displayed in the museum. The enlisted men had a more difficult life. Low platforms covered with straw served as communal beds for as many as ten men who would huddle together for warmth in the poorly heated barracks.

Living-history programs and battle reenactments are ongoing. There are regularly scheduled guided ranger tours, as well as Junior Ranger and other kids' programs. A highlight of the summer season is the Honor American Days Concert, the last Saturday in July. The Syracuse Symphony Orchestra plays a concert of patriotic selections including the "1812 Overture" and "Stars and Stripes Forever." Fireworks conclude the concert, complete with cannon and musket fire from the fort.

RESTAURANTS

Coalyard Charlie's (315-336-9940, www.coalyardcharlies.com, 100 Depeyster St., Rome, NY 13440) The building housing this eatery originally served as a general store and boardinghouse on the Erie Canal more than 150 years ago. A family restaurant that has been serving area diners for more than 50 years, Coalyard Charlie's bills itself as "Rome's Original Erie Canal Tavern." There is an "all you can eat" soup, salad, and bread bar that is included with most entrées. Other offerings include seafood, steak, prime rib, chicken, burgers, salads, and sandwiches, as well as a children's menu. Open Monday to Saturday for dinner; weekdays for lunch.

Savoy Restaurant (315-339-3166, www.romesavoy.com, 255 East Dominick St., Rome, NY 13440) Established in 1908, the Savoy has had more than a century of experience in perfecting the art of hospitality. The menu is comprehensive, with chicken including the Utica-Rome signature Chicken Riggies, veal, steak, prime rib, seafood, pasta, and steak. This is a throwback to an earlier era, with live music and candles on the tables. Open daily for dinner, lunch Monday to Friday.

Teddy's Restaurant (315-336-7839, www.teddysrestaurantny.com, 851 Black River Blvd. North, Rome, NY 13440) Teddy Roosevelt is on the menu cover, and quotes from the president and Rough Rider are inside. Favorites include Teddy's Turkey Club, Teddy's Reuben, Teddy's BLT, a full menu of Italian dishes including award-winning Chicken Riggies, voted number one in Utica's Riggie Fest, chicken, seafood, steak and New York Rough Rider (N.Y. strip loin with onions and cheese). Open Monday to Saturday for lunch and dinner.

Chicken Riggies Give Birth to Riggiefest

Chicken Riggies, a popular dish native to the Utica-Rome area, is essentially chicken, rigatoni, and peppers and onions, in a spicy cream-and-tomato sauce. To answer the perennial debate over which restaurant serves the best Riggies, **Riggiefest** was born in 2005. Three years in a row Teddy's Restaurant in Rome won the number one slot and has since been inducted into the Riggie Hall of Fame. The Food Network and Rachel Ray have featured this unique dish on television.

ATTRACTIONS

Delta Lake State Park (315-337-4670, www.nysparks.state.ny.us, 8797 State Rt. 46, Rome, NY 13440) Lake Delta was created when the state built a dam in 1912 and flooded some 3,000 acres, destroying the village of Delta. The park is located on a peninsula extending into Delta Reservoir, and features a picnic area and hiking and nature trails. There is a boat launch and shoreline fishing for trout, pike, bass, bullhead, and perch. The park offers 101 tent, trailer, or RV camping sites, and a sandy beach with swimming in the summer. Open year round. Camping season is the first Friday in May through Columbus Day. The beach is open for swimming on weekends and holidays from Memorial Day through late June and daily from late June through Labor Day. The boat launch is open 24 hours a day from early May to late November.

Fort Rickey Children's Discovery Zoo (315-336-1930, www.fortrickey.com, 5135 Rome–New London Rd., Rome, NY 13440) This is a special kind of zoo with an emphasis on children and fun. It includes a petting area that allows children to interact with the barnyard animals. There are also pony rides, a playground, and a catfish-feeding area. Animals include spider monkeys, llamas, alpacas, American bison, gray wolves, emus, and fallow deer. Open daily in summer, weekends only September and October; adults $9.50, seniors $8, children free with paying adult and coupon (available on Web site) or $6.50.

Fort Stanwix National Monument (315-338-7730, www.nps.gov/fost, 112 East Park St. [entrance at 100 S. James St.], Rome, NY 13440) Open daily 9–5; free admission.

ILION

The small village of Ilion is a classic canal success story. When Eliphalet Remington Jr. built his first rifle in 1816, he had no idea he was attending the birth of one of the largest firearms companies in the world. For nearly two centuries Remington firearms have helped shape American history.

In 1828 Remington moved the company's operations to a site alongside the newly constructed canal. For a while the village was called Remington Corners, but Remington objected to having his name used for the village. In 1843 the name Ilion, as the ancient city of Troy was called, was proposed, and Remington approved. So the village became Ilion.

This original factory is part of the property on which the Ilion firearms plant sits today—surely the most successful canal business still in its original location. It is also the oldest firm in the United States still manufacturing its original product. Remington Arms Company was an enormous success. The location was pivotal in making it possible for the company to ship the guns, as well as the typewriters, sewing machines, and other goods it

Erie Canal Village

The site where the first shovelful of dirt for the "Big Ditch" was dug on Independence Day in 1817 just outside Rome is preserved in the **Erie Canal Village** (315-337-3999, www.eriecanalvillage.net, 5789 Rome–New London Rd., Rome, NY 13440). This is a restored pioneer community made up of buildings moved from a 50-mile radius and set up to resemble a canal town of the 1840s. The buildings were taken apart board by board and reassembled on the site.

Visitors can stand on the very spot where the course of American and world history was changed forever. Water no longer fills the original canal, which today resembles a ditch, but the second canal is filled with water and visitors are invited to ride on a mule- or horse-drawn packet boat. If you're lucky you might get Sal, a resident mule named after the mule in the old canal song "Low Bridge, Everybody Down," to pull your boat.

Other highlights are the narrow-gauge train that travels around the property, a 3.5-mile multiuse trail, blacksmith demonstrations, an authentic 1850s tavern, and a gift shop filled with canal books, music, and other souvenirs.

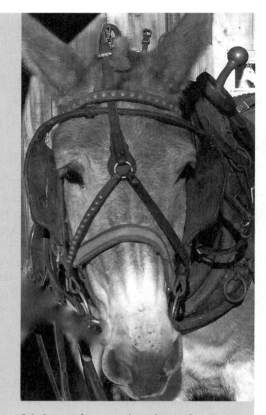

Sal, the most famous mule on the canal

Bennett's Tavern, a Methodist Church, blacksmith's shop, the Crosby House, train station, schoolhouse, canal store, a settler's house, print shop, and the Shull House are among the buildings that comprise the village. Staff in period dress enhance the atmosphere.

There's a museum with push-button exhibits, including a map that lights up to show where the locks are and a recording of "Low Bridge, Everybody Down" played on a wooden flute. A reproduc-

manufactured, around the country and the world. For a number of years the company operated its own canal boats for shipping its products.

The company and the **Remington Firearms Museum** (315-895-3200 or 800-243-9700, www.remington.com, Catherine St., Ilion, NY 13357) bill themselves as "where the history of a company tells the history of a country." The first rifle made at Remington's Ilion factory was a flintlock. There's one just like the original at the Remington museum, plus several of the original Remington percussion rifles that helped settle America.

In the 19th and 20th centuries, Remington meant "first" in fields as diverse as typewrit-

The Erie Canal Village in Rome celebrates where it all began

tion packet boat is displayed in the museum, complete with women's quarters. Red velvet curtains add a touch of elegance to the three-tier bunks, suspended by leather straps.

The **New York State Museum of Cheese,** which originally housed the Weeks & Merry Cheese Factory from 1862 to 1910, is also here. The museum showcases a re-created cheese factory and an exhibition on the development of the state's dairy industry.

A popular feature of the village is a ride aboard the *Chief Engineer of Rome*, which keeps to a regular schedule of 40-minute trips on a restored section of the enlarged canal. It was built of Mohawk Valley oak to the same specifications as the passenger-carrying packet boats of the canal's early years. The packet boat travels along a 1.5-mile section of canal. Time does sometimes stand still, at least here on the old canal.

The Erie Canal Village is open Wednesday to Sunday, Memorial Day weekend through Labor Day. Admission: adults $10, seniors $7, children $5 (packet boat cruise $6 additional).

ers, knives, cash registers, farm equipment, and even bridges. During the last quarter of the 19th century, Remington became known for many firsts in American-made handguns. Many of the most popular and the rarest of the company's revolvers and pistols are on display, including the 1865 Double Derringer that kept many a notorious gambler honest.

Annie Oakley was known as Little Miss Sure Shot with her Remington .22 rifle. Exhibits about Annie and other famous and infamous Remington fans are a highlight of the museum. The museum is open Mon.–Sat.; free admission.

The **Ilion Marina** (315-894-9421, 190 Central Ave., Ilion, NY 13357), open May to

The Remington Arms Company is an original canal-side business

October, has a full range of marina services including a café, showers, store, electricity, water, and free boat launch, and is within walking distance of the Remington Firearms Museum.

HERKIMER

The village of Herkimer is named after the Herkimer family, whose most prominent member was General Nicholas Herkimer, a Revolutionary War hero. His home is preserved in nearby Little Falls.

The area is a favorite rock-collecting area because of the vast deposits of large quartz crystals known as Herkimer diamonds. Although the minerals are not true diamonds and not generally used as gemstones, they have become popular as small trinkets. There are several commercial mines that cater to tourists. These gemstones are believed to be close to 500 million years old. They appear to have been precision-cut and have a diamond-like geometrical shape.

Customers can break up rock or screen the soil to find the crystals. Some believe that Herkimer diamonds are effective for healing, meditation, and spiritual purposes. It is thought that the double-terminated points allow for energy to enter and exit from multiple locations on the crystal, resulting in a more powerful energy flow.

Herkimer is also home to Erie Canal Cruises, which offers regular cruises aboard *Lil' Diamond II* along the canal through Lock 18.

A Famous Writing Instrument

"Like its predecessor, it [Ilion] has a long association with war, weapons, and words through the Remington Arms factory whence emerged not only guns (famous models and ones less so, like the Mule-Ear Carbine, the Zig-Zag Derringer, the rifle-cane) but also the creation of a practical typing machine . . . the first typewritten manuscript accepted for publication came from a Missourian who wrote about a river, and he did it on a contraption made in Ilion. That's got to mean Twain's *Life on the Mississippi*."

—William Least Heat-Moon, *River-Horse: Across America by Boat*

Herkimer offers a variety of canal-side attractions

ATTRACTIONS

Ace of Diamond Mine and Campground (315-891-3855, www.herkimerdiamonds.com, Rt. 28, Middleville, NY 13406) Prospector tools are available for rent or for sale, or visitors can bring their own shovels and hammers, safety glasses, gloves, and collecting containers. Guided mining with specialized equipment is available for $1,500 for the day. There is a store, snack bar, and gift shop. There is also a campground. Open April 1 to October 31; adults $8.50 and children 4–7 $4.

Erie Canal Cruises' passenger boat Lil' Diamond II is named for Herkimer's famous rocks

Erie Canal Cruises (315-717-0350, www.eriecanalcruises.com, 800 Mohawk St., Herkimer, NY 13350) The 90-minute cruises depart daily at 1 and 3 pm. The cruise season is from May 23 to October 13. Adults $18 and children 3–10 $12. (For additional information see listing in "Transportation" chapter.)

Gems Along the Mohawk (315-717-0077 or 866-716-4367, www.gems alongmohawk.com, 800 Mohawk St.,

Herkimer, NY 13350) Located just off the New York State Thruway (I-90), Exit 30, this is a standout location, offering a visitors' center, shopping opportunities, a waterfront restaurant, and a marina (the site is homeport for Erie Canal Cruises). It occupies a strategic location on the canal, on the Thruway, on the New York State Canalway Trail, and at the beginning of the southern Adirondack Scenic Byway. Developed by the owner of Herkimer Diamond Mines, it features products manufactured or created in central New York, including collectibles, artwork, photography, handmade candles, hand-crafted shoes and clothes, books about the area and books by area writers, handcrafted apparel, and gift items from a local alpaca farm. The Waterfront Grill Restaurant has large windows offering panoramic views of the canal, and there is also outdoor dining. Menus include Italian dishes, steak, prime rib, chicken, and veal, with an emphasis on local ingredients when possible. Open daily.

Herkimer Diamond Mines (315-717-0175, www.herkimerdiamond.com, 4601 State Rt. 28, Herkimer, NY 13350) An instructional video gets visitors started on their prospecting. It's a good idea to bring safety eyewear, gloves, and closed-toe shoes. Visitors may also bring chisels, screeners, small shovels, buckets, and extra hammers. The gift shop has 5,000 square feet of space, offering jewelry, gems, rocks, and minerals from all over the world. There is also a café and nearby Herkimer Diamond Mines KOA Campground, with fishing on West Canada Creek, a famous trout stream. Open daily April 15 to October 31; adults $10, children 5–12 $8. This fee includes the use of a rock hammer, museum admission, and bags for your finds.

LITTLE FALLS

With an elevation of 1,060 feet, Little Falls is the highest point on the Albany-to-Buffalo canal route. The city posed one of the greatest challenges to canal building and is one of the only places that has visible remnants of 200 years of canal history, including the 1795 guard lock of the Western Inland Lock Navigation Company.

Cruising along the Erie Canal near Herkimer

Industrial facilities along the Mohawk River have been put to new uses in Little Falls

The Mohawk River descends more than 40 feet as it passes through a narrow gorge at Little Falls while proceeding less than 3 miles. Lock 17 is the highest lock on the Erie Canal. It was constructed to solve this engineering challenge, replacing three locks on the 1825 canal. Until recently it was the highest lift lock in the world.

The Little Falls Canal was the first real canal built in New York State. It was begun in 1783 and completed in 1795. Its locks were made of wood originally, but were rebuilt in 1802 in local stone. The last stage of construction is evident in the surface ruins at the west end of the city. Although economically unsuccessful, this early canal served to demonstrate the importance and possibilities of water transportation.

The site of today's Little Falls was created by the Mohawk River eating through a preglacial divide, creating a deep gorge with imposing walls. At the bottom, the river tumbles down a series of rapids. Little Falls owes its basis for existence to this geographical feature.

The area's earliest European settlers, arriving in the first decades of the 18th century, were involved in river trade and commerce associated with the portage around the rapids. Little Falls was the site of several frontier industries during the 18th century, including a saw mill, grist mills, and a foundry.

In the 19th century a cheese exchange was established, and in the years 1853–75, Little Falls was cheese market to the nation. A 2-ton cheese was sent via the canal to New York and then on to Washington, D.C., for President Andrew Jackson's second inaugural celebration in 1833.

Riverfront brick buildings that once housed a textile factory producing uniforms for Union soldiers during the Civil War have been transformed into art galleries and antiques stores. This historic area has experienced a renaissance as Canal Place, now an art and antiques district.

Little Falls was the site of much industrial growth in the years surrounding the beginning of the 20th century. The development of industry and commerce in the city was due largely to the immense source of available energy. Today, this power source is being tapped by a hydroelectric plant located just west of Lock 17.

There are many natural and geological features in the area. The deep chimney potholes, scoured in the stone by the swirling waters at the end of the last ice age, are a geological marvel. Many of the larger potholes are on Moss Island, adjacent to Lock 17. An original lock of the Erie Canal dating to 1825 has been preserved and may be viewed just below Lock 17. It can be visited by walking down a long stairway at the east end of the lock.

Little Falls diamonds can be located along various outcroppings. Excellent examples of these quartz crystals are on display at the Little Falls Public Library and the Little Falls Historical Society Museum.

RESTAURANTS

Ann Street Restaurant and Deli (315-823-3290, 381 S. Ann St., Little Falls, NY 13365) This is a great place for breakfast or lunch or an early dinner on Friday and Saturday. It features special sandwiches, soups, and homemade desserts. Open Monday to Saturday.

Beardslee Castle (315-823-3000 or 800-487-5861, www.beardsleecastle.com, 123 Old State Rd., Little Falls, NY 13365) Around a bend on Rt. 5 is a setting that seems both out of place and perfect. It is a magnificent stone castle. Built in 1860 as a replica of an Irish castle, Beardslee Castle offers an extensive wine list, single malt scotches, small batch bourbons, and more than 50 beers, in addition to fine American cuisine including wild Alaskan salmon and Angus beef. The restaurant grows many of its own herbs and vegetables in the summer and features organic produce year-round. All-natural wood fire using local cherry and apple wood is using in grilling. There is live music and special events throughout the year and even a resident ghost or two. Open Thursday to Sunday for dinner.

Canal Side Inn (315-823-1170, www.canalsideinn.com, 395 South Ann St., Little Falls, NY 13365) Consistently rated one of the best inns on the Erie Canal, this lovely establishment, located in the historic Canal Place district, looks as if belongs in a French village. It combines a fine restaurant serving imaginative French and American cuisine and three luxuriously sized suites with kitchenettes. The dining room is open for dinner Tuesday to Saturday and a grill menu is served nightly in the lounge.

ATTRACTIONS

Little Falls Antique Center (315-823-4309, www.littlefallsantiquecenter.com, 25 West Mill St., Little Falls, NY 13365) Housed in an 1855 mill building on the Mohawk River and the Erie Canal, this center's 22 dealers sell antique tools, books, postcards, furniture, glass, clothing, jewelry, china, and Civil War memorabilia. Open daily.

Little Falls Historical Society Museum (315-823-0643, www.lfhistoricalsociety.org, 319 S. Ann St., Little Falls, NY 13365) Located in a historic 1833 bank building, this museum features displays about the Erie Canal, the area's early cheese industry, and historical memorabilia. Open Tuesday, Thursday, and Saturday, mid-May to September; free admission.

Visitors to the Little Falls Antique Center can spend hours navigating through these treasures

Herkimer Home and Oriskany Battlefield Site

Nicholas Herkimer came from a family of German Palatinate refugees who settled in the area around Little Falls. A successful farmer and trader, Herkimer built a fashionable English Georgian-style mansion in 1764, now known as the **Herkimer Home State Historic Site** (315-823-0398, www.littlefalls ny.com/HerkimerHome, 200 State Route 169, Little Falls, NY 13365).

Herkimer's place in history was assured by his legendary courage during the American Revolution's crucial summer of 1777, when a three-pronged attack on New York posed particular danger to the sparsely settled Mohawk Valley frontier.

On July 10 the advance of British colonel Barry St. Leger's troops on the Americans at nearby Fort Stanwix was reported. Despite the considerable reluctance of the settlers to muster to their own defense, Herkimer managed to rally eight hundred men and boys by August 4 and hastened toward the besieged fort. Two days later Herkimer and his men were ambushed by Iroquois and British-allied Loyalists. Herkimer was seriously wounded in the leg but he managed to keep command of his militia, which held its ground despite fierce hand-to-hand combat.

Herkimer was carried home and died ten days later after his leg was unskillfully amputated. Immediately regarded as a hero and a martyr to the cause of American freedom, his home became a shrine. He is buried on the property and the inscription on his tombstone reads: "General Nicholas Herkimer, died Aug. 17, 1777, ten days after the battle of Oriskany, in which engagement he received wounds which caused his death."

In considerable disrepair, the home was acquired by New York State in 1913. Preservation was begun and a major restoration was completed in the 1960s. Today, it is operated as a house museum. On Sundays from Memorial Day to Labor Day costumed staff and volunteers are engaged in household and farm activities. There is a dock available to canal boaters and it is just a short walk to the Herkimer Home. Open Wednesday to Sunday, mid-May to October; Tuesday to Sunday, July and August. Admission: adults, $4, seniors and students, $3.

At the **Oriskany Battlefield State Historic Site** (315-768-7224, www.nysparks.state.ny.us, 7801 State Rt. 69, Oriskany, NY 13424), a National Historic Landmark, a granite shaft marks one of the bloodiest battles of the Revolutionary War. Visitors can walk the site, learn the history through interpretive signs, and visit a historic encampment during special events. Open Wednesday to Sunday and holiday Mondays from mid-May to mid-October. Free admission.

Moss Island (end of S. Ann St., Little Falls, NY 13365) Moss Island is the only glacial park east of the Rocky Mountains. It is not actually an island but an intrusion separating the highest lock in the Erie Canal system from the natural bed of the Mohawk River. It is a favorite site among rock climbers and hikers wanting to see the glacial-formed potholes. It has been declared a Natural History Landmark by the National Park Service, one of 400 spots so designated in the United States.

The Shops at 25 West (315-823-0240, www.shopsat25west.com, 25 West Mill St., Little Falls, NY 13365) There are more than 30 artists, craftspeople, and vendors selling their creations in this historic former mill building. There are decorative arts, jewelry, quilts, kitchen gadgets, old-fashioned candy, jams and jellies, paintings, pottery, and clothing. Talk to the artist or creator. Many will take special orders. Open daily.

Turning Stone Casino

Turning Stone Resort & Casino (315-361-7711 or 800-771-7711, www.turningstone.com, 5218 Patrick Rd., Verona, NY 13478) looks like a mirage in the midst of rolling farmlands. The action at the Oneida Indian Nation's Turning Stone started with a small bingo parlor in 1979. Since then, Turning Stone has grown into a major gaming and golf destination. It is just off I-90 between Utica and Syracuse, about 30 miles east of the latter.

This 1,200-acre resort is the largest golf, spa, and entertainment complex in the Northeast. The four hotels, five golf courses, two spas, concert hall, nightclub, casino, and heliport welcome more than 4 million visitors a year, making it one of the top tourist destinations in New York State. It is a city unto itself—minus the city, of course.

The golf courses have received top ratings from *Golf Magazine*. Atunyote, the Tom Fazio–designed trophy course, is Oneida for "eagle." Many consider the star of the courses to be Shenendoah, designed by Rick Smith.

Skana Spa, the nationally recognized spa, is one of the few places in the country to offer an authentic Native American sweat lodge experience. American Indians have used the sacred sweat lodge as a means of cleansing the body and purifying the spirit for centuries. The three-hour ritual features interpretative storytelling, drumming, and chanting led by a Native American guide before culminating in a detoxifying sweat that hits 200 degrees. The dome-shaped structure made of red willow, draped in buffalo hides, and centered on a fire pit is stoked by roasting hot rocks.

Spa Magazine named the spa the Best New Spa of 2007. It features a 33,000-square-foot building with treatments based on American Indian therapies and healing herbs, leaves, and flowers. Signature treatments include the Sage and White Pine Hot Towel Massage and the Dandelion and Mint Foot Cure. Facials and masks are made from natural ingredients such as pumpkin and wild black cherry.

The accommodations are designed to cater to all tastes and budgets. The award-winning Lodge is an elegant 94 all-suites hotel with a gourmet restaurant, Wildflowers; the 279-room Hotel at Turning Stone has luxury and honeymoon suites; the 287-room Tower at Turning Stone is 19 stories and the tallest building between Albany and Syracuse; the 62-room Inn at Turning Stone is handy for families and the budget conscious. There is even a RV park with organized activities for children, a fishing pond, tennis, and other sports activities. A variety of packages are available, centering around golf, spa, and even hot-air ballooning.

Oneida Community

Just a few miles from the lights, action, and glitz of the Turning Stone Casino is quite literally another world: the utopian Oneida Community.

Though the religiously based Perfectionist community existed only from 1848 to 1880, artifacts of the community survive in the handsome 93,000-square-foot National Historic Landmark **Oneida Community Mansion House** (315-363-0745, www.oneidacommunity.org, 170 Kenwood Ave., Oneida, NY 13421). Set amid sweeping lawns, century-old trees, and well-kept gardens, the massive building is itself one of the community's greatest legacies. It operates today as an apartment house, a museum, and one of the most unusual bed & breakfasts anywhere. There are nine large guest rooms, each with a private bath. A stay includes breakfast, access to the large library, and a private tour of the Mansion House. An on-site restaurant is open for lunch and dinner.

Actually, the Oneida Community has had a long history of attracting visitors. During the height of the community's existence, thousands of tourists came regularly by railroad or the Erie Canal and paid 60 cents for one of the community's largely vegetarian dinners or 25 cents for an evening's "grand entertainment" of music and puppet shows.

The founders of the community wanted to create a heaven on earth. For 33 years they believed they had succeeded. They shared everything—including their worldly possessions, their religious fervor, and their sexual partners. Under the direction of Vermont native John Humphrey Noyes they became the most successful commune in American history. Noyes led his followers from the communism of property through the communism of households to the communism of love or, as he called it, complex marriage.

They were highly successful inventors and businesspeople and became quite wealthy. They were also the world's largest producer of silverware. Though the silverware is no longer made in Oneida, there is still a silverware presence at the **Oneida Ltd. Factory Store** (315-361-3662, www.oneida .com, Sherrill Shopping Center, 606 Sherrill Rd., Sherrill, NY 13461), which sells Oneida goods including silver, glassware, china, and related items at big discounts (as much as 70 percent). It is just a mile down the road from the Mansion House.

A stay at the Oneida Community Mansion House includes a private tour

A replica of Henry Hudson's famed ship Half Moon docked at Albany

9

ALBANY AND THE EASTERN CANAL REGION

Troy, Schenectady

ALBANY

In 1609 the English navigator Henry Hudson sailed up the river that would later bear his name and discovered the area that became Albany. He was looking for a route to the Pacific Ocean and Asia.

Despite his disappointment on not meeting that goal, he took possession of the lands in the name of Holland, since he was sailing in the service of the Dutch East India Company. Hudson gave glowing accounts of the magnificent river and bountiful area. The year 2009 would see region-wide 400th-anniversary celebrations of Hudson's famed voyage.

The Dutch settled the city and set up trading posts. By 1664, nearly ten thousand Dutch were living at Fort Orange when the English captured the fort and renamed it in honor of the duke of Albany. In 1686 the British granted Albany's founding charter as a city, making it the second-oldest chartered city in the United States. It still operates under its original charter.

By 1750 it was an important trading center, and in 1754 the first general congress of all the colonies was held in Albany. Though it was technically part of the British crown until the Revolution, Dutch merchants continued to influence the city. Under Dutch guidance, Albany played an important role in maintaining communication between the French, the British, and the Iroquois. Albany's annual **Tulip Festival** in historic Washington Park honors this Dutch heritage each spring (for more information visit http://alabanyevents.org).

Albany was named the capital of New York in 1797. Because of its riverside location and the system of turnpikes that fanned out from the city, Albany was the transportation hub of the Northeast. The status was heightened with the construction of the Erie Canal, which helped Albany develop as a business and banking center.

It has long been a popular pastime to malign Albany. H. H. Richardson, a famed architect who designed grand buildings in the city, had this to say in 1870: "Of all the most miserable, wretched, second-class, one-horse towns, this is the most miserable."

But the city, which has sent more presidents to Washington, D.C., than any other city, has undergone a transformation in recent decades. It far exceeds the usual expectations.

The Pulitzer Prize–winning Albany author William Kennedy called his hometown an

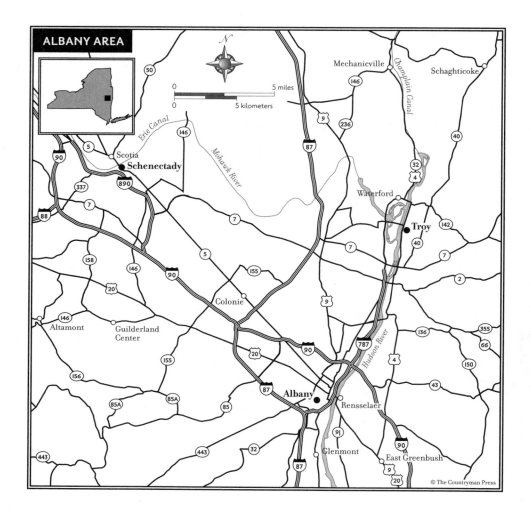

"improbable city of political wizards, fearless ethnics, spectacular aristocrats, splendid nobodies, and underrated scoundrels." He is enamored of the city: "Albany is a wonderful place to live. It's a fascinating, beautiful city." He added that it is a place where one "finds all the elements that a man ever needs for the life of the soul." Kennedy continues to fan the creative fires as director of the New York State Writer's Institute, which features lectures and workshops by some of the world's top writers.

The city is a dream for fans of architecture, and 18th- and 19th-century structures blend gracefully with the dramatic buildings of the Empire State Plaza.

When the chateau-like State Capitol, a massive stone building with Renaissance flourishes, was completed at the then staggering cost of $25 million, it was the most expensive building in the country and one of the lengthiest public works projects in the state. It took five architects and 32 years to complete. It was 1899 before Governor Theodore Roosevelt declared the building complete, although in true Albany fashion the entire project was steeped in controversy.

The 3-acre, five-story building remains the jewel of downtown Albany. It is the last great monumental structure to be built entirely of masonry and cost twice as much as the U.S. Capitol in Washington, D.C.

The Capitol building's staircases are quite extraordinary. The so-called Million Dollar Staircase boasts more then three hundred portraits by stone carvers of famous New Yorkers and the carvers' families and friends; the Senate Staircase, or "Evolutionary Staircase," contains depictions of simpler creatures at the bottom, while the carvings (and creatures) become more complex as the stair rises.

Just down the block from the Capitol stands Albany City Hall, designed by H. H. Richardson. Kennedy called it "one of the most sublime structures ever built for the aggrandizement of politicians."

This capitol expense proved to be relatively small compared with the more than $1-billion Nelson A. Rockefeller Empire State Plaza. Governor Rockefeller was inspired to build the mammoth structure after he was embarrassed by the slums and derelict neighborhoods that he and Holland's Princess Beatrix passed through while she was visiting the city on its 350th anniversary. He pushed for a new headquarters for the state government, calling it, in typical Rockefeller fashion, "The most spectacularly beautiful seat of government in the world."

The governor himself designed part of the plaza. In an airplane with Wallace Harrison, the principal architect of the plaza and also of Manhattan's Rockefeller Center, Rockefeller sketched a plan for the mall on the back of an envelope.

The 11-building, 98-acre Empire State Plaza was fully completed in 1978. In and around the buildings and in the concourses that link them are 92 pieces of modern art. Rockefeller, who had served as president of the Museum of Modern Art before becoming governor, donated a Jackson Pollock painting and personally approved the purchase or

The New York State Capitol

Albany skyline Albany Convention & Visitors Bureau

commission of the rest of the collection. It is the greatest collection of modern American art in any single public site that is not a museum.

Today, the plaza is the center for entertainment and festivities in the city. It has been credited with turning Albany from an ugly duckling into a handsome and somewhat overwhelming swan. It is a public square with reflecting pools, a skating rink in winter, flowers, fountains, and parks; the site of the New York State Vietnam Memorial; a convention center and performing arts facility; a state museum devoted to the environment; a library; a covered concourse one-fourth of a mile long; the headquarters for nearly 50 state agencies, and the Corning Tower.

On the 42nd floor of the Corning Tower, an observation deck provides vistas of the Hudson River and downtown Albany and, on a good day, the mountains to the north. The tower is named in honor of Albany's longtime mayor, Erastus Corning II, another resident for the record books. First elected in 1941, he was mayor until his death in 1983—42 years in all. No other city mayor had a tenure that was even close.

Largest Working Weathervane

The weathervane atop the State University of New York at Albany's Central Administration Building (the original Delaware and Hudson Railroad Station) is a replica of the *Half Moon*, the ship in which Henry Hudson sailed up the Hudson River to what became Albany. The weathervane, weighing in at 400 pounds, is the largest working weathervane in the United States.

LODGING

Albany has a rich collection of historic bed & breakfasts and inns as well as historic hotels. There are also a wide array of chain hotels and motels near the airport and in the State University at Albany neighborhood. Rates as listed are for double occupancy.

Lodging Rates

Inexpensive: Up to $75 per couple
Moderate: $76–$150 per couple
Expensive: $151–$250 per couple
Very Expensive: More than $250 per couple

ALBANY MANSION HILL INN & RESTAURANT

518-465-2038 or 888-299-0455
www.mansionhill.com
115 Philip St., Albany, NY 12202
Price: Expensive
Credit Cards: Yes
Handicapped Access: No
Special Features: Pet friendly

This inn and restaurant bills itself as Albany's best-kept secret. An 1861 Victorian house with guest rooms on the top floors and a restaurant at street level, it was originally the home of brush maker Daniel Brown and is located in the historic district just around the corner from the governor's executive mansion. Founded in 1984 by Maryellen and Steve Stofelano Jr. as the city's first downtown bed & breakfast, the inn has eight comfortable guest rooms with single or double queen beds. Several of the rooms feature the artwork of renowned local artist Len Tantillo. A full complimentary breakfast is served in the dining room. Conveniently located a five-minute walk from the Empire State Plaza and Capitol. Parking is free, a bonus in a downtown location.

ANGELS BED AND BREAKFAST

518-426-4104
www.angelsbedandbreakfast.com
96 Madison Ave., Albany, NY 12202
Price: Expensive
Credit Cards: Yes
Handicapped Access: No
Special Features: Complimentary full gourmet breakfast

This intimate bed & breakfast in the heart of downtown Albany, within convenient walking distance of the major capital sights, began life in 1811 as the John Stafford House. Governor Joseph Yates rented the house in 1822 for use as his official residence. He hosted some of the most prominent people living in or passing through Albany during his governorship. The house has been lovingly restored and was transformed into this luxurious small urban inn in 2003. There are three comfortable second-floor rooms with high ceilings and either a king- or queen-sized bed. Each room has a private bath. On the ground floor is a cute café, and the outdoor roof deck offers a good place to relax.

BEST WESTERN SOVEREIGN HOTEL

518-489-2981 or 800-780-7234
www.bestwestern.com/sovereignhotel albany
1228 Western Ave., Albany, NY 12203
Price: Moderate
Credit Cards: Yes
Handicapped Access: Yes
Special Features: Pet friendly, indoor pool

This 192-room hotel is 3 miles from downtown Albany and next to the State University at Albany. Airport shuttle service is available. There is an indoor swimming pool, exercise room, and complimentary hot breakfast. Every room has a refrigerator and there is a full business center. The **1228 Grill & Bar** is on the premises and is open for breakfast, lunch, and dinner. There is a happy hour daily and free hors d'oeuvres Monday to Thursday.

CRESTHILL SUITES

518-454-0007 or 888-723-1655
www.cresthillsuites.com
1415 Washington Ave., Albany, NY 12206
Price: Moderate
Credit Cards: Yes
Handicapped Access: Yes
Special Features: Pet friendly

Across from the State University at Albany and about ten minutes from downtown, this comfortable, modern two-story, 95-room facility welcomes business and leisure travelers, families, and pets. There are studios and one- and two-bedroom suites with free high-speed Internet, free local telephone calls, and kitchens. A 24-hour convenience center offers snacks and light meals. A hot breakfast and light evening meal and social hour (Monday to Thursday) are complimentary. There is a courtyard with an outdoor pool, patio, and grills, as well as a fully equipped business center and fitness center. Shuttle service provides transportation to and from the airport and bus and train stations.

CROWNE PLAZA ALBANY

518-462-6611 or 800-227-6963

Rooms at the Morgan State House offer history—and comfort

www.cpalbany.com
State and Lodge Sts., Albany, NY 12207
Price: Moderate
Credit Cards: Yes
Handicapped Access: Yes
Special Features: Free shuttle service to Albany Airport and Amtrak Station

This 384-room (including 18 suites with living area, refrigerator, and microwave) high-rise hotel recently underwent a complete renovation. It is in the heart of historic downtown Albany, one block from the New York State Capitol and the Times Union Center. There's an indoor pool and complete health club as well as a full business center. The Sleep Advantage program features a complimentary sleep CD, relaxation tips, and exercises and amenity bag with earplugs and eye mask. There are Quiet Zone floors that are offered Sunday through Thursday to help ensure maximum silence for business-travel guests. Complimentary high-speed Internet access is available throughout the hotel. Dining choices include **Webster's Corner Restaurant**, showcasing regional cuisine and wines by the glass. It is open for breakfast and dinner. **Kelsey's Irish Pub** is the choice for pub fare and drinks.

HAMPTON INN & SUITES ALBANY DOWNTOWN

518-432-7000, 800-HAMPTON
www.hamptonsuitesalbany.com
25 Chapel St., Albany, NY 12210
Price: Expensive
Credit Cards: Yes
Handicapped Access: Yes
Special Features: Women-only Empire Floor; complimentary high-speed Internet

Opened in October 2007, this is one of downtown Albany's newest hotels and has 121 rooms including 35 studio suites with a microwave, refrigerator and wet bar, eight two-room whirlpool king suites and an executive two room full kitchen suite. The innovative Empire Floor, exclusively for women and offering relevant amenities including a private 30-minute session in the Relaxation Club massage chair, sauna, or steam room, is popular with both business and leisure travelers. A portion of the Empire Floor proceeds go to the American Cancer Society's Making Strikes against Breast Cancer campaign. The hotel's complimentary breakfast buffets include hot items and "On the Run" bags for those in a hurry. It is home to the award-winning **Yono's Restaurant.**

74 STATE

518-434-7410
www.74State.com
74 State St., Albany, NY 12207
Price: Moderate–Expensive
Credit Cards: Yes
Handicapped Access: Yes
Special Features: Complimentary high-speed Internet

Opened in 2007, this 74-room hotel is housed in a former office and retail building constructed in 1910. At the ribbon-cutting ceremony, Albany writer William Kennedy said: "I'm glad that 74 State Street is here. It's a herald of the new day and the new night and proof that our town is finally finding a way to spend 24 hours Downtown." The elegant boutique hotel located on Albany's historic State Street features paneled walls, fireplaces, and leather furnishings throughout the public areas. The rooms and suites are all large and luxurious, with Eurotop beds, duvets, and marble-top vanities. Some rooms have fireplaces.

THE DESMOND HOTEL AND CONFERENCE CENTER

518-869-8100 or 800-448-3500
www.desmondhotels.com
660 Albany-Shaker Rd., Albany, NY 12211
Price: Moderate–Expensive

Credit Cards: Yes
Handicapped Access: Yes
Special Features: Three restaurants, home of the rare Scrimshaw Steinway piano

Opened in 1974, the hotel was designed to resemble an 18th-century colonial village. It is built around two large indoor courtyards with skylights, landscaping, and indoor swimming pools. The 324 rooms and suites are fashioned after the homes of sea captains from the 18th century. The rooms feature oriental rugs, original oil paintings, and colonial replica furnishings. Many rooms and suites offer a private balcony overlooking the indoor courtyards, and fireplaces (nonworking). A number of rooms have four-poster beds. The hotel is about five minutes from the Albany Airport, and there is a complimentary shuttle service. There is also complimentary high-speed Internet. The Scrimshaw Steinway piano is one of only two known remaining pianos of the 14 of its kind made more than one hundred years ago by Steinway. It was formerly owned by the world-famous architect Stanford White and is now a regular part of the fine dining in the **Scrimshaw Restaurant.** It has won the *Wine Spectator* Award of Excellence every year since 1997. There is live entertainment nightly. **The Tavern** and **Simpson's** offer more casual fare.

THE INN ON SOUTH LAKE

518-438-7646
www.theinnonsouthlake.com
145 S. Lake Ave., Albany, NY 12208
Price: Moderate
Credit Cards: Yes
Handicapped Access: No
Special Features: Complimentary high-speed Internet

This Victorian house was originally built in 1890. The main floor houses the library, which features a fireplace, wood-beamed ceiling, and stained-glass windows; the dining room includes a window seat, cherry paneling, box-beamed ceiling, and stained-glass window; and the living room showcases ornate woodwork and yet another stained-glass window. The second floor has five spacious bedrooms, three with private baths and two that share a bath. The Blair Suite is named for Dr. Louis Eli Blair, the owner of the home and an 1881 graduate of Albany Medical College. This is a self-contained apartment with a fully equipped kitchen, living room, bedroom, and bathroom—perfect for extended stays. The inn is adjacent to University Heights and within walking distance of Albany Law School, Albany Medical Center, and other medical facilities.

THE MORGAN STATE HOUSE/WASHINGTON PARK STATE HOUSE

518-427-6063 or 888-427-6063
www.statehouse.com
393 State St., Albany, NY 12210
Price: Moderate–Expensive
Credit Cards: Yes
Handicapped Access: Washington Park State House only
Special Features: Complimentary breakfast and YMCA guest pass

This is a gem in downtown Albany. It is an elegant and professionally run European-style boutique hotel in a beautiful town house on "Mansion Row," just a few blocks from the Empire State Plaza and across the street from Washington Park. It was built in 1888 and remained a single-family house until 1975. The six very large rooms are quite extraordinary, with 19th-century period detailing and furnishings. The tile bathrooms have claw-foot tubs and some rooms have fireplaces. The beds are a signature feature with feather mattresses and down comforters and pillows. All the sheets are starched and ironed, a luxury you will rarely find. Free high-speed Internet is available in the rooms and lobby. All rooms have a view of the park or the garden in the back. The two-bedroom suite boasts an elegant library. The third-floor king room has a sitting area and a fireplace with a beautifully carved mantle. Three buildings west of the townhouse is the Washington Park State House under the same ownership and operation, with nine studio condominiums, spacious rooms, and suites with kitchens or kitchenettes. It is a good choice for an extended stay. There is an elevator. No children under 16 are allowed.

RESTAURANTS

Albany has a long tradition of good food and fine dining. Both travelers and fresh foods have been coming to the city for hundreds of years. Restaurant quality has also been influenced by the presence of politicians in residence for the New York State Legislature sessions and lobbyists with generous expense accounts. Excellent ethnic restaurants abound. All restaurants are by New York State law nonsmoking. Prices are estimated per person for dinner entrée without tax, tip, or beverage.

Dining Rates

Inexpensive: Up to $10
Moderate: $11–$25
Expensive: $26–$40
Very Expensive: More than $40

ANGELO'S 677 PRIME

518-427-7463
www.677prime.com
677 Broadway, Albany, NY 12207
Open: Mon.–Sat.
Price: Expensive–Very Expensive
Credit Cards: Yes
Cuisine: American
Serving: L Mon.–Fri.; D Mon.–Sat.
Handicapped Access: Yes
Special Features: Live music Wed.–Sat. nights

In the hub of Albany's theater district just one block from the Palace and Capital Repertory Theaters, Angelo's 677 Prime offers an elegant and stylish wood-paneled dining room that would be at home in midtown Manhattan. In addition to aged prime beef, seafood, and a wide selection of fine wines, patrons of Angelo's are treated to a rotating exhibition of fine art. The restaurant's Collection Series program spotlights a new artist every six months. For true wine lovers it offers the Prime Wine Society, a group of members each with his or her own personalized 12-bottle wine bin as well as other special services. Desserts include such special items as an Ice Cream Playground (mini chocolate chip cookie and ice cream "chipwiches," chocolate vanilla-dipped cone, chocolate crunch bar, and fried vanilla ice cream). There are also decadent chocolate truffles to go.

LE CANARD ENCHAINÉ BRASSERIE (formerly Nicole's Bistro)

518-465-1111
www.le-canardenchaine.com
633 Broadway, Albany, NY 12207
Open: Daily
Price: Expensive
Credit Cards: Yes
Cuisine: French
Serving: L Mon.–Fri.; D Daily
Handicapped Access: No
Special Features: Outdoor courtyard with raw bar

This French bistro is located in the historic Quackenbush House, one of Albany's most treasured landmarks. The early Dutch structure is likely the oldest standing house in the city and dates from about 1730. The house was used as a headquarters in the French and Indian War and as a jail for British general John Burgoyne after the battle of Saratoga. The handsome restaurant is one of Albany's best choices for a special occasion or romantic dinner.

Classic meat dishes include braised lamb shank with port wine raisin sauce and braised beef short ribs with Parmesan fries. The homemade breads set on each table are wonderful. This brasserie offers a taste of Paris at Albany prices. An excellent deal is the three-course prix-fixe dinner special Sunday through Thursday. During warm weather there is outdoor dining in the courtyard, which features a reproduction of a colonial herb garden and raw bar. The restaurant is owned by Jean-Jacques Carquillat and Michael Vrowsky. The partners also operate a restaurant with the same name in Kingston, New York. It has been called the finest restaurant between Manhattan and Montreal.

C. H. EVANS BREWING COMPANY AT ALBANY PUMP STATION

518-456-3540
www.evansale.com
19 Quackenbush Sq., Albany, NY 12207
Open: Daily
Price: Moderate
Credit Cards: Yes
Cuisine: American
Serving: L, D
Handicapped Access: Yes
Special Features: Award-winning microbrewery

Known as the Albany Pump Station because of its location in a cavernous 19th-century former pump station, this establishment is part award-winning microbrewery and part restaurant. The Evans family was in the commercial brewing business for three generations. Its award-winning ales were well known in the Northeast and were even exported to England and France before Prohibition forced the brewery's closing in 1920. Neil Evans revives this rich heritage here, and the walls are decorated with C. H. Evans Brewing Company memorabilia. The menu is quite diverse, with typical pub food such as burgers, pastas, and sandwiches, as well as entrées such as home-style meat-loaf, corned beef brisket, Wurst platter, filet medallions, and Cajun shrimp and scallops. Check out the award-winning Kick-ass Brown Ale and the Quackenbush Blonde. There is a special kids' menu and Sunday family-style dining.

GRANDMA'S COUNTRY RESTAURANT
518-459-4585
1273 Central Ave., Albany, NY 12205
Open: Daily
Price: Inexpensive–Moderate
Credit Cards: Yes
Cuisine: American
Serving: B, L, D
Handicapped Access: Yes
Special Features: Large gift shop and pies available for take-out

This is the place for pie (and other dessert) lovers who come from near and far for these treats. Try the fresh open blueberry (in-season) with layered wild Maine blueberry filling and a touch of vanilla pudding, topped with mounds of fresh whipped cream and large, sweetly glazed fresh blueberries. Or how about the Swiss chocolate almond? It is billed as the "Empress" of Grandma's cream pies, with mounds of fresh whipped cream blended into a creamy rich chocolate filling, all topped with more whipped cream and garnished with hot fudge, toasted almonds, walnuts, and chocolate shavings. There's also pecan, apple, strawberry, banana split cream, sugar-free apple pie, cherry, pumpkin, fresh lemon meringue, Boston cream, Dutch blueberry, coconut custard, and more. It's also the place for breakfast, lunch, and dinner, with such grandma-friendly items as sandwiches, meatloaf, burgers, pasta, and other old favorites.

JACK'S OYSTER HOUSE
518-465-8854
www.jacksoysterhouse.com
42 State St., Albany, NY 12207
Open: Daily
Price: Expensive–Very Expensive
Credit Cards: Yes
Cuisine: American
Serving: L, D
Handicapped Access: Yes
Special Features: Raw bar

This has been an Albany institution since Jack Rosenstein, a former oyster schucker, opened it on January 24, 1913. The Rosenstein family has operated the restaurant ever since. Located downtown at the foot of State Street a short walk from the Capitol, it is easily accessible to locals, lawmakers, and visitors. Now grandson Brad Rosenstein presides over the award-winning dining room and greets all guests, believing that first impressions are critical. Customers in a nostalgic frame of mind still can order selections that would have been found on early menus, like oysters Rockefeller or clams casino. Those with more contemporary tastes can opt for fusion-style preparations like roasted quail, lightly stuffed Normandy-style, and Napoleon of zucchini and ricotta layered with tomato basil jam. Both lunch and dinner menus include a raw bar as well as Jack's famous 1913 Manhattan clam chowder recipe. Other lunch items include burgers, salmon, scrod, crab cakes, and calves liver. Dinner entrées include lobster Newburg, lamb chops, Atlantic scrod, meatloaf, short ribs, and steaks. Desserts include such classics as bananas Foster and New York style cheesecake, as well as Jack's signature specialties. A favorite is the homemade strawberry cotton candy (great fun for table sharing). Reservations are recommended.

JUSTIN'S ON LARK
518-436-7008
www.justinonlark.com
391 Lark St., Albany, NY 12210

Open: Daily
Price: Moderate–Expensive
Credit Cards: Yes
Cuisine: Caribbean/Asian/Southwestern
Serving: L, D
Handicapped Access: Yes
Special Features: Live jazz entertainment
daily (except Tues.)

Justin's offers music, an expansive and
imaginative menu for lunch, brunch
(Saturday and Sunday), dinner, and a late-
night café menu. It has been a star attraction in Albany for 20 years or so. The decor
is wood and brick with lots of artwork on
the walls. There's a handsome bar. On the
café menu there's a fried catfish sandwich,
meatloaf and mac and cheese plate, blackened eggplant sandwich, sesame grilled
game hen, and Jamaican jerk chicken. On
the lunch menu there is a Fast Track Menu,
perfect for those whose lunchtime is limited—the soups and salads are easily prepared. Dinner items include Cajun jumbo
peppered shrimp, seared apricot ginger-
glazed duck breast, and ropa vieja (a Cuban
dish that features braised brisket of beef).

MISS ALBANY DINER

518-465-9148
www.missalbanydiner.com
893 Broadway, Albany, NY 12207
Open: Tues.–Sun.
Price: Inexpensive
Credit Cards: No
Cuisine: Diner
Serving: B, L Mon.–Fri.; brunch Sat. and
Sun.
Handicapped Access: Yes
Special Features: Classic diner appeared in
movie

Just down the road from Nipper, the RCA
dog perched on one of the many nearby
warehouses, Miss Albany is housed in a
classic diner car. It is one of the area's most
celebrated breakfast and lunch places. If it
looks familiar, you may have caught sight of

it in the movie *Ironweed*, based on the novel
by Pulitzer Prize–winning Albany native
William Kennedy. It was restored before its
movie role and is listed on the National
Register of Historic Places. Opened in 1941,
this is a diner with a difference. Try eggs
with curry sauce or the house specialty,
MAD Irish toast: pecan cream cheese
slathered between two thick slices of
French toast, then covered in a butter-
scotch Irish whiskey sauce. You can even get
a real New York City egg cream here. The
diner is usually packed on weekends.

RIVERFRONT BAR & GRILL

518-433-8005
www.riverfrontbarge.com
Corning Preserve, Albany, NY
Open: Daily, seasonal May–Sept.
Price: Inexpensive
Credit Cards: Yes
Cuisine: American
Serving: L, D
Handicapped Access: Yes
Special Features: Live bands Thurs.–Sun.,
outdoor dining

This is Hudson River barge dining and it's a
rocking party place, especially on nights
when the bands play and the weather gods
are smiling. Lots of typical pub fare including chicken wings, steamed clams, crab
cakes, and burgers. Daily specials feature
fish fry, fried clams, fried seafood, and
prime rib on Saturdays. Located in the
Corning Preserve park along the Hudson.

SASO'S JAPANESE NOODLE HOUSE

518-436-7789
www.sasos.com
218 Central Ave., Albany, NY 12206
Open: Tues.–Sat.
Price: Moderate
Credit Cards: Yes
Cuisine: Japanese
Serving: L, D
Handicapped Access: Yes

Special Features: Take-out available

Chef Saso started as a young apprentice in a sushi restaurant in Chiba, Japan, and earned his chef's license in 1975. He later came to the U.S. to work as a hibachi chef, and in 1996 opened Saso's in an unassuming storefront on Central Avenue. The menu includes a bevy of noodle dishes in addition to traditional items. Saso's has a loyal following. Many come for the sushi; others enjoy the bowls of noodles or rice with vegetables and tofu. Diners can finish off their meal with green tea ice cream.

YONO'S RESTAURANT
518-436-7747
www.yonos.com
25 Chapel St., Albany, NY 12210
Open: Mon.–Sat.
Price: Moderate–Expensive
Credit Cards: Yes
Cuisine: Indonesian/Continental
Serving: D
Handicapped Access: Yes
Special Features: Alligator, kangaroo, and ostrich on menu

This is the third incarnation of Yono's, and it is now inside the new Hampton Inn & Suites Hotel in downtown Albany. It has won numerous awards and rates as one of the area's top dining experiences. The owner and chef, Widjiono (Yono) Purnomoi, is a native of Jakarta, Indonesia, and began his chef career on board the legendary Holland America SS *Rotterdam*. He has appeared on the *Today Show* and the Food Network. The dining room is designed with a 19th-century town house in mind, a homage to the original Yono's. The ceilings, original woodwork, bronzed mirrors, crystal chandelier over the service table, elegant tableware, and fresh flowers all work together to convey the feeling of luxury dining from a time gone by. Indonesian food is not Chinese, not Indian, and not Japanese, but it has touches of all these as well as Dutch and Portuguese from the East Indies' colonial days. Diners can choose from the Indonesian or continental side of the menu. There are standard steaks and seafood and such exotic dishes as pan-roasted ostrich medallions and an appetizer of sautéed alligator or roasted kangaroo. The five-course Indonesian Rijsttafel takes diners through a kaleidoscope of flavors and ingredients. Yono's has an extensive wine list, and there are excellent desserts to top off your meal—raspberry walnut torte, Kentucky bourbon nut pie, a sorbet trio.

CULTURE

Albany has a rich history of music and theater dating back to the 19th century. As New York's capital, Albany, as well as the surrounding area, benefits from generous state funding and support of the arts and the many historic buildings and other attractions.

Museums and Historic Sites
ALBANY HERITAGE AREA VISITORS CENTER
518-434-0405 or 800-258-3582
www.albany.org
25 Quackenbush Sq., Albany, NY 12207
Open: Daily
Admission: Free

The museum galleries offer a variety of permanent displays exploring the history of Albany from its beginnings to the present day. The USS *Albany* Heritage Exhibit features ships named for the city from 1846 to the 21st century and archeological items found during the Quackenbush Square excavation. Special history exhibits are scheduled during the year. The **Henry Hudson Planetarium** is an official NASA Space Place. A visitors' center is also on-site.

ALBANY INSTITUTE OF HISTORY & ART

518-463-4478
www.albanyinstitute.org
125 Washington Ave., Albany, NY 12210
Open: Wed.–Sun.
Admission: Adults $10, seniors and students $8, children $6

Founded in 1791, the Albany Institute is the second-oldest museum in the U.S. and it is dedicated to collecting, preserving, interpreting, and promoting interest in the history, art, and culture of Albany and the upper Hudson Valley. Highlights of this museum include some of the finest Hudson River school paintings, colonial Albany, 18th- and 19th-century paintings and sculpture. In the Colonial Albany gallery are furnishings, paintings, and artifacts that tell the story of the Dutch settlement in this area 350 years ago. Ancient Egypt galleries feature a pair of mummies, a priest and priestess, from 304 b.c. and 966 b.c. There's a popular Children's Gallery and a number of family activities including summer art camps, school vacation art making, story times for preschoolers, and a special curriculum for homeschoolers.

DESTROYER USS *SLATER* DE-766

518-431-1943
www.ussslater.org
Broadway at the foot of Madison Ave., (adjacent to Dunn Memorial Bridge), Albany, NY 12201
Open: Wed.–Sun. April–Nov.
Admission: Adults $7, seniors $6, children $5

This is the only Destroyer Escort remaining afloat in the U.S. and the only one with its original battle armament and configuration. Launched in 1944, the *Slater* escorted convoys in the Atlantic and the Pacific. In 1951 she was donated to the Greek Navy and served as a Hellenic Navy Officer Training Vessel until 1991, when Greece gave the ship to the Destroyer Escort Sailors Association. The ship has been used in a number of movies, including *The Guns of Navarone.* There are hour-long guided tours and youth group overnight camping. It is a popular destination for naval reunion groups. The gift shop sells made-on-the-spot dog tags using a vintage World War II machine.

GOVERNOR NELSON A. ROCKEFELLER EMPIRE STATE PLAZA VISITOR CENTER

518-474-2428
www.ogs.state.ny.us/visiting/cultural/defaultplaza.html
Empire State Plaza, North Concourse, Room 110A, Albany, NY 12230
Open: Daily; tours Mon.–Fri.
Admission: Free

One of the country's most spectacular capitol centers, Empire State Plaza has become a cultural center. It is the city's most distinctive downtown feature. From the New York State Capitol to the New York State Museum, the Plaza is full of things to do. Festivals, concerts, seasonal ice-skating, and tours are just a few of the activities. The seat of government operations for New York State, the plaza occupies 98 acres, with 11,000 employees in ten buildings. Free tours are provided twice a day on weekdays. Tour highlights include the world-class Art Collection, which has been described as "the greatest collection of modern American art in any single public site that is not a museum," and stops at various Plaza memorials, including the New York State Vietnam Memorial. The tour concludes on the Corning Tower Observation Deck, which provides a scenic view of the Hudson River and the entire Capital Region as well as the Catskills and Berkshire Mountains.

HISTORIC CHERRY HILL

518-434-4791
www.historiccherryhill.org
523½ S. Pearl St., Albany, NY 12202
Open: Closed until 2010 except for special events

The Van Renssselaer-Rankin family amassed several lifetimes and several households' worth of personal papers and possessions during their 176 years of occupancy at Cherry Hill. In April 1963, when Emily Rankin, the last surviving family member, died, the house and its contents became the Historic Cherry Hill Collection, a completely intact assemblage of one family's material possessions spanning five generations and over three hundred years of American history. The house has many stories to tell. One of the most scandalous happenings was a murder in 1827, and Behind the Scenes Murder Investigation Tours were popular with fans of the television drama *CSI*. The house is currently undergoing an extensive renovation and is expected to reopen in 2010.

HUDSON RIVER WAY

518-434-2032
25 Quackenbush Sq., Albany, NY 12207
Open: Daily
Admission: Free

Opened in 2002 this pedestrian bridge connects downtown to Corning Preserve Park on the banks of the Hudson. It is lined with 30 trompe l'oeil paintings on lampposts that depict the city's history and heritage from prehistoric times and early Dutch merchants to the present.

NEW YORK STATE CAPITOL

518-474-2418
http://assembly.state.ny.us/tour
Washington Ave. and State St., Albany, NY 12230
Open: Mon.–Sat.
Admission: Free

Sitting majestically atop State Street hill, the Capitol is an Albany must-see. Guided tours are offered daily and the tales of its construction and the happenings since the 1880s are

Hudson River Way connects downtown with the city's riverfront Albany Convention & Visitors Bureau

legendary and often quite mind-boggling. Costing more than $25 million in the 19th century, it is one of the most expensive buildings ever erected in the United States. The single largest room in the building is the vast Assembly Chamber and it was the first of the building's grand spaces to be completed and occupied. The Executive Chamber or Red Room was designed by architect H. H. Richardson. Every governor since 1881 has used the desk. The Hall of Governors has portraits of all governors and includes four future presidents: Grover Cleveland, Martin Van Buren, Theodore Roosevelt, and Franklin Delano Roosevelt. The Senate chamber, also designed by Richardson, is acclaimed as one of his finest designs. The walls are covered with gold leaf and there is Siena marble from Italy, granite from Scotland for the pillars, and Mexican onyx on the north and south walls.

NEW YORK STATE MUSEUM

518-474-5877
www.nysm.nysed.gov
Madison Ave. (on Empire State Plaza), Albany, NY 12230
Open: Daily
Admission: Free

A massive museum, it is the largest museum of its kind in the country. It tells the story of New York State, both natural and cultural. The newest permanent gallery, The World Trade Center: Rescue, Recovery, Response, was the first major museum exhibit of artifacts from the September 11, 2001, terrorist attacks. It documents the 24-hour aftermath of the disaster and includes the stunning video shot by two French brothers. Popular permanent exhibits include the Adirondack Wilderness, an Archaeological Perspective of Albany (includes artifacts related to the early Dutch settlement and the daily life of past residents), the Ancient Life of New York focusing on the dinosaur age, Birds of New York, Harlem in the '20s, a carousel from North Tonawanda's Herschell-Spillman Co., the Cohoes Mastodon (excavated in nearby Cohoes in 1866 during construction of a mill), Fire Engine Hall, and Native American Crafts. The **Museum Café** is open for breakfast and lunch and the **Museum Shop** is full of unique New York items.

The Million Dollar Staircase inside the Capitol

SCHUYLER MANSION STATE HISTORIC SITE
518-434-0834
www.nysparks.state.ny.us
32 Catherine St., Albany, NY 12202
Open: Wed.–Sun. mid-Apr.–Oct. (also Tues. June–Aug.); rest of year, by appointment only
Admission: Adults $4, seniors and students $3

The historic home of Revolutionary War General and U.S. Senator Philip Schuyler and his family was built on a bluff overlooking the Hudson River. Schuyler and his wife Catherine Van Rensselaer were descended from affluent and powerful Dutch families. Built between 1761 and 1765, the Georgian style mansion features 18th-century interiors complete with furniture, decorative arts, paintings, and personal artifacts of family members. Throughout the Schuyler family occupancy from 1763 to 1804 the mansion was the site of military strategizing, political intercourse, elegant social affairs, and active family life. The wedding of daughter Elizabeth Schuyler to Alexander Hamilton took place in the house in 1780. A visitor center provides an overview of Philip Schuyler and his 80-acre estate in the 18th century.

Performing Arts
Albany Symphony Orchestra (518-465-4755, www.albanysymphony.com, 19 Clinton
    Ave., Albany, NY 12207) Founded in 1930, this 68-member orchestra performs in three
    locations: the Palace Theatre, the Troy Savings Bank Music Hall and the Canfield Casino
    in Saratoga Springs. The schedule includes classical concerts, an American Music festi-
    val and family concerts.
Capital Repertory Theatre (518-445-7469, www.capitalrep.org, 111 N. Pearl St., Albany,
    NY 12207) This intimate 300-seat theater in the heart of downtown offers professional
    contemporary and classic drama, off Broadway musicals, cutting edge comedy, and
    major premieres.
Palace Performing Arts Center (518-465-3334, www.palacealbany.com, 19 Clinton Ave.,
    Albany, NY 12207) Opened in October 1931, it was originally a RKO movie house pre-
    senting vaudeville acts between features films. The 2,844-seat theater boasts an ornate

Schuyler Mansion State Historic Site John Rozell/NYS Parks, Recreation and Historic Preservation

Austrian Baroque design with atmospheric elements that created the illusion of the auditorium being open to the sky above. It recently underwent a major renovation and hosts popular acts, community events, movies, concerts, even boxing. The most notable concert event happened in 1965 when the now legendary Rolling Stones appeared on stage in their first American tour.

The Egg (518-473-1845, www.theegg.org, 51 S. Pearl St., Albany, NY 12207) Part of the Empire State Plaza and shaped like an egg, this decidedly modernistic-looking building is a performing arts center that is dedicated to providing a showcase for New York State artists as well as providing the stage for a wide range of performing arts including plays, dance, and concerts.

RECREATION

Cruises

Albany Aqua Ducks Tours (518-462-3825, www.albanyaquaducks.com, 1 Quay St., Albany, NY 12201) The Ducks offer a fun way to see the sights of downtown Albany, ending with a splash in the Hudson River and the opportunity to cruise the river and see the waterfront from a different perspective. The Aqua Ducks are 39-foot amphibious vehicles known as Hydra-Terras, manufactured in Rochester, NY. Vehicles like these were originally used during World War II to move cargo from ships and to transport troops including those who landed on the beaches of Normandy on D-day. Open daily Apr.–Nov. Admission: Adults $26, seniors $24, children $15. Tours leave from the

In winter, the Egg provides a dramatic backdrop for ice skaters Albany Convention & Visitors Bureau

Albany Heritage Area Visitors Center at the corner of Broadway and Clinton Ave. in historic Quackenbush Square.

Dutch Apple Cruises (518-463-0220 www.dutchapplecruises.com Madison Ave. and Broadway, Albany, NY 12201) The 65-foot classic *Dutch Apple II* was built in 1986 of local woods and follows the design of popular Hudson River dayliners of an earlier era that ferried passengers to and from ports along the Hudson. There are two-hour sightseeing cruises along the Hudson as well as a variety of entertainment cruises. Open daily April 15 through October; adults $17.95, children $12.95.

Albany Aqua Ducks tours take to the streets—and the river

Parks

Albany Pine Bush Preserve Commission (518-785-1800, www.albanypinebush.org, 195 New Kramer Rd., Albany, NY) The 3,000-acre Pine Bush Preserve is one of just 20 inland pine barren environments in the world. The Discovery Center is a good introduction to the preserve. You can touch a snake skin, make a sand dune, plan a prescribed fire, and learn how to help the environment. The bush is a wide-open landscape filled with dense shrubs, scattered pitch pines, prairie grass and wildflowers all rooted in sweeping sand dunes. It was formed toward the end of the last Ice Age 12,000 to 15,000 years ago. This is a good spot for hiking, cross-country skiing, and snowshoeing. Open daily; free admission. Discovery Center open Tuesday through Sunday.

Albany Riverfront Park at the Corning Preserve (518-434-2032, www.albany.org). On the far side of the Hudson River Way Pedestrian Bridge, the park is home to an 800-seat amphitheatre that hosts numerous events from spring through fall. The visitors' center offers an explanation of the Hudson River's tides. There is also a bike trail and boat launch.

John Boyd Thacher State Park (518-872-1237, www.nysparks.state.ny.us, 1 Hailes Cave Rd., Voorheesville, NY 12186) This park is situated along the Helderberg Escarpment, one of the richest fossil-bearing formations in the world. The park provides a terrific panorama of the Hudson-Mohawk Valleys and the Adirondack and Green Mountains. The park has volleyball courts, playgrounds, ball fields, and numerous picnic areas. Interpretive programs are offered year-round, including guided tours of the famous Indian Ladder Trail. There are more than 12 additional miles of trails for summer hiking and mountain biking and winter cross-country skiing, snowshoeing, hiking and snowmobiling.

Schodack Island State Park (518-732-0187, www.nysparks,state.ny.us, 1 Schodack Way, Schodack Landing, NY 12156) This park sits off the eastern shore of the Hudson River just south of Albany. Approximately 7 miles of Hudson River and Schodack Creek shoreline bound the 1,052-acre site. The park has been designated a State Estuary and a portion of the park shelters a Bird Conservation Area that is home to bald eagles, cerulean warblers and blue herons that nest in the cottonwood trees. Eight miles of multiuse trails wind through a variety of econological communities. The park has an improved bike trail, volleyball, horseshoe fields and a kayak/canoe launch site.

Shopping

Malls and plazas offer the major shopping opportunities. There are also some unique shops that have become destinations unto themselves.

Colonie Center (518-458-9020, www.shopatcoloniecenter.com, 131 Colonie Center, Albany, NY 12205) This two-level enclosed shopping and entertainment center has more than 100 specialty stores including Macy's and Sears. L. L. Bean's first retail store in New York State is here as well as Barnes & Noble. Dining choices include the Cheesecake Factory Restaurant, P. F. Changs China Bistro, and Friendly's Restaurant. Regal Cinemas Stadium 13 boasts state-of-the-art projection theatres.

Crossgates Mall (518-869-3522, www.shopcrossgates.com, 1 Crossgates Mall Rd., Albany, NY 12203) Albany's largest mall with more than 300 shops and restaurants plus 18 cinemas, this mall draws regular shoppers from a wide geographical area. Some of the stores include H&M, Best Buy, Build A Bear, Macy's, Borders, and Victoria's Secret. Restaurants include Johnny Rockets and Houlihans.

Grandma's Country Corners Gift Shop (518-459-1209 or 888-595-4726, www.grandmas cc.com, 1275 Central Ave., Albany, NY 12205) Next door to Grandma's Country Restaurant, this is a huge gift shop with thousands of high-end collectibles including Precious Moments, Cherished Teddies, Fenton Glass, and Swarovski Crystal.

Huck Finn's Warehouse (518-465-3373, www.huckfinnswarehouse.com, 25 Erie Blvd., Albany, NY 12204) This is the area's largest retail outlet specializing in any and everything for the home with more than 240,000 square feet of space. Savings are regularly 20 to 50%. It is also well known for being a fun place to shop. Kids love Huck's school bus, his old-fashioned jukebox, the merry-go-round in the upholstery department, and the horse ride in the sleep center.

Stuyvesant Plaza (518-482-8986, www.stuyvesantplaza.com, 10 Executive Park Dr., Albany, NY 12203). This upscale plaza has more than 50 shops and restaurants. There are one-of-a-kind shops and national retailers such as Talbots, Ann Taylor, Chico's, Coldwater Creek, and Eastern Mountain Sports. The Book House and the Little Book House (for children) are local, independent bookstores. Eateries include Bountiful Bread, Bruegger's, Cold Stone Creamery, EATS Gourmet Marketplace, Peaches Café, and Provence.

Troy

Troy, named for the legendary city made famous in Homer's *Iliad*, is 8 miles north of Albany near the juncture of the Erie and Champlain canals and the Hudson River. It is considered the gateway to the New York State Canal System and offers a beautiful waterfront park and marina.

The city had a joyous celebration on October 8, 1823, to mark the opening of the canal as far as Rochester. A canal boat named *Trojan Trader* left the city carrying 25 tons of the first merchandise to travel west from the Hudson River on the Erie Canal. In 1825 the Marquis de Lafayette was the honored guest and featured speaker for a daylong celebration. He pronounced the canal "an admirable work of science and patriotism."

When the construction of the Erie Canal began, there were no engineering schools in the young country. Taking a lesson from the canal, in 1824 Stephen Van Rensselaer and Amos Eaton founded Rensselaer Polytechnic Institute (RPI), the first engineering school in the country and the oldest technological university in continuous existence in the English-speaking world. The school is now located on the steep hills overlooking downtown. Washington Roebling, chief engineer of the Brooklyn Bridge, lived in Troy while his son attended RPI.

On December 23, 1823, the *Troy Sentinel* newspaper published for the first time Clement Clarke Moore's "A Visit from St. Nicholas," later renamed "'Twas the Night before Christmas." The Columbia University professor's famed work was first published anonymously.

A woman named Hannah Montague brought fame to the city when she decided to cut off the collars and cuffs of her husband's shirts and wash them separately—thus began the fashion of detachable collars and cuffs. In the 1830s Troy became the home of Cluett, Peabody & Company, manufacturers of collars, cuffs, and shirts and later famous for the Arrow shirt and the elegant advertisements that graced magazines and billboards for the next 150 years. Because of its history as a manufacturing center for shorts and shirtwaists, collars and cuffs, Troy is sometimes referred to as the Collar City.

The city suffered two disastrous fires—one in 1820 and another in 1862—that consumed hundreds of buildings. Through the 19th century and into the 20th century, Troy was one of the most prosperous cities in New York and in the country.

The city enjoyed a thriving iron and steel industry and later became home to a wide variety of other businesses. There are dozens of examples of original cast- and wrought-iron railings adorning many of the brownstones from that period. The plates for the Union's Civil War battleship *Monitor* were manufactured here.

The city has been on the National Register of Historic Places since 1986 and has outstanding examples of Queen Anne, Empire, beaux-arts, Romanesque, Italianate, Greek Revival, and Gothic Revival architecture. Troy boasts one of the best-preserved 19th-century downtowns in the United States. There are blocks of town houses, churches, and civic and commercial buildings that look remarkably like they did more than one hundred years ago.

The 1875 Troy Savings Bank and Music Hall, a National Historic Landmark, houses a magnificent 1,200-seat auditorium on the four floors above the bank. Its acoustics are reputed to be among the finest in the world.

The historic downtown is said to have "the mother lode of Tiffany windows." The beaux-arts public library and several of the city's churches have outstanding Tiffany windows. A remarkable Tiffany window forms the backdrop for the circulation desk at the library. Upstairs, the walls of the main reading room are lined with Hudson River school paintings.

Famed American artist Norman Rockwell was so charmed by the city that he featured it in some of his paintings. Back in 1991 when Martin Scorsese needed to re-create the Manhattan of the 1870s for *The Age of Innocence*, he came to Troy, a city that offered the perfect backdrop and little commercial activity to impede shooting. It was also the setting for the films *Ironweed* and *The Bostonians*.

After World War II, Troy's economy declined precipitously and buildings emptied out and stayed empty for decades. The city is currently staging a comeback, with new businesses and visitors discovering its charms. River Street, the city's earliest commercial area, is now home to an antiques district featuring many cafés and art galleries.

LODGING

Olde Judge Mansion Bed and Breakfast (518-274-5698, www.oldejudgemansion.com, 3300 6th Ave., Troy, NY 12180) This ornate 1892 Victorian home in the Gothic/Italinate design was built for Thomas Judge and his family. All five guest bedrooms are on the second floor, with enclosed gated parking in the back. There are three private and one shared bathroom. The house features heavy oak woodwork, pocket doors, 12-foot oak ceilings, and embossed tin walls. Guests have access to a pool table and dartboards in the recreation room. Close to Rensselaer Polytechnic and Russell Sage College.

RESTAURANTS

Brown's Brewing Co. (518-273-2337 www.brownsbrewing.com 417 River St., Troy, NY 12180) Brown's Brewing Company was established in 1993, becoming the first brewery restaurant in the capital region. Housed in a 150-year-old former warehouse building overlooking the mighty Hudson River, the restaurant has evolved using local products whenever possible and menu items that utilize and complement the beer produced. The large 300-seat restaurant with a riverside deck and beer garden has become a social hub for the community, harking back to 19th-century canal times. Live music is a special feature here. The brewery has won a number of awards including Best Brewery in

Antiques district shop in Troy Greg La Civita

Troy's Famous Uncle Sam

One of Troy's most famous citizens was Samuel Wilson, aka Uncle Sam. Wilson was a meatpacker who went into business in the city in 1797. As the story goes, he provided large shipments of meat to the U.S. Army during the War of 1812 in barrels that were stamped "U.S." Supposedly, someone jokingly suggested that the initials stood for "Uncle Sam" Wilson. Thus "Uncle Sam" came to symbolize the federal government.

Naturally, there's an Uncle Sam statue at the northern edge of the historic district. Uncle Sam's traditional appearance with a white goatee and star-spangled suit is an invention of artists and political cartoonists. The single most famous portrait of Uncle Sam is the "I WANT YOU" Army-recruiting poster from World War I.

the Hudson Valley; a gold medal for its Pale Ale, awarded at the prestigious Culinary Institute of America in nearby Hyde Park, N.Y.; and a gold medal for its Oatmeal Stout at the World Beer Cup. Dinner entrées include beer-marinated London broil, shepard's pie, and Brew House chicken. There are heart-healthy items such as grilled shrimp on a skewer and grilled chicken breast. There are also traditional burgers, sandwiches, soups, and salads, as well as a kids' menu. Open daily for lunch and dinner.

ATTRACTIONS

Children's Museum of Science and Technology (518-235-2120, www.cmost.org, 250 Jordan Rd., Troy, NY 12180) The museum offers a wide variety of hands-on programming, with live animals; a Hudson River ecosystem exhibit; the Go Power! energy-pathway exhibit; the Weather Front exhibit, which includes amazing green screen technology; and the PlayMotion! exhibit, which lets children explore the planets in the solar system. Throughout the day there are animal shows, planetarium shows, and workshops. A full-service restaurant, the Eatery in the Park, offers plenty of healthy kid-friendly items. The gift shop offers a number of original and imaginative toys and souvenirs for children of all ages. Open Monday to Saturday July to August; Wednesday to Saturday September to June. Adults and children age two and up $5.

Sacred Falls of Cohoes

Located north of Troy, the 70-foot-high Cohoes Falls hold a sacred significance for the Iroquois and Algonquin people and have direct relevance to the origins of the American Constitution. The People of the Long House (Iroquois) and the Mohawk Nation believe this location is where the "Peacemaker" survived a fall from a tree into the torrents and thus brought the good message to the Mohawks at a time when they were at war with other nations. The Mohawks accepted this message of peace and the Iroquois Confederacy was formed under the Great Law of Peace. The Great Law of Peace was used as a model by the drafters of the U.S. Constitution and was acknowledged by the U.S. Senate in 1987.

Troy RiverSpark Visitor Center (518-270-8667, www.troyvisitorcenter.org, 251 River St., Troy, NY 12180) This is a good place to begin a visit to Troy. An award-winning 20-minute slide show explains the international significance of the area's industrial heritage. Artifacts and interactive exhibits tell the story of highlights such as the invention of the world-famous Burden Water Wheel, the most powerful vertical water wheel in history and most likely the model for the world's first Ferris Wheel. There are pamphlet guides to the Heritage Trail, the Tiffany Window Walking Tour, and the Historic Canal Tour. Open daily; free admission.

Troy Savings Bank Music Hall (518-273-0038, www.troymusichall.org, 30 Second St., Troy, NY 12180) Built in 1875, the 1,180-seat music hall is a National Historic Landmark known the world over for its superb acoustics. Artists book long in advance to record their performances here. As one of only three continuously operating 19th-century concert halls in the U.S., the hall's elegant Old World charm provides the perfect setting for jazz, classical, folk, and international artists as well as an artistic home for many of the region's leading classical music organizations.

Watervliet Arsenal Museum (518-266-5805, www.wva.army.mil/, 10th St., Watervliet, NY 12189) The arsenal, founded in 1813 and operated by the U.S. Army, is across the Hudson River from Troy. This museum tells the story of the arsenal as well as the history of the big guns that are still manufactured here. In addition to the many one-of-a-kind guns from the past four hundred years, there are many new artillery weapons on display. Everything from 60mm lightweight company mortars to the massive 16-inch guns of World War II battleship fame are here. The rarest artifact is a muzzle-loading 24-pound cannon surrendered by British general John Burgoyne at the battle of Saratoga on October 17, 1777, the turning point of the Revolutionary War. The museum tells the story of America's development of the cannon as well as the history of America's oldest, continuously active arsenal. Open Sunday to Thursday. Free admission. Photo ID required.

Troy Savings Bank Music Hall Jill Malouf

SCHENECTADY

This is a city rich in history and accomplishment. The area that is now Schenectady was originally the land of the Mohawk tribe of the Iroquois Nation. When Dutch settlers arrived in the Hudson Valley in the middle of the 17th century, the Mohawk called the settlement at Fort Orange Scau-naugh-ta-da, meaning "over the pine plains." Eventually, this word entered the lexicon of the Dutch settlers, but the meaning was reversed, referring to the bend in the Mohawk River where the city lies today.

Schenectady's Stockade District is lined with historic homes

Arendt Van Curler led the settlement in the area in 1661 and described it as "the fairest land the eyes of man ever rested upon."

On February 8, 1690, the town was attacked and overrun by French forces and their Indian allies, who burned the town and killed all but 60 of the inhabitants. The event is known as the Schenectady Massacre.

The city was quickly rebuilt and the unique collection of 17th-, 18th-, and 19th-century buildings in the current Stockade District are protected by New York State's first local historic preservation ordinance. It is one of the oldest and best-preserved neighborhoods in the country.

In 1795 Union College, the first college chartered in New York State, was founded. The Erie Canal made Schenectady an even more important transportation and commercial center. By 1836 it was the converging point for four railroads. Locomotive engines were manufactured here beginning in 1848.

When the Erie Canal opened, the town became a busy place for passenger stopovers and transshipments of cargo. There were 27 locks between Schenectady and Albany, and the trip required 24 hours when traffic was light, longer when it was crowded—a much more commonplace occurrence. Passengers had the alternative of a three-hour stagecoach ride from Albany to Schenectady. Westward passengers could leave Albany late in the afternoon and enjoy dinner and a comfortable overnight in a tavern or hotel in Schenectady and leave the next morning on a packet boat. This was a popular choice for many canal passengers to shorten their trips and add to their comfort.

Thomas Edison moved his Edison Machine Works to the city in 1887. In 1892 it became the General Electric Company. The city is home to one of the first commercial radio stations in the U.S. General Electric also generated the first television broadcasts in the country in 1928 when an experimental station began regular broadcasts on Thursday and Friday afternoons. George Westinghouse invented the rotary engine and air brakes here.

Schenectady was known as the City that Lights and Hauls the World—a reference to its two prominent businesses—General Electric and the American Locomotive Company, which once made virtually every steam and diesel locomotive in the country.

LODGING

The Parker Inn (518-688-1001, www.parkerinn.com, 434 State St., Schenectady, NY 12305) Built in 1905 as an office building by attorney John Parker, it was transformed into a stylish 23-room boutique hotel in 2002. Its location next to Proctors Theatre is a prime attraction, and the theater and hotel cooperate with meal and overnight packages. Complimentary continental breakfast buffet; dinner and lunch buffets served before theater performances. Rooms include free high-speed Internet and refrigerators. There are six suites including a spacious Presidential Suite.

RESTAURANTS

The Stockade Inn (518-346-3400, www.stockadeinn.com 1 North Church St., Schenectady, NY 12305) The Stockade Inn is in the historic Stockade District and is popular for dinners and special events. There is an elegant, Old World atmosphere in the dining room and entrées include such choices as veal, steak, seared ahi tuna, and roasted halibut. A lighter menu with such items as dim sum for two, Sicilian pizza, crab and lobster cake, sandwiches, and salads is served in the lounge. Open Tuesday to Saturday for dinner; Sunday brunch.

The Waters Edge Lighthouse (518-370-5300, www.thewatersedgelighthouse.com, 2 Freemans Bridge Rd., Glenville, NY 12302) Located less than a mile from Schenectady's Proctors Theatre in a prime spot on the Mohawk River, the building has a long history. It was formerly known as the River House, Little Richard's Tavern, and for 105 years before that, a farmhouse privately owned by the Seeley Family. The Greek Revival farmhouse dates from the 30-year period in the 19th century when the area produced a large portion of the country's brooms. The outdoor patio was voted Best Patio Dining in the Capital Region by readers of *Capital Region Living* magazine. It boasts a wide array of sandwiches, burgers, and pizza, as well as seafood dishes featuring seafood risotto, Mediterranean sea bass, eggplant Parmesan, veal marsala and beef including filet mignon, Lighthouse tournedos, and strip steak. An expansive banquet facility is available for private parties. Open daily for lunch and dinner.

ATTRACTIONS

Schenectady County Historical Society (518-374-0263, www.schist.org, 32 Washington Ave., Schenectady, NY 12301) Located in the heart of the Stockade District and within a few blocks of both the original Erie Canal and today's canal, this is a good spot to begin a walking tour of the area. Free tour brochures are available. The building is an 1895 Colonial Revival house that has an amazing array of historical artifacts relating to the area's rich history. There is a permanent exhibit on the Erie Canal in Schenectady that includes a large collection of old canal postcards. There's also an exhibit on the city's American Locomotive Company and an 1823 dollhouse built for New York governor Joseph Yates's granddaughter. Also here is one of only two surviving Revolutionary War Liberty flags. Open Monday to Saturday; adults $4.

Schenectady Museum & Suits-Bueche Planetarium (518-382-7890, www.schenectady museum.org, 15 Nott Terrace Heights, Schenectady, NY 12308)
Located near Union College about six blocks from the Stockade District, this is a dynamic museum and planetarium that explores the area's rich technological heritage. A family-friendly museum, it celebrates science, invention, and imagination using cutting-edge technology in numerous exciting, interactive exhibits. The Power House exhibit explores the impact of science on everyday lives. Learn about the science of Silly Putty, an accidental invention created at GE's Schenectady plant, and the science behind nanotechnology and the manmade diamond. The MRI exhibit invites visitors to get inside a real machine (the Magnetic Resonance Imaging machine, or MRI, was developed in the area). The planetarium features the GOTO Star Projector; one of only 12 in the country, it offers a real-life view of the night sky not available anywhere else in the Northeast. The archives include 1.6 million images from the General Electric Photograph Collection. The gift shop offers many unusual items including hard-to-find educational toys. Open Tuesday through Sunday and Monday holidays; adults $5 (7.75 includes planetarium), seniors $4 ($6.75), children $3 ($5.75).

Schenectady Stockade Historic District (518-382-5147, www.historicstockade.com)
Located between today's Erie Canal and the original canal, which is now Erie Boulevard, the district is about a half mile from downtown. The Stockade was home to the city's 17th-, 18th-, and 19th-century citizens. More than one hundred architectural landmarks survive virtually intact and offer examples of nearly every architectural type, period, and style of residential and religious buildings dating from 1690 to 1930. Dutch Colonial, English Colonial, Federal, Georgian, Queen Anne, and other Victorian styles are all well represented. It boasts the largest collection of pre-Revolutionary buildings in the country. Restored in the 1950s and 1960s, the Stockade was recognized as New York State's first historic district. The district survived only because of two events. A fire in 1819 destroyed the warehouse and business district. Shortly thereafter, the Erie Canal was built along the course of what is now Erie Boulevard. This isolated and protected the Stockade District from the repeated redevelopment that marks the history

Schenectady County Historical Society entrance

An electrifying display at the Schenectady Museum & Suits-Bueche Planetarium

of nearly all of America's city centers. In June there is a Secret Garden Tour, and the last weekend in September there is the "Walk About," where select homes are open for viewing. Open daily; free self-guided walking tours, charges for guided walking tours and house tours.

Performing Arts

Proctors Theatre (518-382-3884, www.proctors.org, 432 State St., Schenectady, NY 12305) Listed on the National Register of Historic Places, this 2,700-seat theater opened in 1926 and was originally a vaudeville house attracting such legendary performers as Red Skelton, George Burns and Gracie Allen, and magicians Harry

Stockade District walking tour

Blackstone Sr. and Jr. More recently, it is home to the Schenectady Symphony and the Northeast Ballet. In the 1970s the theater was saved from the wrecker's ball and has recently completed a $30-million renovation and expansion. The stage can now accommodate touring Broadway shows and the theater attracts a variety of top entertainers, orchestras, and dance companies; a 436-seat GE Theatre next door is equipped with an Extreme Screen showing three-dimensional movies. The movie screen is one of the largest in the Northeast.

SHOPPING

Tough Traveler Ltd. (518-377-8526, www.toughtraveler.com1012 State St., Schenectady, NY 12307) This is a mecca for travelers and anyone looking to buy a specialty bag. Opened in 1970, all items are locally made in Schenectady. From child carriers to pet carriers to hiking packs to ski bags to camera bags to suitcases of all types, this store has it all. The items have been featured on the *Today Show* and in magazines including *Child, Outside,* and *Backpacker.* Customers rave about the products and the quality of the workmanship.

Whitehall's Skene Manor overlooks the Champlain Canal

10

Champlain Canal

Waterford, Stillwater, Schuylerville, Saratoga Springs, Whitehall

The Champlain Canal crosses through some of America's most historic lands. It connects the Hudson River to Lake Champlain, a distance of about 60 miles from Waterford on the Hudson to Whitehall on Lake Champlain.

There are twelve locks along the route. The first, the Troy, or Federal, Lock (operated by the U.S. Army Corps of Engineers), provides access to both the Champlain and Erie canals. The Champlain Canal itself has eleven locks, although they are numbered 1 to 12 because the lock-identification system wasn't altered to reflect the fact that lock C-10 was never built.

From Waterford north, the canal follows the Hudson to Fort Edward, with locks, dams, and dug channels bypassing falls and rapids in the river. At Fort Edward the canal leaves the Hudson and follows a dug channel to Whitehall, at the head of Lake Champlain.

Renowned for its rich military history, the canal runs alongside many former military outposts dating back to the French and Indian and Revolutionary wars, such as Fort Ann, Fort Edward, and Fort Miller, which draw their names from former army posts in the region.

There are no cities on the canal, although the elegant and historic city of Saratoga Springs is just 12 miles from it. Instead, the Champlain passes through small rural communities, many of them former mill towns. The landscape has changed so little over the years that traveling along the canal, even with the advantage of modern conveniences, is truly a journey into the past. New harbor facilities have been built along the waterway, and canal communities are rediscovering their waterfronts.

The history of the Champlain Canal is closely linked with that of the Erie Canal. Both were begun in 1817 soon after peace came to a region that had known brutal warfare for over a century. The Champlain Canal opened in 1823, two years before the Erie Canal was completed, and it is now the oldest continuously operating canal in the United States.

WATERFORD

Waterford is the oldest incorporated village in the United States. Situated at the junction of the Mohawk and Hudson rivers as well as the Erie and Champlain canals, it played a vital role in the American Revolution and industrial boom of the 19th century.

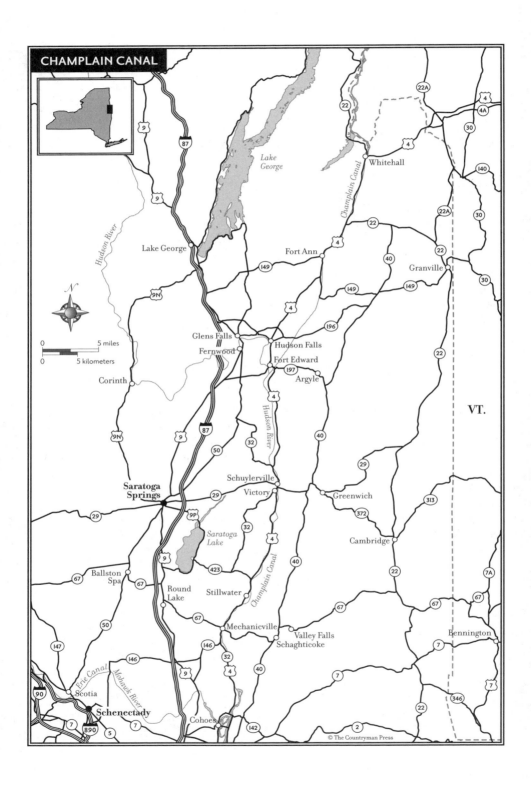

In the 1600s this area was a center for Indian trading, and by the 1800s it was a hub for the Adirondack timber trade. When the canals opened, barges headed east to New York and west to Buffalo and the Great Lakes lined up to get through Waterford's locks.

Located in an 1830 Greek Revival mansion, the Hugh White Homestead, the **Waterford Historical Museum and Cultural Center** (518-238-0809, www.waterfordmuseum.com, 2 Museum Lane, Waterford, NY 12188) has permanent exhibits on the history of Waterford from prehistoric inhabitants to the Dutch traders, the colonial military road, the Industrial Revolution, and the Erie and Champlain canals. There are also two Victorian period rooms and a local-history library. It is open Wednesday to Sunday from May to October.

In recent years Waterford has reclaimed its waterfront, and both boaters and land visitors now have reason to linger. Those with an appreciation for engineering will not want to miss a stop at the Waterford Flight, which lifts boaters 170 feet over 1.5 miles. Walkers or bikers can travel along Flight Lock Road, which follows the path of the Flight. Completed in 1918, it includes five locks that form the largest lifts in the shortest distance of any system in the world. The Flight replaced the "Terrible 16," a series of locks opened in 1825 as part of the original Erie Canal to bypass the massive Cohoes Falls. The observation deck at Lock 6 Park provides a good view of this engineering marvel. Lock 2 Park is a popular spot for waterfront festivals such as the **Tugboat Roundup** (www.tugboatroundup.com) and **Canal Fest.**

Waterford is also home to **Peebles Island State Park and Erie Canalway National Heritage Corridor Visitor Center** (518-237-7000, www.nysparks.state.ny.us/parks, Delaware Ave., off Ontario St., Waterford, NY 12188). Located at the confluence of the Hudson and Mohawk rivers, this park offers miles of paths through gently rolling wooded landscape. It is a popular fishing spot, and in winter a good choice for cross-country skiing and snowshoeing. The headquarters of the Bureau of Historic Sites and Bureau of Historic Preservation Field Services are found here. The building that formerly housed Cluett Peabody Shirt and Collar Manufacturers now provides space for offices and the state's conservation laboratories. Within the park are the remains of the Matton Shipyard, which

Waterford marks the intersection of the Champlain and Erie canals

Locking through at Waterford

built wooden canal boats and steel tugboats. There are also Revolutionary War earthworks that were built to halt the British advance on Albany. Open daily.

STILLWATER

The **Saratoga National Cemetery** opened in 1999 in Stillwater. This cemetery is nestled among the rolling green hills on a bluff overlooking the Hudson River and Champlain Canal. It offers pastoral views of dairy farms and scenic vistas.

Continuing north, keep an eye out for cannons on the shore between the villages of Stillwater and Schuylerville on the grounds of the **Saratoga National Historical Park** (518-664-9821, www.nps.gov, 648 Route 32, Stillwater, NY 12170), site of the famous battle of Saratoga, the turning point in the Revolutionary War that changed the course of world history. Every American schoolchild learns of the surrender, on October 17, 1777, of General John "Gentleman Johnny" Burgoyne to the colonists at Saratoga. It was a vital and sweet victory for the Americans.

Saratoga National Cemetery in Stillwater

The best way to see the whole picture is to stop at the visitors' center. Here you can pick up a battlefield brochure and see the 21-minute-long film *Checkmate on the Hudson*. The small museum gives a feel for the human dimensions of 18th-century warfare. There are weapons, clay pipes, crude eating implements, including a wooden bowl and a little camp stove, even a tooth-brush owned by colonial soldiers.

The Friends of the Saratoga Battlefield developed a CD driving tour complete with authentic Revolutionary War music that offers an excellent guide to the 9-mile-long battlefield tour. Pick it up at the visitors' center (many area hotels also offer copies)—it adds a new dimension to the tour. The road is one-way, so you can't change your mind and turn back midway, but you can always skip stops if you are in a hurry. There are displays with taped audio narration at most stops.

During my latest visit we counted 12 deer in the park. If you visit during the summer, you will likely see militiamen. Living-history encampments are regularly scheduled at the Nielson Farm, which American generals used as their headquarters. The farmhouse still stands.

One of the more popular sites is Number 7, the Breymann Redoubt. General Benedict Arnold was injured in the leg here just as Americans captured the position. The so-called Boot Monument immortalizes the incident. The only such monument like it in the country, it bears neither the likeness nor the name of the commemorated hero—reflecting Arnold's later reputation as a traitor. Had he died here from his wounds he would have gone down in history as one of America's finest generals and patriots.

The battles began on September 19 and ended nearly a month later on October 17, when Burgoyne, vastly outnumbered by the Americans, surrendered. By the terms of the Convention of Saratoga, Burgoyne's depleted army, some 6,000 men, marched out of camp "with the Honors of War" and stacked its weapons along the west bank of the Hudson River.

The visitors' center at the park is open daily; the tour road is open April 1 to November 30, weather permitting. Admission is $5 per car.

SCHUYLERVILLE

South of Lock C-5 is the Schuyler Canal Park Visitor Center. Just steps from the visitors' center is the Surrender Tree marker, which marks the location of a large elm tree under which General Burgoyne signed the Convention of Saratoga, formally surrendering his troops to the American general Horatio Gates.

Canon overlooking the Hudson River at Saratoga National Historical Park

The battles at Saratoga occurred at a time when Americans had begun to think their cause was hopeless. The victory restored American confidence and led France to openly assist the colonists in their fight for liberty.

The 155-foot **Saratoga Battle Monument** (518-664-9821, www.nps.gov) is a short walk from Schuylerville's main street. Three of the four sides of the monument feature sculptures of American generals. The fourth side should have housed a sculpture of Benedict Arnold, who was vital to the success of the battle of Saratoga. However, his later decision to join the side of the British earned the country's scorn as a traitor to the cause of liberty. So the niche remains empty.

The **Schuyler House** (518-664-9821, www.nps.gov), the historic country home of General Schuyler, is a beautiful house museum. After the British burned the original to keep the Americans from using it, the present house was erected shortly after Burgoyne's surrender, and became the center of Schuyler's extensive farming and milling operations.

The house, and the Battle Monument, operate as part of the Saratoga National Historical Park in Stillwater; it is open Wednesday to Sunday from Memorial Day weekend to Labor Day. There is a free guided tour.

Two tour boats, *M/V Sadie* and *M/V Caldwell Belle,* operated by **Champlain Canal Tour Boats** (518-695-5609, www.champlaincanaltours.com, Canal House on Towpath, Schuylerville, NY 12871), offer a variety of cruises on the Champlain Canal, including locking through Lock C5. From the boats, which operate from May to October, cruisers can see Saratoga battle cannons along the shore.

SARATOGA SPRINGS

Saratoga is a Mohawk word meaning "place of swift waters." Some historians believe that American Indian tribes discovered the mineral springs running under swampland as early as the 14th-century and made them a site of pilgrimage. They called them "smelly water."

Everyone from George Washington to Edgar Allan Poe has enjoyed Saratoga's naturally

The Roosevelt Mineral Baths at Saratoga Spa State Park

carbonated springs. Waters travel through shale and limestone, absorbing minerals to become the bubbling, salty, and sometimes pungent water that made Saratoga famous.

It's possible "to take the waters" at the Roosevelt Mineral Baths, one of the imposing buildings in the Saratoga Spa State Park, a national landmark. The 2,300-acre state park offers a swimming pool complex, tennis courts, golf course, ice skating in winter, trails for walking and biking, and the Saratoga Performing Arts Center. The center is the summer home of the New York City Ballet and the Philadelphia Orchestra. The gracious and elegant Gideon Putnam Hotel and Conference Center is also in the park, and the dining room offers fine dining in a classic setting.

Saratoga Springs still retains much of its earlier charm. Broadway, the city's main street, has been named one of the five best main streets in the U.S. by the National Trust for Historic Preservation. It was the place where the fashionable came to take in the spa waters, try their luck at the casino, and bet on their favorite horses. This was the favorite haunt of Diamond Jim Brady and Lillian Russell. Although the roulette wheel doesn't spin here anymore, most everything else is still possible.

Start your day at Saratoga Springs with breakfast at the track, a longtime Saratoga tradition. It's served on the terrace overlooking the track early each morning—between 7 and 9:30—while jockeys exercise their mounts. This tradition began at the turn of the century when partying racehorse owners ended their all-night sprees with an eye-opener at the track before going home to bed.

The jockeys have been riding their mounts since 1863 when John Morrissey built the first thoroughbred racetrack, called Horse Haven. Building the track was easy—finding the horses was more difficult. The Civil War was raging, and every healthy animal had been requisitioned for the war effort. Encouraged by the event's popularity, Morrissey built a new track on the very spot where the Saratoga Racecourse now stands—justifying Saratoga's claim as the oldest track in America.

When the thoroughbreds return, so does the elegance of a bygone era. The thoroughbred racing season is short and sweet in Saratoga. The month of August is devoted to the steed. The entire town focuses on one pastime, one sport, and the town is transformed. The stables are suddenly alive from dawn to dusk. Harness racing has a much longer run, from mid-January to late November, with a short break in April.

The finest thoroughbreds in the country are here for the season along with their fans, including the rich and famous. The atmosphere at the track is somewhere between a country fair and garden party, with the grassy paddock, huge trees, flowerbeds, striped awnings, complimented by open-air food vendors, musicians, families on outings, jockeys in their colored silks, horse players leaning on the paddock fence, and elegant summer patrons sporting their summer straw hats and watching their horses circle the parade ring before the race. Some have said that Saratoga Springs is the only city in the United States that counts over two thousand thoroughbreds as summer guests.

The course itself is gorgeous, with putting-green turf and manicured trees and hedges. There is even a lake in the infield and a canoe, painted in the colors of the latest Travers winner. The top race of the season is the Travers Stakes, the oldest continuously run stakes race for three-year-olds in the country. However, the highlight of the season belongs to the two-year-olds. These are talented novices from the very best stables who are held back in order to make their debuts before the knowledgeable holiday crowd at Saratoga.

Some come to people watch as much as to watch the horses. There is electricity in the air during the season. Of course, prices skyrocket during the racing season, so if horses are not a top priority in your travels, visit outside the racing season for a quieter and less expensive trip.

Lodging

Hotel rates generally are higher (often much higher—doubling or even tripling) during the summer racing season, and many accommodations have two-night-minimum stays in-season and during other popular events such as Skidmore College graduation. Booking six months to a year in advance is recommended for the racing season. There are some historic hotels in the area and a number of lovely bed & breakfasts, as well as a variety of chain hotels. Budget-conscious racing fans often choose to stay in the Albany area to the south. Rates as listed are for double occupancy.

Lodging Rates
Inexpensive: Up to $75
Moderate: $76–$150
Expensive: $151–$250
Very Expensive: More than $250

Hotels

ADELPHI HOTEL

518-587-4688
www.adelphihotel.com
365 Broadway, Saratoga Springs, NY 12866
Price: Moderate—Very Expensive
Credit Cards: Yes
Handicapped Access: No
Special Features: Continental breakfast included

Built in 1877, the Adelphi was considered a jewel from the moment it opened. A century later, the hotel had fallen into disrepair and was saved from the wrecker's ball by a young couple who transformed it into a magnificent High Victorian hotel with modern amenities including an elegant outdoor pool. It is the last of the grand hotels that once lined Broadway, and evokes the Saratoga charm of yesteryear. Designed as an Italian villa, the building has a distinctive second-floor piazza in front that is ideal for people watching and outfitted with antique wicker and Adirondack furniture. There are 34 rooms and suites—all individually designed. The hotel is full of original antiques, and the opulent lobby beckons visitors to enjoy a trip back in time. Period antiques, old engravings and photographs, lacy curtains, and print wallpaper adorn the unique rooms. Styles range from English country house, French provincial, High Victorian, Adirondack, arts and crafts, and folk art. The various styles all work together, and the hotel is a real treat.

ADIRONDACK INN

518-584-3510
www.adirondackinn.com
230 West Ave., Saratoga Springs, NY 12866
Price: Moderate
Credit Cards: Yes
Handicapped Access: Yes
Special Features: Pet friendly, transportation to the racetrack

There is complimentary track shuttle during the racing season as well as complimentary transportation to and from the train station and the private airport. All 50 rooms have refrigerators and microwave ovens. There is an outdoor pool and outdoor grills on the three acres of inn grounds. A continental breakfast is included during the racing season. This is a comfortable inn with large motel-style rooms as well as cottages.

CARRIAGE HOUSE INN

518-584-4220

www.carriagehouseinnsaratoga.com
198 Broadway, Saratoga Springs, NY 12866
Price: Moderate–Expensive
Credit Cards: Yes
Handicapped Access: Yes
Special Features: Complimentary high-speed Internet

This inn's 14 guest rooms could not be more different and are designed to fit a variety of budgets. The standard rooms have two double beds, a refrigerator, microwave, and a sitting area; the deluxe guest rooms are very spacious and include a full kitchen; the queen canopy rooms have antique furnishing, original wooden floors, and high ceilings; the Adirondack king suites feature a grand king-sized log bed; and the Saratoga suites have original 1875 handcrafted wooden high ceilings, Victorian antiques in the living room, a fireplace, refrigerator, and microwave.

GIDEON PUTNAM RESORT & SPA

518-584-3000
www.gideonputnam.com
24 Gideon Putnam Rd., Saratoga Springs,
NY 12866
Price: Moderate–Expensive
Credit Cards: Yes
Handicapped Access: Yes
Special Features: Set in middle of historic park

The hotel bears the name of the founder of Saratoga Springs—Gideon Putnam. After settling near High Rock Spring in 1795, he saw the area's potential and purchased land near Congress Spring to build Putnam's Tavern and Boarding House. He soon enlarged the guest house and went on to design plans for a village, calling it Saratoga Springs. In tribute to his early efforts, in the 1930s New York State built Saratoga Spa State Park, including the Gideon Putnam Resort. Today, the resort is in the center of the 2,300-acre state park, which includes two Olympic-sized outdoor pools, Roosevelt Mineral Baths, golf course, and Performing Arts Center. During the winter there is cross-country skiing and ice skating on two outdoor rinks. There are two restaurants plus outdoor dining during the summer. The 120 rooms are reminiscent of

The Gideon Putnam Resort and Spa

the Georgian era, including 18 elegant parlor and porch suites.

GRAND UNION MOTEL AND CRYSTAL SPA

518-584-9000
www.grandunionmotel.com
120 Broadway, Saratoga Springs, NY 12866
Price: Moderate–Expensive
Credit Cards: Yes
Handicapped Access: Yes
Special Features: Pet friendly

This motel has its own natural water source, the Rosemary Spring. Of course, Rosemary Spring water is served at the motel and at the Crystal Spa. Various spa packages are available, and services include a private mineral bath, various massages including prenatal and postnatal, body treatments like Citrus Sensation and Chocolate Indulgence scrubs and Algae Clay Purifying Wrap, and facials. All 64 rooms and suites feature unique step-down mosaic-tiled tubs that are large enough for two. Many suites have king-sized beds and refrigerators. There is also an outdoor pool.

LONGFELLOW'S INN

518-587-0108
www.longfellows.com
500 Union Ave., Saratoga Springs, NY 12866
Price: Moderate–Very Expensive
Credit Cards: Yes
Handicapped Access: Yes
Special features: Complimentary high-speed Internet

Located in a wooded knoll outside Saratoga Springs, Longfellow's offers dramatic Adirondack Mountain views and 50 luxurious rooms. It started life in 1915 as a dairy barn. The loft rooms take advantage of the great heights in the building with two levels—the king bed is upstairs, and downstairs there is a queen sleeper sofa and a wet bar with refrigerator. The standard rooms have two queen beds. There are exercise facilities, massage rooms, and in-room dining. A continental breakfast is included. **Longfellow's Restaurant** is open for dinner daily and offers open-loft dining, a courtyard, fireside dining, a tavern, and an award-winning wine cellar with fireplace. The classic menu includes seafood, prime rib, macaroni and cheese with black truffles, Gorgonzola-encrusted New York strip steak (Longfellow's signature dish), and rack of lamb.

SARATOGA ARMS

518-584-1775
www.saratogaarms.com
497 Broadway, Saratoga Springs, NY 12866
Price: Expensive–Very Expensive
Credit Cards: Yes
Handicapped Access: Yes
Special Features: Exercise room

This elegant 1870 Second Empire hotel was built by the grandson of Gideon Putnam, founder of Saratoga Springs. Family-owned and -operated, the 31-room boutique hotel has the feel of a bed & breakfast, with a large wraparound porch. A onetime boardinghouse converted to a luxury inn in 1999, it underwent an expansion and renovation in 2005. The rooms are full of antiques as well as modern amenities. There are nice touches like luxury robes. Several rooms have fireplaces. A full breakfast is served daily and guests are invited to postrace parties on the expansive porch. The handwritten tiles in the shower tout facts about Saratoga Springs.

THE INN AT SARATOGA

518-583-1890 or 800-274-3573
www.theinnatsaratoga.com
231 Broadway, Saratoga Springs, NY 12866
Price: Moderate–Very Expensive
Credit Cards: Yes
Handicapped Access: Yes
Special Features: Complimentary bicycles

The oldest operating inn in the city, with 42 rooms and suites, is today a modernized 1843 Victorian inn. A full gourmet breakfast is included. During racing season there is complimentary horse-drawn carriage shuttle service to and from downtown, and there are complimentary bicycles. It was voted Best Inn by *Capital Region Living* magazine.

Bed & Breakfasts

BATCHELLER MANSION INN

518-584-7012
www.batchellermansioninn.com
20 Circular Street, Saratoga Springs, NY 12866
Price: Moderate–Very Expensive
Credit Cards: Yes
Handicapped Access: No
Special Features: Pool table in Diamond Jim Brady Suite

One of the city's outstanding landmarks, the Batcheller is an architectural pastiche of High Victorian eclecticism, combining French Renaissance Revival, Italianate, and Egyptian influences. It is a fairy-tale castle and quite extraordinary from the outside with its riot of turrets and minarets. Built in 1873 by George Sherman Batcheller, an attorney, diplomat, and politician, it has a commanding view of Congress Park. By the late 1960s and early '70s, the house was abandoned and left to weather, vandals, and vagrants. Saved from demolition, it has been transformed into one of the city's most elegant inns. The nine rooms and suites are filled with antiques, and each is individually decorated. The Diamond Jim Brady Suite, named in honor of the man who dominated gambling in the city, sports a regulation-sized pool table as well as a massive Jacuzzi tub.

CHESTNUT TREE INN

866-427-0838
www.chestnuttreeinn.net

9 Whitney Place, Saratoga Springs, NY 12866
Price: Moderate–Very Expensive
Credit Cards: Yes
Handicapped Access: No
Special Features: Complimentary breakfast served in courtyard

Nestled on a quiet street within walking distance to the racetrack, downtown shopping, and museums, this is lovely seven-room Victorian inn is furnished with comfortable, elegant turn-of-the-century antiques. All rooms have private baths. There are king, queen, and double rooms. Guests are invited to enjoy afternoon tea or wine on the expansive porch filled with wicker furniture.

CIRCULAR MANOR

518-583-6393
www.circularmanor.com
120 Circular St, Saratoga Springs, NY 12866
Price: Moderate–Very Expensive
Credit Cards: Yes
Handicapped Access: No
Special Features: Full gourmet breakfast

Built in 1903 by William Case, a prominent contractor and lumber company owner, this inn is in the historic district, within walking distance of both downtown and the Race Course. There is a welcoming Queen Anne circular porch and oak staircase, banisters, floors, and pocket doors. The five guest rooms are handsomely decorated. Most bathrooms have marble floors and antique fixtures including claw-foot tubs. The Hydrangea Suite has a sitting room and French doors.

THE FOX 'N' HOUND BED & BREAKFAST

518-584-5959
www.foxnhoundbandb.com
142 Lake Ave., Saratoga Springs, NY 12866
Price: Moderate–Very Expensive
Credit Cards: Yes
Handicapped Access: No
Special Features: Afternoon tea served daily

This Victorian mansion was built in 1904 for John Wagman. Newton Breeze, the architect responsible for many mansions in Saratoga Springs, designed this magnificent, three-story Queen Anne brick house with a hipped roof and wonderful porches. A Tiffany stained-glass window in the foyer invites guests to the staircase leading to the five guest rooms. The Lilac Suite is filled with lilacs on the walls, bedspreads, and pillows, and has a private balcony. The Springs Room has a custom-made canopy bed. The Saratoga Room has deep blue walls, a brass bed, and cozy writing nook. Innkeeper Marlena Sacca is a Culinary Institute of America graduate and instructor who prepares the gourmet breakfasts that are served in the formal dining room. Her *Breakfast at the Fox 'n' Hound Cookbook* is filled with her inn breakfast recipes. Favorites include fruit parfait, baked apples with caramel sauce, eggs Florentine, cheese pancakes with raspberry sauce, fresh fruit, various crepes, and omelets.

UNION GABLES BED & BREAKFAST

518-584-1558
www.uniongables.com
55 Union Ave., Saratoga Springs, NY 12866
Price: Moderate–Very Expensive
Credit Cards: Yes
Handicapped Access: No
Special Features: Pet friendly

This is a rambling 1901 Queen Anne Victorian marked by distinctive turrets and gables. For many years it was owned by Charles Furness, owner of the *Glens Falls Times*. Then it served as a freshman dormitory for Skidmore College. For the next 17 years the building was used as a group home, and then, after a massive renovation, Union Gables was born in 1992. Ask for a room facing Union Avenue. "Linda" is full of pinks and light green, "Anne" is huge and decorated in lilac and purple, and "Bruce" is more masculine with a peaked attic ceiling. "Cindy" is an adjoining child's room. There are ten rooms in the main house plus two rooms in the Carriage House. The common areas include a massive wraparound porch and large living room. There is a tennis court, exercise room, and outdoor hot tub.

RESTAURANTS

Saratoga Springs has been attracting the rich and famous for several centuries, and fine dining and good food have long been part of the experience. French, Italian, Irish, German, Indian, and, of course, American traditional menus are all here. Saratoga Springs also is the birthplace of the country's favorite snack food—potato chips. All restaurants are by New York State law nonsmoking. Prices are estimated per

Birthplace of the Potato Chip

The thin, salted crisps known as potato chips have long been America's favorite snack food. In the summer of 1853, a guest at the elegant Moon Lake Lodge in Saratoga Springs found Chef George Crum's french fries too thick for his liking. He demanded a thinner batch and then rejected the next batch. Exasperated, Crum decided to rile the guest by producing fries too thin and too crisp to skewer with a fork. The plan backfired. The guest was ecstatic over the paper-thin potatoes, and other diners requested the new dish. They began to appear on the menu as Saratoga Chips, and thus potato chips were born.

person for a dinner entrée without tax, tip, or beverage.

Dining Rates
Inexpensive: Up to $10
Moderate: $11–$25
Expensive: $26–$40
Very Expensive: More than $40

CHEZ SOPHIE BISTRO
518-583-3538
www.chezsophie.com
534 Broadway, Saratoga Springs, NY 12866
Open: Daily
Price: Moderate–Expensive
Credit Cards: Yes
Cuisine: French bistro
Serving: B, L, D
Handicapped Access: Yes
Special Features: Weekend jazz brunch, live music

Located in an elegant space at the Saratoga Hotel and operated by Chef Paul Parker and his wife, Cheryl Clark, this legendary bistro continues the tradition begun by Parker's mother, Sophie, who operated a beloved Saratoga restaurant for years. The freshest ingredients are simply prepared, offering a touch of Paris in upstate New York. The menu is creative without being fussy and changes daily. In honor of the restaurant's heritage as a French diner, it offers a terrific midweek (Monday to Thursday) prix fixe, three-course dinner for $35. A glass-encased floor-to-ceiling wine area at one end of the dining room displays the hundreds of wines available. The award-winning wine list features 400 primarily French wines and 40 Belgian-style beers. The dining rooms and courtyard also serve as galleries for the sculpture, drawing, and paintings of Paul's father, Joseph C. Parker, who founded the original restaurant in 1969 with Sophie.

CHIANTI IL RISTORANTE
518-580-0025
www.dzrestaurant.com
18 Division St., Saratoga Springs, NY 12866
Open: Daily
Price: Moderate
Credit Cards: Yes
Cusine: Northern Italian
Serving: D
Handicapped Access: Yes
Special Features: Outdoor dining

Located in the ground-floor space of a condo building called the Lofts in the heart of downtown, Chianti boasts a priceless bronze plaque. It depicts Christ on the cross and is a copy of one of 16 panels on the Holy Door, an entrance to St. Peter's Basilica at the Vatican in Rome. It is one of only three known copies in the world, a gift from the owner's mother. The owner, David Zecchini, and his sister, General Manager Debora Zecchini, are both natives of Rome, Italy, and the executive chef, Fabrizio Bazzani, is a native of the Verona, Italy, area. The open kitchen is in the center of the restaurant and the decor has been described as rustic elegance. Zecchini said he wants his guests to come twice a week and not once a month. It's not a special-occasion place, but it is a special place. Chianti favorites include carpaccio and pasta dishes. There are a variety of small bowl courses featuring ingredients like lentils and leaks; Sicilian eggplant with raisins and tomatoes; and asparagus with oil and garlic. An extensive wine list includes more than 350 labels.

CIRCUS CAFÉ
518-583-1106
www.circuscafe.com
392 Broadway, Saratoga Springs, NY 12866
Open: Daily
Price: Moderate
Credit Cards: Yes
Cuisine: American
Serving: L, D
Handicapped Access: Yes
Special Features: Live music

This fun restaurant, filled with circus memorabilia, offers a menu of well-prepared American dishes. There's live jazz on Wednesdays, open mike every Thursday, and karaoke every first and third Saturday. It sizzles with personality, from the server wearing a "I Tame Lions" T-shirt, to the hot bowl of fresh popcorn on every table, to the eclectic menu complete with a fun House of Desserts (blue cotton candy anyone?) and an array of specialty drinks. Dishes range from burgers and pot pies to chicken Trevi and Shrimp and Chicken Vera Cruz. The signature dish is tomato basil salmon.

FORNO TOSCANO BISTRO

518-581-2401
www.fornobistro.com
541 Broadway, Saratoga Springs, NY 12866
Open: Mon.–Sat.
Price: Moderate
Credit Cards: Yes
Cuisine: Northern Italian
Serving: L, D
Handicapped Access: Yes
Special Features: Outdoor dining

A sister restaurant to Chianti II Ristorante, Forno Toscano translates to "Tuscan oven." The decor is both European and contemporary, with lots of metal and wood. There's an open kitchen and lively bar area. Offering a variety of Italian dishes, Forno features Tuscan-style food that is rustic and simple. From the thin-crust wood-fired pizza to lasagna to beef tenderloins to the pastries and desserts, the menu is simple yet comprehensive and very Italian.

GAFFNEY'S RESTAURANT

518-587-7359
www.gaffneysrestaurant.com
16 Caroline St., Saratoga Springs, NY 12866
Open: Daily
Price: Moderate
Credit Cards: Yes
Cuisine: American

Serving: L, D
Handicapped Access: Yes
Special Features: Outdoor dining, live entertainment

Housed in a 1903 building that is listed on the National Register of Historic Places, it has been a popular spot since it opened in 1982. There are weekly specials including vegetarian nights, open-mike nights, cigar nights, and wine pairings. The menu includes pub fare such as burgers, wings, and sandwiches, as well as entrées such as Greek scampi, steak, and shrimp Saratoga.

HATTIE'S RESTAURANT

518-584-4790
www.hattiesrestaurant.com
45 Phila St., Saratoga Springs, NY 12866
Open: Daily
Price: Moderate
Credit Cards: Yes
Cuisine: Southern
Serving: L, D
Handicapped Access: Yes
Special Features: Outdoor dining, Hattie's Hot Sauce available for take-out

Since its establishment in 1938, the words *Hattie's* and *Saratoga Springs* are often mentioned in the same breath. Serving fine southern home cooking in a friendly, down-home atmosphere to legions of fans, Hattie's is an institution in Saratoga and well beyond. There's an authentic southern feeling in Hattie's, maybe that's why all the horse people from millionaires to stable boys love it. There are overhead fans, checkered tablecloths, a banging screen door, and a wall of testimonials to the woman who ran the restaurant for almost six decades. Now owned by Culinary Institute of America graduate and chef Jasper Alexander, the fine food and comfortable feeling remains. Menu favorites include Hattie's fried chicken, Jasper's mac & cheese, creole jambalaya, catfish, red beans and rice, and chicken and dumplings.

July in Saratoga

"Balanchine enjoyed his Julys in Saratoga. In the morning after he made his tea he took it out on the verandah. There was always a fresh croissant from Mrs. London's Bakeshop and often a coffee cake of incredible richness."

—Richard Buckle, *George Balanchine: Ballet Master*

LILLIAN'S RESTAURANT

518-587-7766
www.lilliansrestaurant.com
408 Broadway, Saratoga Springs, NY 12866
Open: Daily
Price: Moderate
Credit Cards: Yes
Cuisine: American
Serving: L, D
Handicapped Access: Yes
Special Features: Outdoor dining

Lillian's opened in 1974, borrowing the name from Broadway actress Lillian Russell, summer resident of the spa city. It is decorated in turn-of-the-20th-century decor with Tiffany-style lamps, stained glass, and Victorian accents. Prime rib, steak, pasta, chicken, and grilled salmon are traditional favorites. Desserts include such longtime favorites as cheesecake, toll house pie, chocolate mousse, and chocolate volcano cake.

MRS. LONDON'S BAKERY CAFÉ

518-581-1652
www.mrslondons.com
464 Broadway, Saratoga Springs, NY 12866
Open: Tues.–Sun.
Price: Inexpensive
Credit Cards: Yes
Cuisine: French
Serving: B, L, light dinners
Handicapped Access: Yes
Special Features: Take-out bakery items available

Wendy and Michael London opened Mrs. London's in 1977 and since then it has been a big draw for bread, dessert, and pastry

Sidewalk dining at Mrs. London's Bakery Café on Broadway

fans. Mrs. London's would be right at home on the Right Bank of Paris. There are soups, salads, and sandwiches but what most everyone comes for are the pastries and the breads. There is a large range of morning pastries that are made through the night so they are freshest in the morning. There are croissants, Danish, and brioche in many forms, as well as scrumptious scones, triple chocolate chip cookies, brownies, pies, and cakes. All are available to take home or for picnics.

RAVENOUS

518-581-0560
www.ravenouscrepes.com
21 Phila St., Saratoga Springs, NY 12866
Open: Tues.–Sun.
Price: Inexpensive
Credit Cards: Yes
Cuisine: Crepes
Serving: L, D
Handicapped Access: Yes
Special Features: Weekend brunch

This small, contemporary style café specializes in crepes for lunch, dinner, and weekend brunch. Locals also rave about the Belgian pommes frites—fresh-cut french fries served in paper cones with your choice of dipping sauce. Crepe fillings include traditional French favorites (like ratatouille and ham and Gruyère) as well as other more creative fillings from around the world. Delectable dessert crepes feature fresh fruit, nutella, fromage blanc, and homemade whipped cream. Beer, wine, espresso, and homemade cool drinks round out the menu.

SPERRY'S RESTAURANT

518-584-9618
www.sperrysofsaratoga.com
30½ Caroline St., Saratoga Springs, NY 12866
Open: Mon.–Sat.
Price: Moderate
Credit Cards: Yes
Cuisine: American
Serving: D
Handicapped Access:
Special Features: Outdoor patio

Sperry's is a dependable local favorite that has been around since the 1930s. It is an attractive bistro with an art deco atmosphere and black-and-white tile floors, a few high-backed booths, and a welcoming bar. Known for its steak au poivre cooked to perfection and seasonable soft shell crabs, Sperry's also has an extensive wine list, including wines by the glass. With a nod to diners who prefer smaller portions, there are small plates and some entrées that are available in half portions.

SPRINGWATER BISTRO

518-584-6440
www.springwaterbistro.com
139 Union Ave., Saratoga Springs, NY 12866
Open: Thurs.–Mon.
Price: Moderate
Credit Cards: Yes
Cuisine: American bistro
Serving: D
Handicapped Access: Yes
Special Features: Midweek prix fixe dinners

Cozy, comfortable, and elegant describe the atmosphere of this restored Victorian home. Award-winning chef David Britton says the fare is based on "unpretentious ingredients with a lot of technique and high quality." He is very involved in the farm-to-restaurant program and bases his daily-changing menu on what is available locally. The dining room offers casual ambiance with an upscale mood. There are midweek three-course prix fixe dinners for $28. Dinner menus include braised rabbit, veal London broil, and braised short ribs.

THE OLDE BRYAN INN

518-587-2990
www.oldebryaninn.com

123 Maple Ave., Saratoga Springs, NY 12866
Open: Daily
Price: Moderate
Credit Cards: Yes
Cuisine: American
Serving: L, D
Handicapped Access: Yes
Special Features: Ghost tales abound

This is an establishment full of history and even some ghosts. An inn since 1773, it is named for a Revolutionary War hero and first permanent local settler who purchased it in 1787. What attracted early visitors was the High Rock Spring across Maple Avenue from the inn. Tradition says that Native Americans visited the spring as early as 1300 to gain strength from the "Medicine Spring of the Great Spirit." General Phillip Schuyler spent summers next to the spring and George Washington, Alexander Hamilton, and DeWitt Clinton visited the Saratoga battlefield and were taken to the spring. The inn is a cozy place with brick-lined dining rooms, stone walls, and wood-beamed ceilings. Menu items include traditional turkey dinner, strip steak, and more exotic lobster-and-crab-stuffed haddock and broiled cedar-spiced salmon. Daily lunch, dinner, and dessert specials are available as are take-out meals. There is an award-winning wine list.

CULTURE

Saratoga Springs has a long history of attracting tourists, and a rich cultural tradition far exceeding other similar-sized cities. Beyond a wealth of historical attractions there is big-city entertainment especially during the summer, when the New York City Ballet and the Philadelphia Orchestra are in residence at the Saratoga Spa State Park.

Museums and Historic Sites

CHILDREN'S MUSEUM OF SARATOGA

518-584-5540
www.cmssny.org
69 Caroline St., Saratoga springs, NY 12866
Open: Mon.–Sat. July 1–Labor Day, Tues.–Sun rest of year
Admission: $6 per person; children under age one, free

This museum is designed for children seven and under. They can climb into a tree house and find the habitats of local animals, surround themselves in a life-sized bubble, or create music. They can pretend to be a bank teller, practice their building skills, slide down the pole in the firehouse, jump into a fire truck, go to a child-sized grocery store, and visit a post office. There are many more hands-on exhibits designed to involve children and stimulate their imaginations.

NATIONAL MUSEUM OF DANCE AND HALL OF FAME

518-584-2225
www.dancemuseum.org
99 S. Broadway, Saratoga Springs, NY 12866
Open: Tues.–Sun.
Admission: Adults $6.50, seniors and students $5, children $3

Established in 1986, this is the only museum in the country dedicated to American professional dance. It is located in the former Washington Bath House, a spacious 1918 arts and crafts building in Saratoga Spa State Park. The museum houses a growing collection of photographs, videos, artifacts, costumes, and archives related to dance. The only permanent exhibit is the Hall of Fame. To date more than 30 dancers, teachers, choreographers, designers, critics, and patrons have been recognized for their influence. The Children's Discovery Room is a place where young visitors can try on costumes, dance on a small stage, and play instruments.

NATIONAL MUSEUM OF RACING AND HALL OF FAME
518-584-0400
www.racingmuseum.org
191 Union Ave., Saratoga Springs, NY 12866
Open: Daily April–Oct., rest of year Tues.–Sun.
Admission: Adults $7, seniors and students, $5

Self-guided tours of the museum begin at the starting gate and move through the galleries exploring more than three centuries of racing history. Exhibits explain the physical characteristics of the best thoroughbreds and re-create typical scenes at the racetrack and on the backstretch. Exhibits include equine painting and sculpture. The Anatomy Room explores the unique physiology of the thoroughbred. In the Racing Day Gallery visitors can learn how to bet and discover what is in the jockey's room. The Hall of Fame Gallery displays the colorful racing silks and plaques recognizing each Hall of Famer.

NEW YORK STATE MILITARY MUSEUM AND VETERANS RESEARCH CENTER
518-581-5100
www.dmna.state.ny.us/historic/mil-hist
61 Lake Ave., Saratoga Springs, NY 12866
Open: Tues.–Sun.
Admission: Free

Housed in an 1899 armory, the museum displays more than ten thousand artifacts dating from the Revolutionary War to Desert Storm that relate to New York State's military forces, the state's military history, and the contributions of New York's veterans. The artifacts include uniforms, weapons, artillery pieces, and art. A significant portion of the collection is from the Civil War. There are significant exhibits relating to New York's 27th Division in World War I and World War II and notable state military regiments such as the 7th (Silk Stocking Regiment), 69th (Fighting Irish), 71st, and 369th (Harlem Hell Fighters) New York Infantry. There is the largest collection of state battle flags in the country and the world's largest collection of Civil War flags.

SARATOGA AUTOMOBILE MUSEUM
518-587-1935
www.saratogaautomuseum.org
110 Avenue of the Pines, Saratoga Springs, NY 12866
Open: Daily June–Oct., Tues.–Sun. rest of year
Admission: Adults $8, seniors, active military, students $5, children $3.50

This is the place for car lovers, with such classic as the 1917 Ford Model T Runabout, the 1916 Stanley Steamer, a 1926 Packard, a 1931 Alfa Romeo, a 1938 Jaguar, a 1956 Lancia, a 1966 Corvette—just some of the gems on display in this restored 1935 water bottling plant.

There is a Racing in New York exhibit and an East of Detroit exhibit. New York State was once home to more than one hundred different automobile manufacturers. Most were small, but there were successes like the Franklin and the Pierce-Arrow. This exhibit includes a 1931 Pierce-Arrow, Charles Lindbergh's 1928 Franklin airman, and a 1903 Weebermobile.

SARATOGA SPRINGS HISTORY MUSEUM
518-584-6920
www.saratogahistory.org
Canfield Casino in Congress Park, Saratoga Springs, NY 12866
Open: Daily Memorial Day–Labor Day, Wed.–Sun. rest of year
Admission: Adults $5, seniors and students $4

The museum is housed in Canfield Casino, the 1870 former gambling casino. It is on the National Register of Historic Places. The museum hosts free lectures and educational programs on Saratoga Springs history. The exhibits occupy three floors and feature a diverse collection of 15,000 objects ranging from the 1802 Gideon Putnam Tavern sign to Victorian dresses to memorabilia from the mineral springs. There are also 375,000 photographs of Saratoga Springs from 1855 to 1980.

YADDO GARDENS
518-584-0746
www.yaddo.org
Union Ave., Saratoga Springs, NY 12866
Open: Daily
Admission: Free

Yaddo was founded in 1900 and is an artists' community on a 400-acre estate. The gardens feature a variety of plants that peak throughout the season. The roses are at their peak in June and July and then again in late August. The rock garden is in bloom mid-June through mid-September. The gardens are the only part of the estate that is open to the public.

RECREATION

Golf
Saratoga Lake Golf Club (518-581-6616, www.saratogalakegolf.com, 35 Grace Moore Rd., Stillwater, NY 12170) The challenging 6,400-yard layout was constructed through a forest at the south end of Saratoga Lake with significant elevation changes, water, and wetland hazards.

Saratoga National Golf Course (518-583-4653, www.golfsaratoga.com, 458 Union Ave., Saratoga Springs, 12866) Winner of numerous awards, this course is also home to the highly rated Prime Restaurant, a traditional fine steakhouse.

Saratoga Spa Championship and Executive Golf Course (518-584-2006, www.saratoga spagolf.com, 60 Roosevelt Dr., Saratoga Springs, NY 12866) This course is set in a pine forest, surrounded by the natural beauty of Saratoga Spa State Park. There are 9 holes of executive and 18 holes of championship golf, grass tee driving range, putting green, full-service golf shop, and a restaurant.

Eagle Crest Golf Club (518-877-7082, www.eaglecrestgolf.com, 1004 Rt. 146A, Clifton Park, NY 12065) Just 15 minutes from Saratoga Springs, this 18-hole facility offers a great value. There is a course set up of 5,600 to 7,000 yards with four sets of tees to choose from. There is also a full practice facility, pub grillroom, and pro shop.

Horse Racing

Saratoga Gaming and Raceway (518-584-2110, www.saratogagamingandraceway.com, 342 Jefferson St., Saratoga Springs, NY 12866) It is also called the Saratoga Racino and has more than 1,700 video gaming machines, live harness racing, a nightclub, dining options, and more. You can even pay to have a race named for you or your guests.

Saratoga Polo (518-584-8108, www.saratogapolo.com, Whitney Field [corner of Bloomfield and Denton Rds.], Saratoga Springs, NY 12866) Enjoy the sport of kings Wednesday, Friday, and Sunday nights mid-June through Labor Day. The Saratoga Polo club was established in 1898. Tailgating is popular at the polo matches and the whole family (including the dog) is invited.

Saratoga Race Course (518-584-6200, www.saratoga.org/visitors/saratoga-race-course .asp, 267 Union Rd., Saratoga Springs, NY 12866) This is an elegant, beautiful racetrack and the oldest in the U.S. Here you can get right next to the horses as they are led along a path through the crowd to the paddock, or rub shoulders with the jockeys. The season is late July through Labor Day. During the meet, the world focuses on Saratoga for its world-class thoroughbred horse racing including the Travers Stakes, known as America's Mid-Summer Derby. Named one of the top ten sporting venues in the world by *Sports Illustrated* magazine, it is an architectural treasure. There is no racing on Tuesdays.

Shopping

Until recently Saratoga Springs had no national chain stores in its historic downtown. The stores that have opened here, including Gap, Eddie Bauer, and Banana Republic, were designed to fit in well with the more numerous local independent shops. Art galleries, antiques, jewelry, clothing, home furnishings, and gift shops line Broadway and the other downtown streets.

Art Galleries

Crafters Gallery (518-583-2435, www.craftersgallerysaratoga.com, 427 Broadway, Saratoga Springs, NY 12866) Since 1993, Crafters Gallery has served as a showcase and meeting ground for local artists. In addition, the gallery carries everything from vintage baseball prints to hand-painted folk art from around the globe. The gallery also carries the original candy Peppermint Pig, a holiday tradition that originated in Saratoga Springs more than 120 years ago.

Greenwood Galleries (518-281-6951, www.greenwoodgalleries.com, 74 Beekman St., Saratoga Springs, NY 12866) This gallery features original oil paintings, watercolors, pastels, limited- and open-edition prints, and photography. There is also tribal textile art from Zambia. Their sale benefits the lives of rural Zambians and the HIV-positive orphans they care for.

Mimosa Gallery (518-583-1163, www.mimosagallery.com, 70c Beekman St., Saratoga, NY

Taking the Waters

The naturally occurring mineral springs were the first draw for visitors to Saratoga Springs. Found throughout the area due to a geological fault line, the springs are well preserved to this day. Naturally carbonated, the waters have been an important icon for the Saratoga area since it became popular as a destination. Visitors, jugs in tow, can sample the mineral springs at many area pavilions. Each spring has a unique taste and look based upon the mineral content. Visitors can also take natural spring baths at area spas. Many springs are within the Saratoga Spa State Park. Pick up a comprehensive guide at the **Saratoga Springs Visitors Center** (518-587-3241, www.saratoga.org, 297 Broadway, Saratoga Springs, NY 12866).

Filling up at one of several mineral springs in Saratoga Spa State Park

12866) This is a gallery of "art for home and wear." The jewelry, handbags, scarves, glass, and ceramics are by local as well as nationally renowned artists.

70 **Beekman Art Gallery** (518-542-6688, www.saratoga.org/70beekmanartgallery, 70 Beekman St., Saratoga Springs, NY 12866) This gallery specializes in oriental art and features works from local, regional, and international artists. The gallery sells oil paintings, pastels, sculptures, and jade and wood carvings, as well as artistically designed jewelry and oriental specialty clothing.

Symmetry Gallery (518-584-5090, www.symmetrygallery.com, 348 Broadway, Saratoga Springs, NY 12866) This nationally recognized gallery features American contemporary

A Park with a Difference
Saratoga Spa State Park (518-584-2535, www.saratogaspastatepark.org, 19 Roosevelt Dr., Saratoga Springs, NY 12866) is a park that has it all. The 2,300-acre park is distinguished by its classical architecture and listed as a National Historic Landmark. It is noted for its diverse cultural and recreational resources. In addition to the nationally known Saratoga Performing Arts Center, the Spa Little Theater, the National Museum of Dance, the Gideon Putnam Hotel, mineral springs and the mineral baths, the park offers a multitude of traditional recreation opportunities including a top-rated golf course, tennis courts, and swimming pools. The Saratoga Performing Arts Center (known locally as SPAC) is a music and performing arts venue that features classical programming, festivals, and major concerts. The New York City Ballet and the Philadelphia Orchestra are in residence each summer—the ballet in July and the orchestra in August.

glass and fine crafts. There is glass sculpture, vases, paperweights, bowls, and glass jewelry by more than two hundred artists.

Specialty Shops

deJonghe Original Jewelry (518-587-6422, www.djoriginals.com, 470 Broadway, Saratoga Springs, NY. 12866) Artist-designer Dennis deJonghe specializes in creating one-of-kind pieces on the premises. He is noted for his Saratoga Collection of area landmarks and his Equestrian Collection of jewelry related to horses.

FortyCaroline Antiques (518-424-4201, www.fortycaroline.com, 454 Broadway, Saratoga Springs, NY 12866) Located in the "Downstreet Marketplace," where it is also known as Downstreet Antiques, this is an eclectic old-fashioned curiosity shop with vintage jewelry, small furniture, paintings, old books, old fishing lures, and vintage holiday decorations.

G. Willikers (518-587-2143, www.gwillikerssaratoga.com, 461 Broadway, Saratoga Springs, NY 12866) This store is full of imaginative, creative, and fun toys for all ages including Thomas wooden trains, Madame Alexander dolls, and Cloud B and Baby Gund.

Impressions of Saratoga (518-587-0666, www.impressionssaratoga.com, 368 Broadway, Saratoga Springs, NY 12866) This store has a vast array of collectibles, art, and gifts for horse lovers as well as dollhouses, toys, jewelry, and home accessories.

Menges & Curtis Apothecary (518-584-2046, www.mengesandcurtis.com, 472 Broadway, Saratoga Springs, NY 12866)

A hat shop along Broadway in Saratoga Springs

Established in 1860, this apothecary is one of the oldest in the country. It is a traditional pharmacy and also provides custom compounding services. Travelers come for the line of gifts, candles, soaps, lotions, including pharmacist-formulated Apothecary Essentials line of creams and lotions containing natural Saratoga Springs water.

N. Fox Jewelers (518-587-7777, www.nfoxjewelers.com, 404 Broadway, Saratoga Springs, NY 12866) A Saratoga landmark for more than 60 years, this is an elegant store complete with a spectacular crystal chandelier. It features top lines of diamonds, gold, and other jewelry, as well as appraisals and custom-made jewelry.

Sloppy Kisses (518-587-2207, www.sloppykissesofsaratoga.com, 493 Broadway, Saratoga Springs, NY 12866) A treat boutique for dogs offering everything for the dog owner and dog lover. Dogs are welcome in the store. The bakery features fresh-baked dog treats. Items include doggie clothing, pet carriers, collars, leashes, dog beds, toys, and new-puppy kits.

Sweetheart's Dolls (518-584-6362, www.sweetheartsdolls.com, 368 Broadway, Saratoga Springs, NY 12866) This shop offers a wide range of dolls, including modern collectible dolls, in a wide range of prices. Ethnic dolls are a specialty. There are extensive lines of New York City Ballet dolls, Harry Potter, and Wizard of Oz dolls. Hours vary, so call ahead.

Fort Edward

Past Lock C-5, New York's Adirondack Mountains can be seen to the west and Vermont's Green Mountains are visible to the east. The Hudson River turns westward at Fort Edward and the Champlain Canal continues north via a 23-mile dug channel.

This was an important military outpost during the 18th century. Both British and American troops passed through the area. The Old Fort House, now a museum, was built by Patrick Smyth in 1772 using timbers taken from the ruins of the fortifications at Fort Edward. It served as a headquarters for both British and American generals during the Revolution, although not at the same time. General George Washington dined here on two different occasions in July 1783.

The Old Fort House Museum (518-747-9600, http://ftedward.com/history/oldfort/oldFort.htm, 29 Broadway St., Fort Edward, NY 12828) is a campus of five buildings, including a tollhouse, law office, and an original one-room schoolhouse built around the turn of the century and used until the 1950s. It was moved to the property. The A. Dallas Wait Law Office was built in 1853 by Washington County judge A. Dallas Wait, next to his house in Fort Edward. Also moved to the property, it is filled with period law books, typewriters, and a wood stove. The museum is open daily June to August, and Tuesday to Friday September to mid-October. Adults $5.

WHITEHALL

Settled in 1759, Whitehall is the terminus for the Champlain Canal and is considered the birthplace of the U.S. Navy. The first American fleet was built here in 1776 during the American Revolution.

Englishman Philip Skene founded the village. He named his vast holdings Skenesborough in honor of himself. It was the first English-speaking settlement on Lake Champlain and thrived as Skene built a logging operation, a foundry, and a shipbuilding enterprise. On May 9, 1775, Skenesborough was captured by American forces in the first aggressive Revolutionary War action in New York State. Skene's trading schooner became

Port marker at Whitehall

the first ship of the U.S. Navy when it was taken to Crown Point, armed, and used under the leadership of Colonel Benedict Arnold to capture a British ship renamed Enterprise on May 18, 1775. In 1776 Congress ordered General Philip Schuyler to construct a fleet of ships capable of countering an expected British invasion.

This first U.S. Naval fleet of 13 ships added to the 4 already patrolling Lake Champlain was constructed during the summer of 1776. Well aware that he was heavily outnumbered, Arnold knew that he could not win, or even risk, an open battle on Lake Champlain against so strong a foe. Instead, he decided on a sniper attack at Valcour Island in 1776. Hiding his tiny fleet between the island and the mainland, Arnold waited in the dark for the British fleet to pass the island, at which time he attacked from the rear. Fighting from this protected anchorage allowed Arnold's men to take on the British men-of-war one at a time as they tried to sail into the harbor.

In the face of overwhelming odds, most of Arnold's fleet survived and hurried back to Skenesborough, while the British, knowing that winter was hard on their heels, headed back to Canada to sit out the harsh New England weather. This battle delayed the British arrival at the battlefield at Saratoga until the following October. In that year the Americans had time to regroup and plan their strategy against the British Army. That delay may have been just what they needed to defeat the British at the famous battle of Saratoga in October 1777, known as the turning point of the war. This naval fleet was the only one to see active service in the Revolutionary War.

Whitehall's history is recounted at the **Skenesborough Museum and New York State Heritage Area Visitor Center** (518-499-1155, Skenesborough Dr., Whitehall, NY 12887). The museum was created in 1959 in an unused canal terminal built in 1917. It was renovated in 1991, creating a New York State Heritage Area Visitor Center. There's a 16-foot diorama depicting Philip Skene's home and its outbuildings. Maps, photographs, and artifacts describe the village's involvement in the Revolutionary War and War of 1812. Open daily June to Labor Day, weekends Labor Day to mid-October, other times by appointment. Adults $2, seniors and students $1.

Today, Whitehall bills itself as "where the Champlain Canal meets Lake Champlain." It is a lovely village that has embraced its status as a canal community. Since its opening in 2000, the **Bridge Theater** (518-499-2435, www.bridgetheater-whitehall.com/bridge.htm,

Champlain Canal in Whitehall, with Skene Manor visible on the hill

Whitehall's Bridge Theater spans the Champlain Canal

8 N. Williams St., Whitehall, NY 12887) has brought arts and entertainment to the area. Its location on a bridge directly over the Champlain Canal has earned the venue's billing as "America's most unique theater." The 60-seat theater offers Friday-night cabarets and Saturday performances during July and August.

Skenesborough Museum, Whitehall

Whitehall offers ample docking in the center of the village, antiques, dining and accommodations, and even a castle on a hill. There are free concerts in the park along the canal on Friday and Saturday evenings in July and August.

LODGING

Finch & Chubb Inn and Restaurant
(518-499-2049, www.finchandchubb
.com, 82 N. Williams St., Whitehall, NY
12887) This place has its all. Located on
Lock 12, the facility includes a full-service marina, boat launch and docking,
gift shop, "boatique," store, fishing, free
canoes, cocktail lounge, restaurant, and
a five-room inn including two suites
overlooking the canal. The suites have
two bedrooms and a living room. The
award-winning restaurant serves dinner
daily in the summer and is closed
Monday during the rest of the year.
Menu items include charbroiled steak,

A Ghostly Castle

Skene Manor (518-499-1906, www.members.tripod.com/skenemanor, 8 Potters St., Whitehall, NY 12887), Whitehall's "castle on the hill" is perched high on Skene Mountain, offering spectacular views of the village and the canal. State Supreme Court Justice Joseph H. Potter built the castle in 1874. Local legend says that the manor is haunted by Philip Skene's wife. People have reported seeing the ghost of a young woman dressed in a white Victorian gown and wearing an unusual ring on her left hand, walking the corridors of the manor. The manor is open Wednesday to Sunday, and there are free tours. Luncheon is served in the Tea Room Friday to Sunday.

sautéed duck, venison, broiled salmon, and pan-fried catfish. Homemade desserts include Toll House pie and apple berry crisp. The **Black Pearl** serves casual pub fare and has an outside deck overlooking the water.

Tour boat passengers watch as lock gates close

11

CANAL FACTS

The popular song "Low Bridge! Everybody Down" was written in 1905 by Thomas S. Allen after Erie Canal traffic was converted from mules to engines. Allen (1876–1919) was an American vaudeville composer and violinist and one of the early figures in the Tin Pan Alley era of popular music. The song memorializes the years from 1825 to 1880, when mule barges transformed New York State.

The song has become part of the folk repertoire, recorded by folksingers like Glenn Yarborough and Peter Seeger, as well as Bruce Springsteen. During the canal season, the song echoes the entire length of the canal on boat cruises and at many canal festivals. It is regarded as the unofficial Erie Canal song. Some versions use "fifteen miles" on the Erie Canal instead of "fifteen years."

"Low Bridge! Everybody Down"; or "Fifteen Years on the Erie Canal"
Thomas S. Allen, 1905

I've got a mule, her name is Sal,
Fifteen years on the Erie Canal.
She's a good old worker and a good old pal,
Fifteen years on the Erie Canal.
We've hauled some barges in our day,
Filled with lumber, coal, and hay,
And every inch of the way I know,
From Albany to Buffalo.

Chorus
Low bridge, everybody down,
Low bridge, we must be getting near a town
You can always tell your neighbor,
You can always tell your pal,
If he's ever navigated on the Erie Canal.

We better get on our way, old pal,
Fifteen years on the Erie Canal.
You bet your life I wouldn't never part with Sal,
Fifteen years on the Erie Canal.
Giddap there gal we've passed that lock,

We'll make Rome 'bout six o'clock,
So one more trip and back we'll go,
Right back home to Buffalo.

Chorus
Low bridge, everybody down,
Low bridge, I've got the finest mule in town,
Once a man named Mike McGinty tried to put it over Sal,
Now he's way down at the bottom of the Erie Canal.

Oh, where would I be if I lost my pal?
Fifteen years on the Erie Canal.
Oh, I'd like to see a mule as good as Sal,
Fifteen years on the Erie Canal.
A friend of mine once got her sore,
Now, he's got a broken jaw.
'Cause she let fly with her iron toe
And kicked him back into Buffalo.

Chorus
Low bridge, everybody down,
Low bridge, I've got the finest mule in town,
If you're looking 'round for trouble, better stay away from Sal,
She's the only fighting donkey on the Erie Canal.

I don't have to call when I want my Sal,
Fifteen years on the Erie Canal.
She trots from her stall like a good old gal,
Fifteen years on the Erie Canal.
I eat my meals with Sal each day,
I eat beef and she eats hay,
She ain't so slow if you want to know,
She put the "Buff" in Buffalo.

Chorus
Low bridge, everybody down,
Low bridge, I've got the finest mule in town;
Eats a bale of hay for dinner, and on top of that, my Sal
Tries to drink up all the water in the Erie Canal.

You'll soon hear them sing all about my gal,
Fifteen years on the Erie Canal.
It's a darned fool ditty 'bout my darned fool Sal,
Fifteen years on the Erie Canal.
Oh, every band will play it soon,
Darned fool words and darned fool tune.
You'll hear it sung everywhere you go,

From Mexico to Buffalo.

Chorus
Low bridge, everybody down,
Low bridge, I've got the finest mule in town.
She's a perfect, perfect lady, and she blushes like a gal,
If she hears you sing about her and the Erie Canal.

Another popular canal song:
"The E-ri-e"; or "Forty Miles from Albany

We were forty miles from Albany
Forget it I never shall.
What a terrible storm we had one night
On the E-ri-e Canal.

Oh, the E-ri-e was a-rising
And the gin was a-gettin' low.
And I scarcely think we'll get a drink
'Till we get to Buff-a-lo-o-o
'Till we get to Buffalo.

We were loaded down with barley
We were chock-full up on rye.
The captain he looked down at me
With his goll-darned wicked eye.

Well, two days out of Syracuse
The vessel struck a shoal;
We like to all be drownded
On a chunk o' Lackawanna coal.

We hollered to the captain
On the towpath, treadin' dirt
He jumped on board and stopped the leak
With his old red flannel shirt.

The cook she was a grand old gal
Stood six foot in her socks.
Had a foot just like an elephant
And her breath would open locks.

The wind begins to whistle
The waves begin to roll
We had to reef our royals
On that ragin' canal.

The cook came to our rescue
She had a ragged dress;
We hoisted her upon the pole
As a signal of distress.

The captain, he got married
And the cook, she went to jail;
And I'm the only son-of-a-gun
That's left to tell the tale.

Length:

Canal system is 524 miles long, including lake and river channels, with an average width of
125 feet and a depth of 10 to 12 feet. There are 57 locks and 16 lift bridges. Each lock is
328 feet long and 45 feet wide.
• Erie: 338 miles long, average depth of 10 to 12 feet
• Champlain: 60 miles long, average depth of 9.5 feet
• Oswego: 24 miles long, average depth of 10 to 12 feet
• Cayuga-Seneca: 12 miles long, average depth of 9.5 feet
to Ithaca: 45 miles
to Watkins Glen: 45 miles

Open:

The canal system is open from May 1 until November 15.

How a lock works

A lock chamber accommodates a boat that is a maximum 300 feet long and 43.5 feet wide.
The major components are four hinged gates; four valves that regulate the flow of water
into and out of the chamber; the controls used by the lock operator to supply electricity to
the eight motors that operate the gates and valves; and the reinforced cement chamber
itself. The chamber has tunnels to carry water into and out of the chamber. Gravity, not
pumps, moves water into and out of the locks.

When not in operation, all gates on the lock are closed. When the lock is used to lower a
boat, two valves are opened to allow water to fill the chamber through the tunnels. The
water enters the chamber through smaller tunnels along the side of the walls. Once the
chamber is full, the valves are closed and the two gates leading into the chamber are
opened fully. The boat enters the chamber and positions itself along the walls of the chamber, holding its position with lines that hang from the walls. The gates the boat entered
through are then fully closed. Next, two valves are opened, allowing the water in the chamber to discharge into the lower pool. When the water level in the chamber matches the
level in the lower pool, the exit gates are opened and the vessels drop their lines and exit
the chamber. The process is similar when raising a boat.

The difference in elevation between the upper and lower pools is the lock's "lift." It
ranges from 6 feet to 40.5 feet on the canal system. Less lift means a shorter time locking
through.

Helpful phone numbers and Web sites

New York State Canal Corporation
800-422-6254
www.canals.state.ny.us

Erie Canalway National Heritage Corridor
518-237-7000
www.eriecanalway.org

Canal Society of New York State
www.canalsnys.org

New York State Dept. of Environmental Conservation (campgrounds)
800-456-CAMP
www.reserveamerica.com

New York Dept. of Parks and Recreation (state parks and campgrounds)
518-474-0456
www.nysparks.com

New York State Canalway Trail
518-434-1583
www.ptny.org

New York State Division of Tourism
800-CALLNYS
www.iloveny.state.us

Western canal region: Lockport

Western Canal Information

Buffalo Niagara Convention & Visitors Bureau
716-852-0511, 800-283-3256
www.visitbuffaloniagra.com

Chamber of Commerce of the Tonawandas
716-692-5120
www.the-tonawandas.com

Niagara County Tourism
716-439-7300 or 800-338-7890
www.niagarausa.com

Tourism Niagara (Canada)
800-263-2988
www.tourismniagara.com

Orleans County Tourism
800-724-0314
www.orleansny.com/tourism

Greater Rochester Visitors Association
585-232-4822 or 800-677-7282
www.visitrochester.com

Cayuga-Seneca Canal Information

Finger Lakes Association
315-536-7488 or 800-548-4386
www.fingerlakes.org

Cayuga County Tourism
315-255-1658 or 800-499-9615
www.tourcayuga.com

Geneva Area Chamber of Commerce
315-789-1776
www.genevany.com

Ithaca/Tompkins County Convention & Visitors Bureau
607-272-1313 or 800-284-8422
www.visitithaca.com

Seneca County Tourism
315-568-2906 or 800-732-1848
www.seneca.org

Schuyler County Tourism Bureau
607-535-4300 or 800-607-4552
www.schuylerny.com

Central Canal Information
Syracuse Convention & Visitors Bureau
315-470-1800 or 800-234-4797
www.visitsyracuse.org

Sylvan-Verona Beach Resort Association
315-762-5212
www.sylvanbeach.org

Oswego Canal Information
Oswego County Dept. of Promotion & Tourism
315-349-8322 or 800-248-4386
www.co.oswego.ny.us

Eastern Canal Information
Oneida County Convention & Visitors Bureau
800-426-3132
www.oneidacountycvb.com

Leatherstocking Country, NY
315-866-1500 or 800-233-8778
www.leatherstockingny.com

Albany County Convention & Visitors Bureau
518-434-1217 or 800-258-3582
www.albany.org

Champlain Canal Information
Saratoga County Chamber of Commerce
518-584-3255 or 800-526-8970
www.saratoga.org

Washington County Tourism
518-746-2290 or 888-203-8622
www.washingtoncounty.org

Annual Canal Events
May
Albany Tulip Festival, 518-434-2032, www.albanyevents.org,
Waterford Canal Fest, 518-235-9898
American Carp Society Northeast Regional Carp Tournament, 315-635-4871, Lock 24

Memorial Day Weekend "Kick Off to Summer," 315-762-5212, Sylvan Beach, www.sylvanbeachny.com/events

Lake Ontario Counties Trout and Salmon Derby, 888-733-5246, Oswego, www.loc.org

Native American Living History Weekend, 518-747-3693, Fort Edward, www.rogers island.org

Kites over Fort Ontario, Oswego, www.fortontario.com, 315-343-4711

June

Concerts at Gateway Harbor, 716-692-5120, N. Tonawanda, www.the-tonawandas.com,

Sunday Concerts at the Gazebo, Spencerport, 585-352-4771

Bikes at the Beach, Sylvan Beach, 315-762-5212, www.sylvanbeachny.com/events (Tuesdays)

Summer Concert Series, Pittsford, 585-248-6285

Cruise Nite & Music by the Canal, Medina, 585-798-0220 (Fridays)

Fairport Canal Days, 585-234-4323, www.fairportmerchants.com

Canal Trail Celebration, all canals, 518-436-3055

Finger Lakes Carp Derby, Seneca Falls, 315-568-9063

Canal Town Strawberry Festival, Canastota, 315-697-5002, www.canastota.com

Albany Alive at Five, 518-434-2032, www.albanyevents.org

Waterfront Festival & Cardboard Boat Race, Watkins Glen, 607-732-4400, www.watkinsglen.com/festival

Blessing of the Fleet, Baldwinsville, 315-638-0550

Rose Parade, Newark, 315-331-1451, www.newarkfire.org

Strawberry Festival Duck Race, Albion, 585-589-9176

Wildflowers & Wine Festival, Montezuma Wildlife Refuge, 315-568-5987, www.friendsofmontezuma.org

Baldwinsville Summer Concert Series, 315-635-5999

Ilion Civic Band Summer Concert Series, 315-826-3092

Fort Edward Heritage Days, 518-747-3693

Music & Fireworks in the Park, Phoenix, 315-695-1308, www.bridgehousebrats.us,

July

Riverfront Concert Series, Oswego, 315-343-1600, www.gsteamers.com

Celebrate the Fourth, Erie Canal Village, Rome, 315-337-3999, www.eriecanalvillage.net

Reading of the Declaration of Independence, Stillwater, 518-664-1847

Fourth of July in the Park, Palmyra, 315-597-4849

Annual Steamboat Rally, Waterford, 518-233-9123

AuroraFest, Aurora, 315-364-7610, www.auroranewyork.com

Erie Canal Fishing Derby, Tonawanda-Albion, 716-772-7972, www.eriecanalderby.com

Whitehall Canal Festival, 518-499-1155

Corn Hill Arts Festival, Rochester, 585-262-3142, www.cornhill.org

Lock 7–Lock 12 CanalFest, Schenectady, 518-372-5656

Convention Days, Seneca Falls, 800-732-1848

Annual Ilion Days, 315-894-5459

Canal Fest of the Tonawandas, 716-692-3292, www.the-tonawandas.com

Oswego Harborfest, 315-343-6858, www.oswegoharborfest.com

Fortfest, Oswego, 315-343-4711, www.fortontario.com

Albany celebrates its Dutch heritage during Tulip Festival Albany Convention & Visitors Bureau

August
Rome Canalfest, www.romecanalfest.org, 315-337-1700
Canal Day Festival, DeWitt, 315-364-8202, www.townofdewitt.com
Little Falls Canal Celebration, 315-823-1740, www.littlefallsny.com
Annual Canal Splash, statewide, 518-436-3055, www.canalsplash.com
Festival of the Arts, Oswego, 315-343-4711, www.fortontario.com
Canalfest, Sylvan Beach, 315-762-5212, www.sylvanbeach.com/events
Great New York State Fair, Syracuse, 315-487-7711 www.nysfair.org

September
Annual Tug Boat Roundup, Waterford, 518-233-9123, www.tugboatroundup.com
Golden Harvest Festival, Baldwinsville, 315-638-2519, www.onondagacountyparks.com
Palmyra Canal Town Days, 315-597-4849
Anniversary of the Battles of Saratoga, 518-584-3255, www.saratoga.org
Old Home Day, Medina, 585-798-3311, www.medina-ny.com/historical

Books

The Erie Canal: Cruising America's Waterways, by Debbie Daino Stack and Captain Ronald S. Marquisee (Manlius, NY: Media Artists, 2001). The companion book for PBS's award-winning series *Cruising America's Waterways,* it features 225 color photographs that show-case the waterways in all four seasons and addresses the practical aspects of navigating them.

Cycling the Erie Canal 2nd ed. (Albany, NY: Parks & Trails New York, 2007). This 140-page cycling guidebook has 42 full-color maps and comes in a handy compact size and is spiral bound for easy use. It includes suggested itineraries and places to stay. To order, call 518-434-1583 or visit www.ptny.org.

Erie Canal Legacy: Architectural Treasures of the Empire State, by Richard O. Reisem, photo-graphs by Andy Olenick (Rochester, NY: Landmark Society of Western New York, 2000). This is a large coffee-table book filled with stunning photographs showcasing the architec-tural treasures of the Empire State following the construction of the Erie Canal.

The Artificial River: The Erie Canal and the Paradox of Progress, 1817–1862, by Carol Sheriff (New York: Hill and Wang, 1997). The author examines the construction of the canal and its impact upon the nation and the people involved, from boat captains to farmers.

The Cruising Guide to the New York State Canal System: Champlain, Erie, Oswego, Cayuga-Seneca 3rd ed. (South Burlington, VT: Northern Cartographic, for the New York State Canal Corporation, 2006). This 185-page publication offers detailed maps, information on canal marinas, service listings, and updated bridge clearances. It also includes a pullout map of the Hudson River featuring marinas, services, and attractions along the river.

Wedding of the Waters: The Erie Canal and the Making of a Great Nation, by Peter L. Bernstein (New York: W. W. Norton, 2005). This *New York Times* bestseller tells the improbable story behind the history of the Erie Canal and its profound effects upon the young nation.

General Index

Lodging by Price

Inexpensive: Up to $75
Moderate: $76–$150
Expensive: $151–$250
Very Expensive: More than $250

Buffalo and the Western Canal region

Inexpensive
Hostelling International-Buffalo Niagara, 45

Inexpensive-Moderate
Comfort Inn, 74
Holiday Inn Lockport, 74
Lockport Inn & Suites, 74
Lord Amherst Motor Hotel, 46

Moderate
Beau Fleuve Bed & Breakfast, 42–43
Best Western Inn on the Avenue, 43
Buffalo Niagara Marriott, 43
Comfort Suites Downtown Buffalo, 43–44
Doubletree Club Hotel, 44
Hampton Inn Williamsville, 44
Holiday Inn Buffalo Downtown, 44–45
Millennium Airport Hotel Buffalo, 47
Sleep Inn and Suites Buffalo Airport, 47

Moderate-Expensive
Adam's Mark Buffalo Niagara, 42
Hampton Inn & Suites Buffalo, 44
Homewood Suites by Hilton Buffalo-Airport, 45
Hyatt Regency Buffalo, 45–46

Expensive-Very Expensive
The Mansion, 46–47

Rochester area

Moderate
Adams Basin Inn, 83
Brookwood Inn Pittsford, 105
Canaltown B&B, 110
Country Inn & Suites, 83–84
Del Monte Lodge, 105
428 Mt. Vernon, 84
Holiday Inn Rochester Airport, 85
Liberty House B&B, 110
Palmyra Inn, 110
Radisson Hotel Rochester Airport, 85–86
Radisson Riverside Hotel, 86
RIT Inn & Conference Center, 86
Rochester Plaza Hotel & Conference Center, 86
Thomas Galloway House B&B, 110
Woodcliff Hotel & Spa, 106–7

Moderate-Expensive
Dartmouth House, 84
Genesee Country Inn, 84
Hyatt Regency Rochester, 85

Expensive-Very Expensive
Inn on Broadway, 85

Cayuga-Seneca Canal

Moderate
Aurora Inn and Restaurant, 115–16
Barrister's Bed and Breakfast, 128–29
Belhurst, 134–35
Benjamin Hunt Inn, 139
Farm Sanctuary B&B, 139
Geneva-on-the-Lake Resort, 135–36
Hampton Inn Geneva, 136
Holiday Inn Waterloo, 129
Hubbell House on VanCleef Lake, 129
John Morris Manor Bed & Breakfast, 129
Pearl of Seneca Lake, 139–40
Ramada Geneva Lakefront, 136
Watkins Glen Harbor Hotel, 140

Moderate-Very Expensive
Taughannock Farms Inn, 118

Expensive
William Henry Miller Inn, 118

Expensive-Very Expensive
La Tourelle Resort and Spa, 117
Statler Hotel at Cornell University, 117–18

Syracuse and the Central Canal region

Moderate
Bed & Breakfast Wellington, 158
Cinderella's Café & Suites, 184
Hobbit Hollow Inn, 177
Holiday Inn-Carrier Circle, 159–60
Maplewood Inn, 160
Mirbeau Inn & Spa, 177
Red Mill Inn, 180
Sherwood Inn, 177–78
Sunset Cottages, 184

Moderate-Expensive
Craftsman Inn, 158
Doubletree Hotel Syracuse, 158–59
Genesee Grande Hotel, 159
Renaissance Syracuse Downtown, 160

Expensive
Embassy Suites Hotel, 159
Jefferson Clinton Hotel, 159
Sheraton Syracuse University Hotel & Conference Center, 160

Dining by Price

Inexpensive: Up to $10
Moderate: $11 to $25
Expensive: $26 to $40
Very Expensive: $40 or more

Buffalo and the Western Canal region

Inexpensive
Anderson's Frozen Custard, 49
Frank and Teressa's Anchor Bar, 48
Polish Villa, 52
Quaker Bonnet Eatery, 53
Ted's Hot Dogs, 49
Towne Restaurant, 55

Inexpensive-Moderate
Chef's Restaurant, 49–50
Dug's Dive, 50–51
W. J. Morrissey's Irish Pub, 55

Moderate
Chocolate Bar, 54
Cole's, 50
D'Arcy McGee's Irish Pub, 50
Eagle House, 54–55
Fat Bob's Smokehouse, 51
Pearl Street Grill & Brewery, 52

Moderate-Expensive
Rue Franklin, 53
Shanghai Red's, 53–54

Expensive
Harry's Harbour Place Grille, 51–52
Salvatore's Italian Gardens Restaurant, 53
The Stillwater, 55

Expensive-Very Expensive
E. B. Green's Steakhouse, 51

Rochester area

Inexpensive
Abbott's Frozen Custard, 88
Nick Tahou Hots, 87
Petals Restaurant, 86
Simply Crepes, 105
Tom Wahl's, 88

Inexpensive-Moderate
Dinosaur Bar-B-Que, 88
Lock 29 Tavern, 110
River Club Restaurant, 86
State Street Bar and Grill, 86

Moderate
Golden Port Dim Sum Restaurant, 88–89
Muddy Waters Café, 110

Rohrbach Brewing Company, 90
Siam Restaurant, 91
Triphammer Grill, 92

Moderate-Expensive
Crescent Beach Restaurant, 87
Erie Grill, 105
Pane Vino Ristorante, 89

Expensive
Bamba Bistro, 87
Crystal Barn, 105
Lento Restaurant, 89
Max of Eastman Place, 89
Peter Geyer Steakhouse Restaurant & Pub, 105
Restaurant 2 Vine, 89–90
Richardson's Canal House, 105–6
Rooney's Restaurant, 90–91
Tastings Restaurant, 106

Cayuga-Seneca Canal

Inexpensive
Two Naked Guys Café, 121

Inexpensive-Moderate
Crystal Lake Café, 144
Deerhead Inn, 129–30

Moderate
Abigail's Restaurant, 129
Antlers, 119
Cobblestone Restaurant, 136
Crow's Nest Restaurant, 136
Dijon Bistro, 119–20
Henry B's, 129
Maxie's Supper Club and Oyster Bar, 120
Moosewood Restaurant, 120
Nonna's Trattoria, 136
Savard's Family Restaurant, 140
Seneca Harbor Station, 140
Simply Red Lakeside Bistro, 144
Wildflower Café, 140

Moderate-Expensive
Edgar's, 135
Halsey's Restaurant, 136
Knapp Winery and Vineyard Restaurant, 143
Stonecutters, 135
Taughannock Farms Inn, 120

Expensive
Lancellotti Dining Room, 135

Syracuse and the Central Canal region

Inexpensive
Doug's Fish Fry, 178
Stella's Diner, 164

Inexpensive-Moderate
Eddie's Restaurant, 184
Seasons Bar & Grille, 160

Moderate
Ale 'n' Angus Pub, 161
Canal View Café, 184
Coleman's Authentic Irish Pub, 161–62
Colorado Mine Co. Steakhouse, 162
The Crazy Clam, 185
Danzer's German & American Restaurant, 162
Dinosaur Bar-B-Que, 162
Harpoon Eddie, 184
Lemon Grass, 163
Pascale Wine Bar & Restaurant, 163
Pastabilities, 163–64

Moderate-Expensive
The Krebs, 179
L'Adour Restaurant Francais, 162–63
1060 Restaurant, 159

Expensive
Arad Evans Inn, 161
Limestone Grill, 158
Rachel's Restaurant, 160
Redfield's Restaurant, 160
Rosalie's Cucina, 179
Stillwater Restaurant, 159

Expensive-Very Expensive
Giverny, 178

Oswego Canal
Inexpensive
Fajita Grill, 198
GS Steamers Bar and Grill, 197
Port City Café & Bakery, 199
Press Box, 199
Rudy's Lakeside, 199–200

Inexpensive-Moderate
Riverview Restaurant, 192

Moderate
Bridie Manor, 198
Canale's Restaurant, 198
King Arthur's Steak House & Brew Pub, 198–99
Vona's Restaurant, 200

Utica area
Inexpensive
Ann Street Restaurant and Deli, 230

Moderate
Castronovo's Original Grimaldi's Restaurant, 217
Coalyard Charlie's, 222
Delmonico's Italian Steakhouse, 217
Dominique's Chesterfield Restaurant, 217
Moose River Restaurant, 217
Savoy Restaurant, 222
Teddy's Restaurant, 222
Thornberry's Downtown Grill & Pub, 218
Tom Cavallo's Restaurant, 217–18

Moderate-Expensive
Beardslee Castle, 230
Canal Side Inn, 230

Albany and the Eastern Canal region
Inexpensive
1228 Grill & Bar, 239
Miss Albany Diner, 245
Riverfront Bar & Grill, 245

Inexpensive-Moderate
Grandma's Country Restaurant, 244
Kelsey's Irish Pub, 240

Moderate
Brown's Brewing Co., 256–57
C. H. Evans Brewing Company, 243–44
Saso's Japanese Noodle House, 245–46

Moderate-Expensive
Justin's On Lark, 244–45
Stockade Inn, 260
Waters Edge Lighthouse, 260
Yono's Restaurant, 241, 246

Expensive
Le Canard Enchaîné Brasserie (formerly Nicole's Bistro), 243
Scrimshaw Restaurant, 241
Webster's Corner Restaurant, 240

Expensive-Very Expensive
Angelo's 677 Prime, 242–43
Jack's Oyster House, 244

Champlain Canal
Inexpensive
The Black Pearl, 291
Mrs. London's Bakery Café, 279–80
Ravenous, 280

Moderate
Chianti Il Ristorante, 277
Circus Café, 277–78
Finch & Chubb Inn and Restaurant, 290–91
Forno Toscano Bistro, 278
Gaffney's Restaurant, 278
Hattie's Restaurant, 278
Lillian's Restaurant, 279
Olde Bryan Inn, 280–81
Sperry's Restaurant, 280
Springwater Bistro, 280

Moderate-Expensive
Chez Sophie Bistro, 277

Expensive
Longfellow's Restaurant, 274

Dining by Cuisine

Albany and the Eastern Canal region

Champlain Canal